'SCUSE ME
WHILE I
KISS
THE SKY

© 1981 JIM MARSHALL

'SCUSE ME WHILE I KISS THE SKY
THE LIFE OF JIMI HENDRIX

DAVID HENDERSON

BANTAM BOOKS
TORONTO · NEW YORK · LONDON · SYDNEY

'SCUSE ME WHILE I KISS THE SKY
*A Bantam Book / published by arrangement with
Doubleday & Co., Inc.*

PRINTING HISTORY
Doubleday edition published November 1978
4 printings through June 1980
Bantam edition / October 1981

Cover art by Jeannette Adams.

Book designed by Renée Gelman.

Library of Congress Cataloging in Publication Data

Henderson, David, 1942-
'Scuse me while I kiss the sky.

Condensed and rev. from: Jimi Hendrix : voodoo child of the Aquarian age. Garden City, N.Y. : Doubleday, 1978.

1. Hendrix, Jimi.   2.   Rock musicians—United States—
Biography.   I.   Title.
ML410.H476H46   1981   784.5'4'00924 [B]   81-2591
        ISBN 0-553-01334-3 (pbk.)   AACR2

Published simultaneously in the United States and Canada

PRINTED IN THE UNITED STATES OF AMERICA

0 9 8 7 6 5 4 3 2 1

Dedicated to
the memory of
Walter "Porky" Ellison
of Throgs Neck

ACKNOWLEDGMENTS

Grateful acknowledgment is given to those who have given me the benefit of their direct contact with Jimi Hendrix, in the form of an interview and/or conversation:

Al Brown, Betty Davis, Willie Chambers, Joe Chambers, George Chambers, and Julius (of the Chambers Brothers), Claire, Stella Douglas, Alvenia Bridges, Dave Holland, Albert King, Len Chandler, Ed Kramer, Ronnie Drayton, Myrna Friedman, Jim Brodey, Derek Taylor, Ray Cepeda, Quincy Jones, Jimi Hendrix, Alexis Korner, Devon Wilson, Buddy Miles, Chuck Wein, Denny Green, Ray Warner, James "Vishwamitra" Scott, Richie Havens, Ram John Holder, Ellis Haizlip, Rahman Ali and Miles Davis, Clara Schuff, Hugh Masekela, Noel Redding, Herbie Worthington, Kenny Rankin, Ed Sanders, Phillip Wilson, "Bobo" Shaw, Peter Orlovsky, Arthur Lee, Blanche Sands, JoAnne and Mark, Alan Price, Curtis Jones, Les Perrin, Juma Sultan, Howard Scott, Finney, Yvonne Rankin, Dan Cassidy, Patricia Jiminez, Ronnie Spector, "H," Fayne Pidgeon, Monika Danneman, Dennis Armstead, Sue Cassidy Clark, Timothy Leary, Sam Silver, James Williams, Fred Rollins, Diana Rollins, Joe Boyd, Colette Mimram, Alan Douglas, Don Moye, Avotcja, Nora Hendrix, Cosmo Deaguero, Bill Graham, Marcia Herskovitz, Carl Lee, Jr., Sharon Lawrence, Jim Robertson, Rudy Costa, John Mayall, Chrissie Charles, Bobby Taylor, Rahsaan Roland Kirk, Albert Goldman,

Media Brown and Diama, Floyd Snead, "Snip" Milton, Willie Dixon, Buddy Guy, "Rocki," and Taj Mahal. Dan Foster and Caesar Glebbeck of the Jimi Hendrix Information Centre in Amsterdam, Holland, Jess Hansen of the Jimi Hendrix Archives in Seattle, Washington, and Don Menn of *Guitar Player* magazine in Saratoga, California, made very important files, documents, and tape recordings available. Through Don Menn of *Guitar Player* magazine unedited tape-recorded interviews with Eric Barrett, Chuck Rainey, Cornell Dupree, John Hammond, Jr., and Gerry Stickells were made available to me. Cecil Brown gave me sections from his interviews with Truman Capote that referred to Jimi Hendrix.

I also extend my thanks to those who helped me in various tangible and intangible ways:

Derek Taylor, George Melly, Ed Knowles, Mike Reynolds, Randa Nova, Craig Street, Michael Gray, Joyce Cole, Peter Bradley, Pat Dennison, Lezley Saar, Arne Passeman, Bari Scott, Rex Griffin, Mary Frank, Gail, Calvin C. Hernton, Teri Turner, Nancy Chandler, Ornette Coleman, Cyn. Zarco, Touraine, Marie D. Brown, Yvette Guerrero, Cordell Reagan, Teddy Stewart, Paul Williams, Leo Branton, David Hammons, Garry George, Karen Kennerly, Zaid Darweesh, Butch Morris, Ray Holbert, Olly Wilson, Mike Ashburne, Lyle Hill, Angela Davis, Bruce Talamon, Mr. H. V. Cox, Eliot Mazur, Pat McCurdy, Bruce Langhorne, *Rolling Stone*, Lewis McAdams, John Rockwell, Cecil Hollingsworth, Barbara Harris, Michael Gray, Daphne Muse, Tommy Mims, Bob Merlis, Ellen Sanders, Jerome Rimson, Calvin Keyes, Loren Means, Vernon Gibbs. *Circus*, *Fusion*, KPFA-FM in Berkeley, California, KSAN-FM in San Francisco, California, and all the beautiful people of the Alternative Chorus–Songwriter's Showcase, Hollywood, California.

Special thanks to typists Grace Rutledge, Eleanor Arge, Damali Cruz, Mary Golden, and J. C. Reilly.

Special thanks to Dr. Barbara T. Christian and Ishmael Reed.

And most special gratitude to my family Barbara, Najuma, Malik, Myrtle, Henry, Ray, and Juanita, and my friends who have stood by me throughout.

And to Lawrence Jordan, my editor, with abiding respect and gratitude.

. . . the story
of life is quicker
than the wink of an eye

the story of love
is hello and good-bye
until we meet again

Jimi Hendrix
September 17, 1970

'SCUSE ME
WHILE I
KISS
THE SKY

SAM SILVER

ONE

It is September 2, 1970. Jimi Hendrix is in Denmark at Vijle Rus-kow Hall, Arbus. He stands on the far end of the stage almost teetering over the edge. He is in a leaning crouch, his right hand sweeps the frets of his Stratocaster, his white- acketed arm a blur of white. The song is "Come On (Part One)," a ong he used to play a long time ago in Seattle in his high school days. Only this time it hardly sounds like the song Earle King wrote. Instead of progressive R&B it is manic slurring chords and elongated drones that peak in a freak treble peal that is constant and foreboding. He seems to be exhorting the traditionally mild Swedish audience. He stops playing and barks out at the crowd between some teeth-gnashing grace notes. Then he smooths on off into a rap. He continues to fret wildly zooming the length of the white Strat. He goes into "Room Full of Mirrors," singing the lyrics as if he were telling something on himself. There is a weird strain in the song. He goes into "Hey Baby—Land of the New Rising Sun." It is nothing like that mellow tune he penned up in Woodstock. It sounds a lot like the previous song. It is almost as if something other-worldly is playing his guitar. As if some force were bending the notes toward a melody they wanted to hear. Only the melody being approached is like nothing he has ever played before. He has seldom had trouble controlling the feedback. It has always worked for him. Yet at the Isle of Wight three days ago

3

and now at Vijle Ruskow Hall there is an added element to his feedback sound. An element that has never before entered his sound. It is peaked to freak out. The other side of "Laughing Sam's Dice." He segues quickly into "In from the Storm," and it is right there. It is unbelievable. It sounds like some crazy manic metallic shit, bleeding, eating through the amps. That tone is totally opposite the emotion of the song. It comes out of nowhere, screaming at him something crazy.

Jimi moves into "Message of Love," *"We're traveling a speed of a reborn man . . ."* He stops abruptly and says, "I've been dead a long time." He walks off the stage. The concert is over.

September 18, 1970. London. Bed long. He a body. So still against thin gray mute of London dawn. A room deep somewhere. Misty in soundless sleep. A gray aura murmurs from the long thin body under the blanket and coverlet. Gas heat whispers underground where the earth rumbles of machine against concrete. Rising against the pale blue India print curtains, tiny slits of dawn filter through the top rows of the gauzelike venetian blinds. The potted tree in the tiny sunken courtyard stands against a wide barred window next to the white front door with a gold engraving of a young Buddha. The white door faces a spiraling staircase with a wrought-iron gate at the top. Two lions sit before each of the three gray-white townhouses that form the Samarkand Residential Hotel.

On the long residential street of Lansdowne Crescent, the Samarkand is opposite a block-long private park, fenced and locked. The key belongs only to the residents of the Crescent. Down the well-kempt street, solid brick gray-white townhouses sweep in a curve past the Pakistan Embassy residence, twisting on through the groves of high trees that surround the fine homes of upper Notting Hill Gate. At the top of the hill are lines of shops and stores along Latimer Road where during the dawn hours strange-shaped vans and trucks of English manufacture energetically deliver their wares. The weekend is just about here. The early morning throbs with the energy of people expecting their pay and a holiday.

Past Lansdowne Crescent, the hill begins a steep descent into the flatlands of Notting Hill Gate where the West Indians, East Indians, mulattoes, hippies, and poor whites live. The view from below is uphill where the trees are so prolific they become a solid mass of green rising like a natural mountain of trees.

At 6:40 A.M. solitary figures appear at various points along Talbot

Road where the buses and the Underground station converge. Posters and leaflets line the boarded-up store fronts, wooden fences and posts announcing the latest West Indian dances and house parties. The great flea market of Portobello Road will be held tomorrow. Throngs of bargain seekers and fun lovers will come from all over London to rub shoulders, and mingle in the ghetto at a safe time. Crews of locals will be lined at points along the mile-long route drinking beer in spontaneous outdoor pubs. Street musicians, solo and ensemble, will play before clusters of casual spectators. Bargains ranging from good antiques to various concoctions of West Indian and East Indian foods will be sold.

Back up on the Crescent he turns and settles. He has had a sleeping pill. Sleep comes in a blood-rush warm slow repose, pulsing, spreading the upturned body. The body, opposed to the grind of the daily workers' toil and time, often sleeps through their day to see some of them in its day, which is night. He feels the crushing weight of the effort his body has been through. Frantic shifts of space, people, enthusiasm weigh upon him. He wants to sleep. To crash a long time. For days. To sleep it all off, to sleep beyond sleep's normal duration. He has made sure he will sleep well beyond the tenseness of his nerve endings, the squelch of his liver, his ulcer, and his lungs all smoke-filled with no exercise. His head begins to numb, blood drains and collects in his stomach slowing down from the business of sorting out the disparate substances in its midst. A sigh. A tremor of the body. This is sleep. Now the body and mind can relax. They agree.

Yet he does not sleep. He can sense his body down, flat out in sleep, yet his mind is awake, his eyes open. A sound out in front. The feeling, the sound of the front door opening and closing. Footsteps coming across the room. He tries to get up but his body refuses to respond. He can only lie looking, hearing. He sees the white door of the apartment. Through that door he has come and gone for days that seem like eternity. *Who is coming through the door?* He tries to call Monika but his mouth will not, cannot form the sound. His mouth feels like his jaws are wired shut. He grinds his teeth. He cannot open his mouth. His neck, his entire backbone is welded to the bed. He is a perfect victim, *and someone has entered the apartment.* Panic wells up inside of him: It could be a fan, a groupie-Band-Aid, a burglar, or someone dispatched to do him in. And lately it has been no secret that he has big enemies. His loving friends around him always, yet as spaced out as they usually are, what could they do if he were seriously threatened? All of his weight presses down against the bed. He is on his back spread-eagled like Christ upon the cross. Amid weird echoes, he waits. There is nothing else he can do.

In his mind he sees a storm sweeping voluminous currents and waves. Hundreds of miles across land and water the storm moves at an incredible pace with fantastic colors. Sunrise over the Pacific rim. Seattle. The sun coming down on the city from the hills. Fall, Indian summer; in the quick tinges of wind that hit with swift force, the harbinger of winter nights and the waters of the storm.

Time moving so fast. He is everywhere at once. Backward and forward in his own time, visiting people and places at a glance. He moves into scenes and then out again so quickly as if he were in flight, and his flight the blink of an eye, the shift from one sphere of vision to another.

Seattle 1912. He sees pointing outward from a pinnacle, a hill, the high granite arm of a statue of an Indian man tall and stately, pointing out over the buildings of downtown Seattle, out toward the lakes that lie before the Pacific Ocean.

People are crowded from the edge of the knoll to the top of the hill where, before the statue, a rotund man in a black frock addresses them with a megaphone from a reviewing stand. He is dwarfed by the statue he points to. He gestures broadly, shouting something about Indians.

The statue is Chief Seattle, the Indian chief the city was named after. He is wrapped in a granite robe that appears strangely tattered. His left foot forward, his right arm raised toward the bays, he looks like he might either be beckoning or waving good-bye.

The tiny officious figure orating is the new reform mayor of Seattle, George Cotteril. He takes the occasion to reaffirm his liberal nature and to belittle the former administration, noting that its former chief of police was at this moment serving time in the penitentiary at Walla Walla.

The crowd roars with approval. On the outskirts of the crowd stands a group of blacks. They laugh, throwing up their hands; the two women are dressed in very fashionable clothes from the East; the three men wear tailored dark suits, their hats tilted and broken in Chicago style.

Nora, the youngest, laughs with the rest but she knew they really had little to be happy about. Black vaudevillians stranded in Seattle, they were wearing their stage clothes and wondering about their survival.

A Model T Ford moves along the Pacific Northwest shelf, heading for Canada. The Pacific Ocean coming in and out of view on the left, faded white streamers trail and break off the speeding black car in the dust and wind. "Just Married" has been scrawled in white along the rear of the auto.

Nora and Ross Hendrix are the newlyweds. They have decided to live in Canada and quit the show-business life. Their colleagues accompany them for the ride. They all sing the big song from the hit black play *Darktown Follies*:

> *First you put your two knees close up tight*
> *Then you sway 'em to the left, then you sway 'em to the right*
> *Step around the floor kind of nice and light*
> *Then you twist around and twist around with all your might*
> *Stretch your lovin' arms straight out in space*
> *Then you do the Eagle Rock with style and grace*
> *Swing your foot way 'round then bring it back*
> *Now that's what I call "Ballin' the Jack"*

It was a great song that swept the nation and was adopted by the "colored" jazz musicians of New Orleans who were doing a new thing that they called "jazz."

Ross desired to escape the "Jim Crow" in America, but he had to acknowledge that the black show tunes, dances, and plays were changing the nation, at least as far as entertainment and recreation went.

The rickety black Ford sped for Victoria Station and the ferry that would take them across the waters to another country.

Jimi sees his father talking. His father looking comical in his sincerity—yet he held you spellbound as he spoke, in his offhand way, about the early years of his life. It was not often Al Hendrix spoke this way. It had to be a long quiet Sunday afternoon with perhaps a few beers and a couple of shots of hard stuff. He would look off straight ahead and his eyes, which were usually sheltered by his dark creviced brow and high close cheekbones, would shine with a liquidy light through the mahogany brown. Jimi would sit as still as he could listening, for he knew that the slightest distraction could take Al off on a tangent from which he might never return. So he listens now as Al talks:

Al Hendrix

My mother was born in Georgia and raised in Tennessee. My mother and Dad got stranded here in a show tour. That was before the First World War. And he wanted to go to Canada, so they went up to Canada to live. They took out papers and became Canadian citizens. My mother was a dancer. She was a chorus girl. A chorus girl back in those days used to wear tights and all such as that. My dad didn't do any entertaining.

My father had a long name: Bertran Philander Ross Hendrix. He was born in a small town in Ohio. I can never remember the name. I met a fellow in the army who had been through there. We had a hard time finding it on the map. My daddy had been married before. I don't know if they were separated, divorced, or what. I remember him telling me one time that he had been a special policeman in Chicago.

My mother's sister was in the entertainment business, too. Her name was Belle Lamarr. That was her stage name. They always used some fantastic kind of name.

My older brother Leon taught me how to tap dance. He died in 1932. My dad died in 1934. Duke Ellington came to Vancouver in 1938. That was the first time a big band came to Vancouver in years. Jitterbugging was in then. We used to have jitterbug contests. But they used to separate the whites from the blacks for the contests, because the whites thought they wouldn't have a chance against the blacks. Once four of us entered the contest: Buster Keeling, Alma, myself, and Dorothy King. We were the couples in the black group. They had a hundred dollars for the prize. They brought a jitterbug group from L.A. and they danced on the stage to show the folks what the jitterbug was all about. That's when jitterbugging first became a craze. Man, I picked it up real quick. I mean, shoot, I had all the timing, because I used to do a lot of tap dancing. We went down and put in an application for the contest. That night there were only two black couples in the thing. I thought we had it made. So I said, well heck, we'll split the purse whoever wins and that'll be twenty-five dollars apiece. But the girls went and chickened out and that made us so *mad*. They didn't want to go on. That just about killed me. I was so disgusted. Twenty-five dollars back in those days was equivalent to about a hundred nowadays. I wasn't working or nothing.

I used to go out and dance with a group, with a white band. But they couldn't play my type of music. They didn't have the rhythm. They'd flow the music along. I would try to tell the pianist to play

stop-time music. So you'd get that *do do doot doot . . . duu duu.* I
mean all the breaks in between the music. But man he'd flow it all
together. So I used to go out with them and dance, but I wouldn't
dance to their music. I would be humming to myself in my mind
when I danced. I would go along with it. But I had to steel myself.
Still I enjoyed it. I mean I always thought I would be scared in front
of a crowd. But shoot, the bigger the crowd, the better I felt. I would
be enjoying myself, and entertaining myself too. I used to dance in
between breaks at intermission. This group would go around to
different dances, and they'd call me and I'd go along. I wasn't able to
make a living at it. I had other jobs. But I was able to make more in
one night dancing than I could in a whole week of hauling wood.

When Canada declared war against Germany, I knew it would
only be a matter of time before the United States got into it. I knew
the Canadian Army would come for me, because my brother served
in the Canadian Army. I got my hat and headed for Victoria. I told
Ma, well, I'm on my way. I tried to get a job on the railroad. But the
old guy would never hire me. He'd tell me I was too daggum short. I
wasn't too daggum short, he just wanted to fool with me. I was
around twenty, but I was about at my full growth then. This was
during the Depression and I decided to go on for myself. I told my
mother I ain't coming back this way. I'm gonna go out and make
something. So that's what I did. When I left I went over to Victoria
and worked there for about two weeks, made myself a little capital
shining shoes, and then came to Seattle. I had always planned on
going to New York or Chicago, the big places. I'm glad I didn't go to
those places. They were wild, cold-blooded. So I wound up here.

Al Hendrix liked the unconscious part of jazz dancing the best. It
was like a dream, all the people watching while he lost himself in
the dance, and he would perform by sheer improvisation, reacting
spontaneously to the music.

Al's mother, Nora Hendrix, would laugh at his excitement over
the new dance craze. Years ago, she used to tell Al that before he was
born there was a dance introduced in the Negro musical *Darktown
Follies* called "The Texas Tommy" that was the same as the jitterbug. This was in 1912 and 1913, when Nora and her husband were
still very much in show business.

While others called the jitterbug "The Lindy Hop," it made no
difference to Al. He would add many steps of his own, steps he had
seen done in movies by Bill "Bojangles" Robinson, or Fred Astaire,
or Buck 'n' Bubbles. Preferring to dance alone, Al would start off in

the basic jitterbug steps: two box steps with the accent off the beat, a kick and three hops on each foot, then the breakaway, and he was off on his own, flowing toward the space in his mind where he lost conscious awareness of his own dancing, the crowd, and the music. The music seeping into him as he moved in semitrance, performing feats he could hardly remember when they were described to him afterward.

Al had benefited from his parents' dancing ability. The times had demanded they pursue non-show-business jobs, yet they never skipped an opportunity to work out the way they used to. As a child, Al had seen his parents perform the acrobatic dance steps so favored in vaudeville—African crossover dances such as "Ballin' the Jack," "The Texas Tommy," "The Ring Shout," "Cakewalk," "Charleston," and other dances of the minstrel, vaudeville, and ragtime eras.

Al had a formidable array of dance steps to add to the largely improvised jitterbug. His steps seemed new to the youngsters who crowded around to watch him perform, first at high school dances and then at dance halls and ballrooms. Just over five feet tall, Al dressed in a long jacket, ballooned pants that bellowed out at the thighs and knees, tapering to narrow cuffs. The suit was perfect for the acrobatic steps due to its outsize proportions. On the dance floor Al's size was no problem. Jazz dancing often featured extreme sizes, either very fat, very tall, very slim, or very short. His size did make dance partners a problem, however. Usually Al danced alone. When he could find a partner who could keep up with him, she was usually too big for him to do the acrobatic air steps, such as the "Hip to Hip," "Side Flip," and "Over the Back."

Al could do more floor steps than anyone in Vancouver. Many touring vaudeville troupes would pick up local black youngsters who were very talented dancers and insert a gang of them in their show as an act. Some "picks," as they were called, went on to be big stars, while many, hired only for the town they lived in, were left to descend back into obscurity.

As a solitary "pick," Al would come to the center floor of the dance hall. Space would be cleared for him and a spotlight trained on him. The band would play one of their hottest numbers and Al would go into his thing. A top jazz dancer was certain to turn on the orchestra and the dance patrons, propelling the vibrations to a fever pitch. With dance halls competing for the crowds, an act like Al's was essential. Even though he danced alone, Al could turn the people on.

Benny Goodman had become nationally famous as the King of Swing through his coast-to-coast radio broadcasts. "Swing" had caught on as the name of the new dance fad, and became almost solely identified with Benny Goodman's orchestra.

Fletcher Henderson had actually solved the problems of large orchestras playing hot jazz. But Goodman received much of the credit. Unlike the confusion apparent in Dixieland when several saxophones, trumpets, and other horns tried to mix in the cacophony, Henderson had arranged many of his songs along the call-and-response patterns of African music. The horns alternated riffs and also played the melody as ensemble. When Henderson sold his arrangements to Goodman, the precision of Goodman's style, coupled with the marketing expertise of the Eastern recording companies, made Goodman indeed "The King of Swing." Fletcher Henderson and many other black orchestras had been playing these arrangements for almost ten years in Harlem, but few people outside of New York City had ever heard them play.

Al Hendrix first came in contact with swing through the radio broadcasts from New York, but he had already intuitively recognized in Louis Armstrong the roots of jazz.

One night in Seattle he danced with Armstrong and outdid every solo he had ever done. From the basic lindy steps, he had gone into "Ballin' the Jack," swaying his knees together left and right, doing a beautiful time step as if he were stepping on feathers, then stretching his arms out in space, he did the "Eagle Rock." Arms high over his head he swayed his entire body from head to toe, going into the "Georgia Grind," rotating his pelvis in a circle to the beat of the music, then coming out into a "Charleston" for a moment. He parlayed the kicks into air steps, took a solo flight, landed in a split, and rose without the aid of his hands and arms into the "jitterbug" right on time with the music.

He became the costar of the show that night. He also met a dancing partner who was just the right size. Her name was Lucille Jeter. She was tiny and slight with a great smile and a lot of energy. She loved to dance as if dance were life in essence. She and Al spent the rest of the night showing off for the crowd. Now he could do the flips and rolls and breathtaking air steps—now he had a jitterbugging partner.

Lucille Jeter had delicate features and a slight build with very light brown skin. When only a few days old, she was taken home from the hospital in a severe snowstorm because the Jeters could not afford to stay any longer. She caught pneumonia. That early illness contributed to her frail constitution. Her father's facial expressions and mannerisms reminded Al of actor Wallace Beery. Mr. Jeter seemed to be a stern and unyielding man but Al's sincerity grew on him. Lucille was a local jitterbug champ. Her little frame could really go. She reveled in the nightlife of jazz and had great enthusiasm.

Although the war in Europe had been staring everyone in the world in the face for several years, the United States' entry into the war came as a shock to the citizens of Seattle.

Seattle shared the Pacific Ocean with Asia, so things were especially weird in the Pacific Northwest. Almost overnight Seattle became a closed town. The city had been making civil-defense preparations for some time, and when the U.S. entry into the war was announced, a secret command took over the city.

Some places not far from the center of town became off limits overnight. Curfews sprung up. Blackouts and bomb drills became an immediate way of life. The air of hysteria channeled into passionate patriotism; everyone was threatened. Paranoia became intense. The Japanese were quickly interred in detention centers out in the countryside of Washington State. The storm of war settled over Seattle. Anxiety about life and death became a strong element in everyone's mind. The cruelties of existence under strife that resulted were taken for granted.

Lucille Jeter was only seventeen years old when the war broke out. The war hit her hard, as it did all the others in Seattle just attaining adulthood. They had to make heavy decisions fast, decisions that would span their lifetimes.

Al Hendrix asked Lucille to marry him before he left to fight the war. It was not an unusual request. The couples they had gotten to know, most of them regulars at the jitterbug dances, swing clubs, and ballrooms were faced with the same decision. Every week the ballrooms, would have more and more couples dancing their farewell dances, very often with the male already in military uniform. It seemed as if the entire swing music world had joined the military overnight.

Suddenly the music became a focus for unity among the youth of America. The ones who had loved to dance now had to fight a war. The big swing band became a symbol of the unity of purpose of America. Glenn Miller and Benny Goodman conducted in uniform. The big bands were going overseas to entertain the boys on the front lines.

Jazz had a fantastic impact on the war. Hot jazz or American swing became an immediate rage in England and Europe. It was like the bugle call of the cavalry. Jazz became synonymous with the swinging American youth, the jitterbugs and cultural epicureans, who had adopted the music of the black Afro-American. Europe in her history had felt the distant strains of Moorish martial music before. The dark Africans had ruled much of Europe for several hundred years, and the fighting ability of the Moors was well remembered in European history. The black Americans were jitterbugs, the white Americans swinging lindy-hoppers. Jazz brought a great morale lift to the European fighting forces. Jazz was relatively new music to the Europeans. Although the cultural elite had always expressed an interest, World War II exposed the masses of Europeans to jazz. They flipped. Jazz was a balm that at the same time lifted their spirits. It gave them the intense joyous detachment of the Harlem hipster. Listening to jazz was like meditation, yet it did not cut you off from the world. In fact, jazz made you want to dance, to act, to express. Jazz became the dominant cultural symbol of the triumph of the Allied forces in the war.

Soon after their marriage, Al and Lucille began to hear a new and exciting musician on the national coast-to-coast broadcasts of the Benny Goodman band. Featured with the band was a name new to the devotees of swing, Charlie Christian. Never before had a new and unknown person had such an impact on the music within such a short time. The reason was the amplified guitar Christian played. Christian could play rhythm with the best, chomping along, and adding some nice tone colorings as well. But Christian could also play intricate melodies with his electrified guitar. The sound was thrilling and immediate; it opened up new realms of meaning for the dancing swingers and the followers of the music itself.

Few "colored" musicians had ever had the exposure of Christian. It had been rough going for the white bandleader to even include a black player during those "Jim Crow" times. Benny Goodman had used Teddy Wilson in New York but had to go through a lot of changes to do it in 1936. In 1941 things had changed in the States. War seemed imminent. The Jim Crow in the South and the racism in the North began to quickly recede as national unity became the only posture reasonable in the face of Hitler, who, by the way, thought jazz one of the strongest elements toward the destruction of the pure white Aryan race.

Charlie Christian's electric guitar sent the banjo back to folk music. Electrically amplified, the guitar was able to top the rhythm with beautiful and strong sound, and then to step out of the background and deliver solos that gave definite blue tonality to the blues-inspired jazz, with slurs and fading vibratos and long sustained lines that were perfect for dance and for listening.

At the same time, uptown in Harlem, Christian was also contributing heavily to a new and secret music based on black rhythms, blue tonalities, and shouts with the likes of "Dizzy" Gillespie, Thelonius Monk, and Kenny Clarke. This music, "bebop," would, in a few years, change the face of jazz irrevocably.

The sweet swing music of Goodman tremendously limited the genius of Charlie Christian. He gave more of his tradition than he received in inspiration. Many nights he would go uptown to Harlem after his gig with Goodman to sit in with some young and crazy black musicians who had all of Harlem in an uproar over the new music they played. Minton's, located in the Hotel Cecil on West 118th Street, was the room for the new music. Goodman's rhythm section usually played straight 4⁄4 rhythms with the drummer hardly ever varying from the straight jazz march beat. Uptown in Harlem, Kenny Clarke had pioneered a drumming style that had expanded the drum polyrhythmically. Kenny Clarke's drums would talk to the soloists, exploding bombs according to the peaks of intensity of the music, rather than by "arrangement." Keeping time with his right hand rather than his right foot, Kenny Clarke also expanded the use of the ride cymbal and high-hat, thus giving wide rhythmic material for the soloists to feed off.

Charlie Christian became an underground hero to the jazz aficionados who flocked to Minton's from all over the tristate area to hear the new thing in jazz. At the same time he was a mainstay of the Goodman band downtown. While other guitarists such as Lonnie Johnston with Louis Armstrong and Floyd Smith with the Andy Kirk band had been important in the evolving of the guitar as a solo instrument, it was Charlie Christian who took it all the way in.

For the bop musicians, old standards such as "I Got Rhythm," "Stardust," and others became vehicles for solos, their melodies inferred, just as the blue tonalities in jazz had been inferred for so long. The wild and emotional soloing at Minton's would become the dominant jazz style after the war. In 1941 it had every jazzman looking over his shoulder for the wave that would be sure to engulf them. Even Louis Armstrong put down bebop as Chinese music. But the war would defer the coming of bebop for some years, strengthening its base in black Harlem while the nation and the Allies swung to the Benny Goodman and Glenn Miller bands.

Charlie Christian never lived to see either the full birth and bloom of bebop or the U.S. entry into the Second World War. He died of tuberculosis in late 1941.

Lucille Hendrix gave birth to a boy at 10:15 A.M. on November 27, 1942. Without Al to consult she named the baby Johnny Allen Hendrix.

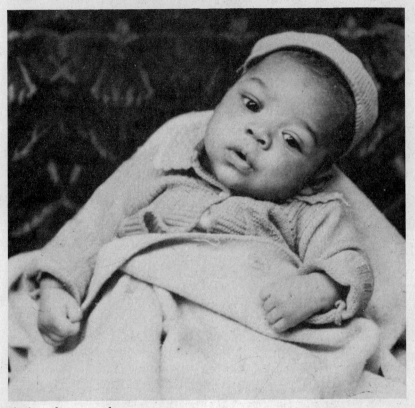

Jimi at eleven weeks   J.A. HENDRIX

It is the Fourth of July 1943. Johnny Allen Hendrix, eight months old, is held to the window of Seattle General Hospital by a white-smocked nurse. The display of fireworks is particularly impressive this war year.

Johnny Allen had awakened to the great flashes of lights in the sky. The nurse had found him there awake, calmly surveying the rush of brilliant lights against the darkening sky. As she changed his diaper in the dim light of the infant-care ward, the nurse wondered what the fate of this little boy would really be. His mother was not all right. The weakness of her constitution and the excitement of the war years was a bad combination, especially for a lonely, very young woman. Taking care of a child required a lot of strength on a steady basis. It would mean an end to the frolic of music and dance. She had gotten back out too soon. Her birth delivery had been difficult. She had been advised to rest for a year but as soon as she had felt strong enough she had gotten back out on the dance floor and tested her small strength to the fullest.

TB was more under control now than it ever had been, especially for poor blacks. Lucille had been consumptive from birth, and now with the manic depression that frequently accompanied TB she would have to be quarantined for quite a while. As for little Johnny Allen, he would have to be elsewhere; he certainly couldn't stay in the infant-care ward for the months necessary for Lucille's recovery.

Al Hendrix

My wife and I separated when I came home from the service in 1945. During the time I was in the service, she had left him with this person and with that person and one thing and another. The people always kept in contact with me, the different ones that had him. I would send her an allotment home. The government had a deal for sending allotments home, and besides I was trying to send *extra* money home. But after she and I separated I wouldn't send nothing to her. Of course she got the government allotment. She was entitled to that. Jimmy was down in Berkeley, California. He was staying here with a woman in Seattle, I forget her name, but she died and then her sisters came from Texas and took him down to Berkeley. She lived in Berkeley. And when I came out of the service—I had kept in contact with this woman, and she had told me about her sister dying—I went down to Berkeley when our ship came in. I had come from the South Pacific. We were supposed to come in on "Navy Day" and I figured I would be discharged in 'Frisco. But on "Navy Day" the harbor was full of ships, and they weren't able to discharge us there. So I got discharged up here in Seattle. I immediately went down to Berkeley and got Jimmy. He was three years old. He had never seen me before. The people there had a picture of me in uniform, but it was a strange thing. I missed all his baby days and that's what I always wanted to see. They never gave me a furlough when he was being born. They told me when I went into the service that during emergencies, sickness, birth, or anything like that you could get a *furlough*. But I was down in Alabama and all they allowed was a fourteen-day furlough. As slow as transportation was at that time, it would have taken me about fourteen days to *get home*. So I tried to get a longer furlough. I talked to the battalion commander and he told me, "Hendrix, by the time you get home you'd have to be turning around to come back." I was *mad*. He could see it. When I walked out he said, "Hendrix, don't think about going over the hill." I turned around and said, "Yes, sir," and I threw him a salute. Daggummit. Not a week from that day we were all getting ready to go to mess, and on the late bulletin they had the names of the guys going into the stockade. There were three of us who went to the stockade on that day. I was one of them. I asked my top kick, I said what the hell am I being put in the stockade for? He told me, "General principles, general principles . . ." I say well daggummit, usually a person has to be convicted of something. I said well I ain't did nothing. Man, I just went to chow and come back. Sure enough the next day they took the three of us to the stockade. I said well ain't this cold. I was in the stockade two months, but I didn't lose any pay. I guess they were afraid I would go AWOL. That's why I was railroaded. The day before our outfit was to leave, the MPs brought me back to the barracks. We were going to embark on the train. I got my gear together, and I went back and spent the night in the stockade. They brought me back to the barracks the next morning, and I got my gear together and we got on the train. And went out there to the California coast to go overseas.

Al Hendrix came back from the war in 1945. He was twenty-seven years old. In Seattle, departing from the troop train, he was just another soldier returned from the war. Disoriented, unemployed, looking for the loved ones he had left behind.

He had heard that Lucille had been sick. He had heard that the boy she had borne him was staying with relatives. He had not heard much more. Months of cursing in the trenches, looking out into the darkness of war, the only reply a shot, an explosion, a crawling or running soldier. A sad resignation lined his face that day. He was used to uncertainty by now; the war had given him a cynicism usually reserved for a much older man. The war had bred a fatalistic calm into him.

He managed to get to his sister's all right, heavy duffel bag and all. She gave him the cries and hugs and tears, but he wanted to know about his boy. She seemed to be saving that for later, trying to act in accordance with the concepts of a soldier hero returning home. But he was not a hero and there was no homecoming. He had been a simple soldier face down in the trenches, and now he was a young man trying to pick up the pieces of a life he had had to leave nearly five years ago.

Before the war, Al Hendrix had never traveled any farther than the distance between Vancouver and Seattle. Now he undertook the third longest journey of his life. He rode the Southern Pacific out of Washington State, through Oregon, and finally into California. Al disembarked at the Oakland depot on Sixteenth Street near the bay. A cab took him over the train tracks and headed down the bay streets into Berkeley.

Al was impressed by the view. The bay waters leading straight across to San Francisco, a silver-blue glistening city softly covered by a billowing fog. Veering from the approach to the Bay Bridge, the cab began driving toward the hills; the incline soon brought the bay back into sight through the receding stucco and brown-shingled homes. Al had the cab driver slow down as he checked the numbers. They cruised along Grove Street until they came to a two-block-square low-rent housing development.

Savo Island Village was relatively new at that time and did not differ that much from the surrounding homes. Al was impressed. Berkeley seemed an affluent town. The Village looked peaceful and dignified—a nice place for his child, thank goodness.

Al Hendrix

Those people didn't want to give him up. But she told me in a letter, "I know you've been thinking about your son all the time you bee: in the service, and I'm not gonna hold him." He knew them, he only knew me by a picture. They'd ask him who was Daddy, and he'd point to the picture and say, "That's Daddy." So when I got there that was a strange feeling. To see your own kid, and he's talking and walking around, and doesn't know you.

I always wanted to be around my first child and raise him and just do things with him. When I got down there I stayed with them for about a week. I used to send the woman money all the time. They were very nice people. I often wonder where they are now. I don't remember the woman's name, but her daughter's name was Celestine. They were Texans. Everybody was taller than me. I said, "You Texans sure do grow tall." They were a nice family. Celestine, she was around my age, and she was way up there. They figured that I should leave Jimmy with them because he knew them. I said, "Yeah, but this is my son, he's the only thing I thought about all the time I was in the service. Shoot, I want the boy," I said, "this is *mine*." She told me in her letters, "I know we are more accustomed to him than you are and it's gonna hurt us when you come down here to get him." She didn't even go down to the train when we left. Nobody went down to the train. I felt bad about it, but I told them this is part of me, and I'm gonna take care of my kid.

Of course, Jimmy was only three years old, he didn't know what was happening. All he knew was that he was going on a train ride. I had to give him his first whipping that night though. He wanted to run up and down the aisles, and I said, "Well father and son got to get to know each other." And he just kept running. Of course, he didn't pay attention to me, he didn't know me from Joe Blow. So I had to whip him. He said, "I'm gonna tell Celestine." I said, "Well you tell her. She would agree with me."

The first thing Al Hendrix did once he had gotten them settled in Seattle, at 124 Tenth Avenue, Room 580, was to change Johnny Allen's name to James Marshall Hendrix. It became official on September 11, 1946. James Marshall Hendrix, after his brother who

Seattle 1946, four years old   J.A. HENDRIX

had died in the twenties. James Marshall Hendrix: a name with dignity and authority.

Al Hendrix

When I brought him back to Seattle, we stayed with my sister-in-law. She had three girls and with Jimmy we did all right. I was getting my rocking-chair money from the government, twenty dollars a week. I was looking around for some work but there wasn't much going on. But Jimmy was with me from then on.

My wife and I got together again and that's when Leon came into the picture. Leon was born in 1948. She came back and found out that I was home and we got together. But it was an on-and-off affair. It didn't work out too well. So we finally just got divorced in 1950. Leon was about a year old when we got divorced. We were staying at the projects up on Yesler Street. I stayed on in the projects with the kids and she moved.

Having no skills, and having spent his formative years in the military, Al had a tough time finding a steady job. Without a job, Al had to make the tough decision to send his children away to his sister, Patricia, in Vancouver. For three years, Jimmy and Leon stayed with their Aunt Patricia. Jimmy attended school for the first time, going to the Dawson Street Annex Elementary School at the age of six. The school was close to their home in the West End of Vancouver near English Bay. Leon was still a toddler and envied his big brother going off to school every day.

Jimmy became even more introverted. Aunt Patricia used to laugh at puzzled visitors who wondered about his silence, and tell them that he never had much to say, even to her. Aunt Patricia's husband passed away in 1952. She buried him and took the children back to Seattle. Al had a small room into which both Leon and Jimmy moved. Al had just landed a good job at the Boeing Aircraft plant. Economically things were looking up. But Al would have to have a suitable home for the children. Due to the divorce, the authorities were on his back about the care of his children.

James Williams and Jimmy Hendrix became fast friends in Leschi Elementary School. Their friendship solidified by a teacher who looked down on black people, Jimmy and James became inseparable. They both had paper routes right next to each other, and every morning they would meet before and after their deliveries.

James. James Williams. Slight James. Big cheeks. Like cheeks of a squirrel filled with nuts. Incredible big cheeks and a soft voice. Slightly self-doubting, but always his friend. James had a serious face that always held a touch of humor, a glimmer, a smile. Big white teeth, not bucked but coming out at you. He would have to grow into those big teeth. Even in James's big smile there was a sadness, a forlorn air that made the bigger Jimmy want to look after him. James's sadness made Jimmy forget his own troubles. And James was a true companion. With you to the end. That is, when he wasn't sick. Often harassed by his older sisters, his mother, or seemingly by life itself, he would seem to take refuge in sickness.

Eight-year-old Jimi and younger brother Leon J.A. HENDRIX

1955 class picture, Seattle's Leschi Elementary School (Jimi 2nd row from bottom, 3rd from left, in striped shirt) COURTESY J.A. HENDRIX

Jimmy would make him laugh. Cheer him up. Think up things for them to do.

They were both very poor at the point in their adolescence when they began to be attracted to the girls of their neighborhood. But their clothes betrayed them, they looked like little hobos.

Jimmy would secretly think of James as his brother—big like him; they were able to do things together. James was the smaller and more sickly of the two. Jimmy, tall and gangly, with amazingly outsized arms and hands, would look out for James. Jimmy had two fights with bullies who had come down on James. He won them both, no one suspecting that behind this gangling, painfully thin exterior existed a fierce and determined boy who had great love for James.

Leon, his little brother, was so much younger, so unknowing of what was happening. Yet Jimmy hardly knew himself what was happening, what had happened, or what would happen in the future. He couldn't tell Leon anything, and even if he could, Leon was too young to understand. James, on the other hand, was like him in many ways. Even if they were both confused about their life and ultimate fate, they at least had their bond. They had their insecurities to measure themselves against and could mitigate their effects by sharing at least their emotions.

They played together on the Fighting Irish football team, Jimmy with his long arms and speed and hands playing end. They joined the Boy Scouts. James, because of his eloquence and low-keyed air, became the captain and Jimmy the co-captain. When it came time for their trip into the wilds, they wound up in Leschi Park and became the laughingstock of all the troops.

One summer they picked butter beans in the fields outside of Seattle, often hitchhiking back to town. That's when Jimmy first began to talk about his mother. He had had disturbing dreams and was afraid she would die. She drank an awful lot, and she was sick a lot, and very depressed.

Then just on the verge of his manhood, Jimmy's mother died. This hurt him deeply, yet he never said much about it.

Lucille had married again, but in 1958 her health had turned worse. Recurrent TB plagued her. She had trouble staying home to convalesce, preferring to go out dancing instead. Soon she was back in the hospital.

Al refused to take Jimmy to see her but did permit Aunt Patricia to take him. Until she came back from Canada with the two children Aunt Patricia had never met Lucille Jeter. She was afraid for Jimmy that his mother would look wasted and deathly in the hospital bed, but to her surprise, Lucille looked very good in the face, very pretty with a shoulder-length pageboy hairdo. As usual, Jimmy did not have much to say. He mainly stared at his mother.

Lucille passed away shortly after their visit. She had been released from the hospital in pretty good shape, and cautioned to take it easy. But she did not follow the doctor's advice.

Al was greatly saddened, his face assuming deep lines of grief. The boys had never spent much time with their mother and now they would never have the chance.

Aunt Patricia attended the funeral expecting to see Al and the boys there. But they never came. Al would not let them go. Leon was too young to go. Jimmy had pleaded to be allowed to go, but there was no one to take him. Al mourned Lucille privately, preferring not to mix with her family and her second husband's people. Aunt Patricia would have taken Jimmy with her, but she did not know that Al was not coming until it was too late.

Jimmy and his father were like two roomers, two old men who moved often from place to place always at the mercy of one authority or the other: a new landlord, the unemployment officer, the schoolteacher, the welfare office, the foster home, and now that Jimmy was a teen-ager, the police.

Al, tiny and squint-eyed, was a strict authority figure because of his tiny five-foot-two frame, and even more so because of his belief that life had given him a bad deal. He seemed powerless against the forces that shaped his and his son's existence. But while it was obvious that they were almost totally controlled by forces beyond their control, he maintained a stern silence about all that had affected them. He was the adult, the one responsible to handle things, but they seemed to be handled so poorly, and Jimmy was a victim.

His father's candor came not in the words he spoke, but in the spontaneous tears that often came after drinks. Jimmy learned to sense emotion rather than fact, and then it was not too hard to deduce that their plight was just about hopeless.

His father was not one with words anyway. An eighth-grade education had left him self-conscious about his verbal skills. Even when he tried to say something, somehow the words did not come. All of the deeper meanings of what affected their lives seemed to be tied up in big words that lawyers, doctors, teachers, and priests knew. Jimmy learned not to be impatient. He studied patience as the discipline that eventually would lead him and his father to a better life. He knew that his father would not tell him the truth about his mother, his brother, his birth, and his early upbringing. It couldn't be all that sad; but the depths of emotion that the subjects wrought in his father made Jimmy afraid to ask, especially about his mother. She achieved mythic proportions, monstrous in intensity, a woman so powerful even in death that she deeply altered the lives of a man and two boys.

His father nursed a hurt that showed on his face much worse than the teen-aged pimples Jimmy had. A hurt that gnarled lines around his eyes and mouth, lines that grew longer and deeper every day, spreading to the cheeks and the forehead, deep-setting the eyes even more. And seeming to descend deeper into a sadness that washed into turbulent waves never to come out clear with the reasons, the truth of the matter. Coming back even stronger day after day.

Whenever his father seemed on the verge of telling the story, when they were close and intimate and it became obvious that the natural direction would be to mention his mother, his father would either become tearful and go outside, or become very authoritarian. He would snap shut the train of thought and bark an order. Clean up

Jimi and his Dad during Thanksgiving time, 1956   J.A. HENDRIX

J.A. HENDRIX

your room, sweep the floor, wash the dishes. Then he would usually go on about his life in the service, or more to the point, the obligation to duty. When the top kick said to do something you do it, or get your head blown off, and that's the way it is here, when I say do something, I want it done or else heads will roll.

Seeing through it, Jimmy thought it funny that his father would equate the military, with its thousands of men and huge bureaucracy, property, and funds, to a boy and his father alone in a room, in the world. But Jimmy would do what was said dutifully. All he could do was to obey his dad. It made his father happy in a way. There was not that much to ask of each other, so many things being out of the question, so he did whatever his father asked, with as much love and effort as he could. It broke his heart, because what he was doing was something anyone could do, and while sweeping the floor or emptying the garbage he vowed to himself that someday he would do something great for his father, something that few people could do, or something that no one else in the world could do.

Al Hendrix

The way I felt about tap dancing is the way Jimmy felt about guitar playing. I mean it was in him to do it. He felt it. It was no job, he enjoyed it. He just picked it up all of a sudden. He had no formal lessons. He used to practice a lot. I'd come home from work and he'd be there *plunk, plunk, plunk.* If I disturbed him or something he'd go on in the bedroom, and he'd be in there *plunk, plunk, plunking.* And I'd say, "Jimmy, sweep the floor," or something, and he'd say, "OK, Dad," and he'd do that. And after he finished doing that he'd go back to *plunk, plunk, plunking.* I used to hear it constantly.

He'd be *plunking* away, and I could almost see his vision of himself playing for a band. I mean, that's finally what he was doing, too. While he played around the house he was visualizing himself doing that.

He got good on that acoustic guitar. He only paid five dollars for it from this guy. He asked me about it and I gave him the money to get it. And after that I went and got him this electric guitar. But before that he used to be plunking away on this old ukulele. I found it doing some of my gardening work. These people wanted me to clean out this basement, and I found it there and got strings for it. He used to plunk away on it before he got a guitar. He used to pick up a lot of pointers from different people. So many people tell me now, "Oh yeah, my son taught your boy how to play." I don't think anyone *taught* him how to play. I mean *any* artist, guitar players or singers, learn so much from *other* people. They just don't go straight up from themselves. Unless they get themselves a regular musical teacher and learn straight all the way. But Jimmy just wasn't in that kind of boat. We didn't have that kind of money. So he just taught himself. He just picked it up. It was just in him, and the guitar became another part of his anatomy.

So while he waited for adulthood, he talked to his guitar. Like a new person in the household his guitar became alive. It made a world of sound. It held all the songs, all the melodies, and secrets of the universe. Though there were agonies, broken sound becoming melody, string after string the laws revealed themselves to him. It was painfully slow, yet he liked the time-eternal agony of making that guitar talk. After all, he had all the time in the world, all the ageless silence of his room late at night or any time of the day. When he got with his guitar all time ceased. He was transported to other worlds and suddenly realized that what he heard in the guitar, what it coaxed him to bring out, was something totally between them, a relationship he had nowhere else. Just the simplest song melody carried his mind deeper into the potentialities of the instrument, the medium between him and the mysteries of the universe. He began to get a time sense of what he could do and how long it would take to reach the sounds in his mind. Melodies he had never heard before came to him on rainy and windy nights and days, startling in their insistence.

He had not wanted or needed any lessons. He liked the ease and the agony of the long-term agreement between him and his instrument, not taking for granted and short-cutting what they had together. After every trial and error, and every head-hurting drill he had to impose upon himself to master a line or passage, the final sound became his own. New precisely at that time, coming out of nowhere, created by that moment, elongated by trial and error to triumph and release. And his guitar began to respect him and he began to love it like no other love he had known. And then the guitar began to talk. It began to talk back to him. It began to chuckle at his mistakes and lead him to new truths at the same time. It began to murmur the sound he had heard in his mind for so long. It understood the frustrations of his situation. It could re-create every moment and then show him the proper relationship and release. The release was within him all the time. The guitar revealed its secrets and filled the void of lonely silence.

Now his father would find him at his guitar. And, as if he had found him communing with a priest, he would often soften his movements in respect. The quiet was pierced only by vibrating contralto sounds. The better he became with the sounds, the more his father respected his space and solitude. Al began to treat him better. His son now had a world of his own, a world he knew, a world he could understand. Jimmy had his own concern now, and when Al would interrupt him to sweep the floor or empty the garbage or clean up a bit, it was no longer a peremptory command out of the blue. Now Al would pop over and do a little song and dance vaudeville routine, or jitterbug to Jimmy's playing for a moment, and then he would say, "Sweep the floor a little bit, son," or "Wash the dishes" or "Empty the garbage." But it was a love command. An interruption to say, "Hey, I love you, you're my son, I'm glad you're doing something of your own. The routine we have is simple and small next to the beauty of the music that makes you so interested and involved. Now our space increases, and we can look at each other from our distance of mysteries, the separate worlds that neither of us can understand of the other. Not like two bare-faced old black men crabbing at each other, but two people, a father and son doing things that they have to do. We can now look at each other and say a couple of things that need saying, the things that keep our lives going, and then we can go back to our concerns: your world of sound and my making our lives work."

Jimmy discovered that the vibrations of music can truly bring people together. He discovered through his closer relationship with his father that music is indeed magic. Music can heal wounds and offer other worlds. The guitar brought them closer together, and it made his father proud of his son. His son was investigating a mystery he himself had always been close to yet had never mastered, though he had always wanted to. A man, a father worrying about not being able to pass along knowledge to his son, now had his prayers answered. His son was entering the secret mystical covenant. Jimmy's music filled the silence, made the walls sing, made the air smell better, and heightened their lives together. A simple man, Al Hendrix did not ask that his son be a Charlie Christian, he was just happy his boy was using his time constructively.

In 1954 Jimmy began to get seriously involved with girls and with music. Awkward and shy, he had difficulty with the girls, but the music was kinder to him, although not any easier. He noticed the girls liked music. This was a great inspiration.

Adolescence seemed to drive Jimmy and James apart. Soon they both realized their adolescence would be markedly different from their boyhoods. Although Jimmy was quiet and shy, he had a Sagittarian aggression that seemed to thrust him near or close to wherever he wanted to be, whether his mind agreed with him or not. Jimmy was very definitely going toward girls, no matter how gawky he appeared. He had also made up his mind about music.

During Jimmy Hendrix's adolescence, rock 'n' roll became an overnight national phenomenon. American popular music finally opened up to its tribal and folk roots, and the American public voted for the new music with cash money. "Jim Crow" was finally legally defeated in the U.S. Supreme Court decision of 1954 striking down public-school segregation. The black masses finally had the legal sanctions of racism removed from their paths. American music began to release its racism as well and reveled in the elemental music of the country. Rock 'n' roll swept the nation. The young people of America, the babies of the Second World War, began participating in this mass puberty rite. A wild musical initiation ceremony of incredible proportions whose momentum would transform these rites into a philosophy of life.

In 1954 black music began appearing on the national charts with increasing regularity. Up until that time white pop music dominated the national charts with only an occasional black entry. White pop music was descendant from the 1940s smooth big-band vocal sound, which had appealed to the youth of the wartime decade. In the early 1950s this sound became the dominant taste in music.

In 1949 the biggest songs in the nation were white pop, with black music subjugated to a narrow race market. The top songs of 1949 were "Mule Train" by Frankie Laine, "Tennessee Waltz" by Patti Page, and "Ghost Riders in the Sky" by Vaughn Monroe. "Ghost Riders in the Sky" continued as the top song into 1950, when it was joined by Mario Lanza's semioperatic "Be My Love." "How High the Moon" by Les Paul and Mary Ford, an advanced composition in its use of overdubbing, echo chambers, and follow-through mastering techniques, became a hit. The monster hit "Cry" by Johnnie Ray entered the charts October 1951 and was No. 1 through all of 1952. Vaughn Monroe's "Old Soldiers Never Die (They Just Fade Away)," taken in part from General MacArthur's retirement speech, became a lament to the Korean War, which was at its height in 1952.

As early as 1947 "Old Man River" by the Ravens had made the crossover from the black radio stations to the national charts. Amos Milburn was a favorite of Al Hendrix. "Rooming House Boogie" in 1949 and "Bad, Bad Whiskey" in 1950 seemed to speak directly to the Hendrixes' experiences. Johnny Otis's band, featuring Little Esther and The Robins (who went on to become Esther Phillips and The Coasters, respectively), had a trio of blues hits in 1950: "Double-crossin' Blues," "Deceivin' Blues," and "Mistrustin' Blues." "Louisiana Blues" and "Long-distance Call" by Muddy Waters were hits on the black stations in 1951. In 1952 Lloyd Price's "Lawdy Miss Clawdy" was No. 1 on the black radio stations across America.

In 1953 The Orioles, a moderately popular group among the blacks since 1949, recorded "Crying in the Chapel." This song became one of the first, if not the first, rhythm and blues hits that crossed over to the national pop charts to be embraced by the entire record-buying public. The group received national publicity and the song became an instant classic.

In 1954 "Gee" by The Crows entered the national charts with resounding force, followed by The Moonglows' "Secret Love," which was "covered" by the McGuire Sisters. This started a "cover" song trend among white pop singers. They would sing the songs over often with a new "pop" arrangement for the white mass audience. In 1954 "Shake Rattle and Roll" by Big Joe Turner was covered by Bill Haley and The Comets. "SchBoom" by The Chords became a classic "cover." As the song veered from the R&B charts onto the national charts, a Canadian group named The Crewcuts covered it. It went on to become *the* monster hit of 1954, with The Chords receiving moderate airplay. "Earth Angel" by The Penguins released in November of 1954 was so R&B-imbued that it was impossible to cover. It took over the No. 1 slot from The Moonglows' "Sincerely" (which was co-written by R&B and rock 'n' roll activist Allan Freed, the New York City DJ who is credited with launching the rock 'n' roll craze.)

By 1955 Tin Pan Alley was in a tizzy. The musical taste of the nation was changing right before their eyes. The national charts became dominated by R&B. *Billboard* magazine, the trade organ for the music industry, began to print under its weekly listings of the top songs: "Keep Pop Alive in '55." Even an R&B version of "White Christmas" sung by The Drifters edged out all the other Christmas songs as the year changed.

In 1955 "Earth Angel" faded from No. 1, only to be succeeded by "Pledging My Love" by Johnny Ace, who had just killed himself while playing Russian roulette. No pop star would ever do that. Johnny Ace's story captivated the nation. R&B was not only dominating the charts, it was becoming legendary as well. "Pledging My Love" was No. 1 for *ten weeks.* Then a flukey blues number by Little Walter called "My Babe," written by Willie Dixon, took over No. 1. Finally white pop regained the coveted spot with "The Ballad of Davy Crockett," the theme song of a weekly Walt Disney television series. The song was played twice a week, before and after the show, on national television. The sale of coonskin caps skyrocketed. Davy Crockett, hero of Texas, had again become a hero by saving the youth of America from the scourge of rock 'n' roll. The press, parents' groups, and many older people had labeled R&B and rock 'n' roll trashy, dirty, primitive music of the lowest order. Even the *Encyclopaedia Britannica Yearbook* said: "The rock 'n roll school in general concentrated on a minimum of melodic line and a maximum of rhythmic noise, deliberately competing with the artistic ideals of the jungle itself."

"Unchained Melody" by both Al Hibbler and Roy Hamilton had a little of both R&B and pop. When it succeeded "Davy Crockett" on the charts, it seemed that happy days for the older generation were here again. They rejoiced when "Cherry Pink and Apple-blossom White" by Perez Prado's orchestra became a substantial No. 1 hit for several weeks. There seemed to be a weird semantic battle going on in the world of song between black R&B performers and white pop singers. "Ain't That a Shame" by Fats Domino took over again, while a slew of new black heavyweights entered the charts: Chuck Berry's "Maybelline," Bo Diddley's "Bo Diddley," The Nutmegs' "Story Untold," The Four Fellows with "Soldier Boy." But then to the chagrin of those of the older generation who believed the music came from the jungle or hell or both, whites started singing that stuff in earnest. "Rock Around the Clock" by Bill Haley and The Comets became the national anthem of rock 'n' roll, signaling to all that many whites had joined the fray—on the other side.

Bill Haley and The Comets used to be called The Saddlemen but changed their name just as the new youth music gathered on the horizon. They had had moderate hits before. They covered Big Joe Turner's "Shake Rattle and Roll" in 1954. Bill Haley, who was also a songwriter, penned a tune called "Rock-a Beatin' Boogie" for a group called The Esquires. It had a refrain that exhorted the listeners, "Rock rock rock everybody roll roll roll everybody." DJ Allan Freed adopted "rock 'n' roll" as the name of the new music of black *and* white youths. Rock 'n' roll, though owing a great deal to rhythm and blues, also came to incorporate white country music as well.

Bill Haley and The Comets' "Rock Around the Clock" became the title tune of a new movie called *Blackboard Jungle*, which featured a juvenile gang on the rampage in a New York City public high school. This confirmed, for the older generation, rock 'n' roll's inexorable connection with youth violence, even though the song had been well on its way to becoming a hit before the movie came out.

"Rock Around the Clock" was succeeded by "Maybelline." Chuck Berry, with his charismatic way of performing, became one of the most popular early rock 'n' rollers. The pop school was given further hope when Mitch Miller's "Yellow Rose of Texas" topped the charts for a moment. But the impetus of the new trend was solid.

The national television show "Your Hit Parade," the showcase for white pop music, became hard pressed to duplicate the R&B and rock 'n' roll hits. Crooners from the old school—Snooky Lanson, Russell Arms, Giselle MacKenzie, and Dorothy Collins—found that their interpretations of R&B and rock 'n' roll songs failed, often miserably.

The "cover" song became an industry with the advent of Dot Records. Gale Storm, a television star of her own series, "My Little Margie," covered "I Hear You Knocking," taking away from Fats

Domino's initial effort. Pat Boone, sporting a clean-cut "Joe College" image from Columbia University, covered in succession "Ain't That a Shame" (by Fats Domino), "Tutti-frutti" (by Little Richard), and "I'll Be Home," a beautiful ballad about returning home from the Korean War, as sung by The Flamingos. By the end of 1955 Pat Boone was the king of the "cover" artists, his flat baritone veering further and further from R&B truth.

By the end of 1955 even Frank Sinatra was "Learning the Blues." *Billboard*'s exhortation to pop lovers seemed to make a difference in 1956. "Sixteen Tons" by Tennessee Ernie Ford was No. 1 on January 1. "The Great Pretender" by The Platters and "Memories Are Made of This" by Dean Martin reversed the trend back to pop in the first weeks of 1956. Kay Starr's "Rock 'n' Roll Waltz" made no bones about the amalgam that Tin Pan Alley was betting heavily on.

The trend might have been totally turned back to pop in 1956 if some country boys had not shown up singing about their "Blue Suede Shoes" (Carl Perkins) and "Heartbreak Hotel" (Elvis Presley). Then came little Frankie Lymon and The Teen-agers' "Why Do Fools Fall in Love?" and The Teen Queens' "Eddie My Love" to prevent a complete sweep by the pop on the charts. An army of "cover" singers of the pop school were keeping the new rock 'n' roll back as many former country artists took to rock 'n' roll.

Elvis Presley and the Everly Brothers would hold up the rock 'n' roll banner until 1960, when the Twist came in and swept the entire nation.

But in the mid-fifties there were black recording artists who were very happy to remain in the narrow race market. Hank Ballard and The Midnighters were doing very fine with their brand of "blue" material. No one would dare copy, cover, or even sell it over the counter. Yet his music spread by word of mouth like wildfire. Their first recording of "sexually frank" material, "Get It," was a big success in every black ghetto from coast to coast. Although it got virtually no air play, "Get It" was followed by a string of singles that used "Annie" as a sex goddess: "Annie Had a Baby," "Work with Me Annie," "Sexy Ways," and "Annie's Aunt Fannie." Etta James fashioned a reply to Ballard and "Annie" called "(Wallflower) Roll with Me Henry," which, while released commercially, was still thought to be too risqué. After several changes the title became "Dance with Me Henry," which was promptly covered by Georgia Gibbs, becoming a big pop hit of 1955. But Hank Ballard and The Midnighters continued on with their suggestive songs, doing good business under the counter.

Annie had a baby
Can't work no more
no no no no no no
Annie had a baby
Can't work no more

She walks with the baby
Instead of me
She talks to the baby
Instead of me

Annie had a baby
Better get it
While the gettin' is good
So good, so good, so good

Hank Ballard wailed on, his high Texas tenor piercing the heavy raunch of The Midnighters. It was more a pure get-down rocker than a risqué song to Jimmy, but his ears glowed anyway because he was not supposed to have heard it.

Having babies and making love were normal in Seattle's Central District. The house rent parties that were given every weekend seemed to play "Work with Me Annie" and "Annie Had a Baby" continuously. Amos Milburn and his "Bad Bad Whiskey" was still popular and Muddy Waters was coming on strong with "Long-distance Blues" and "Hootchie Cootchie Man." But Hank Ballard and The Midnighters, with their happy up-tempo songs about "Annie," a carefree, free-loving, unattached young woman, and her subsequent motherhood, were closer to the reality of how the blacks in the project *really* felt and lived their lives. Of course, the authorities felt very differently about the joy of lovemaking among the blacks in the project, especially since the consequences seemed to make their jobs a nightmare. But the blacks had their own feelings about it that were hidden from the authorities, to be celebrated among themselves. It excited Jimmy to know that the record was banned, was a secret, but sold very well anyway. And its popularity also gave him a new sense of the emergent underground black music. He realized that there was more happy fun where "Work with Me Annie" and "Annie Had a Baby" came from.

The first band Jimmy consistently played with in Seattle was a band formed by Fred Rollins, a high school friend, called The Rocking Kings. At first he had been terribly shy and played rather badly. But his deferential sincerity and his good ear made him a good person for the young band. He listened to every kind of musical expression and idea. When they had a gig he took what was offered with sincere appreciation, whether it was a couple of hamburgers in payment or five or ten dollars. He became the best R&B and rock 'n' roll guitarist in Seattle.

The western part of Canada is only sixty miles from Seattle. Vancouver, British Columbia, the largest city in the area, was starved for the new youth music of the States. The Rocking Kings found work there and went up to play as often as possible.

The ride to Vancouver was beautiful. The boys listened to the radio on the way up. Each had certain favorites. Jimmy's were "Sleep Walk" by Santo and Johnny, "Rocking Crickets" by The Hot Toddies, "Cathy's Clown" by The Everly Brothers, "La Bomba" by The Carlos Brothers, and "Summertime Blues" by Eddie Cochran. He received constant kidding from the fellows; his spacey ways and shy, soft mumblings were always good for an impersonation when the trip got boring. The Rocking Kings played several of The Coasters' hits, things like "Charlie Brown," "Poison Ivy," "Yakety Yak," "Searchin'," and "Along Came Jones"; all were big hits in 1958–59. "Do You Want to Dance?" by Bobby Freeman and "At the Hop" by Danny and The Juniors were sure-fire songs to get a crowd moving, and "The Twist" by Hank Ballard was unbelievable. Jimmy really got off on the "Peter Gunn Theme," but like "Sleep Walk," it was hardly danceable and hardly reflected the big-beat rhythm and blues rock 'n' roll the audiences preferred. *"Petite Fleur,"* written by jazz great Sidney Bechet for the Chris Barber jazz band, was another favorite of Jimmy's. He longed to play his guitar like a horn and saw

The Rocking Kings play at Washington Hall, Seattle, February 20, 1960 (Jimi 2nd from left) J.A. HENDRIX

no reason why that was not possible, but his remarks along those lines never failed to bring sarcastic reactions from his bandmates.

Although spacey and spooky, Jimmy was a hit with the girls. This never failed to irritate the members of The Rocking Kings or the regular guys at Garfield High. When it got around that Jimmy would not engage in fistfights he began to have trouble.

One day after school, Jimmy refused to let a bully handle his guitar. He was chased across the football field in full view of the homeward-bound students, knocked down, and beaten, kicked, and stomped. But he never released his guitar from his protective embrace.

He stopped playing with The Rocking Kings after an intrigue with another band member's girlfriend. Jimmy did not go out of his way to attract the girl, but there was something in the way he moved and joked and jived that she found attractive. Jimmy would always go into his showtime routine onstage while he played. This would enrage all of The Rocking Kings. They thought he was making a fool of himself and them too. Jimmy would always say he was sorry, but would do it again at the next occasion, afterward saying he was sorry again. But the girls ate it up. One night before a gig at Birdland, Jimmy was called into the men's room for a private conference with the band member whose girl dug him. Everyone in the band knew what was up but did nothing to stop it. As the two boys disappeared behind the door the band members speculated on whether Jimmy would fight back or not. When they came out a few minutes later it looked like Jimmy had not bothered to defend himself. He had a bloody nose, his hair was messed up, and he was puffy in a few other places, but he cleaned himself up and went on and did the show anyway. Soon after that incident Jimmy ceased playing with The Rocking Kings.

The Rocking Kings were breaking up anyway. Fred Rollins, the leader of the group, had been scheduled to go into the army and he left soon after the bathroom incident. The next time Jimmy saw Rollins was when he was home on furlough. Rollins was decked out in an army paratrooper's uniform with a screaming eagle emblazoned upon the lapel. Everyone was really impressed and so was Jimmy.

Al Hendrix

Well, Jimmy slumped in school just like I did. When I was going to school I used to tell my mother, "Daggummit," I say, "I ain't learning nothing. I ain't getting no further ahead." I dropped out from Templeton Junior High School in Vancouver. I said the best thing for me to do is to go to work. That was after my dad died, and my mother was on something similar to welfare here. Public assistance of some kind. My brother and I were both going to school, but it was costing too much for us to catch the school bus. So I used to *walk* home in the evening. I used to catch the bus going to school to make sure I'd get there on time, and then I walked home. I had plenty of time; I didn't have to worry about being late coming home.

I think Jimmy stopped in his senior year. I think he only had one more year to finish. I kept getting letters from his teachers saying Jimmy wasn't doing this or that. It seemed like he just lost all interest. I used to tell him, "Man, you better finish. Finish this year." But he didn't. After he dropped out, I went up there one day and the teacher told me, "Well, he's got too many strikes against him. He can't make it." And I said, "OK." So Jimmy came home with me and I said, "You have to go out and work with me. It's all for our common survival." He tried to get jobs in some of the supermarkets as a bag carrier. He applied at a lot of places. And I said, "That's all right, but while we wait for that to come through, you can come and work with Dad."

I had another worker with me named "Shorty," and we got along good. I used to drive him hard. He never asked me what I was paying him. I told him it was for the common cause of survival, to make that rent money and to have some food in our stomach. Of course on the weekend he'd sport around and I'd give him a few dollars. I'd say, "Well OK, I know you going out with the guys, here's five or ten dollars." Of course, cats nowadays say, "Ooooh man, what am I gonna do with that? Where's five dollars gonna take me?" but Jimmy would say, "Yeah, Dad, thanks."

I knew Jimmy had been smoking for some time. In the apartment where we lived we had to go down the hallway to the common bathroom to take a bath or use the toilet. Jimmy would go down there and smoke. Once I was walking up Madison, going to the Honeysuckle to shoot pool, and I saw him and his buddy coming down the street. I saw him before he saw me. He was just walking down the street like Mr. Big Time. I caught up to him right in front of the Honeysuckle Poolhall. "Hey Jimmy," I said. He had his cigarette behind his back. "Well you can bring your cigarette out," I said, "before it burns your fingers." And he looked at me so funny. Real sheepishly. I said, "That's all right man, it's OK." I always told him, "You be truthful to me and I'll be truthful to you." And that's the way he was. But he was surprised that day. I guess he figured I was a kind of strange dad. Sometimes I tell him no on some things and yes on some.

Al Hendrix had not planned on being a gardener, but after working at Bethlehem Steel hauling red-hot steel rods that would singe the double pants he wore, sometimes burning through, Al found gardening to be a relatively placid way to earn a living.

Jimmy's father proved amazingly strong to those who because of his slight height thought him to be half a man. Al was all wringing, twisting, rippling muscles, with light grace. His centaurlike legs making short hustling steps seemed to slide across the garden, as if dancing, his muscles forming without concentration.

Jimmy had the same twisting, sinewy muscles, only he was much taller than his father, although not quite six feet himself. Jimmy's arms draped down almost to his knees. Sometimes his father would stop work and come over and stand by his side comparing arm lengths in jest. Then mock-measuring his arms, Al would shake his head as he gazed down to where Jimmy's arms ended slightly above his knees.

James Williams and Jimmy spent New Year's Eve 1959 together. It was a bitterly cold evening and they, as usual, had nowhere to go. They sat in Jimmy's room. Jimmy always wanted to play and sing. He didn't care what kind of music it was as long as it made song and melody. James liked to sing, to croon. He could sound just like Dean Martin, so they did "Memories Are Made of This," the crooner's latest hit, which was accompanied by a stylish acoustic guitar on the 78 rpm recording.

Take one fresh and tender kiss
and one golden night of bliss

Jimmy played guitar and sang the accompanying chorus. He approximated the chorus: "Sweet, sweet the memories you gave to me/Can't beat the memories you gave to me. . . ." Over and over they sang that song. James did not like those wild rhythm and blues songs, but he loved the slow sentimental ballads that his father and mother preferred.

Singing such a sentimental song evoked images of loves and lost loves. Jimmy stopped to make a phone call. It became a long and involved call and soon Jimmy beckoned James to the phone. Clamping the receiver with his palm Jimmy told James that he was talking to Betty Jean, his one big love. Unable to take her out, he had called; she was too young to really party anyway. But she knew what to feed a man for a good night of lovemaking.

"Now what you gonna give me to eat when I come over?" Jimmy asked her again. "Go on, tell me everything." She began to recite as Jimmy excitedly let James eavesdrop. As if from memory she crooned: some eggs, soft-boiled, oysters and clams, raw on the shell, lots of butter and toast . . .

James was confused, Jimmy nearly convulsed with laughter, converting it into the good cheer he projected into the receiver. He hung up. James asked him what that was all about. "That's what a woman gives her man for his sex," Jimmy replied, "that's love food that builds up the potency."

It was late for seventeen-year-olds, nearly midnight. Jimmy, who seemed to have no rules circumscribing his movements, walked James most of the way home through the chilling night winds. There was no food in the house and Jimmy wanted to eat. The Kingfish Cafe was close to James's house, so they headed in that direction. When they arrived, Jimmy asked James for some money to get food. James, who had just gotten paid, gave Jimmy ten dollars. They said good-bye again, waving. James looked back as he walked away and saw through the steaming window Jimmy sitting gingerly, shyly at the counter. It was New Year's Day 1960. They never saw each other again.

Al Hendrix

"Dad, I have been going down to the recruiting office," Jimmy told me one day. He knew he was 1-A. He knew if he volunteered he would get the category he wanted. He kept going down to see this recruiting officer, and then one day he told me, "Dad, I'm going in." I said, "That's all right, that's all right. There's nothing wrong with that. Get it over with." There were no wars going on, it was after the Korean War and before the Vietnam deal. He said he wanted to get into the Screaming Eagles, and I said, "Oh wow! You going on further than ol' Dad did." I remember I told him when I was in Fort Benning, Georgia, we used to watch them guys jump in their practice parachutes. Man, them paratroopers were double-timing. They weren't allowed to stand at attention or anything. Double-time every place they went on the base. And I said, "Man." When Jimmy told me that he wanted to be a paratrooper, I said, "Oh no!"

1961: Jimi in the service uniform of the Screaming Eagles paratroopers COURTESY J.A. HENDRIX

"Son, you gonna be double-timing your whole time." He said, "I want to get one of them Screaming Eagles, Dad." "Well, that makes me feel real proud," I said. That made me feel real proud of him. He was trying to do something.

He went to ship out, and I went down there with him and gave him some money. A helper-out. It made me feel real good. About as good as I would have felt if my dad had seen me going into the service.

When Jimmy went into the service he didn't take his guitar with him. He had an electric guitar, but he didn't have any amplifier or anything of that sort. I said, "Well I'll send it to you after your basic training. Just let me know."

Blessings on thee little square
O barefoot hag with uncombed hair
with thy solid peg-legged pants
and thy solid hep cat stance
with thy cheeks so fine and mellow

Kiss thy cheeks so fine and mellow
I was just a little square
like the cat with unconked hair
now I'm hip to the chicks
and far from a drip
the cats on the square
call me Joe Ad-Lib
to show how the cats will rap your
scratchings if you're not on into
their latchings
statched at the main crib
Crib on hep cat square
When I just hit this trip
I was laughed for a square

I'm telling you Jack
these cats are on with half a chance
They'll give you the gong
The hats with the gats
and the scopes with them grapes
pitch a fog very dim
over some dregs
My first encounter with some of these frills
When I was down at Joe's I was flatched to the gills

She had a candied cutie
Over a solid coke frame
I was so loaded to the gills
I didn't get her name

Jimi Hendrix,
eighteen years old, 1960

TWO

Thinking about the army brought up an ambivalence in his emotions that made him stop and wonder why his feelings were so torn. Fort Campbell had really been the place where he had first made it on his own. He had dug jumping out of planes. Sometimes he would even take pictures with a camera while jumping. He realized that he was not afraid of what for them as paratroopers was their big ordeal: jumping out of planes. He had reveled in the sound of the big plane lumbering through the air with the intense weight of its human cargo. The sound of the door opening was even more enthralling. The rush of air into the cabin, the howling singing of the wind surging in, augmenting the sound of the engine. It had been a true marriage of machine and nature: the sound, the energy. And then falling. Falling away from that sound, farther and farther toward the earth, where he would float like an angel toward its silence and its life.

When he got his guitar from his father he began to experiment with duplicating the sound of the heavens. It was like the electric guitar had an earth existence and an air existence. He saw that the feat was to be able to make the guitar fly. He understood wind instruments totally after that and tried to emulate not the sound so much as the meaning of the sound to a human. Like the engines of the plane and the resistance of the air made another unique quality, another unique sound, more than the air, more than the engine, more than a wind—it made a sound that sang. It often made him think that there was something being said. It was the sound of speeds and heights the human body could not attain itself. The substance of that sound and the loftiness his body occupied in relation to the earth gave him a rare experience. He wondered how it would be to venture higher. Like a human spaceship beyond the stratosphere.

He could mark his life by the tunes in his head. He was able to transfer the sounds to his guitar—his traveling companion, his life companion. Sometimes he played far outside the sounds the rhythm and blues cats played, yet totally into the weird sounds of the country blues, and the weird emotions the sounds produced in him. Now he was hearing the rural acoustic blues, not the stuff on the radio. No one he had heard on the radio had captured the eerie mystical potentials of the blues sounds in the rough. One man playing a wooden box with cat guts strung across it. From town to town the rural blues men traveled, playing not the huge arenas, but deep down inland, back-home places where, for decades, these blues men had been *the music.* Now driven into obscurity, the solid base of the people, the solid country blues had been forgotten by the big recording and broadcasting companies. Yet, almost like a secret tradition, it lingered carefully, tenuously, only to be revealed to the true seeker.

It had not taken him long to discover after his guitar arrived that all he really wanted to do in life was play guitar. The guitar had been his entire life. It was his sister, his woman, his muse, and his release. Most of the musicians in his unit were part-time. He would amaze them with the absorption and passion with which he played. He sensed a lot of resentment beginning to build about him after he got his own instrument. Before, he would borrow someone else's guitar, or else resort to checking out the antiquated one they had at the base. Once he had borrowed a guy's guitar and while he was playing it, the guy got agitated and asked for it back, saying he was messing it up, that he was going to break it. That was stupid. The guy had been jealous because Jimmy played it so much better than he. It didn't take long for Jimmy to realize that most of the guys were pretty childish. His isolation as a child had kept him away from being close to a large group of people as he was at Fort Campbell. As a teen-ager he kept pretty much to himself, even though he played a lot of music. He restricted his relationships—apart from women—as he grew older to strictly musical ones. He was known to all the young groups in Seattle as the best guitar player of their age and experience. They dug him for his ability, yet he would always be apart from their scenes. His relationship with them had been purely musical, and often they did not understand this, expecting him to hang out and pal around. Now in the army he found most of the fellows to be pretty much on the same level. Once they had worked together or jumped together or even did KP together there would be an assumed collective bond that he did not often share. Once he had his guitar it became, for many of them, an object that symbolized his separateness. And many people sought to destroy him through his guitar. Just for the hell of it.

He started sleeping with his guitar. It was no big thing. Some of the older players who had shown him a thing or two would mention sleeping with their guitars. Then he had seen an interview with Mississippi John Hurt where he talked about sleeping with his guitar. It was kind of a funny topic because the implication there was that the guitar replaced a woman in your bed.

His fellow paratroopers began to tire of his duplications of the sounds of the heavens, heavy metal flying. They began to scorn and deride his efforts. Not only was he a constant fixture in the music room, but in the barracks he was constantly working on new sounds, even without an amp. The men in his barracks began to complain that they could not sleep at night for Jimmy's arpeggios. They took to hiding his guitar and making Jimmy get down on his knees and beg for it back. He would always say he was sorry, but that would not prevent him from doing it again. One day, several of the men jacked him up and beat him up. Jimmy protected his guitar more than himself. But unfortunately for the attackers, Jimmy's boyhood friend from Seattle was Raymond Ross, the 101st Airborne's heavyweight boxing champion. He came into Jimmy's barracks soon after the incident. "I hear y'all messing with my homeboy," he said. Ross then went down the aisle beating up everyone involved and some who were not.

Although he was not attacked physically again, they still made fun of Jimmy. To them he was weird. He slept with his guitar. He talked to his guitar. He played it all the time, relating to it more than he related to the guys. He painted the name "Betty Jean" on his guitar and began calling it by name. The men in the barracks began to say that he was crazy.

Fort Campbell, Kentucky, was in the heart of the South. Great swarms of blackbirds would swoop over the skies making a fantastic appearance on the low horizon. The beauty of the land kept his mind on the rural blues players. The more he learned about the blues, the more he admired the rural blues players, the Delta sound,

and the guys in Chicago who had transplanted that sound to the
city. He would go to Nashville—only 60 miles away—every chance
he got to hear some music or just walk around. The town reeked of
music. A lot of country music abounded and a new hip sound that
groups like the Mar-Keys and Booker T. and the MGs were into.
Their sound was hip and contemporary, yet they had a country
element that was very different from the urban rhythm and blues. It
was a laid-back, easily accessible music that had beautiful turns to it
that captivated you after a while. He felt a kinship with that kind of
sound more than the copies of the Top Ten stuff he had been playing
in Seattle. Nashville, out of the way and small like Seattle, nevertheless had a distinct musical personality. He felt Nashville would
be a good transition for him on his way to New York, and more
importantly, he felt that he could live and learn in Nashville without the big hassles a big city would present him with.

He had not wanted to make it seem like he quit on the army. He
still had a desire to make his father proud of him by remaining in the
elite Screaming Eagles. Yet, once he had been away from home for a
while, away from all that had made him what he was up until that
point, he began to realize what he wanted to do in life.

Fred Rollins, who had played in The Rocking Kings, had gone into
the Screaming Eagles before Jimmy. Although he was on a different
part of the base he kept abreast of what was happening with Jimmy.
He had not known Jimmy's girlfriend in Seattle, but Jimmy gave
him the impression that they were very seriously involved. He
assumed that Jimmy had received a "Dear John" letter when word
got back to him that Jimmy was flipping out. That was the only
reason he could think of for Jimmy sleeping with his guitar, talking
to it, playing it as soon as he woke up in the morning, and making
such weird sounds with it. Even when Jimmy went to mess he
strummed the air and made noises as if his guitar were there with
him.

Word got around that Jimmy was getting out. Rollins had heard
that he had been to see every psychiatrist on the base. Others related
that Jimmy had had an accident while making a jump one day.
Whatever the reason, Jimmy was transferred to the section of the
base reserved for those soon to be released.

Billy Cox, who was in the same section waiting for his walking
papers, heard Hendrix playing one day and was really impressed. A
serious student of European classical music, as well as R&B and
blues, Cox recognized, upon hearing Jimmy play, a genius that

ranged between "Beethoven and John Lee Hooker." Although what Cox heard indicated that Jimmy was limited to only about five keys, "and was still getting his shit together." He also recognized that Jimmy had largely mastered and extended his sound into virtuoso statements.

Cox introduced himself, checked out a bass, and they immediately began to jam. They picked up a drummer named Gary Ferguson, and a second guitarist named Johnny Jones, and they had a group. They gigged for a while in the service clubs on base and in clubs in Clarksdale and other neighboring towns. They played mainly the hits of the day like "Tossin' and Turnin' " by Bobby Lewis, "Daddy's Home" by Shep and the Limelights, "Mother-in-law" by Ernie K. Doe, "Quarter to Three" by Gary "U.S." Bonds, and "Last Night" by the Mar-Keys. Jimmy, Billy, Johnny, and Gary called themselves The Casuals.

Jimmy won a small following for himself in the small towns near Fort Campbell. They would sit through set after set just to hear him solo a few times. Like Charlie Christian, Hendrix was interested in shaping his overall approach to the electric guitar along the lines of horns. He would tell his small band of aficionados that one day he would have the sound of a trumpet with a mute on it. They loved it.

Hendrix and Cox, once discharged from the Army, gigged around, sleeping and eating where and when they could until they reached Nashville. They got quarters over Joyce's House of Glamour on Jefferson Street.

Soon they were in a group with some Nashville natives led by Johnny Snead called the Imperials. Johnny Snead had named the group after the barbershop where the members all had their hair done in elaborate marcels. The proprietor of the shop acted as their manager. Jimmy met Johnny at the barbershop and once Johnny heard him play he became Jimmy's employer, protector, and benefactor. They became fairly popular in the local clubs and even made some television appearances. They were very poor, having hardly enough money for rent and food, but they attracted a following among the people in the neighborhood.

Some of the young girls in the neighborhood became Jimmy's unofficial fan club. They looked out for Jimmy, making sure that he did not go *too* long between meals. Sandra Mathews was the ringleader. She took to calling herself and the girls who hung around Jimmy the Buttons. They would sing the blues behind Jimmy's constant playing. All he played was the blues. They also mended his clothing; that was how they got to calling themselves the Buttons. It was a private joke between them and Jimmy. He would always be

missing a button or two and even worse. Jimmy kept his stage
clothes together, a dark suit with a narrow Ivy League tie and white
shirt, but otherwise he cared little about how he appeared when he
was not onstage.

Once Fred Rollins came into town on a pass from Fort Campbell.
He knew that Jimmy and Billy were gigging regularly and went
straight to the club where they played with the Imperials. They
were on when he got there. Fred went straight to the bandstand and
took out his sax. Pretty soon he caught their eyes and was invited up
to sit in. Halfway through the number Fred realized that Jimmy and
Billy had advanced far beyond him musically. It was embarrassing
for everyone all around. Rollins excused himself from the bandstand
and sat down.

A few days later Rollins went by Hendrix's place. Jimmy was
there with his girlfriend, a small black woman. Jimmy was virtually
penniless. Rollins offered to treat both Hendrix and his girlfriend to
dinner. They went to a local diner where Jimmy's girlfriend began to
feel ill. They ate anyway, Jimmy eating her meal too. Rollins was
appalled that he had bought Jimmy two dinners. Disgusted over
what he felt was Hendrix's greed and lack of will to work for a
living, Fred Rollins told Jimmy off with finality.

One day Jimmy met Steve Cropper in a soul food restaurant. They
got to talking guitar and soon they were in a small studio that
Cropper knew about. Steve Cropper was the biggest star Jimmy had
ever hung out with. Lead guitarist for Booker T. and the MGs. Cropper, although he was white and from a country-music background,
had become one of the best R&B guitarists of the Memphis sound.
They jammed for a spell, then Cropper had the engineer, who was
also a friend, record them. It was amazing. Here, out of the blue, was
Jimmy jamming with Steve Cropper.

An acetate demo record was made of the session. Jimmy took it
around, but there were no takers. Discouraged, Jimmy decided to
return to the Pacific Northwest.

Jimmy made his way back to Vancouver in the winter of 1962.
One night he wandered into a club he had heard about called
Dante's Inferno and found an unlikely duo in Tommie Chong and
Bobby Taylor fronting a band. Jimmy had known Floyd Snead, Wes,
Tommy, and Tommie Chong before, and with the addition of Bobby
Taylor, the band was really outasight. It was not unusual in the
Pacific Northwest to find a Chinese and a brother playing in a soul
band, but it was kind of weird to hear Chong sing background in

falsetto tenor that was authentic soul. The band cooked. It was not long before Jimmy was sitting in. And it was not long before Jimmy was asked to join the band.

Tommie Chong and Bobby Taylor were partners—owners of the band as well as the club. They had a good thing going. The club was packed and swung with Canadian Twist enthusiasts every night. The band had an unusual fervor. And then at midnight, when public clubs had to close, they had another club that was private right above Dante's Inferno called the Elegant Parlor.

Bobby Taylor had recently graduated from the master's degree program in music at the University of California, Berkeley, and had

Another of Jimi's early bands (Jimi at left, Billy Cox at center) J.A. HENDRIX

come to Vancouver at the request of Tommie Chong, who had offered him an across-the-board partnership in exchange for Taylor's incredible singing voice, keyboard musicianship, and composition abilities. Bobby Taylor also knew how to run a club properly. Called "Bobby Taylor and the Vancouvers," the band did arrangements of popular songs of the day that were better than the originals. They had a large and consistent following.

Jimmy would play with the Vancouvers on weekends and on weekdays at the Black and Tan Club in Seattle. He stayed with his grandmother Nora and her family. It was perfect for Jimmy. He was able to cool out, play guitar, and get his energy up. Jimmy was very laid back and quiet. What impressed Bobby Taylor the most about Jimmy was his mental strength. Jimmy said he couldn't sing but that he loved to. He would make up songs as he played, like the calypso singers. He didn't do his with rhyme, he did his with meaning.

He worked with them on and off for about a year, then Little Richard came through and raided the Vancouvers, taking Jimmy along, too.

Little Richard called himself "the father of rock 'n' roll." From Macon, Georgia, Little Richard added a high keening gospel sound to the then prevalent rockabilly and came up with the most notorious of the early rock 'n' roll hits: "Tutti-frutti," "Long Tall Sally," "Good Golly Miss Molly," "Jenny, Jenny, Jenny," "Slippin' and Slidin'," "Ready Teddy," "Lucille," "Send Me Some Lovin'," "Keep A-knockin'," and more.

While Pat Boone and other white singers received a great deal of the credit and the loot for their versions of Little Richard's compositions, Little Richard was confined to the same race crowd that had spawned his creativity. The same is true of Elvis Presley spinoffs from Big Bill Crudup, Bo Diddley, and Big Mama Thornton. "If I could only find me a white boy who can sing colored," Sam Phillips had lamented, until he found Presley. While Chuck Berry was hard to cover, his incarceration in Texas for four years during the height of the rock 'n' roll craze kept him effectively out of the picture.

When Jimmy Hendrix joined Little Richard in 1963, the rock 'n' roll craze had subsided into the Kennedy years, and Little Richard had returned to the withering rhythm and blues circuit of the small towns of the Deep South and the West Coast. But Richard Penniman was not one to internalize his hurts. Jimmy Hendrix received lecture after lecture on the hardships pressed upon Little Richard by a public and an industry that did not reward the originators of their joy and fortune. If Little Richard was not making money, Hendrix was making less. Traveling by bus from gig to gig, sometimes stranded in strange, out-of-the-way towns, subjected to the degradations of a hurt and complex man, Hendrix nonetheless persisted, playing that same strange amalgam of rockabilly and gospel, whose simple changes offered no challenge whatsoever to his musical ability. In fact, he and others in the band like Black Arthur and Henry Oden would often rebel in the midst of the insipid changes and take the music out there. This would never fail to enrage Little Richard, who considered the music little more than a background for his singing and dancing and his general display of outrageous finery. He was so uptight about someone else stealing his spotlight that he became upset if they even looked good in the clothes they wore. Once Jimmy wore a fine ruffled shirt onstage. Little Richard was irate. He called a meeting. "I am Little Richard," he screamed, "I am Little Richard, the King, the King of rock and rhythm. I am the only one allowed to be pretty. Take off those shirts. . . ."

Sometimes Richard Penniman would calm down and talk about his background. A friend of his family killed his father, who had operated a club called The Tippin' Inn in Macon, Georgia. Little Richard was "discovered" through a demo recording he sent to an executive of Specialty Records while he was washing dishes in a Greyhound bus depot in Macon. Bumps Blackwell came there to take him to New Orleans, where they recorded several songs. They went one over the limit with a new song Richard had. It was called "Tutti-frutti." Almost overnight Richard Penniman was thrust into stardom. It seemed as if it had been too much for him. For two years it seemed like everything he wrote was a hit. He hardly had time to catch his breath. Another artist who recorded for Specialty told Little Richard one day that the type of music he was playing was evil. That thought stayed with Richard. He never thought that the pronouncement might have been inspired by jealousy. While Little Richard was on tour in Australia in 1957, the Soviets launched Sputnik. He thought of the Tower of Babel and left show business to study for the ministry with the Seventh-Day Adventists. Instead of playing music, he would tell his audiences about his conversion to God. Only two years after his first hit he left the world of music. But songs he had had in the can kept him in hits into 1959, although the last two hit songs, "Baby Face" and "Kansas City," were written by the others and were not nearly as outrageous as his own tunes had been.

Little Richard would talk about his innocence during that time. He was a naïve twenty-three when "Tutti-frutti" became a hit. The first time he was exposed to anything other than alcohol was a mind-blowing experience for him. "I screamed like Aunt Jemima with no pancakes when I first tried marijuana," he would say. He would often emphasize an incident by saying, "I screamed like a white lady." Little Richard was really into screaming. He would tell Jimmy how he taught these young white boys, who had played backup for him when he toured England in Liverpool, how to scream. They were called the Beatles. Now every time they turned on the radio they would hear the Beatles screaming like white ladies. Jimmy had a lot of sympathy for Little Richard, and a lot of respect, too. Many times it seemed like Little Richard was still a lad from Macon recovering from seeing his father killed by a friend.

Jimmy Hendrix jumped Little Richard's band in St. Louis and went to Chappie's Lounge to see Ike Turner's Blues Band, which was one of the hottest R&B bands in the South. Jimmy sat in and they made fun of him and his antics as usual, but he met Albert King afterward and that made the whole thing worthwhile. Jimmy had heard about this left-handed blues guitarist, who roamed among Memphis, St. Louis, and Arkansas, through several recordings of his: "Blues at Sunrise," "Ooh-ee Baby," and "Traveling to California." Jimmy would not play with Ike Turner but he could be with a virtuoso blues guitarist who played left-handed (he played a right-handed guitar upside down) like him and had come from the blues depths.

King too was amused by Jimmy, yet he was kind and talkative. He was almost old enough to be Jimmy's father. He talked about Blind Lemon Jefferson, whom he had seen play in the parks around Forest City when he was a boy. He also saw Memphis Minnie, who would sing to a player piano that had custom rolls of her tunes. King grew up and began to seek his own sound as a guitarist. He played drums with Jimmy Reed for a spell but the guitar was his heart. He was influenced by Howling Wolf and Lonnie Johnson. T-Bone Walker's sound entranced and eluded him until he began bending strings to compensate for the intricate runs Walker was able to do that he was not capable of. He squeezed the strings with his massive fingers rather than in the traditional bend and got a sound that was completely his own. He played without a pick and developed a tremendously tactile touch. He showed Jimmy some fingerings using the thumb and frettings that bent the strings horizontally instead of vertically. His trademark was a sound that slurred up and then dropped down. Albert King was fascinated with horn sounds.

Jimmy had been intrigued by some of the scenes they had encountered at some of the big shows on the package tours. The saxophone players who blew the tenor usually generated the most excitement, often inciting the largely rural crowds to riot, so intense was the reaction. Jimmy wondered why the guitar could not do the same thing. Playing with Little Richard the guitar was used as a rhythm instrument, yet the new Fender electrics were capable of an incredible distortion-free sound, as loud as you wanted. Sometimes Jimmy had defied Little Richard and soloed, getting down on his knees and going through his whole routine. But he would get it when it was over. And there was nothing like having Little Richard shout at you for two hours. Nothing.

Jimmy wanted to get a feeling for what was being played off the beaten track, away from the top forty tunes of the day, back in the woods where there were no mass inhibitions.

Jimmy was always on the alert for a hot guitarist but now he also wanted to check out these saxophone honkers up close and get that sound imbedded in his mind. Hendrix was always amazed by the power of horns. Suddenly in the midst of a hot rock 'n' roll number, during the horn chorus where they riff to one note, one horn disengages from the chorus, a tenor sax, then it begins to honk, squeal, and bleat on the beat, toward a different vector than the chorus. The tenor goes beyond the music and stops the music as he gets into the pure sound of the honking reed, the sound of the slaying of a lamb, a cow, a bull, the screaming, weird sound of sacrifice heavy in the augmented air. On the hypnotic beat, the honker is on his knees, the crowd begins a low roar from the back of the outdoor arena. In the darkness a mass frenzy builds, a chain reaction. The honker is down on his back with the saxophone held straight above him steadily bleating, staggering the beat now, splitting notes and jacking chromatics. The crowd is surging against the stage now, circling bodies begin to bob up and down as the crowd turns within itself. High crying notes in the sky, a couple roll on the ground in a mad embrace, a bottle smashes against a bald head glistening with sweat, a fight starts, the crowd rushes forward and away at the same time, cries of joy and sorrow rise in the air, and the tenor saxophone is the only thing visible on stage. It seems to be levitating, enchanted by its own sound. Then the saxophone begins to glide along the stage, going crazy in squealing elemental abandonment. Now the crowd seems to understand; it charges the stage. The honking has tranced into manic legato tenor dorians; the saxophonist has gone beyond. The crowd is both angry and thrilled; they rock the stage, clambering aboard hallucinating mass destruction. The tenor player barely escapes.

A typical tenor saxophone climax to an outdoor concert. Hendrix, with his fascination for horns, must have seen many such frenzied endings during his music wanderings adrift from Little Richard's band.

Jimmy Hendrix rejoined Little Richard in Atlanta, Georgia, after a recording session he led there suddenly fell apart. He had become as established as any young brilliant guitarist could get in Nashville and the R&B chitt'lin' circuit, yet it seemed as if he could move no further. Little Richard's funky comeback tour had an expectant enthusiasm to it. Little Richard was crazy, but he was also wise, although the way he expressed his wisdom was outrage at its height.

Atlanta had been the only big town on the tour. The band rode the bus while Little Richard flew. They toured a lot of the out-of-the-way places in the Southwest as well. The big cities like Denver, San Francisco, Atlanta, L.A., and Las Vegas were often only connection points for the smaller towns they actually played. And when they went into the South, they went into the heart of the civil-rights upheavals.

Little Richard was very effeminate and sometimes he could really act weird. The comeback was difficult for a man who had been a top star. Often Little Richard went into tirades, and very often the money was short all around. Many of the band members were young musicians like Jimmy. They shared the fear of being left stranded in some little one-horse town, especially in the South. Little Richard was often petulant and unpredictable. Some members of the band felt that he did not like women. But all of them needed whatever money they were paid and were afraid to protest even when they felt they were receiving poor treatment.

Jimmy maintained himself as best he could. He loved to play. Little Richard was convinced that the rockabilly change that had propelled him to stardom in the fifties would prevail in the sixties, but the audience's musical tastes were changing.

Jimmy wore a conked hairdo that he maintained himself, often with a Sterno kit and hot comb. There was hardly enough money to have it done properly by a hairdresser, and often they were nowhere near a town big enough to have a barber shop that specialized in processed hair.

Sometimes Little Richard would make them wait around his hotel room before he paid them. He liked young boys to hang around him and sometimes would go through scenes with them in front of the band while they waited to be paid. He liked Jimmy a lot and sometimes it would seem that he was directing these antics at Jimmy.

At the Olympia September 10, 1967 © JEAN-PIERRE LELOIR

Once in Oakland Little Richard held the band in his room waiting for their pay while he berated a girlfriend of one of the band members. The scene got very ugly. Somebody called the cops, and the four members of the band decided to leave. They did not know whether they would have their jobs later or not. But many, including Jimmy, felt that they had had enough.

Jimmy continued on down to Los Angeles with Little Richard to do some recording with him. But once they got into the studio Jimmy found that the material was the same old stuff they had been doing on the road.

Jimmy left Little Richard's band in Los Angeles. There he went on to work with a young musician named Arthur Lee and a singer named Rosa Parks on several sessions that produced a forty-five record called "My Diary." Thinking that he could find more session work, Jimmy stayed around Los Angeles for a few weeks, but nothing was forthcoming. Joining another package tour, this time with Solomon Burke, Jimmy went on to tour the U.S.A. with various R&B and soul groups and singers such as Chuck Jackson, the Supremes, Ike and Tina Turner, Jackie Wilson, B. B. King, and—this was the last straw—the blond-wigged wrestler Gorgeous George.

Finally, Jimmy found himself in Chicago. He wanted to get back through Nashville and see some friends before he pushed on to the Big Apple, but while he was in Chicago he had to go by Chess Studios and see what was going on.

Chess Records in Chicago was the home of the recorded urban blues. He did not want to seem impressed, but milling around with him were many of the greatest names in blues: Muddy Waters, Little Milton, Bo Diddley, Willie Dixon, Little Walter, Lafayette Leek, Howard Ashby, Al Duncan, and Robert, Jr., Lockwood. And a whole bunch of dudes who just sat around looking heavy. He had asked one of the cats, who walked around the studio like he owned it, about the chances of recording with his own group. Tall and paunchy, the dude just kinda grinned at him like he was crazy. Later in the day while he was fooling around the studio between sessions he saw the same dude in the booth. Jimmy started playing some of his way-out blues, changing keys while he hammered a weird obbligato, then holding a single note while he up-tempoed on the bass strings, and then sliding back into the former key, and hitting some scratch rhythm chords. He thought it was pretty good. But when he went into the booth to maybe get a reaction, they started talking about the good old days. Although they pretended to be just talking, they were commenting on his playing. He got a lecture on the blues, much to the delight of the old blues men. Willie Dixon, the tall paunchy guy, held forth.

Right then, Muddy Waters walked in. Jimmy could not believe it—his idol stood in the tiny room nodding to everyone, moving his large frame in slow rural grace. Jimmy did not know whether Muddy Waters knew of him or not, but Muddy's remarks seemed to be only for his ears, although you would never have known it by looking at Muddy. They all started drinking some Chivas Regal. Muddy sat up there just like one of the boys, but you could tell by a subtle respect that hung in the room that he was their leader. It was not that he demanded that they pay attention to him. If one of the other guys had an essential point to make, he would think nothing of riding over what Muddy Waters was about to say. But when Muddy got to talking about the old days there was no one who had something more important to say.

He talked about Robert Johnson. He called him Robert. Alan Lomax had been looking for the legendary Robert Johnson when he had come upon Muddy Waters on the plantation where Muddy worked. Robert was dead by that time, something he had always sung about: to be killed by a woman. Only he had been killed *over* a woman by her husband. But one of the hands told Lomax about Muddy. Muddy even sang one of Robert Johnson's songs: "Kindhearted Woman." Muddy Waters had been the youngest fellow playing in the little group they had in Stovall, Mississippi, but he was very confident of himself mainly because he could sing. Even then, he had a powerful voice that did not pamper the blues or whine the lyrics. He sang like a man and had had just begun picking up his sliding style. At first he had mainly blown harmonica (he called it "the French harp"), but then he bought his first guitar from a friend for $2.50 and that same night got a gig where he was paid $2.00. He knew then he had done right saving nickels and dimes to get his first manufactured guitar—a Stella. Pretty soon the man at the all-night place raised him to $2.50 a night.

Although he had been "found" by one of the most significant "talent scouts" of authentic blues, Alan Lomax, it was not overnight stardom for Muddy. But by that time he had saved up and bought a Sears, Roebuck guitar that cost $11. He found that he could make a fantastic amount of money ($30 to $40) playing the streets of Clarksdale. Muddy Waters's idol had been Robert Johnson. After Johnson died, Muddy's "copy" was Son House, who lived just across from him on another plantation. He would go and hear Son House often. There were a lot of blacks in the Delta who had mastered the bottleneck style, but few had the dedication of Son House, who traveled all over the Delta playing the slide guitar. Few also had the raw determination of Muddy Waters, who, although just a youngster, was determined to be "known before the world."

Muddy Waters did not know how the slide guitar first began to be played. It looked easy. Maybe easier than picking. But in order to be a master of the slide guitar you had to know the blues deeply. You had to know the feel for duration and the way the meaning was being interpreted, for when you slide you "go down in and get some of it and get out of it." It is a subtle but powerful effect that sets songs on the edge of a particular emotion. The effect can overwhelm not only the listeners but the player as well; he has to know when to get up off it or else he ruins the whole sensibility of the song.

Muddy had picked cotton, milked cows, all the things that a sharecropper or fieldhand does, but his ambition was to play slide guitar on a par with the greats: Robert Johnson and Son House. He had recorded for Alan Lomax, with his little group at the Stovall plantation, but he got to Chicago on his own. He worked in a paper factory and played the house parties the workers gave on the weekends. Soon the word spread and he was hired to be in the house band of a small club called The Flame. He played as a sideman for Sunnyland Slim, Eddie Boyd, and a couple of times with Memphis Slim ("Memphis Slim was the big man, he was the big man"). Pretty soon Muddy Waters put his band together. His sound was based on the Delta sound. He found that players from Texas, Alabama, and Georgia did not fit as well with Mississippi Delta sound as those from Mississippi or Louisiana. Muddy based his style somewhere between Robert Johnson and Son House, adding a strong vocal, whereas they had depended on their playing.

Sunnyland Slim told Leonard Chess about Muddy. The first tunes Muddy cut for an unsure Leonard Chess were: "Feel Like Goin' Home," "Can't Be Satisfied," "Little Annie Mae," and "Gypsy Woman." All written by Muddy Waters.

Muddy had extended the blues by adhering to strict time, speeding it up to get a drive to it. There was a lot of competition in Chicago. In the midst of World War II, a lot of people were picking up on bebop. The big blues men were Tampa Red, Big Maceo, Memphis Slim, and the original Sonny Boy Williamson, who had that "particular twinkle in his voice that got to people." Blues had a lot of competition, but those who knew the blues still loved the blues.

"The big drop after the beat on the drum formed the foundation of my blues. Nothing fancy—just a straight heavy beat with it," Muddy said. He remembered Charlie Patton. "He was a real clown with the guitar. He'd pat the guitar, hit the guitar, whirl it over his head." He remembered some of the old records he heard as a kid: Blind Blake, Blind Boy Fuller, Blind Lemon Jefferson, Charlie Patton, and, of course, Robert Johnson and Son House. He seemed to have a thing about Robert Johnson. He figured Robert was the only man who could beat him sliding. Probably Son House could too when he was younger. But Muddy felt that it was on his shoulders to bring that lowdown Mississippi Delta sound up North.

"That's what makes the blues so good. When you know your blues, if you try to put direct time like you would do in pop music, I don't think the blues will sell as good. Some of my songs just have thirteen bars. I don't even count them myself, I just feel them out. We learned the beat, learned what people was moving off of. Even if it was the blues, we still had to drive behind it.

"But you see blues, it's tone—deep tone with a heavy beat. I kept that back beat on the drums plus full action on the guitar and harmonica and the piano in the back, then you've got a big sound. I think the best blues singers came from the church. I even thought of being a preacher myself, the blues is close to preaching. I got all my good moaning and trembling going for me right out of church."

Jimmy sat there listening in awe. He would not get to record at Chess, but he was happy he had stopped by. He took the bus back to Nashville, and picking up a friend, decided to try his luck in New York.

Jimmy Hendrix arrived in Harlem with a male friend from Nashville. They both got rooms in the Hotel Theresa on 125th Street and Seventh Avenue. Jimmy and his friend started hanging out in the Palm Café, which was less than a block away. All of the musicians who were playing at the Apollo at the time hung out in the Palm Café, and there was a live broadcast of the house band over WLIB-AM every weekend. Jimmy made it known among the bartenders and regulars that he was looking for work as a lead guitarist. He would run down a list of the performers he had worked with and the tours he had been on, but no one believed him. The Palm Café attracted many a weirdo. It was located on the main drag of Harlem, 125th Street, off Seventh Avenue, and the constant stream of weirdos, combined with the natural skepticism of the average Harlemite, made it hard to believe Hendrix. He looked like he was fifteen or sixteen, at most, to the hardened veterans of Manhattan Island's black city. He spoke so softly and acted so spacey that they just knew he was some kind of nut. And besides, none of the Supremes, or members of Little Richard's or Ike and Tina Turner's bands were there to back up his story. And what the hell was Seattle?

But one night they finally let him up on the bandstand to play with the house band. They fully expected some kind of weird shit and were not disappointed. After he got up on the bandstand and plugged in his guitar, they discovered he was left-handed yet was playing a right-handed guitar—upside down, yet! Now who ever heard of a left-handed guitarist? Then he tuned up in the weirdest way by playing a crazy run of screeching notes. The Palm Café house band played a sedate mode of Harlem jazz, heavy on the bottom and mellow on the top. Jimmy blasted his way through their sound right away, playing weird tonics against the key and incorporating mild feedback into his soloing. His rhythm chords were on time but sounded off to the members of the band, who were of another generation. They started messing up behind him, dragging the beat, and looking at each other in disgust, as if to say that amateur hour was at the Apollo every Wednesday night, not at the Palm Café. Jimmy played on determinedly, even getting into his showtime routine and flicking his tongue at the girls in the first

row. He got a few titters and a little applause as he walked off. But
he had touched one of the young ladies there.

Fayne Pidgeon came over to his table where he sat with his friend
from Nashville and gave him her best foxy smile. She just wanted to
let him know that she enjoyed his playing and that those jerks up on
the bandstand deserved to be kicked dead in their asses, one by one.
Fayne was offered a drink and sat down. Jimmy was very dejected
about his performance, but Fayne urged him to cheer up. She knew
the cats in the band and would make them give him another chance.
She had really liked Jimmy's performance. It was unusual. And his
stage routine was really something else, especially the wagging of
his tongue in time to the vibrato he played with one hand while
down on his knees. She dug it very much. Cheered by Fayne's
boisterous enthusiasm, Jimmy told her about himself and the various bands he had played with across the country. Fayne was impressed by all the places he had been and the people he had played
with. Besides, he had no reason to lie. She decided right there that he
was probably some kind of genius and that she would befriend him.
He was also kind of cute—he might be able to do more with that
long tongue besides fluttering it onstage.

One day Ronnie Isley of the Isley Brothers was scouring New York
looking for a new guitarist. They had several important gigs in
Canada and Bermuda and just had to have someone on lead guitar
who could really play. If they disappointed their fans outside the
U.S.A., they might not be able to get those gigs again. Ronnie went
into the Palm Café and spotted a man named Tony Rice, who used
to work with Joe Tex. He let him know right away about the problem. Tony Rice had been present when Jimmy Hendrix had sat in
with the house band and had been impressed. Ronnie pressed Tony;
he had to be sure this guy was really good. Ronnie ran off a list of top
lead guitarists who were in the R&B bag. Tony said that this Hendrix cat was better than all of them. Convinced that he was not
being put on, Ronnie went up to Room 406 of the Hotel Theresa and
met with Jimmy. They came back to the Palm Café to see if Jimmy
could audition for Ronnie with the house band. Tony Rice went up
to the bandstand and asked if Jimmy could sit in. They could not
believe their ears—of course not. Then Ronnie Isley himself went
up to ask them and the answer was still no, even to an Isley Brother.
Jimmy was mortified. He knew that behind that kind of recom-
mendation he would not get the job. But both Ronnie and Tony had
spotted some heavy jealousy among the house band members. Ronnie told Jimmy not to sweat. Would Jimmy come out to their place
in New Jersey that weekend? Jimmy was glad to, although he had to

admit to Ronnie that he did not have enough strings on his guitar to be able to audition properly.

Jimmy met Ronnie in Englewood, where the band had rented a house. The Isley Brothers stayed in Teaneck. Ronnie went out and bought Jimmy some strings. Jimmy tuned up in his weird way—wonk, woonk, wheee—and then went straight into "Twist and Shout," "Respectable," "Shout," and "Who's That Lady?" the Isleys' last release for United Artists. He knew their songs already. There was no doubt about it, Jimmy Hendrix had the job. Ronnie was amazed to have found someone who played so well and who knew their songs too. Jimmy Hendrix was a godsend.

Jimmy joined the Isley Brothers in the spring of 1964 and immediately got to play two gigs out of the country, in Canada and Bermuda. Jimmy loved to travel to places he had never been before. Bermuda was fantastic. The Isley Brothers were very big in that British Commonwealth country and played to an SRO-packed baseball stadium. There were even people standing on the hills overlooking the stadium. The Isley Brothers' band backed the other groups on the bill. Jimmy Hendrix caused a sensation when he went into his showtime guitar biting and playing on his haunches with one hand. The entire stadium uproared.

The Isley Brothers got attached to Jimmy. He was so unassuming and noncomplaining. He received thirty dollars a night just like everyone else in the backup band and never carped about it. He would ask for an extra ten sometimes for something he needed for the gigs, like strings or an extra touch to his stage clothes—he was really into frilly shirts and chains. The Isley Brothers took to calling him "the Creeper" because he "moved so softly."

Buddy Miles was a young, underaged drummer playing with Wilson Pickett's band when he encountered the new guitarist the Isley Brothers had with them at the Uptown Club in Montreal. "Shout" was the Isley Brothers' big number, and when they got into it their lead guitarist, off to the side, would put on a show of his own. He did flip-flops, played the guitar behind his back, ate the strings, and did splits—all at the same time, it seemed. He had a ribbon tied to his arm and one tied to his leg, and he wore an earring in one ear and had an outrageous pompadour. He turned on the crowd and the Isley Brothers too; he lent a showman novelty to the group as well as an excellent lead guitar.

Later Buddy went backstage to meet this cat. He was Jimmy Hendrix, a real strange, retiring cat. Buddy was so fascinated that he kept touching Jimmy as if to make sure he was real. Not at all like his image onstage. Buddy, who was from Minnesota, and a newcomer to

Jimi talks with Buddy Miles at Monterey Pop, 1967 © 1981 JIM MARSHALL

the East, began to hang out with Jimmy. Jimmy was a strange bird all right. Never much for hanging out or doing the things that most of the guys in the other bands would do. Jimmy would spend hours alone in his room at the Manhattan Hotel in Times Square playing on his guitar without an amp. Usually when Buddy saw him it was when Jimmy was ready to step out. He would dress in the weirdest fashions Buddy had ever seen. Zebra sunglasses, fancy vests, and red hats. Once, Jimmy said, he had even dyed his hair orange.

Thin as a rail and seemingly never hungry, Jimmy was always bustling with energy. One day, Jimmy turned Buddy on. He called it crystals. But out of his bag he produced a baby bottle with nipple, cap, and all. Thinking the white substance inside was milk, Buddy was really taken aback when Jimmy undid the cap and poured out some of the contents: sparkling white powder. Buddy cracked up. The methedrine crystals gave a weird, high-powered high. It made you want to do nothing but play. You heard the strangest of all possible sounds—and you tried to play them. Weird, high-pitched, almost supersonic whistle peals, and teeth-grinding bass notes that lathered and rumbled at the utter bottom. Jimmy loved the new tune Wilson Pickett was doing: "Midnight Hour." It was in many ways a musician's tune. Full of wailing horns, testifying vocals, and hip guitar licks that evoked a quest through the black ghetto for love.

Pickett had just signed with Atlantic Records. He had sung lead on "I Found a Love" when he was with the Falcons and used that song as the pinnacle of his live show.

Jimmy had been recording with the Isley Brothers as well. All of their releases in the year 1964 had him playing guitar. They were also signed to Atlantic, which released the singles: "The Last Girl" and "Looking for a Love," "Wild as a Tiger" and "Simon Says," and "Move Over and Let Me Dance" and "Have You Ever Been Disappointed?" The Isley Brothers had started their own label in '64 called T-neck. They released one single that year and Jimmy was on lead guitar for "Testify (Parts I and II)." Their biggest hits up until that time had been "Shout" in 1959 and "Twist and Shout" in 1962. But when the Beatles did "Twist and Shout" in 1964, it became No. 1 on the national charts.

Jimmy's Harlem woman, Fayne Pidgeon, dug him, stood up for him, protected him as only a Harlem woman could, but seemed always to be laughing at him. She often thought of herself as the woman *and* the man in their relationship because she was always the one to "jump up in some nigger's face" about Jimmy's playing. Jimmy was always bugging somebody with the way he walked, his soft-spoken shyness, and especially the way he played. Fayne felt protective of him. He seemed out of place in Harlem. People would always ask him where he was from. Many had never heard of Seattle, and this increased their disbelief. Some thought he was a sissy or a faggot, but he just didn't care how people took him. He was only interested in playing. Alone he played mostly old blues to himself, but he knew all the rhythm and blues changes and just about everything else that was played over the radio.

As soon as Fayne met Jimmy Hendrix she felt a protective thing for him. She pulled him out of the scene he was in then to come live with her and the twins, Arthur and Albert Allen, Fayne's childhood friends, and her baby. After living together for quite a while, they finally began going together.

Fayne laughed a lot. She would always laugh at Jimmy. She had never met such an oddball. And he had big titties too, that really cracked her up. And Jimmy would be so embarrassed that she would almost die laughing. He was always good for a rise. But it was the oddity that attracted her. Used to doing her own thing, independent and bold, she was a fine and foxy fixture on the Harlem music scene. The Apollo, the Palm Café, Small's Paradise, Frank's, Sugar Ray's, and the fast three-for-one bars with their flashy exteriors and plush interiors, she knew them all. As fine and loud and funny as she was, she had the run of Harlem and was perfect for Jimmy, who would have been like a lamb going to slaughter alone in Harlem.

They lived all over Harlem. At first, in 1964, they lived with a friend named Bootsie at 210 West 118th Street between St. Nicholas and Eighth avenues. They lived in Room 213 of the Cecil Hotel over Minton's, the famous club where bebop was invented, where Charlie Christian had established the electric guitar as a major jazz instrument capable of solos instead of just rhythm-keeping. The patrons and the personnel there would tell Jimmy and Fayne the history of the place, and Jimmy, interested in all music, would check it out. Jimmy got a chance to check out Sugar Hill when they moved up to 154th and St. Nicholas, where all the "uppity niggers" used to live years ago. There were big, palatial apartment houses, where people like W. E. B. DuBois once lived. Some were tenement slums, others still held on to the beauty of the past.

Hendrix was amazed at Harlem. This small section of Manhattan had more blacks than all of Seattle. No white folks lived up there. It was a black city. And Fayne moved through Harlem as though she owned it.

But Hendrix could not get a gig in Harlem. He could tour as lead guitarist with the biggest names in rhythm and blues and still be ignored.

Fayne was always her own woman. Enamored of rhythm-and-blues stars and just pretty young boys, she found that Hendrix fit her fancy in the young-boy department, but it was her romantic involvement with Sam Cooke that finally got him that gig. She took him backstage at the Apollo to meet the great singer. Through Fayne, Hendrix met many New York rhythm and blues artists and through his own ability he often got gigs with them, but they were unwilling to work with his musical ideas. He was just gigging—playing the same changes that thousands of young black guitarists with conked hair could play.

Fayne and her weirdo, Jimmy, came to know all the local bands that played the Harlem weekends. Most of the clubs featured live weekend music, and Jimmy thought that it would be a different scene from touring with a big-name star who had an obligation to the audience to play their hit songs the same way they were heard over the radio. But he found the club bands just as rigid. They resented him coming up to sit in and then putting on his act. Licking the guitar, collapsing to his haunches, and playing a lot of *off-the-*

wall riffs. He acted as if he were somewhere else, onstage by himself, as if he were the star, instead of just another guitar player begging to sit in. Fayne would just give them hell for freezing up on Jimmy. They often got mad at Jimmy, but Fayne was always ready to take them on.

Both Fayne and her mother regarded Jimmy as a trip. But his inoffensive and sweet disposition always won them over and kept them in his corner. He was simply not a threat to man or beast on a social level. All he wanted to do was play. He lived and breathed to play his guitar.

While Fayne was heavy into Harlem, she did not trust anything out of Harlem. Midtown, the Village, those were the "white" sections. She was ill at ease outside of Harlem and sarcastic at Jimmy's naïve curiosity. And when he brought home a weird hillbilly record by some dude named Bobby Dylan, she just *knew* Jimmy had gone completely crazy.

Hendrix left the Isley Brothers and soon picked up with Curtis Knight and the Squires just before Christmas 1964. Adding needed flash to their unit (as he had done for the Isley Brothers), Hendrix was a welcome addition to the group. While it was difficult to become known while playing with the Isley Brothers, with Curtis Knight and the Squires it was much simpler. They played the local clubs of New York City and New Jersey, and as an emergent band they gave him the attention he craved and felt he deserved.

Their repertory included top forty R&B, some originals, and some up-tempo songs for extended boogie. They performed two of these— "Driving South" and "Killing Floor"—often. Because they played primarily discos and small dance halls, they had to maintain extended danceable numbers. While Hendrix had more chances to solo, his main job was to augment the rhythm section and melody lines in unusual ways for the dancers.

Hendrix appeared with the Squires at the post-Christmas show at Georges Club 20 in Hackensack, New Jersey. The relief of finally being past Christmas was evident. The crowd was lively and plenty drunk. Curtis Knight was delighted to have such a top-notch guitarist in his group. ". . . I'd like to let everyone know that you're being recorded. This is being recorded live here at the fabulous Georges Club 20 in Hackensack, New Jersey. . . . What are you going to do for the people, Jimmy, on Christmas plus one?" Hendrix slurs in a Louis Armstrong grate, "A little thing called 'Driving South.' " Cur-

tis Knight picks up: "A little thing called 'Driving South'—in D. If
you ain't never been there you gonna take a trip with us now, baby.
If you ain't got no car, put on some skates." The Squires hit some
butt-bumping rhythm and are gone. "Driving South," a one-chord
back-beating tune with plenty of room on the top for continuous
soloing by Hendrix, as Knight names off cities and states, going
deeper and deeper into the Southland. "Eat it! Eat it!" Curtis Knight
shouts to Hendrix, as Jimmy displays his novelty attraction, playing
the guitar with his teeth.

Hendrix's attack is sharp and piercing on treble reach. His soloing
is bluesy with long loping lines that ride over several beats of the
up-tempo song. As the towns get deeper and deeper into the South,
Hendrix's guitar gets bluesier and bluesier, getting down into the
deeper registers of the Delta sound, where the guitar plays bass
notes as well as lead figures. Hendrix climbs out of the Delta with a
long upward-sliding wail that skirts the psychedelic. Toward the
end, Jimmy joins the rhythm by noodling bass figures against the
beat. Then Knight shouts, "Eat it! Eat it!" again, and Jimmy goes
back into a riffing guitar frenzy for a while, then back to noodling
with the rhythm as "Driving South" goes out.

Howling Wolf's "Killing Floor" starts out in a light whimsical
rhythm with a high-ranged bass line pizzicato "Batman"-like
theme, nearly happy-go-lucky. Then Curtis Knight's rhythm guitar
speaks out, right on the beat, with a rhythm guitar electric chik,
chik-chik, chik, chik-chik and then starts scratching like a twitch-
ing electrical charge inside a tube, piercing the rhythm with syncopated washboardlike percussion swinging in on the four, advancing
the rhythm subliminally. And then Jimmy comes in on his Fender
Duo-sonic Telecaster playing a longer rhythm figure in harmony
with the rhythm guitar. Then he joins the percussive scratching, his
Telecaster sounding like a rattlesnake, harmonizing metamusically,
creating an echo subtone scratching against the backbone in buck
dance rhythm licks. Hendrix applies a slow arc of contrasting harmonies against Knight's steady rhythm; they swing in a modal arc
as Hendrix explores the sound. He does not dominate the rhythm
guitar; rather, he lays back in that Charlie Christian space, unobtru-
sive in an echo vector dewailing on the other side of the sound.
Jimmy arcs the harmony completely perpendicular, his Telecaster
creates a flashing lightninglike stroke of complete fusion before returning to the melody stroke. Jimmy starts his solo in a low-register
geechie stutter, then goes on in a legato statement that is blues,
poetic, and beautiful. He ranges into his personal style at the top
toward another place in the melody, and then quickly returns to an

earthy declamatory style full of the articulations of the blues, and comes down to hit the head of the lyric right on.

Lord knows I should've been gone
Lord knows I should've been gone
I'm justa messin' round
Cryin' on the killing floor

Jimmy goes crazy as they take it out in staccato rhythm. He climbs the wall with the whimsical yet sinister melody and joins the rhythm as well with heavy contrasting comments on the bottom of the floor. His wails scale against the ceiling, the nonchalance of the melody turning into a flash of manic murder intensity at the peak. They descend, and the song ends to a cacophony of applause, shouts, cusses, and banging glasses.

Some of the other clubs Hendrix played with Curtis Knight and the Squires were: The Purple Onion, a Greenwich Village discothèque; The Queen's Inn; The Cheetah in Times Square; and Ondines on the chic Upper East Side.

At The Cheetah they became known to a larger circle of people, some of them well known in the music business. Knight had band uniforms made out of the same cheetah-skin pattern that decorated the club's interior. It looked like the Squires were coming out of the walls. Murray the K on his AM radio show pushed The Cheetah heavily, with ads and personal testimony. Jimmy also stayed at The Cheetah to play with Carl Holmes and The Commandos. Ondines was the cream of discothèques. The beautiful people went there. Jimmy met Ronnie Spector, the leader of the Ronettes and the wife of legendary producer Phil Spector. She told him in a beautiful laughing offhand way that he was gonna make it, that he would someday be a star. He loved her for that.

Jimmy Hendrix toured with Joey Dee and the Starlighters near the end of 1965. He was to write his father from Boston on November 24.

Dear Dad,
We're in Boston, Mass. We'll be here for about 10 days. We're actually playing in Beveve. Tell Ernie I'm in her home state. I hope everything is all right. We're right next to the ocean. Right across the street.

—Jimmy

When he arrived back in New York City after the tour, he was set up in a boss pad when Fayne saw him again. The money didn't last long but the impression remained. This was the first time he had toured with a predominantly white band. He had played with few white bands in Seattle, but with Joey Dee he got to savor the "Twist" craze right up close. The hysteria that the augmented rockabilly beat drove the myriad crowds to was amazing. It was like Joey Dee was a high priest, a messenger bringing a sacred message to all. Right there he witnessed the power of word and music, especially as promoted by big-town machinery, but more so, as ordained by the people's need for release. The Twist included all ages and all kinds of people, and it was not necessarily youth-oriented. The Beatles in '65 were still the kings of the English sound, but they were essentially a listening experience, a pleasant experience compared to the uncouth Twist parties.

Doris Troy, then riding high on her monstrous hit "Just One Look," was present when Jimmy Hendrix auditioned for King Curtis's band. King Curtis had mellowed his sound to an approach to rhythm and blues that had resulted in a big national hit, "Soul Serenade," in 1964. Jimmy, inspired by King Curtis's style, sought to emulate it in his playing. He drove his Fender Telecaster to its highest limits in trying to give back the horn lines that had inspired him. Usually the people Hendrix desired most to play with did not like his strong musical presence; they wanted a backup guitarist, and Hendrix's interest in heavy metal funk ensemble playing was far ahead of its time. He had begun to get the message that he would have to start his own group if his ideas were to come to fruition. But he was hired. King Curtis's band was the heaviest of the R&B crossover bands on the set. Hendrix had achieved the ultimate band of his idiom. At that point he knew he would have to go out soon and do his own thing. After the King Curtis band, there would be no place else to go but out on his own.

The King Curtis band was a heavyweight aggregation that was as close to jazz as rhythm and blues could come. Their big hit, "Soul Serenade," featured King Curtis's plaintive saxophone sliding into a get-down funk, wailing out. Jimmy shared the lead work with Cornell Dupree and fed King Curtis the pretty rhythm chords and fills that were so essential to the melody.

Jimmy got to be friends with Cornell Dupree, and with Chuck Rainey, who played Fender bass. He did not often make friends, being quiet and keeping to himself a lot, but the frequency of contact with the cats in the bands drew them together.

Jimmy grew on the cats. Jimmy, nonchalant, very easy to get

The Jimi Hendrix Experience at the height of their popularity
LINDA MCCARTNEY PHOTO

along with, and always happy to be on any gig, even if it was only as second guitar, was never known to say anything negative. But it was hard to get close to him; he was almost too good to believe.

Jimmy had perfect pitch. This required a lot of tuning, but he was able to do it quickly. He often tuned differently for different numbers, and on occasion he employed an open tuning where he only needed to bar up the frets to change chords.

For King Curtis, Jimmy got a new Stratocaster. He needed it for such a heavyweight group.

Jimmy made several recordings in 1964 and 1965, but none of them were really where his head was at. There was never enough time to do what he wanted to do, and when he was doing things he liked, he never had enough time to explore the studios. The recordings with Little Richard were standard studio rehashes of Richard's hits of the late fifties, with a few new numbers. But Jimmy's rhythm work was so innovative and his brief solos so fresh, it was amazing Little Richard did not expand Jimmy's contribution. He recorded with the Isley Brothers. "Wild Little Tiger" was more or less a vehicle for Jimmy's guitar. He concocted a wild screeching hook and then drove the tune with a rhythm line that reflected the up-tempo refrain. Jimmy achieved his effects by shaking the guitar and rolling the strings over one another. "Move Over and Let Me Dance" was another R&B rocking, shouting number of the Isley Brothers that featured Jimmy Hendrix. They gave him more freedom than Little Richard did, but could no more integrate his sound into Top Forty R&B than Little Richard could in his own brand of rockabilly.

The most dramatic of Jimmy's early work is the instrumental "House of the Rising Sun," Leadbelly's favorite, cut during an independent session. Recorded on fairly good equipment in Atlanta, Georgia, it was the hit of those sessions. In it he uses a light up-tempo rhythm that greatly differs from the tragic vocal tones of the lyrics. It gives the feeling of transcendence.

Jimmy also recorded with Curtis Knight and Lonnie Youngblood, a saxophone player, in 1965, but as in most of his sessions during this period, only as a side man.

Harlem had been like a mother to him, his birth into New York City. The Harlem rebellion of 1964 showed him a big picture of the tremendous pent-up frustration inherent in ghetto living. It reminded him more and more of living in the Central District of Seattle. He soon found Harlem as stifling as his hometown. It was impossible for him to play and make a name for himself there. He had stayed long enough to check it out thoroughly. The problem of his leaving was not with music but with Fayne. They had grown close after months of hanging out together and doing their own thing. She was a beautiful, unique, classical black woman. But she seemed to be stuck in Harlem. Her child, her mother, her cousins; they all lived almost communally. It seemed that she would be content to stay in Harlem year after year and never really *see* the way he saw things. He had to move. Leaving Harlem meant leaving Fayne.

THREE

Hendrix spent weeks walking the Village and East Village, from the Hudson to the East River. From Gansvoort Pier down West Eleventh to West Tenth then all the way across town to where West Tenth ran into the brown austere Women's House of Detention, then past Eighth Street and Sixth Avenue where all the street people hung out. The streets near the rivers were always empty, but here in the heart of Greenwich Village, the tempo began. Blacks, whites, Puerto Ricans, freaks, hippies, and desperadoes milled about, with camera-toting tourists smiling their way past the multitudes. He walked on Eighth Street until it became shaded by the eastern light, and the office buildings of Broadway and Astor Place loomed tall above the skyline. The continuous flow of traffic down the street that never stopped: Broadway. He thought of the Drifters' song about Broadway: *How ya gonna make some time/When all you got is one thin dime/ . . . and I won't quit till I'm a star on Broadway.* Yeah.

And then the tenements of the East Village low downtown. St. Mark's Place and Cooper Square where all the art students hung out—all the starving artists of the Lower East Side. Weird nationalities like Ukrainians, Poles, Yiddish-speaking Jews, Puerto Ricans, and on the last avenue, Avenue D, blacks. This little ghetto in downtown Manhattan was right near the East River.

Jimmy became more aware of the great underground movement in jazz the more he hung out. Charlie Parker was a legend in the Village. Although he had been dead for several years, people still talked about him as if he were still around. The Village Gate featured jazz, but usually only big names. Jimmy often heard the names of Sun-Ra, John Coltrane, Eric Dolphy, Cecil Taylor, Archie Shepp, Charles Mingus, Ornette Coleman, and Albert Ayler spoken with awe and reverence. Most of them usually played in the clubs on the East Side like the Five Spot, the Jazz Gallery, and Slugs Saloon. Sometimes he saw advertisements for Sun-Ra at the Charles Theater on Avenue B and in other places. Sometimes Mingus played at the Village Vanguard. Jimmy was aware of them. Sometimes he would be at someone's house and hear some of their recordings. But he was having enough of a hard time with his own music to try to consciously incorporate some of the ideas he heard. Many of the old-time "folkies" were mad with Dylan for taking up the electric guitar. Music was a controversial thing and he tried to avoid disputes. He listened when he could to the new and avant-garde jazz, but there were few guitarists playing in that vein. After Charlie Christian there was Wes Montgomery, but few jazz guitarists had become really well known. Sometimes he fantasized about playing jazz. But it was like a classical form of music. Usually jazz musicians read music. He could not read and would definitely not take the time out of his own development to learn. There seemed to be not much reason for it where he was coming from. In his heart he was closest to the old blues forms, and that was where he wanted to stay. But he also knew that some of the freak sounds he heard in his head, and tried to play through guitar, were closer to a jazz thing than what he was supposed to be playing.

Hendrix by now could play any rhythm and blues classic or current hit blindfolded. His departure from Harlem was not only an attempt to get away from having to play them at all, but also to stretch out more in the direction his imagination dictated. Not only was rhythm and blues still grounded in the same rigid chord changes and nuances borne out of the blues, but also most black musicians had ignored the musical possibilities of the bastard forms of rockabilly and rock. While the young white rock 'n' rollers had often managed to copy and cajole the correct changes of black music, they nevertheless failed to present in their stage presentation "The Show."

"The Show" was the staple of every performance, especially on the southern tours and at places like the Apollo. "The Show" was when the artists or band would do some wild, way-out stuff. "The

Show" was the height of the performance, and like the saxophone "honkers," this display often put both the audience and the performer in a transcendental state where improvisation came to the fore and the unexpected took everybody out. Very much akin to the building emotional patterns of black holiness churches, this crescendo, once reached, could be stretched and augmented and built upon all night if necessary. But for the true followers of black music, it was this transcendental moment everyone waited for. Most of the white musicians of rock 'n' roll, still heir to their racial memories and culture, remained almost classically distant in their approach to rock 'n' roll. Playing all the notes purely, but almost stock still, they seemed incapable of delivering or unable to deliver the *physical* key to the higher spheres of the music.

When Hendrix put on a show, he blew minds and terrified the audience. He would just go out. Dipping down into simulated splits, whirling his guitar, gobbling his tongue, screaming with the pulsing Telecaster signal. He had the ability to get down with "The Show" and push the audience higher.

Hendrix, a restless, questing spirit, could not rest on his laurels as a top lead guitarist. Besides, while his rep allowed him a modest following of fellow musicians and friends, it allowed him no monetary rewards beyond the survival wages he earned as an independent lead guitarist for hire. He had nothing to lose.

Jimmy felt that he might get a chance to lead his own band at the Cafe Wha?, a basement club right across the street from the Gaslight. The Wha? had the most varied bill of any club in the Village. The club opened in the early afternoon with a hootenanny favored mainly by the hookey players from various high schools. A flexible bill that rarely featured anybody, it reflected the transient audience it attracted. Very often the audience would also be the performers. The "hoot" in the afternoon was one way for a performer to eventually be placed on the bill for the evening's entertainment. The "hoot" cost nothing to get into, and the purchase of one item on the menu was enough to be allowed to sit in the cavelike darkness all afternoon.

On weekends the cover charge was a dollar. Tex would stand at the doorway hawking the tourists inside. The audience on weekdays was split between those who liked to discover good talent at a low admission price, and made it a point to go several times a week, and tourists who wanted to go *somewhere* mainly to be able to say they had been someplace in "the Village," but who lacked the funds for the more expensive clubs, or lacked hip, intellectual, or arty conversation for the Figaro or Fat Black Pussy Cat coffeehouse scenes.

The Cafe Wha? was the perfect place for Jimmy. Dark as all get-out (a good place to mack), the shy could disappear either in the audience or on the stage. A very tolerant audience in the best tradition of the hoot, they would sit and struggle with the shy artist until he got himself together.

Only in the Village at the Cafe Wha? could he display his innovative approach to R&B, traditional blues, and the new rock. Only at the Cafe Wha? was he able to explore his imagination at length without interruption, while playing for the predominantly white audiences. The Cafe Wha? was like a woodshed for him where he worked out and exposed his compositions, and his being there regularly enabled more music people to come check him out.

Jimmy became a fixture at the Cafe Wha? Soon he had a large following, and his musical abilities attracted other musicians who wanted to play with him. Finally he had his own band: Jimmy James and the Blue Flames. Most of the Blue Flames were pickup musicians, except for Randy Wolfe, a white blues devotee who played second guitar, often in the bottleneck style.

Over the Cafe Wha? at the Players' Theater, the Fugs, a local poets' band from the East Village, held forth every night. Tex, a barker of sorts for the Cafe Wha?, introduced Jimmy to Ed Sanders, Tuli Kupferberg, and Ken Weaver: the Fugs.

Jimmy and the Fugs naturally picked up on each other. Both were moving into new and exciting things although now merely low men on the totem pole of the MacDougal Street hierarchy. Jimmy was shedding his R&B roadshow image as fast as he could, growing his hair long. The Fugs were moving from poetry into music. Ed Sanders and Tuli Kupferberg were well-known poets who decided to get into some kind of rock 'n' roll. Ken Weaver, their buddy, was the drummer, and Jim Pines was the guitarist. They picked up whatever musicians they could to round out their act, which at first had been very raw.

Ed Sanders, who knew how difficult it was to get a band together, sympathized with Jimmy. Ed would see him turned around onstage directing Randy Wolfe, who played rhythm guitar behind his lead, and the rest of the ragtag group—the Blue Flames, named after Junior Parker's old band. The Fugs, too, were slowly honing their raw melodies down to a personal style of performance, in the show-business sense. The Fugs all lived in the East Village (the Lower East Side), where it was far cheaper to live than in the Village. They hung out with the poets and other postbeatniks of the neighborhood. They would talk about poetry, dope, antiwar politics, and fucking all in the same breath.

Once Ed Sanders went with Jim Pines over to a loft on Hudson Street where Jimmy was staying with Buzzy Linhart, Roger McGuinn, and David Crosby, who were trying to get a group together. That was the first time Sanders had actually visited Jimmy in a place where he lived. Usually Jimmy would be staying with some lady or another from place to place.

Jimmy offstage was as crazy as they were with his methedrine in a baby bottle, and his comic-book riffs, which would delight and puzzle. But Ken Weaver and Ed Sanders would take all of it in with true poet soul and insight. Jimmy's brand of blues was unfamiliar to them, but they were experienced enough to recognize the real thing, especially when Jim Pines ran some things down to them about the music. Jimmy had started spending almost all of his time downtown, but every now and then he would take off for parts unknown for a gig. They didn't know that he doubled as one of the leading R&B guitarists, highly in demand.

But Jimmy felt at home in the funky Village. A lot of people in the Village were into blues. His weird ways and talk were not made fun of, nor was his highly personal way of interpreting the blues. Pulling off of the same bedrock as the older blues players, he was also able to infuse the blues with a heavy contemporary R&B feeling that brought the blues up to date. And he had a flair for the contemporary freak sound that screamed silently to be expressed throughout the narrow streets of the Village. He received consistently rising respect from the people of the Village, from the people of MacDougal Street, the people who lived and worked there who had watched Dylan go by not too long ago.

MacDougal Street and points circular to its center were the foci for the troubador "folk" singers of the time. Len Chandler, with Arlo Guthrie opening the show, was a constant at the Gaslight Cafe. Ram John Holder, the West Indian folksinger, Bill Elliot, Dave Van Ronk, Mississippi John Hurt, Brownie Terry and Sonny McGhee, Barbara Dane, and many others, including a peripheral Bob Dylan, orbited out from the Gaslight.

Richie Havens and Johnny Hammond and Buzzy Linhart were the Cafe Au Go Go people. Peter, Paul and Mary played the Bitter End. Gerde's Folk City was the traditional folk club. Tim Hardin, Roosevelt Sykes, and others, including Dylan, preferred the out-of-the-way, offbeat insularity of Gerde's Folk City. Izzy Young and his Fretted Instrument Shop was the connection for strings, advice, a sandwich, and some plain-out energy. Both Izzy Young and *Broadside* magazine were printing commentaries quickly and often on the emergent folk scene. Izzy Young's minusculely typed and printed pamphlets, filled with philosophy and quotes from Izzy himself, alerted the underground to the new energy on the folk scene. *Broadside* magazine printed new songs, commentaries, and an occasional letter on a more consistent monthly pace. Len Chandler wrote of his visit to Woody Guthrie on his motor scooter with little Bobby Dylan on the back holding on. But for all of the *Broadside* set, the folk music and blues were acoustical and often solitary. Brownie McGhee and Sonny Terry were correct while Muddy Waters and the Chicago gang were still oddities.

The lowest club on the totem pole was the Cafe Wha? While the Night Owl Cafe was considered gross for its loud electric music and the drunk, raucous teen-agers running in and out of it far into the night, they at least would feature the Lovin' Spoonful, The Raves, Lothar and the Hand People, and occasionally the Holy Modal Rounders. The Cafe Wha?, a misnomer, was considered too low for words. During a fill between songs for the folk crowd that liked a little low-keyed titter or two, a joke about the weird club down the street was always good for a laugh. The folk and blues crowd was kin to the beat-poetry followers who flocked to see Ted Joans and his crew of rentable hipsters perform at the "SCENE" Cafe. Beholden to the word: phased-out over clear decipherable acoustic guitar runs, or words uttered from the lips of a beat poet, it was almost asking too much to ask these emerging hippies to behold a screaming electric blues guitar, no matter how tame.

It was Johnny Hammond's fate to link up with the "craziest guitarist on MacDougal Street." The son of the legendary producer for Columbia Records, John Hammond, Sr., he had come out of the same bag, the blues, that had made his father's name synonymous with Bessie Smith and her tremendous popularity and also with Robert Johnson. John Hammond, Jr., was meandering between folk and blues during the early sixties. Jimmy was to give him a heavy prophecy as to where the blues was going.

One night, Johnny Hammond wandered down into the Cafe Wha?'s cellar. He had heard an unusual blues band was playing down there, and having the natural curiosity and outgoingness of his father, Hammond went down into the dark steep basement to check it out. Brought up on the blues, John, Jr., realized the inventiveness of Jimmy's licks. Not much on vocals, but bold and moving instrumentals. He decided to return later and see if he felt the same way again. At that time, 1965 going into 1966, folk artists were more than adamant about not using electric instruments. But something had to be done about the Beatles. Nevertheless, using electric instruments was considered tantamount to selling out to the pop establishment. But it was the darkness before dawn.

The next time John Hammond, Jr., went to see Jimmy James and the Blue Flames, Hammond was headlining across the street at the Gaslight playing acoustic folk. Jimmy James had obviously mastered all the progressive R&B licks, had a good store of somber blues runs, and had an impish fluidity mixed with a quick bright sound. Johnny had wanted to go heavily electric for some time. Even then he often doubled on a soft electric guitar to play several of Jimmy Reed's urban blues in the small folk clubs. "Bright Lights Big City" was his favorite of Reed's tunes. He knew Jimmy James would be an excellent lead guitarist with him, and it just so happened that he had a gig the following week at the Cafe Au Go Go. Feeling freaky inside the Cafe Wha?, Hammond got to Jimmy as soon as he had finished his set. Jimmy knew John Hammond, Jr., and his music from Mac-Dougal Street. So Jimmy also got right to the point. The money he received for playing all night at the Cafe Wha? was below the starvation level (that was a policy of the club; that added to its reputation). Could Hammond get him a gig anywhere anytime? He was dying to get out of that hole, even for a minute. He was sorry to be asking for a favor, but he was entirely too desperate to come on any other way. Johnny felt a rush of sympathy for Jimmy (besides, he had been wondering how they would sound together). He was happy to be able to invite Jimmy to play with him at the Cafe Au Go Go. The sideman fee Jimmy would receive would top his weekly take at the Wha?.

They rehearsed a few tunes together. Jimmy was quick and always on top of the note. He would work out fine. Jimmy was so shy that the undemonstrative act of Hammond would not be thrown out of kilter. Jimmy was so thin it was amazing he had any energy at all.

The Cafe Au Go Go was the classiest club on MacDougal Street. Close to the Cafe Figaro right off MacDougal on Bleecker Street, the Cafe Au Go Go was also a basement club, but not nearly as steep as the coal-shute-angle plunge into the Cafe Wha?. Circling elegantly to a long deep room with ample table and chair space, the Cafe Au Go Go had an array of lighting effects that many off-Broadway theaters could not match. Sexy, friendly waitresses and a menu of good food made you happy to be there.

The first set they played was a feeling-out session with Hammond using tunes from his *So Many Roads* blues album. Jimmy sedately laid back, soaking in the plushness of the place as compared to the zany Cafe Wha?. Many celebrities were in attendance, including a contingent of English pop stars: the Rolling Stones and the Animals, the hottest English acts in the U.S.A. at the time. But to Jimmy the heaviest person there was Mike Bloomfield, who played lead guitar for Dylan on "Like a Rolling Stone." During the last set Jimmy went into his act. Suddenly during his solo number, "I'm a Man," he's down on his knees flicking his tongue as his guitar obbligatos, stroking the strings with his teeth, using his ax as a battering ram, while playing the most complex of blues changes, with strange guttural feedback sounds delicately balanced against peaking dissolving riffs.

The audience was aghast at Jimmy James's wild antics, especially John Hammond, Jr. The British boys were stunned also. They had seldom witnessed a black performer put on a "Show." Although they were connoisseurs of rural and urban blues, their knowledge had been gained via mail-order postal. Rare and obscure recordings of the old and new blues were their inspiration, especially Muddy Waters. But never in the flesh had they encountered a man as young as Jimmy who had so heavily pulled it all into a pure style of his own.

Jimmy James's sound was his own. The showmanship performance dance was there, all right, but there was a unique sound as well.

Like Dylan, Hendrix had totally synthesized his realm of musical experience into something revolutionary.

With their stateside business pressing them, most of the Stones and the Animals, in their polite English way, congratulated Jimmy James on his performance. Politely suggesting he come to England, they promptly went on about the business of making money, music, and discovering the American scene. Amid all the hullabaloo attendant upon them, the Animals had not *really heard* what Jimmy was playing. While his showtime dance movement caught their attention, the advanced nature of his music was lost in the crowd, lost in the constant ordering of drinks, greeting and meeting new friends, and soaking all of it in.

Two of the Stones stayed behind to rap with Johnny and Jimmy—Bill Wyman and Charlie Watts—and so did Keith Richards's old lady, Linda Keith. Someone suggested they play some at the Gaslight. The small basement club was clear and they got a nice jam together. Linda Keith really enjoyed it. She was quite taken with Jimmy.

Linda Keith, a stunning brunette, was well-to-do in her own right, not just a "groupie" along for the free ride. She was also an intelligent and cultured being just as hungry for the real experience of black urban blues as the English musicians she came to the States

The Experience on tour   *WIDE WORLD PHOTOS*

with. But then she had the leisure time to follow through on the music.

She began to go to the Cafe Wha? every night. The cavelike atmosphere of the Cafe Wha? reinforced the feeling that Jimmy's music was just as underground there on MacDougal Street as it would be if it were in a black ghetto or in a small southern town. Open to all and not caring about the "in" things to do or the taboos of the hip Village scene, Linda Keith drank in the depths of the Cafe Wha?. In Jimmy's long open-ended sets she heard his incredible versatility range through everything from blues to pop to rock 'n' roll to rhythm and blues to young Dylan. It was obvious that Jimmy's ear could assimilate any sound. What was amazing was that after listening to him go through it all, he could then express his own personal virtuoso style. There was no doubt in her mind. He would be a star.

She began looking after Jimmy, actually treating him the same way she would treat her old man, Keith Richards, who had continued on tour with the Rolling Stones. Her fancy hotel suite belonged to Jimmy, her record collection, meals, short cash, a winter coat, a ride downtown, a brand-new Stratocaster; these were small attendant favors to her, while to Jimmy they were godsends. He had been starving to death. He had developed vicious ulcers from lack of food combined with the methedrine crystals he took just to keep going. Linda Keith's ministrations gave him energy, strengthened his blood sugar, and gave him hope. And she gave him recognition, finally, on MacDougal Street, where heads would turn as her limousine dropped him off and remained parked outside, chauffeur interred, while he played. He became human. After more than a year of pure struggle mounting his own music, he began to receive the small favors of the important people. Better days were coming.

Linda Keith would not let Chas Chandler rest. She forced his professed interest in managing and producing to a confrontation.

She took Chas Chandler down to the Cafe Wha? one night. As they walked in, Jimmy was playing a wild version of "Hey Joe," a song by Tim Rose that was an underground favorite. It all came together for Chas as he sat in that basement club watching Hendrix perform on the low stage. Jimmy had known that Linda would bring Chas down and he was pulling out all the stops.

Chas wasted no time. He and Jimmy sat down together and Chas came right to the point: "I believe you'll be a sensation in Britain. If you agree, I want only you. I'll pay your fare to London, look after you, and manage your affairs." After long debate, Jimmy agreed, and the first vital movement was over.

Jimmy signed a contract that called for Chas Chandler and his partner, Mike Jeffery, a manager of the Animals and a former commando in the British Army, to receive 30 percent of his total earnings and 7 percent of his record royalties.

Chandler was taking Hendrix to England because his contacts were there, and they were considerably wide and carried all the important weight of the emergent youth culture. An important cult had developed around the blues, especially electric blues guitar. America was still like a mirage to the English groups. In 1966 few of them had settled here, as many would later do. Their contact with America was mainly a business arrangement intended to make the most amount of money in the least amount of time. In London the underground was small and very hip. They unanimously endorsed the underground American black music, but in England itself there were no black American stars. Here in one man, Jimmy Hendrix, was all of it and more. Chandler could not wait to watch the impact Hendrix would have on his fellow countrymen.

Chandler's reason for leaving the music business as a performer had a lot to do with the very exploitative mess that quickly usurped many of the best young minds of the British music scene. Self-respect, personal pride, and hard-won intelligent sophistication made Chandler rebel against the hasty English musical establishment, especially the limits it placed upon him as an individual. Like Andrew Loog Oldham, or Brian Epstein, Chandler wanted to use his mind and will to help manage the course of the great musical awakening of the young, not only in England but in America as well. Hendrix, it was clear to Chandler, could handle both very well. But first, England.

It was amazing that Jimmy could just up and decide to go with Chandler. Hendrix had no ties, no strings, and no luggage to speak of. He had not visited his home in Seattle in five years. To get an older, more established blues man to pull up roots and go was highly improbable; and it would still be an uphill fight to get the young to accept them, as they were much older, more set in their ways. But Hendrix, who could play blues with the best of them, was also young, appealing, and had his own concepts of music, which would grow. Very shy, quiet, personable, and polite, he would not shatter the brittle British sensibility. But then Chandler found out just how much trouble a rolling stone could be. Their departure for England had to be delayed several weeks while they awaited arrival of a copy of Hendrix's birth certificate from Seattle. Jimmy had never had use for such an official document as a birth certificate before. Jimmy's carelessness with official documents began to plague Chandler. When that birth certificate finally arrived, they were then able to acquire the most important document of Jimmy's life: a passport.

FOUR

They arrived in England September 21, 1966. Midway across the Atlantic Jimmy James had become Jimi Hendrix. Chas Chandler immediately took "Jimi" by British blues man Zoot Money's house where he was, in effect, greeted with a jam.

The English authorities denied Hendrix a work permit. The best they could do was a five-day visa. Chas Chandler had to move quickly. He was about to launch a star—a star on a par with Bob Dylan, the Beatles, the Rolling Stones—and would accept nothing less.

The jam got word moving through the grapevine. Through transatlantic calls from the States and now during the first few days in London, Chandler made sure that his contacts were well informed as to who Jimi was, what they intended to do, and that they intended to succeed.

Chandler knew better than to allow Hendrix to ponder their hazardous course. Hendrix for his part was so gassed to be in England that he indulged in sightseeing as if he were a tourist. It was essential that they get the band together right away. Hendrix solved a lot of the problems of band members himself. He was able to play so much guitar that they would need only the barest number of sidemen; in fact, two: a drummer and a bass player.

Linda Keith spread the word as well, especially among the ladies. Hendrix was a treat they deliciously anticipated.

Working papers were another problem—a big problem. They had to convince the authorities that Hendrix possessed a talent that could not be duplicated by any working or idle Englishman. The music people did not have to be convinced; the government authorities did.

They rushed to get it together. When Chas Chandler called for bass players and drummers to audition, many quite naturally felt that they were auditioning for the Animals. When they saw Jimi that thought quickly disappeared—the Animals were not likely to change their style for this American black, and change they would have to, because this black dude was quite something else.

Noel Redding was chosen largely because of the way he looked. Bouffant frizzly red Caucasoid-Afro hair, framing a sensitive and intelligent face. He would be receptive. Primarily a guitarist with the fluidity of a guitarist, he became a bass player immediately upon meeting Hendrix. Actually it was a lucky stroke. They had had a lot of trouble finding a bass player. Hendrix knew what he wanted. And what he wanted there was no model for. It had become apparent that playing with Hendrix was not easy. Hendrix, an excellent bass player himself, was able to tell Noel Redding exactly what to play. Noel Redding, having never played the bass before, had only to follow his lead. He looked right, he acted right, and played what he was told. Perfect.

Mitch Mitchell, on the other hand, was cocky, brash, and very confident of his abilities on drums. A typical drummer's attitude. He had played with the best of jazz and rock bands in England and was a jazz enthusiast as well. Unable to hide a strange contempt for Jimi, he channeled it into his playing, where he more than kept up; he challenged. He provided a driving tension that never let up—even beyond performance.

The Jimi Hendrix Experience was born October 12, 1966. Once the group was decided upon—Jimi Hendrix, Noel Redding, and Mitch Mitchell—Chas Chandler began his plans to four-wall them in all the hip clubs in London. Special showcases, as opposed to duration runs with several sets per night, were preferred. Miniconcerts from the onset. From the beginning the message of this phenomenon was: This is a special act. The hip, the intelligent, the connoisseur—take heed: This is a very special talent being handled in a very special way. But Chandler knew that nothing would really happen without a record.

On October 15, 1966, Jimi sat in with Brian Auger and the Oblivion Express at Blaises Club. At once there was a quick flurry of success. They were spotted by *the* Johnny Halliday, the hottest singer on the Continent, who flew them to Paris to appear with him in a tremendous show he was headlining at the Olympia on October 18, 1966. It was sold out; 14,500 in the audience saw the fresh, newly established Experience, who had not played together a month. They played rhythm and blues standards "Midnight Hour" and "Land of a Thousand Dances," "Respect," and also "Everybody Needs Somebody to Love"—they tore the house up—the French fans loved them.

The Jimi Hendrix Experience's first gig in London was on the same bill with Cream at Central Polytechnic. Next they appeared on the popular TV show "Ready, Steady, Go," where they debuted "Hey Joe," their first single recording.

The showcases came after that, The Marquee, The Court of St. James's, Blaises, The Upper Cut. Linda Keith always in evidence with a bevy of guests, mainly young and important women, with their old men in tow. Hendrix was an immediate happening in the underground, the "in" crowd. But then there was the rest of the people who had to be convinced, especially the recording companies.

Chandler carefully nurtured the local recording deal. The advance would be nothing as compared with America—but it would mean solid finance. A chance to recoup and then really get out there.

While the initial press was great—a smash in Paris, a smash in Soho, a smash in the underground (which, it seems, had been waiting for the Experience)—the smash with the "money" was another story. The English did not quite know what to make of this black phenomenon. The press began to ridicule him. Fleet Street stuck Hendrix with the label "The Wild Man of Pop." Could he withstand the viciousness of the establishment press? Could the London underground, which was just emerging itself, successfully champion Hendrix? The money was standing back, seeing what would transpire. Chas Chandler decided to fight. Fire with fire. He encouraged the establishment press to ridicule Hendrix. The more outrageous Hendrix would appear in the *Daily Mirror*, the more the rebellious youth would side with him. The question was, when would they eventually make that catalyst work?

And once the Fleet Street papers got a good look, they made him the perfect antihero. One London paper called him a "Mau-Mau" in banner headlines, while another called him a "Wild Man from Borneo." Jimi Hendrix was denounced by Mrs. Mary Whitehouse, the leader of the National Viewers' and Listeners' Association. Donald Bruce wrote in *Pop Shop:* "For one thing, Jimi is scarcely likely to qualify for a best-looking-bloke competition." And in boldface type: "So why should Jimi worry if he looks like a wild-eyed revolutionary from the Caribbean and that he talks with the shuteye still in his big mouth? . . ."

The youth, the first generation stripped of England's vast colonial wealth, had to deal with the hard facts of a lower standard of living. The press made sure they knew this. The underground was an important vanguard, but very small in actual numbers. The major youth divisions were the Mods and the Rockers. A press invention based on upper-middle-class and lower-middle-class youths. The Skinheads, the rowdy working-class kids, were considered out of it: They dug reggae and violence. They even took to hanging out with the West Indian rude boys in the reggae clubs.

But few English youths could escape the traditional hatred of blacks, even Noel Redding and Mitch Mitchell.

The incongruity of these young fey Englishmen having taken up with "The Wild Man of Pop" did even more to project Hendrix's image in the United Kingdom. While this cooled out some of the hostility he might have received (the group was two-thirds homebred), it also was outrageous theater. Noel and Mitch, both sporting the early John Lennon short German cut when they started with Jimi, soon affected long and wild hair.

Rather staid young Englishmen, both Mitchell and Redding dug jazz and blues (as any English musician did who wanted to be heavy in the pop world), and both wanted badly to make it. Before Jimi they had never become tight with a black man, and especially never considered one their superior. Although the money increased, and all the side benefits were good, Noel and Mitch found it difficult to ignore the fact that they were second to Hendrix.

The circumstance of their hiring (like a hiring hall scene) notwithstanding, Noel and Mitch began to challenge Jimi personally and in the press about their lack of prestige in the Experience. Jimi made many placating statements to the English press, but the conflict persisted. Both Mitchell and Redding were no newcomers to "pop" music. Mitchell had played with several popular and respected groups, his last being Georgie Fame's Blue Flames. Noel Redding had played with The Loving Kind.

Noel and Mitch often used racial slurs when they talked to Jimi. They would call him "nigger" and "coon" and make it all seem like intimate banter, but it had an effect on Jimi and further increased the conflict among them.

Up on the stage, the conflict assumed different proportions. They openly challenged Hendrix at every juncture—playing their young asses off—and that's exactly what Hendrix wanted. Redding, who considered himself primarily a guitarist, burned up the bass line, often tuned to full volume, pushing Hendrix as far as he could. Virtuoso Hendrix seemed to revel to go higher in the fire.

Mitch Mitchell played every rhythm possible, extending from simple timekeeping all the way to Elvin Jones's circular rhythm jazz drumming. Noel Redding, his bass guitar often jacked up to the highest treble intensity, seemed to vie with Jimi's lead guitar and vocals. This energy, fueled by class and color conflict, gave the Experience the full-range sound Hendrix wanted.

By 1966–67 the Beatles had already established their worldwide fame. Taking a chance that paid off big, they began writing and performing songs with more English flavor; very much away from international pop, with its strong dose of Chuck Berry rockabilly rhythm and blues, which had made them until that point. The Beatles, in terms of class-conscious London society, had achieved aristocracy (at least on paper), while the Rolling Stones were yet to emerge as a No. 1 supergroup. The Stones had hit after hit but were still strongly into the blues idiom. The Stones (with the exception of Brian Jones) looked on Hendrix's emergence with consternation, as did Eric Clapton and Peter Townshend of the Who.

Hendrix had pressed the English music world to the wall, thus precipitating a brief debate over how they should react. While the English authorities put Hendrix through the mill, the English rock world got it together much quicker. Townshend and Clapton conferred, as did the Stones and the Beatles—truth won out: Hendrix's music *was* unique and powerful, and his act was outasight. And more importantly, Hendrix did not have a name in the States at all, aside from being known in the business as a good traditional rhythm and blues guitarist. So why not accept him? Make him their own, and lend even more power and veracity to English rock. They were right. Hendrix, as an English commodity, took over where the Beatles left off, and gave English music the strongest dose of real black music it had ever had.

One of Chas Chandler's first moves with Hendrix was to insulate him in the word-passing in-group of English rock masterminds: Les Perrin, Derek Taylor, Brian Epstein, Andrew Loog Oldham, and—for the crucial money at the crucial juncture—his partner Michael Jeffery.

The first party Jimi went to in London blew his mind. Everyone there looked and talked like English royalty, like they were heirs to the throne. Jimi just sat in a corner cross-legged on the floor and took everything in. He was unsure of what would happen in the future there, and the hip set was still unsure as to whether they would accept him.

Marianne Faithfull had just begun to live with Mick Jagger when Jimi Hendrix first appeared in London, but she was well aware of his arrival. Not only had Linda Keith informed her, but also there had been talk of an audition that Hendrix had done for Mick, who was establishing his own production company at the time. Although Jagger had rejected Hendrix, the London hip society of musicians very much was taken with him. Brian Jones raved about Hendrix. Some took that as a signal of the widening rift between Jones and Jagger, but there were others, like Eric Clapton and John Mayall, whose words of awe could hardly be disputed.

Marianne and Mick had attended the opening of a new club, the 7½, and Hendrix had played. Jagger, as "King of the Scene," as John Lennon had dubbed him, had gone primarily out of a sense of duty. This was one of Marianne and Mick's first appearances in public and they had not stayed long. There was still the stigma of Chrissie Schrimpton's attempted suicide hanging over Jagger, and they had not wanted it to look as if they were flaunting anything. But they did want to establish their relationship in the eyes of the public and their peers.

Marianne was intrigued by what little she had heard of Jimi's playing. She had never before heard anyone play in his style, with his speed and apparent root knowledge of the blues.

A couple of days later Hendrix reappeared at the 7½ Club for a three-day gig. Marianne had been killing time while Mick was in the studio recording. She decided to go have an anonymous drink at the club. Although there were several empty tables the atmosphere was charged with excitement. She sat on the floor through the set enthralled. She returned the next night. She felt some kind of bond between herself and Hendrix. It was something impossible to put into words. She felt drawn to him in a special way. Not particularly sexual, the attraction was more like a mutual recognition of each other's soul. That second night they were introduced. She knew it would be impossible not to be recognized and now that they were staring at each other she affirmed their affinity.

Jimi was very polite, as usual, but he was also coming on to her. She was used to being come on to. She was attractive, famous, upper-class, and well-to-do. Sometimes men came on to her because they felt they were supposed to. As if there was some kind of propriety her beauty demanded that made it the thing to do. Jimi came on to her rather strongly. If it had not been for the affinity she felt they shared she might have been taken aback. But she took it as a recognition on his part that they had something strongly in common. She, too, wanted to affirm the feeling. She did not necessarily want to go to bed with Jimi. She had only been living with Jagger a few weeks; they were very happy and very turned on to each other. At another time in her life it might have been a beautiful thing to do, but that night it could not happen. Instead, she asked Jimi if he might like to come to a get-together. She would invite some of her friends and they would hang out after the gig, get high, and talk. Although it was a substitution or a sublimation, it was also an affirmation.

Brian Jones came. He was not too involved in the latest sessions the Stones were doing. They were laying tracks. He would come in later and add touches and whatnot (although it seemed as if he were being frozen into that role—further and further away from ever contributing songs to the Stones' effort). Linda Keith attended, as did Paul McCartney, Chas Chandler, and some young socialites. It was no big thing. They sat around and smoked and got acquainted. There were others there, Mitch and Noel not knowing quite how to act, and Kathy Etchingham, who appeared to be Jimi's old lady, although he seemed to have eyes only for the blond and delicately featured Marianne. They had a nice low-keyed time, but Jimi had seemed somewhat disappointed, although his shyness made some of his emotions ambiguous. Marianne was firmly with Mick, there was no disputing that. But she was glad she and Jimi had had a chance to get together and chat. For Jimi it was almost like having tea, at two o'clock in the morning.

"Hey Joe" had been a song that Chas and Jimi had agreed upon almost by telepathy even before they had left the States for London. It expressed a simple, emotional defiance of authority through a tale of a crime of passion. A perfect vehicle for Jimi's husky-toned voice, "Hey Joe" also had a *feel* to it that they were both confident of. It didn't really showcase Jimi's guitar as much as they would have liked, but it was a rather safe vehicle for the London market.

> *Hey Joe, where ya going with that gun in your hand?*
> *I'm going out to shoot my ol' lady*
> *I caught her making love with another man*

The lines would have been impossible to sing legato, but Jimi's slurring rap placed the ballad perfectly in the minds of the listeners. Not only could they visualize the scene, but they could also relate— like Frankie and Johnny, the theme was universal.

The bridge was the hippest thing happening musically. Jimi and Noel dubbing long bass runs. Jimi's rhythm licks were subtle but effective, giving a hint of his virtuosity without taking away from the song as a whole.

Jimi's vocal uses two voices, the voice of Joe and the voice of a commentator. But the last voice in the song is Joe's as he flees South to Mexico, where no hangman will put a noose around his neck. Jimi gets a chance to take the song to another level, shouting and emoting as the song slowly fades.

Edwin Kramer, slight, blond-haired young engineer, had just started on his new job at Olympic Studios when in walked Jimi Hendrix—the most incredible electric guitarist in England.

Chas and Jimi were not satisfied with the "Hey Joe" recording they had made at another studio. They wanted to feature Jimi's guitar work more, but the more way-out stuff was difficult to record. At this point they knew that an amount of experimentation would have to take place in order to get the recorded sound they wanted. They had had their fill of the staid middle-aged engineers. They liked Kramer from the beginning. He was different, young, and enthusiastic. He would be willing to put in the extra time and effort, as opposed to the company men who freaked out when it was past teatime and they were still in the studio. Besides, Kramer looked like an angel, a cherub, a cupid. His vibes were right.

It would be a job just to get what Jimi did onstage on a four-track tape in the studio. But they wanted more than that. They wanted to *extend* his sound via magnetic tape. They wanted the best recordings and then some. What Jimi was hearing would involve elaborate overdubbing and the most advanced devices to deliver both his quick picking and his distortion and feedback harmonics. But the total Experience sound needed something more as well. The bass had to have absolute depth without distortion in the small speakers common to radio. The drums also needed a boost in order to feature their dynamic interplay with Jimi's lead. With only four-track machines to work with, Hendrix's music was a problem. Kramer took "Hey Joe" home with him and played it all night. The next day he had some ideas and suggestions. That really sold Chas and Jimi. Edwin worked like an elf.

The Jimi Hendrix Experience's first gig at the Olympia in Paris had been grander than they could ever have hoped for. It was a good sign, an august beginning. But Chas Chandler knew that it was necessary to deal with London—and that no matter how much they had going for them it was still going to be an uphill battle. While the JHE recorded at a frantic pace, Chas was talking record deals. Chas and Jimi would frequent the hip after-hours clubs: hobnobbing and scouting. Jimi would usually be requested to sit in, or whatever. In many ways, the requests were a part of the etiquette of polite English society. But Jimi and Chas began to take them up. Taking on a few select offers, the JHE played the exclusive Cromwellian Club and the hip Bag O' Nails Club. There was no serious money involved, only the right kind of exposure. One night Jimi and company played the Scotch of St. James. Rod Harrod, the host, owed a great deal to Chas, who, as one of the Animals, had supported him when he left the Cromwellian because of a dispute with its owners. The Scotch of St. James was located in a yard off of St. James Court. The ground floor had a bar and a restaurant, and the basement level was a dance floor surrounded by tables. The Beatles and the Stones had their own private tables, which were roped off and slightly elevated. It was not unusual for Princess Margaret and Lord Snowdon to show up. The decor was Scottish baronial, with plenty of sporrans, swords, and antlers. There was a couch on one side of the bandstand. Harrod had gone out of his way (discreetly, of course) to make sure that as many of the right people as possible were there. The basement was crowded with patrons, mainly standing on tiptoes to see the action. Jimi, Mitch, and Noel played a superb set that featured "Hey Joe." As soon as Kit Lambert, manager of the Who, and an activist in the new pop youth culture, heard it, he knew the song would be a hit and wasted no time in letting Chas know that he wanted the JHE to be on the new label he was launching, Track Records.

Chas and Kit went upstairs to discuss it further. Lambert was so enthusiastic over JHE that he was almost knocking over tables in his haste to sit down with Chas.

Chas was as enthusiastic about Track Records as Lambert was, but he tried to hide it. Track would not be launched until March. There was no doubt in Chas's mind that "Hey Joe" would be out before Christmas. But he told Lambert that he could promise the JHE to Track Records regardless of the deal made with another company, or whomever. Chas had been talking to record companies about the release of the JHE's first single. They were interested in more than a single, but since Chas was producing the master himself, with no upfront money on the record companies' part, he really owed them nothing.

Soon Chas had the single in the can: "Hey Joe," and "Stone Free" as the B side. He took it to Decca, one of the companies he had been talking to. The A&R man there turned it down flatly, adding that he did not think Jimi had anything special. Panicked, Chas went directly back to Lambert, who reassured him of the validity of the recording, adding, as a vote of confidence, that he would take the record around to the record shops himself if necessary—but he doubted it would be. Reassured, Chas went off to Polydor Records with confidence. He secured a one-shot pressing and distribution deal, with further talks scheduled for the future.

"Hey Joe" was released December 16, 1966, just before the Christmas holidays. It got radio air play at once, but there was really no way of telling how it would sell. The sound was strange and new, with supermusical effects hinting that something explosive would follow. Now the JHE had a product out on the market. Now was the time to begin to gig in earnest. On December 21 the JHE played Blaises Club—their lucky club. Although the Who was gigging at the Upper Cut, it was only a short distance from Blaises, and Peter Townshend showed up. Jeff Beck was there too, in the standing-room-only crowd.

The JHE got its first real writeup in *Melody Maker* in its "Caught in the Act" column. They talked of the star-packed crowd and the blown minds. They used words like "fantastic" and "exceptional" in describing Jimi's guitar playing, and also mentioning Jimi's playing with his teeth, *Melody Maker* forecasted him as "one of the big club names of 1967."

But Chas was edgy. It was difficult for him to enjoy the Christmas holiday. They were broke. The record was out. Now was the time to push through. He had to do something that would establish JHE in the New Year in London. Besides, they had no work lined up and there was no telling what would transpire in 1967. They were at a low ebb; they had to do something, and soon.

Chas decided to throw a party at the Bag O' Nails Club. Although it would ostensibly be a celebration, it would also be a showcase for Jimi. Chas invited all the promoters and tour bookers and the "in" people among whom they would be most comfortable. It was a gamble in which there was also a touch of desperation. Chas knew that if this push did not take hold, then it would be virtually the end of the Jimi Hendrix Experience. The only way for him to pay for their "reception" was to pawn five of his six guitars.

On the night of Chas's party, January 11, 1967, "Hey Joe" entered the charts. Although it was only No. 48, it was a very good sign. It was moving up fast. Now for the first time there was the possibility of Jimi being more than a passing curiosity or an interesting freak, but someone on the way up.

Chas chose the Bag O' Nails because it was right off Carnaby Street, the most fashionable street of the emergent "Flower Power" youth. Many rock stars were in attendance, seated at long tables facing the stage. It was evident they were "following" Jimi. A better following was impossible to buy. But there were numerous other novelties this crowd had followed and then tossed aside after a while. George Melly, the respected English cultural commentator, author, and jazz singer, has said, "Like great fish the top groups glide from club to club, and those whose pleasure is to follow in their wake swim with them."

Chas was looking for work, not in-crowd adulation. Phillip Haywood, club owner and booker, invited the group to play as a support group to the New Animals at a series of out-of-London and in-London gigs for twenty-five pounds a night. Chas was relieved. They would be able to eat.

The next night the JHE played second on the bill to the New Animals at one of Haywood's clubs, the 7½. Immediately it was obvious that it was impossible to bill Jimi as a second, or support act. There was no question who the press and rock stars had returned to see. The 7½, a new club just off Piccadilly, was delighted to have in the audience Mick Jagger, Marianne Faithfull, Peter Townshend, Anita Pallenberg, Eric Clapton, Linda Keith, and Glen Campbell.

Jimi played his standard set of songs: "Hey Joe," "Stone Free," "Can You See Me?" "Rock Me Baby," "Like a Rolling Stone," "Third Stone from the Sun," and "Wild Thing." At this point it was a pleasure for them to be working for steady money with a breaking act on tour. It was like a dress rehearsal for their break, and the way Chas was gambling, they would break out as stars or not at all.

Jimi played the 7½ Club most of that week, with a one-day excursion to the Beachcomber Club in Nottingham on the fourteenth. On January 19 he played the Speakeasy. On the twenty-fifth, the Marquee Club. Things were beginning to snowball. He was playing the top clubs as if he were already an established artist.

At the Marquee, Kit Lambert asked Chas to allow him to bill the Jimi Hendrix Experience with the Who at Brian Epstein's Saville Theater. Chas was delighted. The Saville was tops, and so were the Who. Finally Jimi was sharing the bill with a group of his caliber. It began to get around London that there would be a battle royal on the twenty-ninth of January 1967. A battle of the groups.

The Who vs. the Jimi Hendrix Experience concert, a tribute to Brian Epstein, was held on a Sunday. In attendance were Eric Clapton, Klaus Voorman, Linda Keith, John Lennon, Spencer Davis, Jack Bruce, Paul McCartney, and Lulu. Right from the announcement everyone knew it would be a famous concert. The two most outrageous groups in London dueling in feedback frenzy, full amps billowing forth decibels through theater walls.

On February 4, "Hey Joe" came in No. 4 on the *Melody Maker* chart. That was it; "Hey Joe" was a hit. The February 5, 1967, gig at the Flamingo Club was like the premiere of the Jimi Hendrix Experience as a star attraction.

The Flamingo Club was notorious for its lackadaisical approach to the best of British rock. A hip room, the Flamingo catered to a steady clientele of beatniklike insiders of the London underground. They were all too hip to the machinations of the British recording industry and its sundry promotion men. This club was the last in a long line of hip London clubs Hendrix and company had had to conquer and it was the toughest. The crowd at the Flamingo usually refrained from applauding in anything but the most token fashion.

Jimi opens at once with a jam meandering in heavy tempo. Then signaling in the blues with a long-distance call tremolo, he takes the band into "Killing Floor." Straight-down boogie, up-tempo R&B chords—like an Apollo showtime theme truncated into an introduction to the Jimi Hendrix Experience. Then Jimi speaks from the wall of sound, "Thank you very much." The music ceases. . . . "We'd like to continue on with a little tune, a very straight, ha, ha . . . Top Forty R&B rock 'n' roll record. A little thing called 'Have Mercy,' have mercy on me . . . BABY."

Noel Redding comes out with a "Woolly Boolly" bass beat, Jimi chording blues rhythm licks and filling in the lead, they come to the bridge, the blues chord inverted theme that explains, as so often in R&B, with words and tune changes, the meaning of the plea.

"Can You See Me?" Jimi's own tune, has the first really brilliant solo of the set spaced within an ample middle-bridge section that extends into the break where an elongated twang sustains for eight beats on the up-tempo, and then the ensemble returns to the back-beating wall of sound. Finally Jimi slows the pace, strumming soft chords against a simple run that sounds like a coffeehouse folk song.

"Right now I'd like to try to do a song for you, a little thing by Bob Dylan and 'Like a Rolling Stone.' . . . I want to dedicate this song to a few people in this club."

It comes out more like a ballad with the guitar the dominant sound, picking out the melody.

Jimi's arrangement of "Rock Me Baby" is far from B. B. King's blues-style version. It is definitely supertempo rock 'n' roll all the way for the Experience.

Jimi slurs his announcement of the next number: "Thank you very much; and I'd like to try and do a little mixture of a whole lot of

things in this one here . . . a little Muddy Waters version slightly."
Jimi goes into the beginning of Muddy Waters's version of the traditional blues, "Two Trains Running" (which Muddy Waters called
"Still a Fool"). From there he goes into a short solo circling about
the few notes that compose the introductory phrases and extending
them. And then just as easily slipping back into the original raunchy
chords with short stroking chops to sing a couple of verses. And
then straight and straight up into a psychedelic solo full of blue
tonality yet not sounding like the blues at all. Then back to the
verse, Jimi playing both the Muddy Waters lead and the Jimmie
Rodgers second guitar of the original version at the same time.

Well now there's two trains runnin'
And neither one's going my way
You know there's a one train runnin' at night
The other one runs before day
Runs before day, runs before day, runs before day . . .

Jimi plays with a little feedback at the end and then the song
climaxes into pure distortion, which ends in an abrupt halt. The
crowd comes alive for the first time. They cheer! Jimi answers with
his Stratocaster whoozing a "thank you."

Jimi buzzes into "Stone Free," the *B* side of their record. The song
builds slowly as he mumbles lyrics about being put down for his
hair, for his clothes, and by his women, but he wants everyone to
know—as the song builds to a screeching intensity—that he is
STONE FREE. Without missing a beat the JHE segues right into
their hit "Hey Joe."

His solo is fantastic. His customized Fuzz Face full out creates
endless peak distortions and sustains long lines that create their
own vibrato from sheer force of volume. It is a thrilling sound that
goes right through you. On the tag-out Jimi makes his guitar say
"You better believe it, baby."

"Wild Thing" starts off with the fuzz hook that it was known for
when the Troggs had it as their big hit. But Hendrix made "Wild
Thing" a heavy funky, mad metallic moan, full of the human
sounds of the blues in primordial emotion. You *feel* "Wild Thing."
In the middle passage, he goes into a little bit of the Beatles' "Day
Tripper," contrasting the heavy sexual blues-laden drone of his
"Wild Thing" with the flower-pop hit. Then he takes the song out.
Rolling feedback in lava folds across an incredible terrain. Mitch
Mitchell rolling, tramming, thunderous bombs against tingling
cymbals that sound like a giant-ship emergency bell. Monster fuck-

ing sounds. Fire in pink noise. Thrashing in gargantuan moans, the overdriving amps blown full out reporting the oscillating feedback. Pulling back into a stellar void, the deep tonic of the bass becomes apparent as Jimi sets his guitar back into the drone note that began the song.

The Flamingo Club house emcee picks up in the chaos: "Oh . . . let's hear it please for the Jimi Hendrix Experience. . . ." But the great howl makes his shout a tiny voice. The audience has responded, but their applause and occasional cheers are overwhelmed by the protesting sound system. "OK, ladies and gentlemen. The three gentlemen you've seen on the stage have given you their very best. How about your very best for them? Would you gentlemen, everybody this time, put your hands together for JIMI HENDRIX JIMI HENDRIX EXPERIENCE?"

The crowd erupts again in a very nice hand, with scattered cheers. An incredible hand for the Flamingo.

The emcee continues, ". . . who were working out *so hard* that time. Thank you. I'm afraid that's all from those three gentlemen for the evening, but back on the stand later on goes The All-night Workers. Thank you very much for being so great and clapping so great for Jimi. . . . Here we go for a few sounds, this one dedicated to Jimi, 'Please Don't Go.' "

A British cover of "Baby, Please Don't Go" screeches out from the speakers. It sweeps the club, penetrating to Jimi's dressing-room door, as the dressing room becomes more and more jammed with well-wishers and celebrities. Well, that was it. The Jimi Hendrix Experience is officially open for business—all offers and comers queued up.

One night at the Upper Cut Club Jimi took a little purple mini-pill and had an acid flash. Working in his dressing room he wrote a long poem called *Purple Haze*. It had a great number of verses, and burned with the intensity of that moment. Chas took them right down into the studio.

The bass and guitar dub the same two-note intro that runs duo octaves. Jimi's guitar plays flat against the major chord, giving a strange, almost discordant effect. Mitch on drums is behind the bass sotto. They walk the two-note intro for four beats. Then Jimi gives a slight bend that sets up the theme and resolves the strange discordance into Eastern-sounding fifths. The theme in full-blown wavering fuzz meets the drums full up, strong slaps of the snare with the bass drum kicking in triplets gives it a hip and subtle swing. The bass continues to bop two notes walking an entire octave. Jimi begins to swoop on his bass strings augmenting the bass. Then they set up the entrance of the vocal. Jimi goes into rhythm licks full up on the fuzz that is at the razor edge of distort, giving the effect of sparks flying. At the same time he lets his bass strings sustain a deep fuzz tone. His sustain merges with the bass line and holds for four beats on the same note, then plunges down into deep-moving figures for a quickening of the tempo, as he cuts off his bass string fuzz sustain to concentrate on the rhythm for four beats. They do this twice. Meanwhile, Mitch is drumming his ass off. And then Jimi shouts *"PURPLE HAZE!"* as if he is up on a mountaintop echoing down. Mitch's circular drumming ends in mighty cymbal clashes.

> *. . . all in my brain*
> *Lately things just don't seem the same*
> *Acting funny but I don't know why*
> *'scuse me while I kiss the sky*

A big break occurs on the last phrase, the echo resounding. Jimi plays a figure and then Mitch brings the ensemble back in with a half-circle bash.

> *Purple Haze all around*
> *Don't know if I'm comin' up or down*
> *Am I happy or in misery?*
> *Whatever it is, that girl put a spell on me*

In the second break Jimi hollers, "Help me, help me—aw no," as the chords change driving the song higher toward their resolution. Then the bridge comes in two parts, the fuzz tone changes to a Leslie tone, giving a higher watery organlike effect. Jimi's solo guitar scales the top and then back to the ragging fuzz of the theme.

> *Purple Haze all in my eyes*
> *Don't know if it's day or night*
> *You got me going blowing my mind*
> *Is it tomorrow or just the end of time?*

Jimi yelling in the void of the slight break, and then with the bash of the cymbals crying "Oh no, help me, help me, aw yeah yeah Purple Haze, aw no . . ." The tag-out begins to rage, arcing ecstatic lines. Jimi bending and drumming the treble note into the Leslie climbing higher and higher, the fuzz below dubbing with the bass, the bass taking off from there and plunging down in boogie agony. A long tag sustains in the high registers almost as if flight is at hand. Mitch swirling his snares, switching to cymbals for the higher registers. Jimi hits a harmonic through the Leslie and produces an uncanny piercing tone that takes off, Eastern-sounding beyond the range of guitar, as if another force out of nowhere entered. Occulting and mystical. Purple Haze out.

They listen to the "Purple Haze" tracks back. The first take was good. They try several more, but it's obvious that the first take has a fresh, spontaneous lilt to it (although the rhythm drags slightly at the end) and that freshness is difficult to recapture. Jimi adds a few touches, and that's it—"Purple Haze."

They listen to several playbacks. Jimi's consciousness sinks deeply into what he is saying. He would have liked to see it go much longer in accordance with the many verses he had written, but Chas prevails. They want to keep the time down for the single.

The days in London melted one into the other; he had lost track of time. His life accelerated. He was concentrating so totally on his music that he felt as if he were playing one long gig in one long single night that could just as easily be an eternity. Living by night. Looking out his blackout-curtained window, and it always was twilight. The lights of the city of London coming up over the twilight haze. The dark gray townhouses of London town queued up, low blocks stretching forever. Medieval buses tramming through the narrow streets bringing the commoners, the workers home to their pubs, to their evening meals. But their plight was always boring to him. They crammed into the pub below his window at six o'clock on the dot. His eyes would always turn to the sky, as if trying to discern some light, and the color for him that became the true color of his existence that year, 1967 in London, was that weird purple before the advent of night. That extreme side of the spectral haze— purple into the nights, the endless nights of his life.

Edwin Kramer seemed to have been waiting for Jimi. Not only did he have constructive criticism, he was also dying to try some new things out. Recording with Jimi in the studio convinced him that here was a man who would revolutionize the music and the technology as well. After their first sessions together, Kramer and Hendrix were most taken with each other. Studying the recordings in his time off and working with Hendrix daily in the studio, Kramer was convinced that there were some things they could do in the Olympic four-track studio that had never been done before.

They worked night and day every day for a month putting the first album and much of a second Hendrix album together. Being in the studio for extensive amounts of time where his sound could be immediately played back to him made Hendrix a studio addict. Tunes he had written in the Village and performed at the Cafe Wha? now achieved fruition from their frail beginnings.

The studio opened Hendrix's head up musically more than it had ever been before. Finally there was a source, a place where it could all be put together.

Kramer became so important to Hendrix that it was strange they did not become close friends. They worked well together, were extremely polite to each other—but at the end of their working days/nights, they would each go back to their respective scenes.

Hendrix did not want to do anything that might alienate Kramer. Kramer was a man—and at that time one of the few men in England—who could optimize the sounds in Jimi's way-out head. He would take no risk with Kramer. Kramer was too important for Hendrix to dilute their intense work with play.

They worked out phase shifts, double-tracking, space sounds, wind sounds, even a more controlled feedback sound that could melt right into notes. Underwater sounds, spaceship and rocket sounds, refined white, pink, and blue noises—red noises. They did sound paintings right out of the avant-garde composers' backyard. Since they were using all kinds of sound contraptions to run Hendrix's guitar through, why leave the drums behind? The drums came right along and were as up as Jimi's multiple guitars on every attack. Kramer was able to get a phased timbre on Mitchell's drums that had the double-kit set almost tuned to the two guitars. Bright, liquid, and slapping, the drums walked right out of the recordings at you double-tracked and phase-shifted, just like the guitars. And in stereo, too. Although they did not publicize it, they began to mix everything in stereo. Redding's bass received several electronic boosts as well. Special fuzz tones were developed. But most importantly they were able to get the deepest bass effects possible without distorting the speakers. Whereas in reggae, for instance, it would be years before the bass could be recorded at the depths where it was most effective. The genius of Ed Kramer made it possible for even the five-inch speaker of a common AM portable radio to be able to deliver the full import of the Experience sound. And he was a wizard at lining up two, three, and even four guitar overdubs on one track of the four-track tapes. They had the fourth member of the Experience: Ed Kramer. Through this small elfin blond they were finally able to extend Jimi's guitar into the outer heavens it had been aimed at in the first place.

The Jimi Hendrix Experience began to move, began to fly. People

joined up with the crew out of the night. Gerry Stickells was just hanging out and he had a truck, so he became the equipment manager. A weird electronic genius named "O," who made far-out "toys" for electric guitars, became an essential part of the JHE. "O" improved on Jimi's homemade wah-wah, which had been inspired by the Fugs. "O" also built a little machine they called the Octavia, which could change octaves at a touch. They were working on the highest keening treble range possible with an enhanced report to give the sound the same presence as a middle-range tone. They tested it with some overdubs on a tune called "The Stars That Play with Laughing Sam's Dice," code for "STP-LSD." No "Lucy in the Sky with Diamonds," Jimi was heading for interstellar space through an inward galaxy. The high keening harmonic sounds at full report gave the feel of moving upward, at the upper pitches and upper registers of decibel it was possible to feel the sounds with the body and the emotions at an enhanced rate.

"The Stars That Play with Laughing Sam's Dice" was a joke. But Jimi was serious in the same way that an LSD trip is amusing but quite serious, as the power drug pulls one out of ordinary reality into a nether world of perception. "STP-LSD" is a guided tour to the taking of psychedelics.

The song starts with basic rock 'n' roll, a few Sergeant Pepper licks and Mitch Mitchell's slight back-beat on tom-tom creating a simplistic milieu.

> *The stars up above that play with laughing Sam's dice*
> *They make us feel the world was made for us*
> *The zodiac glass that gleams come through the skies*
> *It will happen soon . . . for you. . . .*

And then the song changes as if the psychotropic drug substances have hit the nervous system, and the myriad voices of the cosmos rise straight up on the wings of perceptions: "aaaaaaaaaaaaaaaaaaaaaaaaaaaAAAAAAAAAAAAAAAAAAAHHH-HHHHHHHHHHHH And away we gooooooo. . . ." The rock 'n' roll switches to psychedelic as the song climbs the scale over into higher keys, and the guitar blossoms to its upper limits. "Thank you very much, thank you very much, thank you, and now we'd like to bring you our friendly neighborhood experience workers. . . ." Beatle-like voices chant "Yeah, Yeah, Yeah," and Jimi, the tour guide, sings-raps:

Opposite: Jimi and Devon © 1970 FRED W. MCDARRAH

The Milky Way express is loaded—ALL ABOARD
I promise each and every one of you you wŏn't be bored

The guitar scaling and writhing at its upper limits, the tremolo bar jacking the sound to oscillating overdrive.

What I'm really concerned about
Is my brand-new pair of butterfly roller skates

Jimi shouts now as the spaceship reaches outer space, the electric guitar in one writhing long riff strains against the heavy metal atmosphere.

No throwing cigarette butts out the window
No throwing cigarette butts out the window
Now if you look to your right you'll see Saturn. . . .
If you look to the left you'll see Mars
I hope you brought your parachutes with you. . . .
HEY LOOK OUT!
LOOK OUT FOR THAT DOOR
DON'T OPEN THAT DOOR
DON'T OPEN THAT DOOR—
Oh well . . .

Jimi takes a treble note almost to feedback and holds it there quavering, then hits a harmonic that takes the signal straight up— sustaining. Whanging furiously on the tremolo bar, Fuzz tone turned all the way up through the Octavia, the guitar produces a looney wail, overdriving the amps as the song fades.

Kathy Etchingham became Jimi's first real girlfriend in London. She was a hard-drinking English girl with a sensuous mouth, fine figure, and shoulder-length red hair, which fell into her eyes and hung straight to her shoulders. She was outspoken and a "wild thing" by English standards, but to Jimi she was not much different from the white girls of the Village scene in New York.

It would have been a hang-up for Chas for Jimi to have a girl living with him while Jimi stayed at his place. As soon as Jimi was making steady money, he rented a pretty good hotel room at first; finally he got a flat over a pub near the Speakeasy in the extended Times Square-like Soho of downtown London.

Jimi promptly painted the living room black and bought black satin sheets for his bed and blackout curtains for the windows. He wanted to create his own environment in a space not of cloudy London but of pure space, the galaxy. Now his staying up all night, or his penchant for staying in bed for days at a time, would not bother Chas. Nor did he have to answer the telephone anymore, as you do when you are someone's guest living in their home. He controlled the number, changed it at will, or simply refused to answer the phone at all.

Even Kathy Etchingham was astounded at his long bouts of bed rest. Sometimes he didn't even want to have sex. She *knew* that was strange. But she was as spirited as she was flexible. She would be down to go for a walk through Hyde Park at dawn, or to listen to the Salvation Army band on Sundays—a ritual he loved.

Kathy was really into drinking and she might have led him more into it. When he first came to London, he had only drunk soda pop. She spaced on the acid though, acid took Jimi to another place.

Another person who quickly became friends with Jimi was Brian Jones. Brian Jones was the unofficial leader of the Rolling Stones when Jimi arrived in London that September of 1966. It was a natural that they would become friends. All Brian had to do was hear Jimi's interpretation of Muddy Waters's "Two Trains . . ." and that was it. It had been Jones who had brought Muddy Waters to the Stones. Muddy Waters had been Jagger, Richards, and Jones's musical inspiration during their lean days in London.

Brian Jones's best friend, Tara Browne, had died in an auto accident right around the time that Jimi began appearing in the clubs of London. Lonely and also turned on by authentic black blues and R&B musicians, Jones turned a lot of his attention toward Jimi. Brian was kinglike, grand, gracious, and sensitive as well. Brian Jones and Jimi Hendrix became friends. Not in public, but in private. They would drink together, smoke dope together, and just hang out. No publicity or anything like that. Just two musicians with big ears. Brian was a big fan of Charlie Parker and Billie Holliday. It thrilled him that Jimi had lived in Manhattan, and down in the Village, where Parker and Holliday were legends. There was something about the way those two lived that fascinated Jones, especially "Yardbird" Parker. They pushed their bodies and minds to the limit through massive doses of drugs and booze. It was as if they had reached mystical heights through what some called self-abuse, yet no one doubted that their self-torture was real. There are some things you just cannot fake. In a world of greed, antiart, and Big Brother authoritarianism, they had consciously sacrificed themselves to the music. In their wretchedness, in their *angst*, no one

could possibly say that they were bullshitting. And the musical
heights Charlie Parker and Billie Holliday achieved in spite of all the
odds—social and self-imposed—gave one the feeling that they had
triumphed on a truly spiritual plane. They had refused any middle
ground.

Jimi and Brian often went to the Cool Elephant Club, where they
would be virtually anonymous among the older clientele. The Cool
Elephant had a jazz policy and plenty of recordings from the bebop
era that so many ignorant hip young Londoners thought passé.
Jones's musical quest was for the truly unique in sound. He embo-
died in his ideas a unity, a synthesis of blues, Eastern music, Moroccan trance music, and Druidian folk fragments of forgotten ages.
Jimi was amused and turned on by Jones, whose enthusiasm was
boundless. Brian Jones was a true *bon vivant*, reveling in joyous
mind-fuzz classical decadence—at least for England. His flare for the
outrageous supported Jimi during his first uncertain months when
he was unsure of the public image to project. Brian Jones was into
saying "fuck it." He would let it all hang out and would not back
down, no matter what the odds. Jimi's first gigs in London were
models of sedateness. He was letting his guitar do the talking. But as
the stories drifted to him of Brian Jones's reckless, seemingly insane
come-ons to the crowds he played before, and the resultant riots and
mass hysteria, Jimi began to feel that he, too, could let it all hang
out. And that was the secret. London, so excruciatingly class-
conscious, would bow before the one who acted like a king, and kill
the one who *tried* to act like a king. Brian was at the top, yet totter
and teeter as he might, there was no disrupting his eminence. "Ruby
Tuesday" became No. 1 as they hung out together. Brian was ecstatic over its success. He loved to hear it by surprise, on the radio in
his Rolls-Royce, in a club, or out of a solitary window they happened
to pass. Brian would tell with great relish of how he and Keith
Richards worked and worked on coloring, adding dramatic yet wispy
touches here and there, altering the mix between lead voice and
background vocal harmonies, while interplaying exotic instruments. Sounds that were impossible to identify gave "Ruby Tuesday" an eternal air of mystery and yearning.

And they would both laugh uproariously about sleeping with their
guitars.

But Hendrix hated a guitar that could not play. Once, while playing before an enthusiastic German audience, he had fallen off the
stage. In the excitement he had tossed his Stratocaster back onstage
ahead of him and realized he had broken the instrument.

It was a stupid thing to do. Angry at himself for an unprofessional mistake, angry at himself for blowing the excitement, and mad at the useless, broken guitar, he grabbed it by the neck, and slung it around the stage, whomping the amps a couple of times. And then he bashed it to smithereens on the stage floor. The sounds of the guitar playing back its own destruction fascinated him. But his fascination was quickly dispelled by the sound of the crowd—*they were going crazy*. Their roar was freaky and manic.

The faces of the few German youths he could see in the front rows stayed with him for a long time afterward. Noel, who had played Germany quite a bit before he joined Jimi's group, dismissed the incident as merely being part of the overall general zaniness of the German rock 'n' rollers. But Jimi was feeling beyond that. He had felt the *emotion* of the crowd as he had felt the emotions of hundreds of audiences before this. What he felt from that German crowd was something he had never felt before playing any gig as third guitar or as leader.

The audience had been shocked out of their minds by the sheer act of destruction. The instrument they had come to hear and had been hearing for the entire evening destroyed before their very eyes. It was like a sacrifice, but more like a dadaist final act of truth. The ultimate testimony of an artist—to destroy his tools, as a final act ending the creation of that moment forever. It was also an incredible renegade act: total rejection of the mechanization of man and art—before many.

Back in London, "Purple Haze" was nearing its release date. Spring was approaching. Talk of "Flower Power" was going hot and heavy in America and beginning to catch on in London. The *Daily Mirror* played up the German destruction bit to the hilt, especially since the Jimi Hendrix Experience was due to begin a big tour with the Walker Brothers, Cat Stevens, and Engelbert Humperdinck. The Fleet Street papers sought to link "Flower Power" with destruction and it seemed that Jimi Hendrix was the perfect symbol. The press seemed to be daring Jimi to destruct at Finsbury Park, where the tour would commence. Dick Katz and the tour press agents loved it, although they knew the arena authorities and theater owners would hate it. Hendrix's office leaked a rumor that Jimi would indeed destruct.

There was a massive turnout at Finsbury Park that March 31, 1967. It was common knowledge that the Walker Brothers, teen idols, would split up after the tour—a virtual guarantee that the young girls would be there in flocks.

Sitting in the dressing room while Jimi waited to go on, Chas Chandler and journalist Keith Altham were discussing some kind of

punch to put into the act. Up until that time Jimi had been doing
straight guitar playing, with the playing-with-the-teeth bit and his
general showtime acrobatics the only departures from the norm.
While this was cool for his musician and underground followers,
Chas knew the teenybopper fans who would be on this tour would
need something extra. Engelbert Humperdinck, Cat Stevens, and
the Walker Brothers were all lady-killer sex symbols. Jimi would
have to be superextraordinary just to keep up. Jimi had a tune called
"Fire" that suggested to a symbolic young girl that she leave her
mama's side and come to him so he could warm his body before her
fire. Keith Altham thought that perhaps something could be done
with "Fire" that would dramatize it more to the kids. It did not take
much discussion for the assembled to figure out that the only way to
dramatize fire was to create one. They sent Gerry Stickells out to get
some lighter fluid and got ready.

The Jimi Hendrix Experience opened the show. "Purple Haze"
and "Fire" were the new songs of the lot, with "Fire" the inevitable
finale. It was basically a vehicle for shouted phrases of sexual in-
nuendo that went as close to the borderline as possible. The lyrics
were not muffled and laid back, as had been his custom, but full-
throated and haranguing. The music was simple up-tempo rock,
built around Jimi's soloing and Mitch's circular drumming.

First the ensemble hits a simple boogie melody, then Jimi shouts
the lyrics against the back-beating drums up to full volume.

> *All right*
> *Now listen, baby!*
> *You don't care for me*
> *I don't care about that*
> *Gotta new fool!—Ha!*
> *I like it like that,*
> *I have only one burning desire—*
> *Let me stand next to your fire*

Mitch and Noel join him singing the refrain in unison, *"Let me
stand next to your fire"* several times, then Jimi hits the lyrics
again.

> *Listen here, baby*
> *And stop acting so crazy!*
> *You say your mum ain't home*
> *It ain't my concern*
> *Just play with me*

And you won't get burned
I have only one itching desire
Let me stand next to your fire

Jimi shouts, *"Oh move over, Rover, and let Jimi take over,"* as he goes into a mad solo complete with all the stage tricks he can throw at the crowd! *"Yeah, you know what I'm talking about. Yeah, get it on, baby."* Jimi jacks his treble reach to its limit and sends the sound careening through the sky, pointing his Strat straight up from a deep crouch. *"That's what I'm talking about."*

Now dig this!—Ha!
Now listen, baby!
You try to gimme your money
You better save it, babe
Save it for a rainy day
I have only one burning desire
Let me stand next to your fire

Jimi soloed on the upbeat tag-out that stretched on until he got the lighter fluid out. He almost blew it. Jimi went down on his back to pour the lighter fluid over the guitar. Lighting the matches seemed to take forever. Finally he got a light. Rolling over and hovering over his guitar he applied the match to the lighter fluid and immediately flames leaped, twelve feet high. He rocked back on his haunches and then over on his back, clutching his hands. People on both sides of the stage went berserk. To many in the audience it seemed as if Jimi Hendrix had self-immolated his body, like the Buddhists were doing in Vietnam—burning themselves in public. There was awe, freaky terror, and delight in the crowd as Jimi bounded up and disappeared backstage. The ovation was shattering. They howled in shock.

Backstage the theater manager was threatening a lawsuit and demanding the guitar as evidence. He was outraged. The audience was still applauding.

The next day Jimi was front-page news. "Purple Haze" was burning down the charts.

The JHE organization had pulled out all the stops, now they started refining the technique. They could not let a chance like this go by. A twenty-five-day tour all over England before legions of teenyboppers with their solid British sex-symbol idols before them. They knew Jimi could not burn his guitar every night. But what he could do was a direct-action burlesque/satire of the whole "pop" sex-symbol scene—and blow everybody's mind. Before, Jimi had only played around with the guitar: slinging it under his legs as he flickered his tongue. Now he developed it. Falling suddenly to his knees like James Brown during "Please, Please" and lip-synching a scream as his Stratocaster emits an orgasmic howl. Then moving the guitar across his body, standing straight up from his haunches panning the instrument before him like a machine gun cock emitting staccato bursts; humping his ax as it rumbles into low-pitched feedback, and then letting it all out as he falls back to his knees, and then over backward, feedback spilling white-hot noise all over him.

Soon the tour promoter was forced to act. There were complaints that Hendrix's sexual behavior onstage was vulgar and erotic. He publicly demanded that Hendrix clean up his act. Meanwhile, his tour quickly sold out.

Jimi began to incur the wrath of the headliners, the Walker Brothers. He was getting all the attention and publicity. When a French TV crew came to film only Hendrix the Walker Brothers really blew their tops. There were all kinds of sabotage from theater owners, stage managers, and sound and light people, but the Experience stuck it through.

When they returned to London "Purple Haze" was in the Top Ten at No. 3 and Jimi had become the No. 1 male sex symbol of London.

The *Sunday Mirror* dispatched a reporter to get a quote from Jimi about the accusations that he performed suggestive movements in his act. Jimi replied: "I think 'act' is maybe the wrong word. I play and move as I feel. It's no act. Perhaps it's sexy . . . but what music with a big beat isn't?"

The next day, May 20, 1967, the Jimi Hendrix Experience signed with Reprise Records (U.S.A.) for a £50,000 advance ($120,000).

Hendrix sat in with jazz great Roland Kirk at Ronnie Scott's club in Soho. This was a very meaningful experience for Jimi. Because he was unsure of his reception among jazz artists, Roland Kirk's acceptance of his musicianship increased his confidence at an important time. While lurid details of Jimi's personality and his threat to English culture were circulated almost daily in the press, this meaningful exchange was ignored.

Before they played together Kirk came to visit Jimi at his apartment. At that time London was ablaze with Jimi Hendrix posters, rumors, and statements. Hendrix had two singles in the Top Ten, and everyone knew he was the biggest new thing happening. But

Hendrix, always self-deprecating, sought out Kirk, a brother, a fellow musician from the States, to simply come visit. Kirk found the flat surprisingly modest. Above a pub, it was the flat of a worker, not a star.

Hendrix had known of Roland Kirk's music in the States. Kirk had played at the Five Spot while Jimi was at Cafe Wha? six blocks away. Jimi, who was able to play three different guitar parts at once, felt an affinity for Kirk, who had gained notoriety in the press by being able to play three wind instruments at one time. Weird instruments, too, like the stritch, a medieval horn that looked like a soprano saxophone, but stretching straight down and longer, with a trumpetlike bell that curved out at the end. Kirk could play a saxophone, a mazello, and the stritch at the same time, three-part harmonizing, and also do circular breathing, which allowed unusually long sustained lines and even three-part phrases. From his neck hung a *wheee* whistle, which he would blow after an incredible solo. Kirk also played flute with his nose. The English press, of course, played up those freaky parts of Kirk's performances. Understanding the importance of novelty in attracting an audience, Kirk's and Hendrix's musical abilities were the bedrock on which these "tricks" rested.

Kirk, burly, bold, blind, outspoken, held radical views concerning jazz. Many jazz men knock the rock and blues players for doing what they consider a facile music. But Kirk did not consider himself a "jazz musician," although he is considered one of the best in the business. Kirk talked only about "the music." Whether it be jazz, blues, rhythm and blues, or rock—it was the music. From the start Kirk and Hendrix communicated on a mutual plane. Their conversations were not about what differentiated them, but about their mutuality, their involvement in the music of black people. Roland Kirk recognized Hendrix as essentially a blues man. While it was necessary for the publicists to put the rock banner on Jimi's music, the funky syncopated foundation and wide choices of phrasings and colorings rested in the blues tradition. Kirk, who is able to deliver powerful blues blowing himself, realized, musician to musician, where Hendrix was coming from.

Jimi's flat over the pub on Brook Street bore a plaque proclaiming that Handel once lived there. They sat there the entire afternoon, listening to records and talking about music and about London as compared to America. They both laughed over the lack of American soul food and jammed most of the time. Jimi played what he usually played and Roland Kirk played what he usually played and it worked out fine. They were joined by the African conga player Kwasi Dzid-zornu, known as "Rocki."

Kirk invited Jimi to come and sit in with him at Ronnie Scott's jazz club in Soho. They dug each other so much that they played together again the next night. No publicity, no recordings, simply the music, for the love of music—and the memories of doing it together.

Ram John Holder and Jimi Hendrix were bound to meet. They had both recently come to London from the Village. They were both guitarists, and they both became involved with Monika Danneman.

Ram met Jimi at the Scotch of St. James, an "in" private club. Ram had wandered in to get a drink and heard that a brother from the States was playing, and that he should check it out. Downstairs Jimi Hendrix was playing some shit that even made the band stop. The audience stood in amazement. At that moment, Ram felt he never wanted to play his guitar again. He felt like burning it.

Later, when he talked with Jimi, he found that they knew some of the same people. Ram had been the co-owner of the Cafe Rafio in the Village. A small club, the Cafe Rafio featured solo guitarists on acoustic in the folk tradition. Dave Van Ronk, Dino Valenti, Tom Paxton, and Richie Havens all had played the Cafe Rafio, as did Ram himself. Ram sang the blues with West Indian intonations that were lost in his sincerity. He loved the blues. He *loved* Hendrix. As a musician himself he recognized Hendrix's blues background and inspiration.

Ram John Holder had come to London to find himself. The son of a preacher from a tiny Caribbean country, he had been educated at all-black Lincoln University and had studied for advanced degrees at New York University. He had become involved in New Left politics as an outgrowth of the civil rights movement. An accomplished guitarist, he was also drawn to the stage as an actor. Ram had to decide in what direction to take his life.

Compared to Jimi, Ram was a scholar. Ram was well read and politically well informed on worldwide liberation struggles. Coming to London had been depressing for him at first. He hated the way in which black West Indians were treated in the United Kingdom. Ghettoized largely in grim towns outside of London, the blacks were no longer needed to work in the factories that had boomed when England was a world colonial power. In fact, the black population, as it continued to grow, was viewed with alarm by the staid English establishment.

Ram was tempted to jump into the political arena and champion the rights of the blacks. He was well aware of the black spokesmen, and there were too few. The outstanding West Indian spokesmen were light-years apart. He admired C. L. R. James, the Marxist West Indian scholar who had written *The Black Jacobins*, the definitive book on the Haitian Revolution. He followed his writings carefully, but as an activist-speaker, James was too old to be really effective. In his late seventies, C. L. R. James did his best, but he was over-shadowed by Michael X, who was much younger and somewhat "in" to the hip London underground. Although Michael X never really committed himself to any specific political group, his pro-nouncements in the press often linked the repression of blacks in London with the suppression of "Flower Power." Fiery, sometimes crazy, and usually unpredictable, Michael X was the only young black able to move through many different echelons of London soci-ety (R. D. Laing thought he was great) and was, therefore, at least potentially important. But in many ways Michael X was not politi-cal enough to organize. He fashioned himself after Malcolm X and "Black Power," whereas Dr. James was a Norman Thomas-type fig-ure, committed to leftist politics. The gulf that separated Michael X from C. L. R. James was symptomatic of the crisis of black lead-ership in Britain.

Ram John was sorely tempted to take the whole thing on.

But then again, looking at it head on, Ram felt in his heart that it would be a hopeless task. That is why he gave what support he could to Michael X. It was a hapless situation that could indeed drive one crazy. Ram tried to understand Michael X and read and relate to Dr. James, but the most he could do at the time was keep himself informed of the global situation.

Ram and Jimi became good friends. They would always hug when they met. There were not too many brothers on the set. Jimi found it amusing that Ram was an inveterate cricket fan and would rush off at a moment's notice to catch a match on the "telly." Jimi could have been an actor himself. He was an excellent mimic, especially of Harlem drag queens, and he told incredibly funny stories of his various tours with small-time bands in small-time places. Like two brothers on the block, they, each in their own eccentricities, brought each other qualities they missed in being away from home.

Ram had met Jimi the first month he arrived. They saw each other almost every day. They both dug hanging out, but as Hendrix's thing began to come together he became more distant and more hassled. The big push was on, and it was not easy, or even particularly pretty to watch.

Around New Year's 1967, Ram caught an interview with Jimi in one of the smaller London papers. Jimi's rap was very spacey. As an educated man looking for substance, all Ram found were platitudes. When he came to the paragraphs where Jimi glossed over politics, revolution, and the plight of the man of color, he blew his top. It was like Jimi had sold out. Ram John was furious. He would have to see Jimi right away.

Ram John would have found Jimi sooner had he not been involved with Monika Danneman. Ram had met Monika one night in early '66 in one of the rare London clubs that featured black music, and where a lot of black American and West Indian musicians hung out. She had come right over and introduced herself. They talked over a few drinks and found each other attractive and intelligent. She invited him for a ride in her sleek sports car. To her flat. A fast friendship ensued.

Later in 1966 Monika had written him from Germany, where she lived with her parents, telling him she was returning to London in early 1967, and could he help her find a flat for a few months? Ram had felt that her request was also a sly way of suggesting she stay with him. He had tried to find her a flat to no avail. Money was no problem to her. She was the daughter of a wealthy Dusseldorf businessman.

They got together when she got to London. She rented a semiposh garden apartment in the European-style Samarkand Hotel in the elegant upper part of Notting Hill Gate. It was a very nice place; a Buddha was engraved on a golden plaque on the white front door. From the street you could not see her apartment. You had to walk down a circular flight of stairs and go through some fairly thick potted trees before you came to her door. There was a heavy seclusion to the place.

Ram John had "sussed" that she was a confused young rich German chick who sought her identity, as many middle-class American white kids did, in the music of the downtrodden black. They had long talks about their childhoods and future plans. Ram had not yet decided on the road he would take in his life. Monika had not either. But she had the option of retiring to her family fortune.

Her father caused her a lot of anxiety. He was intensely jealous of her, and since she had taken to championing and following the music of American blacks, he had become unbearable. They lived in a large mansion-type complex that held separate units for members of the family. She would often bring black musicians who happened to be in Dusseldorf. She went through hell when her father found out. She had to be very careful of her family name.

She had studied all of the arts and had won several awards as an accomplished ice skater. She also painted, wrote poetry, and sang a bit. She was probably better at painting now that she had given up ice skating.

Monika was a good conversationalist and a better listener. Ram told her about his disaffection with Hendrix. As he talked he realized that it was helping him to decide the direction he wanted to take in his career. Monika listened very carefully. To Ram, Jimi had become captured by the media imagery that surrounded him. In fact, he was helping along the senseless "Wild Man from Borneo" typecast. Ram saw how easy it was to become lax, noncaring, and unaware of what was happening around you when you became involved in the heady regions of the London pop culture. The English establishment would allow pop and even "Flower Power," as long as it made money and was not political. Even though they put him down, Hendrix would play along for "his image." Ram could not do that. He decided right there that he would pursue a career as an actor. He would know that he was playing a role, like everyone else, and he would also be free to be himself, continuing his political work. He would still be able to perform and operate intellectually without toning down either part of his expressions.

After Ram John left Monika, he cooled down a bit. He was relieved to get that off his chest. He had high ideals and *expected* those close to him to live up to them. Ram felt it was important to know that about yourself. The same went for Monika. He would not call her for a long while.

A few days later he encountered Jimi Hendrix. Monika was with him. What a trip! Jimi started to give him their usual hug; Ram caught him right there and let him have it. With the power of an orator, he bore through Jimi with his powerful voice. Everyone in the club looked around to see what the row was about. "How could Jimi be so stupid as to put down the very people who were on his side, ultimately more on his side than those who pimped him?" Chas came up, looking more like a bodyguard than a manager. Jimi waved him away, seemingly absorbed in Ram's tirade. Monika looked away, as if embarrassed to look in Ram's eyes.

"They treat you like a nigger freak, the 'Wild Man of Pop' they call you, the 'Wild Man from Borneo.' And you go right along with it. You're stupid, man!"

Jimi took it all, his head slightly down, turned as if ashamed. But he listened carefully to all that Ram said. Probably no one else would say things like that to his face, especially in polite London.

Yet he knew he had no political sophistication. He knew Ram was right. He also knew the chance he was taking. And he well knew he would be alone no matter what the outcome.

Very strong and energetic, and determined to get over, Hendrix faced the weird London society with a Harlem smoothie's cool. Everything was cool, and he would let nothing bother his cool. Things were happening fast. His main concern was to keep his ax sharp and be ready. Cause it was coming, happening hot and heavy.

"I was Lord Kitchener's valet." Carnaby Street clothier. Jimi being feted and fitted at the same time. It is important that he is there. The acceptance of the new London clothing styles by the "pop stars" was immeasurably important to the *blitzkrieg* Carnaby Street fashion designers were wagering against the traditional London clothiers. Hip London. And who is more hip than the emergent Jimi Hendrix? He is from the States. He is photographed most often in the most appealing circumstances. Since Carnaby Street is also fighting the recent upsurge of "hippie" and "Flower Power" casualness, Jimi Hendrix's endorsement of eighteenth-century-style fop is very important to its survival. And moreover, an important endorsement of "hip London" style.

The shop is in a flurry over him. Almost all other business is suspended, the entire shop seems to be participating in his fitting. He is of different proportions than the usual Londoner. Broad-shouldered, with extremely long legs and arms, narrow-waisted, with a protruding behind. Yet fit him they will, even if they have to completely resew entire garments. Hands are all over him. Salesgirls kneeling, salesgirls standing on all sides, the gay proprietor shouting to scurrying figures.

He feels like a racing car in a pit at the Indianapolis 500 being overhauled before going back into the race.

An Australian lady pop writer very politely introduces herself. Her name is Lillian Roxon. She really digs what he is doing.

He sits, now stands, arms up, now akimbo, now at his sides, legs apart, now together, then he sits again. The fine hands of tailors nitting, picking, and measuring, smoothing and tugging.

He remembers when he first got to London. His Harlem rags cross-pollinating with his Village fashions. Fake satin shades of Lester's on 125th Street and Paul Sargeant's slim cuts on West Fourth Street. Stovepipe Levi's chinos, and gaudy buckled Flagg's half shoes. He found everyone in London so impeccably fitted and pressed next to his rugged store-bought wear. Even the uniforms of the various bands he had played with seemed out of place. And his hair in ragged conk; huge pimples on his face. That was all changing quickly.

His first London stage costume had been a light blue nineteenth-century English cavalry jacket over black pants. The best they could do at the time. But now he could really get into it, really get into *a look*. Might as well go all the way—the way of Sergeant Pepper.

The mainstay of the London hip underground was blues pundit Alexis Korner, who had discovered the Stones. Korner's blues band had formed in the late fifties and survived through the successive "Dixieland jazz" and "folk" crazes in London in the early 1960s. Alexis Korner had been the first blues band leader to hire Brian Jones and to showcase Mick Jagger. He also hired Jack Bruce and Ginger Baker for his band. Jones, Jagger, Clapton, John Mayall, and a few others were the young musicians in London who were really serious in their appreciation and interpretation of the blues.

Korner was annoyed when Chas Chandler began to publicly challenge Eric Clapton's "top guitarist" status. Chas told Korner that Hendrix was a cat who was going to show Clapton where it's at. Chandler persisted. Korner had hoped that Hendrix and Clapton would come together and just jam, but Chandler's remarks had destroyed the vibes for the happening, at least in Korner's mind.

Finally Hendrix went to a club where Clapton was playing and asked to sit in. No guitarist *ever* asked Clapton, the King of Blues Guitar, to sit in. As soon as Hendrix began to play and do his show-time act, Clapton knew he had met his match. And Clapton knew that he would have to change.

Chrissie Charles had been John Mayall's old lady. She was a free spirit. As a part of the blues purist circle, she involved herself in activities that promoted the new music of London as culture and sought to elevate blues and jazz and rock 'n' roll in the minds of the English people.

She met Jimi Hendrix while she was involved in putting together a TV special on the English rock scene. They really hit it off together. Even though the special fell through, they continued to see each other. Soon they had an arrangement.

Chrissie had her own flat outside of London. When Jimi wanted to escape from the hassles of his own scene he would give her a call to make sure everything was cool and then split to her place. Things never stopped happening at his own place. He took little holidays out at Chrissie's. The folks in the neighborhood did not know who he was. They went to out-of-the-way places, had picnics, took long walks, just had a good time.

Chrissie wore her soft blond hair close-cropped. Tiny and perky, with a stunningly developed body, she possessed a winning way about her. She could be small and delicate, or energetic and motherly. Endearing as she was intelligent, she had a real sensitivity to the music Jimi played, and a sorrow for the plight of black people in America. Jimi did not like her to become intellectual. Like when she tried to read or psychoanalyze him. He would always make her stop. He preferred her beautiful enthusiastic spirit.

They would always make love in the dark, on Jimi's insistence. This would always remind Chrissie of Jimi's room with its black sheets and black walls. Jimi was extremely shy about his long arms and big hands and feet. Sometimes he took out a psychological race thing on Chrissie, as a representative of the white race. But mostly he was too sweet to be true.

One night Chrissie and Jimi were having a leisurely dinner in an out-of-the-way restaurant. Jimi was being interviewed by a dude from *Beat Instrumental* magazine, but he was young and mellow and they were relaxed and easygoing about the whole thing. Suddenly Eric Clapton walked in. Chrissie whooped him over. It was actually the first time Jimi and Eric formally met. Eric Clapton, retiring and shy, was something of a recluse, and eccentric at that. Only admiration shone in their eyes as Chrissie savored the introductions. Jimi and Eric clasped both hands across the table. Holding each other's hands, they simply drank each other in joyously— hands in hands.

They all talked and got stoned. The man from *Beat Instrumental* was supposed to be interviewing Jimi, but they all got drunk instead. They had a good chat, which lasted into the dawn. The fellow from the magazine kept the tape rolling haphazardly throughout the evening.

The conversation meandered around women, music, and money, a sense of "place" hovering over it all: Where they would be tomorrow or twenty years down the road? Both Clapton and Hendrix were beginning to see the rewards of their tremendous popularity and they were trying to put it in perspective. Hendrix dominated the conversation, but Clapton got in some telling remarks, indicating that he was not as stoned as Jimi.

"Do you expect to do this for the rest of your life in the same place?" Jimi asks. ". . . If I got a gig doing five hundred pounds a week, and I got bored, I'm gonna quit it, man, and go on to something else. . . . I want to see the North Pole, I want to see the South Pole. . . . I want to see Moscow, you know. I want to witness a slight bit of pain of what I hear about." Hendrix qualifies this, he doesn't want propaganda or to be hurt by it. "I want to witness that for at least about a minute or two."

The table breaks up as Clapton comes in. ". . . to witness it, man, for months and really die, you know—that's the way. I'd die a million times."

"Well over a million times walking through London," Hendrix specifies, ". . . I look at the girls . . . you fall in love a thousand times a day."

Someone says, ". . . this is an immediate hang-up."

Jimi counters, "There's no pain in falling in love for a second or even for three minutes . . . it's so good to indulge the beauty of a girl you've never seen before."

Someone asks, "What happens when you meet them?"

". . . that's *social*. I'm not talking about meeting them, I'm talking about *seeing* them."

After a while Chrissie speaks directly into the microphone, "Am I here?"

Everyone laughs as Jimi says, "Don't be stupid. You are here." There's a confusion of giggles and banter as he continues, "Anyway, that's the voice of Christine, lovely Christine."

Then from out of nowhere and to nobody in particular Jimi murmurs, ". . . I find out—even when I get sober—I find out that I tell more of the truth on my own self when I am like this than when I'm sober. Music and life, the flow, goes together so closely. . . . Music, man, it means so many things. It doesn't mean necessarily physical notes that you hear by ear. It could be notes that you hear by feeling or thought or by imagination or even by emotions. . . ."

Clapton says, "I am going to be a millionaire. I plan to buy myself huge cars. It sort of brings you down terribly. At the same time I have a kind of idea that money is kinda necessary."

"Highway Chile" comes up over the loudspeaker in the background; although heavy into the subject, Hendrix cannot help but pause. ". . . just in case anybody can hear the guitar in the background, that's me playing—starving [laughter]. Anyway, getting right back, you can't let money rule, you have to rule money: the way you want to use it."

Jimi goes into a long rap about Christine, declaring how beautiful she is and how her mind is so together. "But see, I don't even want to get caught up to her actually, you know. . . . It's not that I'm hoggish, but I want to have this freedom feeling regardless of what comes to me, good or bad." Everyone listens quietly. "I want to be with her *all* the time, possibly. . . . But man, I might get stoned completely out my mind [laughter]—you know. Completely. And then also I might go into this funny other bag that she might not understand. . . ."

There is a lot of movement around the table, giggles and laughter.

". . . make love to him, yeah," Jimi jeers. "There you go making love to fairies with plastic names [lots of laughter]. . . . I'm so happy now I kissed Eric Clapton, I kissed him. . . . I kissed the fairest soul brother of England."

Clapton laughs along with everyone else.

The fellow from the magazine asks if they think about what is going to happen when they're forty-five.

"Yeah, of course not," Clapton cracks.

Jimi kids him about being scared that when he reaches forty-five he might not have any money in the bank. Everyone laughs. Clapton remarks that it's "a sick thing" for a young guy to be worrying about being an old guy. "Because sooner or later you're just going to say to yourself—right?—'I'm not young anymore' and you'll say that simply because you don't think that you were done when you were young. Then you're gonna set up some values . . . and you'll be an old man . . . and all you're going to do, man, is croak. . . ."

"So Jimi, you just grow a new set of plastic wings," someone says.

Clapton says, "That's what destroys me—how to put on real wings now. Because I don't like flying with plastic wings. . . ."

Jimi speaks: ". . . Let's say, OK, you only hung up about memories, but the things you're doing now, that's the only way you can live is for now. . . . By the time you get to be an old man, just like you said, man, your life changes and you might get different ideas. But you start *then*, man."

Someone asks Jimi if he has any plans for the future, saying, "You're not going to go on making this bread forever."

The sun has risen as Jimi concludes: "Oh well, quite naturally . . . I'll be very surprised . . . plus I'll be happy if it lasts this winter, you know. I'll be so happy if it does . . . until this dies down, you know. And then get maybe, try my best to get real estate and maybe get a few clubs and manage a few groups that have creative ideas and minds. And not plastic wings. . . . I don't like for money to tie me down no kinda way, you know. I don't like anything to tie me down. They always ask . . . you know, this is the longest I've ever lived in any one place in five or six years—in England. For six months, you know. And they always ask, 'Well, why do you like to move on a lot?' You know—'cause I don't like nothing to tie me down. I don't like to depend on anything actually. But you have to sometimes."

May 1967. Jimi had not seen Marianne Faithfull for months. In that time he had become the star that many knew he would be. Marianne, in her own way, had helped him. He still felt the same attraction he had felt at first for her. Perhaps it was assisted by Jagger's rejection of him when he was an unknown, but Marianne in her own right was a fabulous sight.

On May 16, 1967, Jimi Hendrix and company headlined the Speakeasy. He had three songs on the charts. "Hey Joe" was still hanging in there, "Purple Haze" was in the Top Ten, and the new release "The Wind Cries Mary" had just entered the charts and was making fast headway. Onstage he was surprised to see Marianne and Mick sitting at a table right in front of him. He recalled the nights seemingly long ago when Marianne had camped out at the 7½ Club for three days straight just checking him out. They had just gotten "Hey Joe" out and he did not have the star following he had now, nor did he have his sexual burlesque stage act together. Now he physically reacted to his feedback moans. Humping the guitar, playing it between his legs, grinding the strings against the microphone, and then banging the guitar against the amps as he whanged the tremolo bar. This night he really put on a show. He got down on his knees and screamed in ecstasy as the guitar moaned, then in fucking motions he panned the Stratocaster before the audience as if it were his cock, his mouth open lip-synching with the high-velocity howl of thousands of souls in orgasm.

After the set he went straight to Marianne and Mick, ignoring the imploring arms of those who wished a word or a vibe. He ignored Mick as he sat between them. He positioned his chair in such a way that his back was to Mick and his body was directly in front of Marianne's. He had wanted for months to tell Marianne outright the way he felt. Later for all the propriety and fencing and feeling subtle vibrations. As the recorded music played over the sound system, drowning out all except the closest and most intimate of conversations, he told her, his face pressed nearly against hers, that he wanted to fuck her and that she should leave Mick who was a cunt and come with him, right now. She was taken with his audacity. She wondered if in spite of the din Mick could hear what was being said. Even if he couldn't she felt that he could suss it out anyway. She could do nothing but turn Jimi down completely. There was little else she could do unless she just got up and walked out of the Speakeasy with Jimi. Perhaps she was tempted. Given another time and another place, maybe a little more subtlety—she just might have taken him up on his straightforward proposition. Jimi insisted, repeating his demands over and over. Marianne had to completely refuse. She sensed Jagger getting jealous. She also sensed that for Jimi it was a showdown. He was tired of the dallying around. And he resented Jagger not only for the audition but also for his best friend Brian Jones, whom he felt Jagger was driving out of the Rolling Stones, a group Jones had started—not Jagger. Jimi stood up abruptly, not even going through any formalities, not even attempting to smooth things over with Jagger, and split.

The next time Marianne and Mick saw Jimi perform, Mick flatly refused to go backstage and say hello. Marianne understood why.

People related differently to Jimi once his act broke big and "Hey Joe" and "Purple Haze" were on the charts. All the other stars were happy to see him. Another star in the sky, he increased the magnitude, the brilliance, of the entire constellation. And he gave each and all of the English bands an authenticity just by his being on the scene and grooving with them. He was of the blues and for the blues. He was a hip stateside black whom, all of a sudden, everybody wanted to know, to be near to, to say important things to. He was invited to the best parties.

It amazed him to hear Peter Townshend talk about auto-destruct, pop art, and decibel levels of music, from the point of view of an avant-garde artist, just like Andy Warhol and John Cage and Ed Sanders. Townshend would say, "We concentrate on the concepts of dynamics and the use of crescendo." And then top it all off by saying, "Our music is cybernetic." Townshend would get so intense he would look cross-eyed.

Eric Clapton, Townshend's opposite, other side, and running buddy, would listen intently, uttering demure sounds of awe. After Jimi and he had jammed together Clapton had felt his own music changing: "My attitude toward music changed. He influenced me an incredible amount." Clapton would always quietly swing the conversation around to the blues, the old blues.

Jimi would tell them about playing the "chitt'lin' circuit" with Little Richard and Solomon Burke, about his day in Chicago at Chess Records with Willie Dixon and Muddy Waters, and about the new younger cats under them like Little Walter, Buddy Guy, and

© 1981 JIM MARSHALL

Junior Wells. And then about some obscure blues men like Billy Butler and Robert, Jr., Lockwood. When he spoke about Charlie Patton, Son House, Mississippi John Hurt, Robert Johnson, and Elmore James, they, especially the blues purists, knew what he was talking about. But they puzzled over the obscure guys Hendrix mentioned who did not front their own group, lead sessions, and put out albums under their own names. Billy Butler and Robert, Jr., Lockwood were accompanying guitarists, Jimi would explain, of the highest development. They would add touches and colors that expanded the melody and at the same time would feed vocalists notes that excited their imaginations. But most importantly, to Jimi, they could play rhythm. The rhythm of the guitar, Jimi felt, was the key to the blues, jazz, and rock.

Clapton could never seem to understand what Hendrix was getting at when he would stress rhythm accompaniment. But the guitar had been a strict rhythm instrument until Charles Christian and Django Reinhardt showed up on the scene in different parts of the world in the late 1930s and early 1940s. Now the guitar had evolved, becoming more and more a widely accepted solo instrument. Hendrix felt that Clapton was too intellectual about it, and forged his own early classical background on the subject by insisting the guitar was now an instrument of the virtuoso, just like in classical music. Jimi tried to get across the message that the funk, the feel, and the boogie of the blues came from a subtle rhythmic combination of which the guitar played an essential role but never got the credit, especially in live performances on the "chitt'lin' circuit," where the guitar put the electric fire crackling over the bass and drums, creating the dynamic that made folks want to dance and shout and get it all out.

Clapton and Hendrix, both rather shy, would never follow their disagreement through, but it always hung in the air when they met. But their points of view always excited others.

Mick Jagger, with his American teen-ager, English street urchin rap, would talk about his anticipation, before going to America for the first time, of seeing Muddy Waters and Bo Diddley and Chuck Berry, his idols, as stars in their own land. Only he found out that they were scarcely known to the American masses, who usually had first heard these blues people's music through groups like the Rolling Stones. Even the Beatles had had the same experience. It was an unspoken part of English rock and the blues pundits to give back to the international music world the forgotten blues and rock of the old black blues men.

Chas Chandler would talk about his meeting with John Lee Hooker in the States. In a way, Chas's mention of Hooker underscored Jimi's point that rhythm and feel were, in many ways, more important than brilliant virtuoso sooings. John Lee Hooker hardly played any guitar at all. But his raunchy rhythm licks, though they often sounded the same, made you get up off your feet and get to the feeling.

Elmore James had only about three solos that he used on all his recorded material. But the excitement he was able to generate with bottleneck licks in rhythm set up the audiences for his mind-boggling bottleneck flurries during his solos. People would start to shout, jump up and down, and even throw money at him.

As soon as Paul McCartney opened his mouth, everyone looked his way, even if he was trying to be unobtrusively one of the gang. He had only wanted to tell Jimi about this TV special they were working on. The Beatles were going to rent a bus and ride around the countryside playing some new songs and visiting places and seeing things they thought were way out. Would Jimi be interested in being a part of it? Paul was so cute and polite, all Jimi could say was, "Sure. Yeah." They would talk more about it later.

In the reverent hush following Paul's rap, Marianne Faithfull got a chance to talk about the new film she was working on. It was not a big-time London studios job, but an avant-garde venture with Kenneth Anger, an American underground filmmaker. Anger was also an Aleister Crowley scholar who had come to London to be closer to his studies. He was the author of the notorious (by word of mouth) *Hollywood Babylon*, a stunning inside look at the film capital's biggest stars. His film was about demon possession and soul transmutation using many of the rituals culled from Crowley's occult writings.

Brian Jones came up, grinning like an imbecile, floating like a near-drunk angel. Jones was the first serious young English cat on the scene to be heavily into the blues. When Alexis Korner saw him for the first time Brian had already been doing his own thing with the blues for quite a while. Jones met Jagger through Alexis. Known for his love of exotic-instrument sounds against the raunchiness of electronic rock, Brian Jones was a master in the recording studio, an alchemist mixing and sweetening and bringing out the lovely points of melody in amazing directions. He liked to talk about coloring with his autoharp, its obscurity affecting the listeners more by their not being able to identify its sound. The sound first hit their aural centers and made them curious because they could not identify the instrument. Brian was once head and master of the Stones, but now he did not seem to care. He always seemed close to trance. That's the way he played. That's the way he was in the studio.

Kit Lambert walked by, hustling always, talking to a dowager-looking man who reeked of having had money and lots of it for a long time. Lambert was saying as he walked by: "I certainly haven't heard a decent symphony or a decent new opera in the last eighteen months. . . . I think the whole impetus has passed to the younger generation and to the excitement that is generated in pop. . . ."

Always shy because of his appearance, his tremendously long arms and legs, his thinness, his angular big head—even these aspects of his person were used in the development and enhancement of his heavy visual image. If Hendrix felt funny in the States about his appearance, London even further emphasized his outsize; but in England it was a novelty. He had heard the veteran soldiers in the army talk about the amazement of going into a European village during World War II, a village where they had never seen a black person before; now he experienced the awe of a people face-to-face with a person rare to their parts. He got out of a lot of his shyness by seeing that it could be used to his advantage—even the silly comments he would throw off would become a big thing, his mythological head raps became repeated and commented upon. Fleet Street journalists, especially the younger ones on the make who were supposed to be knowledgeable about the youth revolution in London, sought out Hendrix and vied to juxtapose his uniquely way-out appearance and comments with their prose of the "insider." While the young journalists were more often simply youth delegates from the conservative Fleet Street newspapers, a few insightful journalists like Tony Palmer and George Melly supported Hendrix's more serious artistic manifestations.

The Hendrix hairdo, frizzy and bountiful, was viewed by many cultural onlookers as one of the most truly remarkable visual revolts of London. For the British trendy public, who hardly ever outwardly acculturated another race's appearance, another culture, to have their youths sporting bouffant Afros and digging blues was a bit much.

Even the skinheads, who were considered an oddity for supporting reggae and the rock steady of the Jamaicans, did not emulate the Afro or make even a token protest against the oppressive racial policies directed by the English government against West Indians. In fact, they were at the other extreme: Bald (or skinheaded), they were more a revolt against the middle-class mod and rocker movements among the youth of England's early sixties, who had, by the time Hendrix arrived, flowed into the Carnaby Street English rock pop explosion. While the Bee Gees carried on the remnants of the image of the mod element, the Stones were to emulate more the skinhead, especially Jagger in his exaggeration of their lower-class speech. Both the Stones and the Beatles offset their mod-rocker dress with lower-class accents—Cockney, Liverpudlian, East End hood. This effect was more pronounced when they first began to receive serious attention. On their way up, both of the groups manifested working-class dress forms. For the Beatles, the leather and cowboy getups were a large part of their initial acceptance outside of London, in Liverpool and in Germany. The Stones were considered downright scruffy, rude, and contemptible. But around the time of Hendrix's appearance on the scene, both had cleaned up: the Beatles due to great wealth and worldwide diplomacy, the Stones in order to reach a larger public and share in the wealth of the greatest English export since colonialism—rock.

The Great Britain release of the JHE's first album, *Are You Experienced?* came in on the charts June 3 at No. 5. Side one is the top-heavy side, featuring all the hitherto concealed genius of Jimi's guitar.

It opens with a tiny signal streaking across the horizon, peaking in freaky three-part treble harmony. A commanding abyss mode explodes before your eyes, billowing outward *"FOXY LADY,"* Jimi's atonal chord gracing the top end of the figure. The boogie nation's pull-song anthem; lady thrill song trilling, whispering, *foxy foxy* in a perfumed ear. Treble ecstatic. Slick mixed-down R&B rhythm scratching licks against the consciousness.

> *You know you're a cute*
> *Little heartbreaker—Foxy yeah*
> *And you know you're a sweet*
> *Little lovemaker—Foxy*
>
> *I wanna take you home*
> *I won't do you no harm—no*
> *You got to be all mine all mine*
> *Whew! Foxy lady*

The atonal chord staggering the rhythm and keeping funk in the straight jam. The peal comes twinkling into the coda, streaking off in an extended and developed report, and then back to the standard funk as the phased guitar wings across the sky. Hendrix's guitar has an amazing fluidity—an actual human sound of high spirituality, of high evolvement.

"Manic Depression"—with Jimmy playing bass also—is built off of a massive bass drone, implying the accompanying note of the drone in atonal syncopated figures. He dubs with the bass especially during the emphasized breaks. The song becomes an extended jam, offering him a lot of room to just play, as he raps the words:

> *Manic depression is touching my soul*
> *I know what I want but I just don't know*
>   (Honey, how to go about getting it)
> *Feeling sweet feeling*
> *Drops from my fingers fenders*
> *Manic depression is a captured my soul*
>
> *Woman so willing the sweet cause in vain*
> *You make love you break love it's all the same*
>   (when it's over)
> *Music sweet music I wish I could caress caress caress*
> *Manic depression is a frustrating mess*

Tenor voices harmonize upward into the break where the guitar takes over, bucking, tossing, and tumbling.

> *I think I'll go on and turn myself off*
>   *and go on down* (all the way down)
> *Really ain't no use in me hanging around*

(Oh I gotta see you, you know what I'm
   trying to say)

The drum kit churns. It does not keep linear time, but circular, it accents as if by random theory Jimi's rap.

Music sweet music I wish I could caress
   a kiss a kiss
Manic depression is a frustrating mess WOW!
Sweet music sweet music

"Third Stone from the Sun" opens with Noel's bass creating a tranquil and hypnotic two-note drone, while Mitch's drums tap along in the same moderate 4/4 time. Jimi strokes lightly on his guitar as background for a voice that drones off-speed at 16 rpms, as if from outer space. Speeded up to 78 rpms the voice is saying:

". . . Star fleet to scout ship, please give
   your position. Over . . ."
"I am in orbit around the third planet
   from the star called the Sun. Over . . ."
"You mean it's the Earth. Over."
"Positive. It is known to have some form
   of intelligent species. Over."
". . . I think we should take a look. . . ."

The bass drops an octave creating a lovely surprise, then takes a step up to the first bridge, where the drums take over the time, giving the effect of a speeding up of tempo. Jimi plays the lead figure in fifths against the bass, giving the sound an Eastern effect. They come to a second bridge, where Mitch's drums move the pace even quicker, although the bass is still droning a variation of the same two-note figure and pace. Mitch's drums are mixed back down into the en-sembled sound where Jimi is playing some pretty accompaniment that is as meditative as the bass is hypnotic. Here the sounds of the heavens opening up comes out in full force and they all are playing softly against its effect. They take a long break and the sound be-comes airy, flying wind sounds against which Jimi very tastefully blends a subtle fuzz distort within the total sound. Then he hits a warning midrange treble emergency signal that pulsates slowly. He speaks his lines against the hypnotic march.

Oh strange beautiful grass of green
With your majestic silken scenes

Your mysterious mountains I wish to see closer
May I land my kinky machine¿

The mellow bass line continues with the time as the drums dictate the pace. Painting whoozy sound against the endless terrain, Jimi adding touches of distorting fuzz and airy treble tremolos:

Although your world wonders me
With your majestic superior crackling hen
Your people I do not understand
So to you I wish to put an end
And you'll never hear surf music again

Jimi hits the lead theme again, elongating the notes over several bars. Then free squawk crescendo taxiing out to space, the guitar splinters raw fire and static—an electrical monster in free rein. Then silence except for a flat fuzz signal that flows into a space-tracking sound that fades out slowly.

On "Love or Confusion" the setup hook chord delineates the entire song. The strange harmony between the long sustained sitar-like chord and the overdriving Fuzz-Face and Cry-Baby combination creates a tremolo that double-times against the 4/4 time, thus belonging to both the rhythm and the harmony. Jimi makes his guitar do a Sagittarian bow thrust, like the sound heard in cartoons when the Road Runner takes off. Mitch beats out a snare-in-the-round intro. In a fast 4/4 the funky hambone bass lines are joined by Jimi's skipping rhythm work. The bass evokes cavernous underground insurgency in echo. Jimi gets an exotic sitar sound on one guitar track and a harmonizing sustain tremolo on another. The major chord drone dips into a lovely minor mode as he shouts out:

Is that the stars in the sky—or is it raining
    far from now¿
Will it burn me if I touch the sun¿
So big—so round
Will I be truthful, yeah,
In choosing you as the one for me¿

The Fuzz-Face–Cry-Baby combination is jacked to the upper registers where the looney distorted Cry-Baby peal takes over. Driving to a peak of oscillating intensity, it begins to solo as Jimi shouts, his voice integrated into the sound on an equal par with the rest of the instruments: *Is it love¡ Baby, or just a confusion¿* . . . The hambone figures on the bass are counterpointed against Jimi's skipping rhythm figures. Keyed to rhythm against sound, rather than melody against note, Jimi's rap becomes even more powerful mixed down within the sound. The combination of guitars playing rhythm against the long drone chord, and the looney wailing distress signal of the Fuzz-Face–Cry-Baby, are fantastic. The treble peaked over-driving tremolo is both a note of the bizarre harmony and an ele-ment of the 4/4 rhythm, vibrating from double time to quadruple time. Jimi peaks it into a rapturous solo. The *clave* chord kicks off the guitar battery again. Sounding like the rhythms of several Afri-can congas. The electronic metallic overdriving oscillating Strato-caster keeps the rhythm throb close to the pulsations of a red emergency light. With the effortless power and speed of a bird sing-ing natural, it becomes a totally new sound terrain. At the bridge the beat turns over on itself, giving a backward effect, moving into a higher key. Slicing, gargantuan fuzzy treble figure. Jimi's solo is driven by bottom fuzz overtones to even greater heights. So sharp the solo seems to be on the sheer edge of flame. Gliss-sliding and double-picking, he ranges between harmónica effects and synthe-sizer sounds. After the bridge the caravan takes off again in its time-suspended journey. The oscillating overdrive report goes into white noise that holds the harmony just as well. Jimi begins to concentrate on the rhythm as the song goes into short breaks—only to speed off again. The coda is in several segments, all almost iden-tical. Going beyond a normal 4/4 coda, it pushes forward after every break to the point where you are continuously surprised when it starts up again. It stops in full Fuzz-Face chaos.

In *Are You Experienced?* Jimi goes right to the ladies:

If you can just get your mind together
Then come across to me
We'll hold hands and then we'll watch the sun rise
From the bottom of the sea
But first—Are you experienced?
Have you ever been experienced?
Well, I have—

I know—I know
You'll probably scream and cry
That your little world won't let you go
But who in your measly little world are you trying
*   to prove that*
You're made out of gold and can't be sold—

The bell knell keeping time like a tuned cowbell *clave* throughout. The drums shuffle and bop, running up in full flurry and then back down again. The off-time bass line staggering a third beat. Then Jimi solos against the drums that are phased and recorded backward on tape. The drums go forward as the lyric picks up again.

> *So—ah— Are you experienced?*
> *AH! Have you ever been experienced?*
> *Well, I have—*
> *Ah, let me prove it to you*
>
> *Trumpets and violins I can hear in the distance*
> *I think they're calling our names*
> *Maybe now you can't hear them*
> *But you will if you just take hold of my hand*
>
> *AH but are you experienced?*
> *Have you ever been experienced?*
> *Not necessarily stoned but beautiful*

The backward guitar phased sound is elongated otherworldly, suspending time. Treble fuzz going to the peak ping of the harmonic. The *clave* knell fades down, then swells up again and out.

In "Red House" he spins an old twelve-bar blues tale he wrote years ago to tell the ladies that if they don't come through he knows "their sisters will." "Red House" was also a direct feed to the blues purists (Jagger, Jones, Clapton, Page, and Mayall) who always had traditional blues pieces in their albums. In such a predictable form as the twelve-bar blues there is nothing to do but play—virtuosity is needed to bring something new to the standard.

> *There's a red house over yonder*
> *Yeah, that's where my baby stays*

"Red House" is also sensual and fiery love. Jimi is determined to enjoy the sensual life, the "birds" of London notwithstanding.

"I Don't Live Today" pans distances with machine-chugging vibratos that come back again embellished sharper. "Remember" is a ballad, and "May This Be Love" is as close to corn as possible for Jimi. Obviously a song for teen-age girls, but relaxed and pretty, it fills out the JHE's first album.

And in the last song of the album, the title song, "Are You Experienced?" Jimi intones to all in a musk-laden sensual voice, ". . . *I am.*"

FIVE

"The First International Monterey Pop Festival." From the first hint of it—leaflets passed out at the first Human Be-in in San Francisco earlier that spring of 1967—it spread throughout the underground like wildfire. The Human Be-in had been a free-for-all affair; the Monterey Pop Festival would be a more organized affair, honing and directing the energy. There was the feeling of powerful events under way, an entire recognition of the power of flower consciousness in the making.

Many of the underground newspapers that had sprung up across the country, like *The Oracle* in San Francisco and the Los Angeles *Free Press*, gave complete endorsement to the festival as a logical follow-up to the massive Human Be-in.

Thousands of young heads had been astounded at the Human Be-in to find thousands of others just like them. All across the country the returns came in on the Be-in. It was like a national election. It read: We are in power, our shit is working, we can do what we want.

From the beginning "Monterey Pop" had been conceived of as a nonprofit affair that would benefit local, national, and international causes through an ad hoc foundation set up for the occasion. Paul McCartney, Mick Jagger, Brian Jones, Brian Wilson, Donovan, John Phillips, Johnny Rivers, Smokey Robinson, and others served on the

139

board of directors. To the usual music promoters who were used to shooting for great payoffs for their investors, a nonprofit festival was out of the question. It took the intervention of the underground press, which had been thoroughly investigating the entire setup from the beginning, to secure the important support of two beautiful people who had, hands down, the endorsement of the new youth community: John Phillips, of the Mamas and Papas, the local music hero, and Lou Adler, a producer who could handle the finance and other business, and who was known to be honest, and more importantly, into the vibe of what was to be accomplished.

There were also other people working on Monterey Pop who were just as essential as the titular head and the business pro. Derek Taylor, the famous publicist who had accompanied the Beatles on their first tour of America, was chosen to handle the press. Used to the mass insanity, which often meant that a thousand and one things were not done as they should be, Taylor gave his witty intensity wholeheartedly to the event. One important result of his presence was that most of the underground press people (a new phenomenon) were given press credentials, just like the establishment press. In many cases they were treated better than the establishment press, often being allowed to bring in entire entourages. Tuned in to the meaning of the event, Derek Taylor ensured that the reportage would reflect the aim of the festival: international consciousness of the power of youth.

Taylor was an important liaison with the English musical scene. Used to dealing with all aspects of the music business, Taylor did not stand behind his title and deny himself to other tasks. He acted as go-between and follower-througher, and this brought the hippest array of new and established "head" entertainers to Monterey Pop. One of the new acts to appear was the Jimi Hendrix Experience. What might have been passed over as a casual remark made by Paul McCartney to John Phillips via international long-distance telephone was converted into reality. Their power, the power of music, was consciousness. The First International Monterey Pop Festival became the official recorded version of the Human Be-in.

Laura Nyro and the Jimi Hendrix Experience were the new acts at the festival.

Brian Jones and Nico saunter through the brilliantly placid Monterey Fairgrounds of California. Both he and Nico, dressed in flowing robes, look like medieval monk royalty. They each hold a can of Budweiser beer. A large iron cross swings from Brian's neck. They both affect a disdain born of their kindred personalities: Brian Jones in the supererect stature of a serious asthmatic, Nico in the shyness of a lonely child.

They are followed by a bevy of photographers. The photographers are followed by Peter Tork of the Monkees. He is waiting for Brian and Nico to stop so he can pose for a picture with them. The Monkees have a weekly nationally syndicated TV show situation comedy. On TV they are crazy rock 'n' roll stars, their roles based roughly on the Beatles' *A Hard Day's Night*. At the Monterey Fairgrounds they act as if the film crew there making a movie of Monterey Pop is filming one of their shows.

It is difficult for Brian and Nico to stop. Every time they even hesitate in their stroll, they are assailed by a mob, half of whom are working-press people of one sort or another, the other half groupies and minor rock artists.

Brian Jones has flown to California from London for the express purpose of introducing Jimi to the world. This beautiful act of recognition blew Jimi's mind. Jimi Hendrix would be eternally grateful to Brian Jones for this act of great faith. To Brian it was simply a testament of his belief. Besides, he loves the idea of having a holiday, attending a concert without the pressures of having to perform.

He was the first of the Rolling Stones to love the blues, to love the expressions of music coming from the history of black folk in America. To Brian, it was an honor to introduce Jimi.

Backstage everyone is smoking some excellent Mexican marijuana. Otis Redding is amazed. Jimi is happily stoned already.

Onstage, before a record-breaking twenty thousand people, Brian Jones, leader of the Rolling Stones, saunters through the dying smoke-bomb finale of The Who. The crowd hushes in mass awe. Jones laughs looking out at the crowd through the lights. He looks back at Jimi standing in the wings and smiles. There is a direct connection. Brian Jones, laid back in his low-keyed kingly fashion, tells the audience that he has a special treat for them. Direct from England, appearing in the States for the first time—"Jimi Hendrix, the Jimi Hendrix Experience."

The JHE runs onstage. The crowd roars happy approval. Thousands of tabs of Owsley's acid are taking off. "Killing Floor" moves out, down-home rockabilly rhythm 'n' blues—its strange soprano licks almost contradicting the message.

Above them, the sky of California seems huge, endless, as the final hues of sundown disappear low upon the far horizon. The rolling muscles of a darkened mountain range form the backdrop for the stage. The sky a great rolling purple, with a light fog coming up

Brian Jones with Jimi at Monterey Pop   © 1981 JIM MARSHALL

over the sundown. He feels as if he had dropped from the skies. From his London flat to a space of California he had never been within before. There was a primeval feel in the air, a fresh breath of the earth in its pure smell. And the smell is wild, from way back, the untamed smell of trees, ocean, earth, stream, and rock, pretty much the way it had always been.

Against a sky like this the sound seems to vibrate endlessly out into the darkness, the blackness. But it is so incredibly warm, the crowd so alive and eager. He is afraid. He has never played to a crowd of this size and intensity. And never before has he had this much before him in America. It was so fucking ironic. To have come all the way from England, to have seemingly all of America before him, all of America stretching out across the vast expanse. In the darkness of the cool California night, heads faintly illuminated receding back endless, the subtle warmth of the earth blown by a slight breeze as if the warmth, the breeze was their breath.

He is at home, yet far away. They do not know him. He is a stranger to his own land, a stranger to his own people. "Killing Floor" is his musical cudgel. A song to play to challenge from the onset. But midway through it he begins to mellow. This is a beautiful audience. They are with him.

"Hey Joe" was a hit in London, but only a few here have heard it. He wonders if this will get them. So far they have been enthusiastic, but only at the same level as they have been for most of the high-caliber acts. The entire affair is high. The music is out of sight and the audience is generous and happy. They must be killed. Killed in the same sense that "Killing Floor" is a song rather than a death threat. He must do something to blow their minds and they're very high already. But he's building.

He's building. Rushing through "Hey Joe." Trying to slow down and give the ballad the pace it needs, but he's thinking about the finale, "Wild Thing." He does not want to let the audience go down. He tries to put some poise into "Hey Joe," but the vibes are too heavy. It's not his own song. The solo is nice but restrained, too keyed to the melody. He misses the dramatic vocal as he recites, but his dance is something else. He dances the story as he plays. He moves shimmering in the lights as he intones as if disembodied—*"and I got me a gun, and* I SHOT *her."* The dramatic bridge, the guitar pointing straight up in the air, Jimi's arm suspends in the air after the last chord chop. The solo begins by his fretting with his right hand while his left remains in the air, his head averted, his teeth gritting against the looney peal of the first note, looping and wildly oscillating against the ceiling threshold of possible sound. Then in a slight hunch he continues, his head going back at every thrust to the top notes. You hear something of where his head is at and what he can do delineated in the solo bridge over the drone of the straightforward ballad. You hear his interpretation of the simple melody of the ballad as he screams out in agony against the helplessness and hopelessness, the horror of the murder, and the clashed-up love between it all. His guitar talks, it emotes. More than note-by-note melody line perfect, Jimi Hendrix's guitar tells its own story of love in quick, subtle, and versatile runs that peak in histrionic mourning pathos, etched high within the screams of passion and death.

By now Jimi is ready. He starts off "Like a Rolling Stone," playing the intro chords to "Wild Thing." This throws the audience off for a moment. As he talks, he begins to pick out the opening notes to "Like a Rolling Stone," laughing and joking. He mentions the name Bob Dylan and the crowd perks up; he's going to do one of his songs, but they can't figure out which one. His third reference to Mitch Mitchell looking like Bob Dylan's grandmother draws another laugh from the crowd. Then as Jimi slurs out the first few lines in perfect Manhattan street rap, everyone begins to recognize the song, and the vibrations of the audience begin to soar.

"Once upon a time you dressed so fine/threw the bums a dime/in your prime, didn't you? . . ." Right there in that moment Jimi saw himself as he had lived in America. Yeah, he had been the fine-dressing R&B entertainer, and then suffered what many of his friends of the time thought was a great fall. Hanging out down in the Village with all those beatniks and hippies. Taking all that speed for energy and to stave off starvation. The slick veneer front of the R&B musician destroyed for him in the Village. Disdain from his friends "uptown"—"he's looking scruffy and acting crazy."

He saw himself walking MacDougal Street hearing the song, and every time always so amazed at how it hit so close to home. "Like a Rolling Stone" had seemed to come forth from every window, every bar.

Although he had toured the Village like many outsiders he came to realize that anyone who did not *live* in the Village was a tourist.

> *You used to* (ha, ha) *laugh about*
> *everybody who was hanging out . . .*
>
> *Go on now he calls you, you can't refuse*
> *when you got nothing you got nothing to*
> *lose . . .*
>
> *How does it feel*
> *How does it FEEEEEL, baaaby*
> *To be on your own*
> *with no direction home* (Look at you)
> *A complete unknown*
> *Yeah!* Like *a Rolling*
> *Stone.*

He felt his New York City starving days strong enough to put tears in his eyes, to put that touch of emotion in his voice for the people to know that he was not bullshitting. "Rolling Stone" is the kind of song you cannot sing unless you have been through some shit. It was a song that only Dylan could sing—until now.

> *Nobody here taught you how to live out in the streets*
> *and now you got to get used to it . . .*

The days and the nights of not knowing where you were going to stay. Walking the streets, guitar dangling from your back, passing restaurants, watching happy smiling people eat and drink, wondering who you could call on, wondering who your friends are, trying to dredge out of your memory a face, a friendly face, a face you may have forgotten that hasn't forgotten you, sure there is someone you forgot, looking in all faces that pass . . .

> *You said you'd never compromise*
> *with the mystery* tramp
> *but now you got to realize . . .*
> *he's not sellin' any alibis*
> *As he stands in the vacuum of his eyes,*
> *And he says 'Hey, baby,*
> *Would you like to make a deal?*

Jimi begins to laugh between phrases, a blues "ha ha," very much like Junior Wells. Not in humor or in jest, but in its punctuation and indications, a gesture, a grace phrase to the lyric that emphasizes the grim; something only Junior Wells had perfected. Jimi is surprised that this laugh is coming out of him. He begins to blow the lyrics as he sees vivid images of his destitute period in New York City, a period that brought him to the utter bedrock of reality and showed him humanity. In a perfect pause within the verses he tells the audience that yes, he knows he missed some of the lyrics, but he doesn't really care, so caught up is he in the emotional import of the song—and neither does the audience.

Mitch Mitchell is drumming his ass off. Each roll between phrases razor metallic sharp, the continuous tapping of the cymbal perfectly opposite his deep rolls, but in a strange way maintaining the emotional polarity between song and tragedy.

All of the assembled know in their hearts what "Rolling Stone" is talking about. Brian Jones in the wings smiling his weird, blissful smile, bobbing his long head in time, nodding yes, yes, yes.

The song ends with Jimi strumming and sustaining the strange chord that holds "Like a Rolling Stone" and "Wild Thing" together. That same chord that gets stranger as it sustains and begins to feed back ever so subtly, ever so ecstatic in its sinister mode.

Jimi had forgotten where he was, he had become so caught up in the song and the images it brought forth. It was like coming out of a trance to great applause, and shouts. He had lost himself as had the audience. They dug it.

"Rock Me Baby," another modern blues classic by B. B. King, done in quadruple time by the JHE transforms Monterey Fairgrounds for a moment into the Apollo during a production number by the ace rhythm and blues group of the time. Jimi's voice dubbing note for note with his guitar on the choruses.

"Can You See Me?" is Jimi's own tune, the only one he plays this night. A nice back-beating rocker with big round breaks that blossom and then explode back to the boogie. Jimi screaming distant against the funk, *"Can you see me? Can you see me?"* The audience responding "Yeeaaahhh."

He strokes a few chords from "The Burning of the Midnight Lamp" as he introduces "Wild Thing," his last number. He cautions the audience not to think he's losing his mind. He will play the combined English and American national anthems. "Don't get mad, don't get mad. I want everyone to join in . . . all those beautiful people out there."

The last phrase is mumbled as the feedback starts. A totally non-musical frequency signal bellows from the amps, static builds underneath an overtone, harmonizes with the signal, and then a tweak of the tremolo bar leaps the signal several steps as a bass hum, as deep as can be, forms a bottom. The transformers begin to over-drive, gathering momentum upward. He teases the feedback, drawing it out, banging the guitar against his hip, shaking it quite rudely, producing the call of an electrical monster, bansheelike in the air, peaking against itself. Pink noise is driven to screams, as he runs his fingers up and down the frets rapidly getting effects that sound as if the electricity is talking. Mini-electric explosions occur. He strokes the back of the neck, tapping and raising it to certain levels in relation to the position of the amps, manipulating the feedback. Then he quiets all sound, and strums a few notes to make sure of his tuning. Then he sends a tiny signal to the feedback point, but holds it suspended in space, and then the first massive chord chop—"Wild Thing."

Noel singing along, dubbing flat on the note, Jimi sings on a slightly higher overtone. The controls turned straight up to peak, the chord sounds every note distinctly, as if there were three or four guitars playing at once. The audience didn't know what he was going to play and is quite amazed to hear the chords to "Wild Thing" coming out of the wild pink noises. The bass and drum join as Jimi sustains the chords. *"Wild Thing/You make my heart sing/you make everything kinda grrrooooovy/WILD THING. . . ."* The song breaks, and then: *". . . Wild Thing I think you move me but I want to know for sure/Come and a'sock it to me one time/YOU MOVE ME. . . ."* The monotony of the chords has a hypnotic effect; they seem to build within themselves, with each stroke becoming bigger within the darkened landscape of the fairgrounds. Jimi repeats the verse again and then begins to freak out midway into the second part, speeding the rhythm to double time and hitting licks even faster than that. He makes bottom strings of the guitar feed back while he plays lightning-fast rhythm licks on the top strings. Banking left to ensure feedback control, falling down on his haunches, and then coming straight up, bobbing his head like a strobe, flicking his tongue in time with his looney vibrato fretting. Then they break back into the "Wild Thing" melody, and the crowd begins to lose control, roaring almost unconsciously, their sophisticated minds truly blown. Jimi signals the Experience back in from the break, the weird animal-sounding neighing of his guitar catches the audience off guard. They quiet down as he repeats the lyric, then he goes back into the free musical landscape where the bass is the only instrument droning something of the tune.

Within the free landscape Jimi plays a snatch from "Strangers in the Night." Jimi down on his knees, lays the guitar down, quickly squirts lighter fluid over it, and lights a match to it as he bobs on his knees as if praying. The first leap of flames absolutely shatters the crowd. They go crazy as the flames engulf the guitar and it begins to give out a signal of its own in weird demise. Jimi leaves the stage as the guitar burns, playing a weird death knell for itself as the controls are consumed in the flames. It plays on, as if magically controlled. The flames leap higher and higher, the audience is hollering, bellowing, screaming. The sound of the burning guitar stabilizes in a metallic tone, with full sustain.

Jimi falls into Brian Jones's arms in the wings, totally exhausted. The applause grows and grows. It builds higher and higher. The duration is out of proportion to any other act. It rises in crescendo, voices begin to howl.

The audience applauds and cheers for a good twenty minutes. They have to be hushed up. The Grateful Dead are on next. They're sick. The audience has been killed *dead*.

Backstage was mobbed. Jimi floated through it. The audience still roared, it seemed as if they would never stop. The Grateful Dead hung in the wings, hesitant to go on. Brian Jones was chuckling in his wheezy asthmatic way as if it had been him out there. He was truly glad. He loved it. Everyone was crazy. Brian's ecstatic laugh feeding the chaotic insanity. Even Nico was moved. She gave Jimi a big hug and kiss. Everyone wanted to touch him, to share in the electric joy. Mike Jeffery was tripping about something. He was so excited he was pissed off about a mike stand or something. Jimi, Noel, and Mitch just laughed at him as they accepted the congratulations. Hugh Masekela was shouting, "You killed them, YOU KILLED THEM!" Bill Graham was saying something about San Francisco. Jimi was looking for Chas, but he was nowhere to be seen in the multitudes. Jimi couldn't believe that many people could get backstage. It seemed as if the entire audience were crowding backstage. Then he realized they were the performers, the security guards, the roadies, and the concessionaires—the people who put it on were also blown out. He had done it. *He had done it.*

It seemed as if the roar of the crowd would never leave his ears. The audience had freaked out. They roared and screamed. They sounded as if they were going to tear up the peaceful fairgrounds. Hugh Masekela was still yelling, *"You killed them, man, you killed them!"*

Almost like a magical formula, Howling Wolf's "Killing Floor" had been at least a prophecy.

Several of the groups flew back to Los Angeles that night. For them the festival was still on, the vibes were so high. Everyone knew that they had made history. Every performance had been peak. Hugh Masekela, on the rebound from his amazing No. 1 single "Grazing in the Grass," had scored heavily with a total African sound. Steven Stills, as a part of Buffalo Springfield, had done an incredible version of "Stop Look Around." The Who had wailed. Otis Redding, with his soul sincerity, had suddenly and overnight opened up "the love people" as he called them to an entire lore of soul music. But the undisputed hit of the show was Jimi Hendrix. Everyone was totaled out on what he had done. What was so groovy about it was that it was part of a new movement. Jimi had the hippest people in American music surrounding him after one stroke.

Steven Stills proposed that everyone come to his house and continue the good feelings. Everyone was into it and gave Stevie a resounding "Yeah."

Los Angeles International. Stevie Stills's beach house in Malibu was directly up the coast, only a few miles from the airport. They partied through the airport and out into the car. Most managed to get there; but by the time they reached the house, the crowd had thinned.

The party at Steven Stills's beach house became a legend. They jammed for fourteen hours straight. Those who had decided to go home and crash came back the next day to find the party still going strong.

Stevie and Jimi really hit it off together. Either they both played guitar, switching off between lead and rhythm, or one of them played bass while the other showed off his best licks. There were pure moments of bliss when the music would take over and they would go with it wherever it led. Hugh Masekela coming in on trumpet so fine, so crystal-piercing against the ocean's roar. It was like they were playing along with the ocean. The heaviest mama of all, she would go on endlessly; if there was a lull in the music the ocean would solo—playing bass in her elemental roar.

Masekela couldn't believe Hendrix. His music or his costume. Hugh Masekela escaped South Africa's totalitarian racism in the late fifties with a lot of help from black and white Americans. Hendrix's dress reminded Masekela of the African gold miners who would be allowed to go to town every six months or so and proceed to get very drunk. They would buy those black Spanish brims with gold bands around the crown. They would also go in for flowing red shirts and tight black bell-bottoms just like Jimi's stuff. Of course, Jimi had come from England, the source of most of South Africa's goods as well.

If Hendrix got such a response through his personal insanity, Masekela could just as readily abandon hip pop for his own inspirational and ancestral music. When they jammed, Hendrix played nothing but blues. Funky old black American get-down blues. Just as Masekela could take recent hits or standards and give them the African sound, a little hi-life, that swinging nightclub atmosphere, with his wild deep African voice making every word sound new, and then the soaring trumpet putting the icing on the cake. Hendrix had already demonstrated his abilities to deal with hits and standards and make them his own. "Wild Thing" and "Rock Me Baby" were completely transformed by Hendrix into *his* sound. He had mastered that, just as Masekela had. They had a lot to say to each other.

The day after Jimi Hendrix blew thousands of minds at Monterey he was famous in L.A. The kind of fame everyone in Hollywood believes in: the instantaneous smash! The overnight star! If Monterey had been out of sight, then Hollywood was interstellar. Instead of receiving a symbolic key to the city, he received real keys to the city. Invitations came from all quarters to stay at luxurious houses either at the beach or in town, keys to cars, recording studios, and boudoirs. Jimi was the toast of the town.

Peter Tork, the chief Monkee and buddy of Stevie Stills, had just about demanded Jimi stay at his estate in Laurel Canyon. Jimi took him up on his kind offer. He had an immediate entourage composed of rock stars, old friends, and hangers-on, for Laurel Canyon was like a musician's ghetto. Cass Elliot, Judy Collins, Joni Mitchell, David Crosby, and many others lived there. Mike Bloomfield was there, exulting in their reminiscences of the Village days, where Jimi had seemed hopelessly impoverished less than a year ago. Bloomfield was going on and on about how Jimi's playing had improved—even though he had been the most incredible guitarist Bloomfield had ever met, even back then. Buddy Miles was there. Vishwa, a young black cat with long curly black hair and a well-bred manner who sang, wrote, and meditated, was there. He had a flawless way of relating to people. He was very cool. The Chambers Brothers were around, too.

Everyone wanted to see the Jimi Hendrix Experience. KRLA, L.A.'s hip Top-Forty radio station, was playing "Purple Haze" every hour on the hour. Offers were coming in by the hour. Bill Graham wanted them for the Fillmore West in San Francisco. Dick Clark and Peter Tork wanted them to tour with the Monkees. Premier Talent wanted to book them for concerts in New York. Steve Paul wanted them to play the New Scene Club in New York. TV offers abounded. Bill Cosby wanted Jimi to play on an album he was recording. Cosby had taken the melody to "Purple Haze" and written new lyrics called "Hooray for the Salvation Army Band." Jimi was glad he had a couple of managers to handle the deluge. He was content to do all the hanging out he could do. It had been almost a year since he had been back to the States, and over two years since he had been on the West Coast. The last time he was in L.A. was in 1965 during one of Little Richard's endless road tours. Jimi had done a studio gig with a cat called Arthur Lee. He wondered where Arthur Lee was. Lee was a brilliant singer and musician, and one of the few bloods Jimi had met who had been into rock in 1965. Jimi heard that Arthur Lee had started a group called Love.

Stevie Stills played Jimi a tape that he and Buddy Miles had recorded on a lark. It was good; Buddy had grown as a drummer. They were looking for Buddy Miles when they met Devon Wilson at the Whiskey A Go Go. Devon and Jimi had been introduced by Buddy Miles during an Isley Brothers and Wilson Pickett tour of New Jersey in 1965. Jimi remembered Devon vaguely. She had been fast, young, and kind of crazy. She seemed like just another runaway teen-ager in the Village in 1965. But now she was fine and worldly. She was an instant pleasure to be with. Jimi had been hanging out with the boys and was getting tired of the constant gang of people. Devon lived in the Canyon too. She lived in one of the houses Houdini had owned, with a mellow dude named Cosmo, a musician, who would understand that Jimi just wanted to cool out, relax, and be free from hassles.

Jimi excused himself from the boys and went with Devon. Right off of Sunset Boulevard they took a road that led upward on a narrow winding lane. In thirty seconds they were into hill country. She lived right at the Willow Glen Road pass, straight up a private road to the Houdini complex. The mansion was white and remote, overlooking winding Laurel Canyon Boulevard and seemingly all of Los Angeles. Devon seemed to know exactly how to make Jimi comfortable. After introducing Jimi to Cosmo, a diminutive Italian musician who had a group called the Afro-blues Quintet (and whose mind was obviously blown), Devon led Jimi to a quiet wing of the huge mansion where low floor pillows, incense, and music set a wonderful scene. Jimi spent all that evening, and a large part of the next day, there with Devon. He left with the impression that she was a very cool person. He would see her again after all the hustle and bustle ceased. She knew he would.

On July 3, in New York City, Jimi played the struggling Scene Club to the eternal gratitude of Steve Paul. On July 11 the JHE played between Len Chandler and the Young Rascals in Central Park. Chandler remembered Jimi from the MacDougal Street Village days. The crowd laughed when the JHE walked on. Soon the crowd was in shock. Hendrix made the audience feel that the subway had come above ground with all its roaring cave echoes and howls. Jimi knelt and played the Stratocaster like a *koto*, then ripped the strings with his teeth and threw the guitar back over his head into the amps. They played a party Chas threw for the press at the Cafe Au Go Go basement, where Hendrix had blown John Hammond, Jr., off the stage a year ago. At the Au Go Go party Jimi and Noel had a spat. Jimi was angry at him for departing from the bass lines. Noel retorted that he did not need to be told what to play.

Jimi was asked to play at the opening of a new discothèque that would be called The Salvation, at 1 Sheridan Square, right smack in the middle of the Village. This was the kind of hip action the JHE needed. The JHE got included on several bills at big arenas; at the Forest Hills tennis stadium in Queens, New York; at the Hollywood Bowl; and at the Civic Opera House in Chicago.

A communiqué from the Jimi Hendrix Experience's mobile "office" somewhere in the U.S.A to Les Perrin, their publicist in London:

Jimi Hendrix played the Whisky A Go Go in Los Angeles with the big rave there called Sam and Dave—he blew them off the stage. They have been offered the Avalon and Fillmore Auditorium in the future. Last night (Monday) they played the Scene Club, New York City. On the bill were the Seeds, they blew them off the stage. While they were in Los Angeles Jimi stayed in Peter Tork's, of the Monkees, home. After their appearance at the Monterey Festival they were offered, within 4 hours, to tour with the Monkees on their American trip. It opens at Jacksonville, Florida, on Friday and goes on until August 20. How long did negotiations with Chas Chandler take? Half an hour. Jimi Hendrix is at LT 1-7000. While he was in Los Angeles he borrowed Peter Tork's GTO car. It pulled up at a filling station at Malibu and a car hit it, spun it three times and Jimi Hendrix has received a bad injury to his right ankle—the one that was broken and had him invalided from the U.S. Army. Also in the car were Mike Bloomfield, of the Bloomfield Band, it was driven by Stevie Stills of the Buffalo Springfield Band, Billy Narls and also Dave Crosby of the Byrds. Jimi Hendrix's description of Peter Tork's house—"It was about a thousand rooms, a couple of baths, two balconies which overlook the world and Piccadilly Circus. There is a carport in which there is a Mercedes, a GTO and something that looks like an old copper stove. In the house there is a stereo that makes you feel you are in a recording emporium. There is an electric piano, amplifier and guitars all over the place— a cute lovely little yellow puppy type dog."

The Monkees had "Pleasant Valley Sunday" in the Top Ten. More teenyboppers than the Jimi Hendrix Experience had ever seen before screamed for the song everywhere they toured. At first it had seemed like a great idea to tour with the Monkees. Peter Tork's hospitality notwithstanding, the Monkees were a top pop act in the United States, second only to the Beatles in national appeal. The Monkees' TV series was seen by millions every week. Yet it was clear that the JHE belonged to another audience. While the Monkees, by virtue of their TV exposure, appealed more to the stay-at-home subteens, the JHE was more appealing to the hippies, runaways, and rebels. The thirteen- and fourteen-year-olds they toured before were puzzled, but they seemed to accept the heavy sexual set the JHE performed. However, their parents and the middle-of-the-road theater managers were scandalized. They felt Jimi was too erotic. It did not take long for everybody to agree that the JHE and the Monkees were better off apart. The JHE only had a limited time to follow through on their sensational impact. They had a tour already booked through Europe in September. They wanted to make the most of the "Summer of Love" in the U.S.A. Dick Clark, the tour promoter, let the JHE leave the tour with no hard feelings. Although they concocted a story for the press of DAR protestations, it had been clear to all parties involved that the JHE billed with the Monkees was a mistake. Peter Tork, the main instigator behind the JHE's inclusion on the tour, had often felt stifled by the Monkees' clown-pop image. He was more at home with the serious music coming out of the Laurel Canyon musician-and-writer colony than the contrived tunes the Monkees were forced to perform on TV. Hendrix's leaving the tour confirmed for Tork the artistic conflict he felt with the Monkees. He let it be known that this would be his last tour and last appearance as a Monkee.

Jimi and company went on to play the Fillmore West. On the same bill with Gabor Szabo and the Jefferson Airplane, they played before the hippies of Haight-Ashbury and the psychedelic "flower people" of the San Francisco Bay area. The Airplane begged off early in the gig. As the headline act, they were in a dilemma. They could not follow Jimi and they could not play before him. They left the gig to Jimi and went home to practice—just as most of the rock musicians who had been in Jimi's wake were also doing. Bill Graham gave antique watches to each of the JHE and an extra grand in appreciation for their taking on the unexpected extra burden.

As the summer neared its end, the action slowed considerably as everyone got ready for the labor days of autumn. Jimi grew moody. He did not necessarily want to return to London, although Mitch and Noel and Chas were eager to return home. But for Jimi, the U.S.A. was his home. He wanted to follow through immediately on his initial success. He wanted people to see that he was more than the *act* that had gotten him over into their consciousness, but also a musician, a writer, a composer. But there was no way out of their European tour. He began to sense interest in the JHE slacken off in the U.S.A. Riding somewhere on the plane, he wrote a lyric about himself as a writer and composer. Forming the object of his conquest in the form of a female, he wrote of a portrait on the wall and a forgotten earring on the floor and of himself. In one of his most poetic lyrics, Jimi feels his isolation begin to mount as his star rises.

Playing around with a clavichord, he found the haunting classical-like theme to the music. He used a mellotron to get the women

voices; the various loops of tape in this machine were able to con-
coct a female choir. They recorded the tune in New York at the
Mayfair Recording Studio, July 20, 1967:

> *The morning is dead*
> *and the day is through*

> *There's nothing up here to lead me*
> *but the velvet moon*

> *All my loneliness*
> *I have felt today*

> *It's a little*
> *more than enough*

> *To make a man throw himself away*

> *But I continue*
> *to burn the Midnight Lamp . . . Alone*

SIX

The JHE had no time to relax and contemplate their smash debut in the States. It seemed as if they were in England only long enough to switch planes. As they were leaving for Sweden they heard that "Burning of the Midnight Lamp" had come in at No. 23 on the London charts.

They had been committed for some time to two small gigs in Sweden at the beginning of September. They had to be back in London for the "Guitar Festival" at Royal Festival Hall on September 25. And there had to be an album finished by November because they were booked throughout Britain for all of November and December right up to Christmas. And then they had to return to Sweden and tour other European countries all of January 1968. In February they were booked to lead a huge English rock tour across America.

In New York Jimi had signed a contract with Sunn. They provided the Experience with any kind of sound equipment needed in exchange for Jimi's input on their research and development. Now the JHE had a sound system consisting of new Sunns alongside their old and battered Marshalls.

On September 3 they played a small room in conservative Gothenburg, Sweden, called Liseberg. There the audience sat completely contained, politely awaiting the start of the concert. What a

157

Backstage reading *Rock and Folk Magazine*, the Olympia, September 9, 1967 © JEAN-PIERRE LELOIR

contrast with Monterey and New York! Overwhelmed by their civilized demeanor, Jimi became even more timid and terse than usual. They are greeted by even applause with a couple of whistles and one cheer. Jimi's Stratocaster salutes the crowd with a Sagittarian bow-thrust and they are off into "Sergeant Pepper." As he sings the lyric, the beat staggers, giving the delayed effect, Jimi hitting the last figure in writhing tremolos.

The sound is splendid. Jimi gets a bell-clear summit treble, his bends balanced beautifully against the clear high tones. Now Jimi had a sound system he could work with. A cabinet Sunn with a JBL D-130 in the bottom and an L-E 100-S driver horn in the top blended with a Marshall 100-watt stack he shared with Noel's bass to seek a full-range sound at the highest power. From treble peak clusters to fuzz bottom rags, with both Cry-Baby and Fuzz-Face pressed flat to the floor, and all the knobs on Jimi's Stratocaster at 10, the system sounded good.

The guitar pipes *thank you*. Jimi murmurs, "Thank you very much and now while your ears are still ringing we'll go on and do another little thing called 'I Don't Live Today,' dedicated to the American Indian."

The beat is 2/4 tom-tom American Indian war dance with lots of accents.

> *Will I live tomorrow?*
> *Well I just can't say*
> *Will I live tomorrow?*
> *Well I just can't say*
> *But I know for sure*
> *I don't live today*

Over the double-note bass drone that is almost in unison with the drums he sounds like he is hitting two chords at once. One chord dubbing the same note he sings and the other chord a screaming soprano lament, *"I don't"*—Noel's voice rushing in to join Jimi's— *"live today."* Jimi's rap off to the side like casual remarks in passing: *". . . maybe tomorrow, uh, just can't tell you, baby—but, uh, I DON'T . . . live today!* It's a shame to throw your precious life away like this. . . ." Jimi's solo begins behind the beat in a meditative hook that moves out into long languorous lines with vibratos at the end of phrases. The sound streaks out into a perfectly controlled synthesizer line of feedback, then quickly back to the note, only to streak out again into feedback at the very ceiling of its signal. Then a twelve-o'clock high-distort wail swoons back into the message. *"I,"* Noel comes in as Jimi lays out, *"don't"* and they both: *"live today."*

> *I wish you'd hurry up and execute me*
> *So I can be on my miserable way*

The time is doubled as they take the song out in a long tag. The feedback has a beautiful feel in the upper registers. The surflike effects of the Sunn amps make the feedback sing in the upper ranges like a mezzo-soprano. Perfect sustained tones rolling out almost liquid. Unfortunately, the lower registers of the Sunn amps do almost nothing, leaving it all on the Marshall, which is supporting all of Noel's sound as well. The Sunn amps make a dull flat tone for Jimi's Strat at midrange and nothing below. Jimi has to content himself with the upper registers. There is not enough contrast with

the lower registers for him to venture down any more. He stays up on top of the accelerated beat and discovers a contrast between treble *wheeee* reports and sideways feedback. He rides the beat shouting *"awww . . . there ain't no life nowhere."* He shakes the Stratocaster rudely, jabbering a vibrato by force. The guitar becomes thousands of native American Indian souls screaming in the historic void of their violent deaths. The guitar neighing like horses shot from under Indian warriors, bows in outstretched arms blasted by Winchesters in millions of movie frames, going back in time to the original action. They churn upward, Jimi's feedback soaring above Noel's charging jag and Mitch's circular back-beat. Jimi exults in the high registers of the sound system as the rhythm section bashes to a close.

They end the set with "Wild Thing," which is beginning to sound almost traditional alongside the new material.

Jimi and company are in BBC Rehearsal Studio One, supposedly rehearsing a jingle for the "Radio One" show. But he, Mitch, and Noel had long ago reached a beautiful understanding in the emotional needs of their music—to rehearse for a jingle was ludicrous. They had played for eleven months straight and were tight. They stayed in the rehearsal room to make Chas and the BBC executives happy. But rather than waste time, they jammed. Every once in a while they hit something they played in their show repertoire and would go through it for a few bars. Everything in Jimi's music fit into the constant moment of a thought, a jam, an emotion, just as physical time—past, present, future—all came from a primordial time. All of the music he had written, and would ever write, all came from this central place, heavy on blues phrasing and hip rhythm licks, with the drums driving like a jazz night train, and the oscillating deep earth throb of the bass. They would speed up to blurs of quadruple time, and then slow down to roadhouse slow drag intimacy, Jimi providing hair-trigger changes in direction, or key by going off on a weird atonal figure, and then whanging back into the tonal tonic of the key, which was almost always E minor.

Chas brought a whole bunch of Motown people back to see them, including Little Stevie Wonder, and Tommie Chong, of Bobby Taylor and the Vancouvers. Bobby Taylor was not there, but Tommie said that he definitely would come by and check Jimi out.

Little Stevie stayed behind and got to licking on the drums. He

Opposite: Jimi plays Paris   © JEAN-PIERRE LELOIR

'Radio One' discovers Jimi   © JEAN-PIERRE LELOIR

played the same kind of deep metallic almost bass-tone beats that
his drum mentor, Benny Benjamin, the original Motown sessions
drummer, was famous for. "Can't Help Myself," "My World Is
Empty Without You," "Don't Mess with Bill," and "I Heard It
Through the Grapevine" were all recorded with Benjamin on drums.
You did not need a bass with Benny on drums. Benny would pop the
tom-toms in such a way that the sound would augment the low
registers and reinforce the song microtonally.

Jimi joined in and they jammed in strict time, Stevie's clean head
moving sideways in time to the music, Jimi playing rhythm and lead
and sometimes the bass parts, too.

Pretty soon it is time to do the jingle. The JHE goes into a heavy
metal funky rag, and out of it Jimi slurs in menace:

Just turn that dial
Make the music worthwhile
Radio One
You stole my gal
But I love you just the same

Radio One
You're the only one
. . . For me

JIMI HENDRIX
GIG LIST

October 7, 1967	Wellington Club, Dereham, Norfolk, England
October 8, 1967	Saville Theatre, London, England
October 9, 1967	L'Olympia, Paris, France
October 22, 1967	Pier Ballroom, Hastings, Sussex, England
October 28, 1967	California Ballroom, Dunstable, Bedford, England
November 10, 1967	Ahoy Hal, Rotterdam, Holland
November 11, 1967	Sussex University, Brighton, Sussex, England
November 14, 1967	Royal Albert Hall, London, England
November 15, 1967	Winter Gardens, Bournemouth, Hampshire, England (Two gigs)
November 17, 1967	City Hall, Sheffield, Yorkshire, England (Two gigs)
November 18, 1967	The Empire, Liverpool, Lancashire, England (Two gigs)
November 19, 1967	Coventry Theatre, Coventry, Warwick, England (Two gigs)
November 22, 1967	Guildhall, Portsmouth, Hampshire, England (Two gigs)
November 23, 1967	Sophia Gardens, Cardiff, Glamorgan, Wales (Two gigs)
November 24, 1967	Colston Hall, Bristol, Gloucester, England (Two gigs)
November 25, 1967	Opera House, Blackpool, Lancashire, England (Two gigs)
November 26, 1967	Palace Theatre, Manchester, Lancashire, England (Two gigs)
November 27, 1967	Festival of Arts, Belfast, Northern Ireland
December 1, 1967	Town Hall, Chatham, Kent, England (Two gigs)
December 2, 1967	The Dome, Brighton, Sussex, England (Two gigs)

December 3, 1967	Theatre Royal, Nottingham, Nottingham, England (Two gigs)
December 4, 1967	City Hall, Newcastle, Stafford, England (Two gigs)
December 5, 1967	Green's Playhouse, Glasgow, Lanark, Scotland (Two gigs)
December 8, 1967	Town Hall, Chatham, Kent, England
December 9, 1967	The Dome, Brighton, Sussex, England
December 10, 1967	Theatre Royal, Chatham, Kent, England
December 11, 1967	City Hall, Newcastle, Stafford, England
December 12, 1967	Green's Playhouse, Glasgow, Lanark, Scotland
December 22, 1967	Olympia, Christmas on Earth, London, England
January 4, 1968	Lorensberg Cirkus, Gothenburg, Sweden (Two gigs)
January 5–6, 1968	Jernallen Sports Hall, Sandviken, Sweden
January 7, 1968	Falkoner Hall, Copenhagen, Denmark
January 8, 1968	Konserthus, Stockholm, Sweden (Two gigs)
January 29, 1968	L'Olympia, Paris, France

Jimi took the frustrations of the hectic tour out on a Gothenburg hotel room on January 4, 1968. He had started drinking with the intent of getting drunk. Before he knew it he was a moving blackout. First he started on the glasses and lamps, smashing them to smithereens. Then the chairs began to go out of the windows. Noel Redding had the room next to him and was the first to realize what was happening. Jimi was stoned drunk and not easy to handle. He had a wild wiriness with incredibly strong arms. Gerry Stickells came in and soon he and Noel had wrestled Jimi to the floor and sat on him. The hotel authorities were outraged. This was where the royal family of Sweden stayed when they came through. Although Chas Chandler offered to make full payment for the wrecked room, the hotel authorities insisted on arresting Jimi. They could not have it be said that their hotel was an establishment that tolerated rock 'n' roll stars tearing up their premises. The police insisted on handcuffing him, arguing that he was violent. They made one concession: They allowed Jimi to wear his handcuffs in front of him instead of behind his back. Jimi was photographed for worldwide consumption being escorted from the Opelan Hotel accompanied by two police-

Busted! Jimi being escorted to jail in Stockholm after destroying the contents of his hotel room, January 5, 1968 *WIDE WORLD PHOTOS*

men. He walked between them with a white midlength fur coat thrown over his shoulders.

Of course, Jimi was released, but only after a mandatory night in jail. He was shocked by the confinement and very contrite when he got out the next morning. He insisted to Chas that he had remembered nothing of the incident—it had been a complete blackout. But to the youth of Sweden the incident had increased his hero stature; to them he was a true rebel. A few days later in Stockholm the Jimi Hendrix Experience was refused rooms at thirty hotels.

The movie camera slowly rode in on Jimi as he sat on a stool in the white room, made even whiter by the brilliant lighting. He wore his Sergeant Pepper red jacket and his black bolero hat and pants to match. Hunched over an instrument he never played in public—an old acoustic twelve-string—he played a soft talkinglike blues. This was a private song he had composed when he first arrived in London. A song he usually sang only to girl friends alone in his bedroom deep into the night as they sat upon his black satin sheets:

Well I'm waitin' at the train station
Waitin' for that train
Waitin' for the train yeah
Take me Yeah
From this—lonesome place
Well now a whole lot of people put me down a lot
*   of changes*
My girl done—called me a disgrace

The tears burning
Tears burnin' me
Tears burnin' me
Way down—in my heart
Well you know it's too bad little girl
It's too bad
Too bad—we had to part

Gonna leave this town—Yeah
Got to leave this town
Gonna make a whole lot of money
Gonna be big yeah
Gonna be big yeah
Gonna buy this town
Gonna buy this town
Put it all in my shoe
Might even give a piece to you
That's what I'm gonna do—what I'm gonna do
*   —what I'm gonna do . . .*

The movie was called *The Experience* and would be released as a promo for the JHE's first major American tour.

During the fall/winter itinerary Jimi sat in on a Stevie Stills session and played lead on a song called "Good Times, Old Times," they completed *The Experience* movie, appeared in writer Tony Palmer's movie *All My Lovin'*, made their own "home movies" about various sex scenes with groupies, and completed work on the new album *Axis: Bold as Love*, their second album. The album would be released in the States to coincide with their giant tour starting in February 1968.

Jimi would headline a tour featuring the Soft Machine, Eric Burdon and the (New) Animals, the Alan Price Set, and Nova Express.

A planeload of thirty-two English rock musicians plus entourages, managers, and roadies disembarked from their BOAC charter at Kennedy Airport and split up into limos, vans, and trucks. They had to hurry. They were expected to arrive by helicopter atop the Pan Am Building. But the helicopters, which would have taken them into the hub of midtown Manhattan, had been grounded because of poor visibility. It would take at least an hour to drive in.

They arrived at the 'Copter Club of the Pan Am Building more than an hour late. The party was in full tilt. The press reporters, cameramen, photographers, promo men, groupies, stringers, hanger-outers, and hangers-on had had time to get pretty well stoned at the bar.

Jimi's was the only black face in the crowd of English accents. He wore full finery: a black wide-brim bolero with a purple plume from which flowed his long black locks that blended into his black cape, iridescent studded black bell-bottoms, and soft-gloss boots from the Chelsea Cobbler. A totally black-caped figure from head to toe, but his cape flowed open to reveal a sky-blue silken lining, and embroidered on the back were two doves aligned vertically in upward flight. He was very soft-spoken and polite as he addressed the assembled. His reserved manner exasperated many reporters, who yelled at him to speak louder. Eric Burdon, leading the New Animals, spoke louder, as did Alan Price (an original Animal), who was leading a new group called the Alan Price Set. Also on the tour were the Soft Machine and Nova Express.

Soon Jimi got off to the side and got into a good rap with Al Aronowicz, who had his *New York Post* identification pinned awkwardly to his lapel. Aronowicz was a friend of Brian Jones, and they exchanged words about how he was doing.

Jones's recent drug bust prevented him from working outside of England, and they both knew how demoralized he had become. And they felt a bond of sadness. Al Aronowicz would stab his pen at a pad every now and then but it was more like he was just going through the motions of being a columnist for the major afternoon paper in New York City, while his main interest was in simply being people with Jimi. Jimi appreciated the alliance as they both surveyed the chaotic scene going on about them. The people were going nuts in the grand tradition of the New York mass-hysteria press rout. It was definitely an event to check out and chuckle over.

A fistfight broke out across the floor just as a bearded, scholarly-looking man came up and introduced himself. He was Professor Jay Ruby, who was doing a study of various social aspects of present-day rock music. He took out his tape recorder and got right into an interview, asking "What's the musical scene like in England? Is it different from here?"

Jimi answered: "Well, yes, it is. It's a little more together as far as the musicians are concerned. They all know each other and they get a small place and everybody congregates around London. It's not that much different really. They have their own scene and we've got our own scene over here."

"You like it better over there?" Ruby wondered.

"As a musician, not necessarily," Jimi replied thoughtfully. "I like to jam a lot and they don't do that much over there. I like to play with other cats, but you just can't do that over there sometimes."

Ruby compared him to Eric Clapton. Jimi didn't like that, saying, "But like, the blues is what we're supposed to dig. But you see, there are other things we can play too. And we just don't think alike . . . sometimes the notes might sound like it, but it's a completely different scene between those notes."

Was the JHE primarily a live or a studio group? Professor Ruby saw no difficulty with them in the transition from one to the other.

Jimi replied, "Either you can dig it as a record or in person. Like some want to hear one thing—when you make a record you put a certain sound in the record or a certain little freaky thing—like the sound of raindrops reversed and echoed and phased and all that. It's because you are trying to emphasize a certain point in the record. So people already have this in their minds when they go to see you, and they expect to hear that. But the main thing is the words, and they can feel the other thing and not necessarily hear it."

Ruby asked about the effects on Jimi's recordings.

"All those things are our own mind . . . all those things are coming out of us. . . . We do a lot of things. Like, on the last track of the last LP [*Axis: Bold as Love*], it's called phasing. It makes it sound like planes going through your membranes and chromosomes. A cat got that together accidentally and he turned us on to it. That's the sound we wanted, it was a special sound, and we didn't want to use tapes of airplanes, we wanted to have the music itself warped."

Ruby wanted to know how Jimi defined the blues.

"You can have your own blues. It doesn't necessarily mean that folk blues is the only type of blues in the world. I heard some Irish folk songs that were *so* funky, the words were so together and the feel. That was a great scene. We do this blues . . . called 'If Six Were Nine.' That's what you call a great feeling of blues. We don't even try to give it a name. Everybody has some kind of blues to offer, you know."

After the interview Jimi and Al talked about the barrenness of English food. Jimi said that he could really do with some soul food right now. Aronowicz said, "Let's go." They split the 'Copter Club and went down to the Village. They stopped at Seventh and Bleecker, where the Pink Teacup served the best soul cooking below Harlem.

Jimi talked about the axis long before he formulated an album around the theme. The axis is like the Christian cross or the voodoo peristyle—a link between the heavens and the Earth. The axis of the Earth holds everything together. If the axis of the Earth were altered, everything would be different. Entirely new continents, new directions for north and south, and seas inundating shores that once lay peaceful. The axis made electricity possible, the electromagnetic energy that fed Jimi's guitar. Jimi also felt that a record spinning on a turntable was directly related to the Earth's spinning on its axis. At one point he said, "Well, like the axis of the Earth, you know. If it changes, well, it changes the whole face of the Earth like every few thousand years, you know. It's like love in a human being if he really falls in love deep enough, it will change him, you know, it might change his whole life. So both of them can really go together. . . ."

Manly Hall once wrote, "The *Axis* is a mysterious individual who, unknown and unsuspected, mingles with mankind and who, according to tradition has his favorite seat on the roof of the Caaba. . . .

"When an 'Axis' quits this earthly existence, he is succeeded by the 'Faithful One,' who has occupied the place at his right hand. . . . For to these holy men, who also bear the collective titles of 'Lords of Souls' and 'Directors,' is committed a spiritual supremacy over mankind far exceeding the temporal authority of earthly rulers."

An Encyclopediac Outline of Secret Tradition

Flying to London and then flying to California for Monterey Jimi had experienced a mystical peace up above the Earth. He had understood something deep about the Earth just being above the clouds, looking down upon the land and upon the waters. As if the Earth itself was moving him to and fro, back and forth toward recognition. Making it possible for him to be able to transmit the blues on a higher level, just as Muddy Waters had done with the Mississippi Delta blues. Jimi was now extending the blues into universal dimensions, axis of the Earth, balance of the solar system. For he loved the music more than he loved himself, and for him to be able to lift it up and give it to others was the greatest gift he ever imagined receiving.

The album had just been released in America. "Bold as Love" was the title song of the album.

The first chord Jimi strikes is the musical equivalent of anger, brusquely bringing you to attention. Then the song as quickly mellows into the story he tells. It is a ballad with the internal rhymes and alliterations all intact, like the ancient troubadours.

> *ANGER!*
> *He smiles, towering in*
> *Shiny metallic purple armor*
> *Queen jealousy, envy waits behind him*
> *Her fiery green gown sneers at the grassy ground*
>
> *Blue are the life-giving waters*
> *taking for granted*
> *they quietly understand*
> *Once happy turquoise armies lay opposite ready*
> *but wonder why the fight is on*
>
> *But they're all Bold as Love*
> *But they're all Bold as Love*
> *But they're all Bold as Love*
> > *Just ask the Axis*

Jimi conjures the image of a proud warrior; in his shadow, a jealous queen, even the green of her envy is contemptuous of the common green of the grass. (Jimi's chords are tense on "envy.") But

then again he returns to crooning elegance. He recites the colors of
the human aura that can be interpreted by one who *sees.*

"Blue are the life-giving waters"—he riffs convoluted contours of
the sylphs in liquid motion—*"taking for granted."* But the waters
know in their serene passage that life is continuous. He riffs moody
currents, riding the bass like a dolphin rides the waves. The stars at
times compel the Sagittarian to war within himself. Although
opposing parts of him are really innocent—*"they wonder why the
fight is on."* The drums smash martial snares in quick succession as
the riffs run together and change into a higher key, where, on the
pinnacle, he delivers the message of the "intelligences": *"But
they're all Bold as Love. . . . Just ask the Axis. . . . He knows everything."* All his emotions, all of the colors of his mind are keen,
striving for love.

> *My red is so confident*
> *He flashes trophies of war and ribbons of euphoria*

This Mars-like color signifies sexual conquest, victory on the
material plane of genital flesh. Yet there is also the plumed serpent
of Scorpio's highest evolution. He says with up-front blues integrity:

> *Orange is young, full of daring but very unsteady*
>   *for the first go-round*
> *My yellow in this case is not so mellow*
> *In fact, I'm trying to say that it's frightened like me*
> *And all these emotions of mine*
> *Keep holding me from giving my life*
>   *To a rainbow like you*

> *We're all Bold as Love*
> *Bold as love*
> *Well, I'm Bold as Love . . . hear me talkin' to you*
> *Just ask the Axis . . .*

The love that holds the earth on its axis—that mystical force that
continues life through the will of love:

> *He knows everything.*

The song goes out, modulating upward, spiraling faster and faster,
until he hits its center mode. A silent missile's exhaust trailing

away as it escapes into the stratosphere, the message taking the eyes aloft in yogic *Trakham*, fixation on the third eye. Beyond resolution is the pure emotion. The cry of the guitar solo, ranging between tears and ecstasy.

"Spanish Castle Magic," right away incredible three-guitar chorus all in unison playing racing, challenging rhythm licks. An electric guitar choir taking you right up, creating a vortical chant. Harmonizing against electronic atonal overtones, combined with the ultrasonics of the high-volume decibel force, making another disparate, though unified, sound totally unique to the supporting bass and drum. Like supersonic locomotives flying.

Ed Kramer and Jimi laid track after track of guitar onto one track of their four-track master tape. The first guitar track is counterpoint old blues-style picking, with all of Jimi's accumulated speed. The second guitar track strums rhythm chords against the picking. The third guitar track accents single lines and takes sly mixed-down solos. Noel plays a Hagstrom eight-string bass, Jimi often in unison on a Stratocaster. It comes out like a web straining along, rapidly forming matrix after matrix. Hypnotic tones from preelectric blues guitar revved up, creating electronic music with flat-footed blues underneath speeding endlessly through time and space. Sound waves spiraling outward, through human heart and solar energy, challenging the cycles of heavenly lights.

Playing against the beat laid down by the bass, Jimi's guitars chatter and race against each other. The drums kick and shuffle in double time, Mitch's snare raps are precise. Jimi begins to solo. He joins the twin guitars for a moment, hitting them in the middle of their licks, creating cross-rhythms like African drum talk. The accenting lick sustains in the break. He pauses a moment, then moves off.

He makes his Stratocaster growl in the upper range, snarl and turn as if it's a savage beast he is controlling. Jimi dubs in fifths with the bass, as he loves to do, and tells us,

> It's very far away
> Takes the better part of a day
> To get there
> If we travel by . . . dragonfly

The drums solo in double time, maintaining the drive while Jimi raps,

> No it's not in Spain
> But all the same you know

It has a groovy name
And the wind's just right HEY!

Mitch's snares make you stand at attention in the short break as Jimi shouts,

Hang on my darling
Hang on if you want to go

Then the song takes off; the guitar dubbing with the bass gets more intense and then splits off forming a surprising fuzz wail that blends perfectly at the end of their dual figure,

. . . just a little bit of
Spanish Castle Magic

He raps again as Mitch punctuates on the running bass drum.

The clouds are really low
And they overflow
With cotton candy and battlegrounds
Red and brown
But it's all in your mind
Don't think your time
On bad things
Just float your little mind around
LOOK OUT!

His guitar growls a turn, Mitch barks the orders, snare rap on the door, and they plunge deep, Jimi churning the bass guitars into the theme plateau, away from the melody and refrain. Deep across the Spanish Sahara on horseback bearded Moors charging for Tangier, the Straits of Gibraltar, Spain, the magic within her mantle. *"It's all in your mind,"* he shouts against the wall of the music, sounding like a Pentecostal preacher as the song begins to tag out. His guitar snorts fire in staccato rays, the fuzz tone splitting chords spluttering upward. *"A little bit of daydreamin' here and there."* On a one-chord jag the bass comes up, its three-note drone syncopating into five. Rocking out. The guitar tracks in the background move up too, their chant creating a whirlwind. Jimi reaches the top of his summit in rooting licks. He intones, *"Everything's gonna be all right,"* as they go on out, the clanging of the bell as the train leaves the station. Bells diminished, mixed down knell. *Clave.*

"If Six Was Nine" had been part of a studio jam session Jimi had with Noel and Mitch. It just came out of the blue—reflecting how Jimi was feeling at that particular time. They pulled the jam out of the studio tapes and Jimi sang some words over the tracks. He had wanted to do the tracks over again, but Chas said that it was fine the way it was.

> *If the sun*
> *refuse to shine*
> *I don't mind*
> *I don't mind*
>
> *If the mountains*
> *fell in the sea*
> *Let it be*
> *It ain't me*
>
> *Got my own world to look through*
> *and I ain't gonna copy you*
>
> *Now if six*
> *turned out to be nine*
> *I don't mind*
> *I don't mind*
>
> *Now if the hippies*
> *cut off all their hair*
> *I don't care*
> *I don't care*
>
> *Got my own world to look through*
> *And I ain't gonna copy you*
>
> (White-collared conservative flashing down the street
> Pointing their plastic finger at me—
> They're hoping soon my kind will drop and die)
>
> *But I'm gonna wave*
> *My freak flag high HIGH*
>
> (I'm the one who has to die when it's time for me to die
> So let me live my life the way I want to.)

Jimi's tag is with Moroccan flutes going out in free, jazzlike peaks. Trembling in higher frequencies and challenging the heights of sound humanly heard, like the end pitch of a siren or a woman's scream in the night.

Sing on, brother
Play on, drummer

Chas Chandler's "footprints" are heard on the tag-out.

"Little Wing" is so sad yet so hopeful, a ballad not of any particular category, yet blending beautifully between lyric and melody. A simple statement about Jimi's guardian angel, which he always formulates in the feminine, yet it could also apply to any lover or friend.

Well, she's walking
Through the clouds
With a circus mind
That's running wild
Butterflies and zebras and moonbeams
and fairy tales . . . (that's all she ever thinks about)
riding with the wind

When I'm sad
she comes to me
with a thousand smiles
she gives to me free
It's all right she says, it's all right
Take anything you want from me
Anything . . .

Jimi heard the entire song up on the high outreaching stage of the Monterey Fairgrounds as the throngs whooped and hollered themselves crazy. A sad bliss had come over him. He had made it. He had made it in his own land, yet in triumph there was that sad wistful bluesy bliss. A strange country-and-western tinge comes up in the last chorus of his solo, so utterly surprising, yet hinted at in the very beginnings of the piece. This is a piece direct from his muse—*Fly on, Little Wing, fly on. . . .*

Axis entered the Top Twenty on the American charts on February 24, 1968. Now Jimi had new songs to play, and new equipment for the tour as well. They had junked the Sunn amps for the old reliable Marshalls, and had incorporated an entire array of new devices.

Jimi Hendrix's new equipment consisted of a Univox univibe, a Dallas-Arbiter Fuzz-Face, a Vox wah-wah pedal, a Leslie, an Octavia, and twelve stacks of Marshall amps with forty-eight beefed-up speaker cabinets. The fuzz tone, like a pre-amp, boosted the power tremendously and accounted for the distortion effect. He used the wah-wah pedal clear, achieving a watery effect. Parts of that effect can be attributed to the univibe and the Leslie going at the same time, simulating rotating speakers.

Hendrix played a right-handed Stratocaster upside down and re-strung, since he was a lefty. He could have bought a left-handed Stratocaster, but the right-handed one afforded him the speed and efficiency so crucial to the cleanliness and speed of his attack. When a right-handed person uses a standard right-handed electric guitar, the controls are on the bottom, making it necessary to cross over the instrument to work them and thus limiting speed. But with Hendrix's controls on top, actually under his playing hand, he could work the bar and all the control knobs often simultaneously, while playing and manipulating the sliding pickup switch with his palm.

On this tour Hendrix carried along what amounted to a portable recording studio, including boxes of extra fuzz tones, wah-wah pedals, univibes, guitar straps, and assorted boxes of "toys" such as the "Octavia," which were built especially for him. He also carried an assortment of guitars, including his old beat-up Hofner, a twelve-string Hagstrom, a Les Paul Flying V, an old Fender Telecaster, and several brand-new Stratocasters.

On tour. February 7, 1968. Twenty thousand attended their concert at Arizona State University's Union.

Their publicist, Les Perrin, traveling with them from London, had set up a telephone interview for Jimi with the *Sunday Mirror* back in England. The interview had to be done as they all prepared to leave for Anaheim, California, where they were scheduled to appear on the ninth. The call came through. The reason the *Sunday Mirror* was so anxious to run a story about him was that Petula Clark had recently declared Jimi Hendrix "a great big hoax." Jimi's reply was true to form. "Well, I figure it's nice for her to have thought enough about me to say anything."

February 8, Anaheim, California.

Eric Burdon and the Animals had a complete light show. During their song "San Francisco Nights," filmed scenes of San Francisco and close-up shots of Eric Burdon were projected on the screen.

The Jimi Hendrix Experience had to play harder. They had no light show to enhance their performance. They played at intensities that burned out amplifiers. Mitch was drumming so hard that at one point his cymbal went flying out into the audience.

On February 11 they flew into Seattle. Jimi's father, Al, his

Jimi with his father, Seattle, 1968 J.A. HENDRIX

brother, Leon, and his new stepmother, Ayako, and half sister, Janie, met Jimi at the airport. The press was there to record the event. Jimi was to be honored by the city at his old high school and receive an honorary diploma. He had not seen his father or Leon for seven years. He had never before seen his new mother and half sister.

There was a reception of sorts at Al's house. Al was beaming ecstatically throughout. He had a few beers while he reminisced. With people coming in and out, he talked with awe, as if he were telling a dream.

Jimi, unnoticed, sat for a while and watched his father being interviewed by several reporters. Al was loose and loving it. Al Hendrix rapped naturally and good-naturedly, sipping from a can of beer from time to time.

When he called me that night from London, he said, "Dad, I could buy a home, I want to buy you a home this winter" . . . and so on and so on. We both started to cry. And I said, "Now, lookit, Jimmy— *now don't get too excited.* You take care of your scene first. You get yourself established. Ole Dad is doing okay."

He told me a long time ago when I was still gardening and Jimmy was gardening with me then. He had been playing his guitar around a few times then. And he said, "Oh Daddy, one of these days I'm gonna be big and famous." And I told him, "I hope you hurry up and do it before Dad gets too old to enjoy it." We were just kidding and yak-yakking, and he said, "I'm gonna make it, man." And I said, "Well, I believe you will." I said, "If you got the stamina I got, you gonna make it. Ha, ha. 'Cause I'm gonna keep on going, no matter how many obstacles are in my way. I'm gonna keep on going. I'm always gonna be plugging ahead."

I used to tell him, when I first come to Seattle I used to sleep in boxcars and open fields, and one thing and another. Eat my meals around skid row with the bowl of beans. I said, "I ain't no shamed. Shoot, I'm living." I held my head higher. I said, "I'm gonna get outa that." And that's what I always used to preach to him: "Always go high, get yourself higher." You got to do it now on account of there's nothing better. "Man," I'd say, "you got your sights set higher. Go higher."

I remember the first time I heard his record. Some of our neighbors had it in an adjoining apartment, and I knew it was Jimmy's record, even though I had never heard it before. And then they found out I was Jimmy's dad. "Wow! Ooohh! Weeeee! Wow!" They went and give me the record. They said they'd go buy another one. "GEEE, you really Jimi Hendrix's dad?" And I said, "Sure." See, I was looking for soul music, and he come out with a psychedelic job. Something new, way out.

They were playing the record in the apartment right next door.

They had pillows all over the floor, I mean, they were "way out." I said to my wife, "That sounds like Jimmy's record." Now, I don't know why, it's just the way that Jimmy plays his guitar, and I hadn't heard him go for a long time. But he would call from London and play us some new stuff they had just recorded.

I watched him when he played at Birdland, the place that used to be on Madison Street here. That's where he learned a lot playing guitar. He got one stolen from him there, and I went and bought him another one. They didn't sell hard liquor at Birdland. They used to sell pop and it was more or less a place for the kids. But they used to dance to the music. And he used to be playing with a bunch of kids. I used to think to myself, "I see Jimmy playing in a cabaret," or something like that. I didn't know he was gonna get so international.

The next night Jimi played the Seattle Center Arena. His father's face beamed up at him from the first row. Jimi put on a show. He drove the audience to a frenzy that scared the police.

Jimi went to Garfield High School at eight o'clock the following morning. On the way he recalled vividly his high school days. An assembly had been called for the honorary degree ceremony and the entire student populace was there. First the principal made a speech, then Pat O'Day, of KJR, made some remarks and then called Jimi to the microphone. Jimi mumbled that he was glad to be back home. He was lost for words after that and quickly asked if there were any questions. After a long, embarrassing silence, Jimi pleaded, "There must be somebody." After another long pause a girl finally asked, "How long have you been away from Seattle?" Jimi thought for a while and then murmured, "Oh, about five thousand years." He stood there for a moment and then quickly walked off the stage and out of the building. The assembly was hastily dismissed. Jimi never did get his high school diploma.

On February 14 they played the Whiskey A Go Go on Hollywood's Sunset Strip, then they flew straight to Dallas. They had left most of their stuff in L.A. since they were booked at the Shrine Auditorium in a few days. Chas Chandler and Michael Jeffery thought they would be making about seven thousand dollars on a percentage deal in Dallas—the take was twenty-seven thousand dollars. They were smashing house records.

On February 16 they played the Shrine Auditorium in L.A. Mike Bloomfield and Buddy Miles were on the bill with Electric Flag, their new group. Blue Cheer and Electric Flag had replaced Eric Burdon and the Animals and the Alan Price Set, who had continued on touring through the South. The JHE blew L.A.'s mind. Jimi wore a Spanish gypsy tasseled vest, a paisley-nouveau silk blouse, and tight bolero pants with flared studded bell-bottoms. They cut the amp during the "Wild Thing" finale; all at once an incredible wall of sound went silent. The crowd, caught unawares, uttered a collective surprised "Ooooooh."

On February 22 they arrived back in Dallas for a few days. Les Perrin received a clipping of the article in the *Sunday Mirror* that had been written around the telephone interview. He took it to Jimi and they both had a laugh at the big bold headline: "WILD MAN," with an ugly distorted inset photo of Jimi that resembled an ape in English military uniform.

Later, in Miami, Jimi experimented with his hair, lacing several blond patches through it. Linda Eastman was taking pictures and Annie Fisher from the *Village Voice* was taking notes. Linda was gassed by his blond streaks and pink puffed-sleeve shirt. She shot in color. They were ten stories up above a swimming pool area where a square dance was about to start. Mitch ran out on the balcony with his Super 8 to get some shots. Noel was hanging out in leopard-skin skivvies. He had refused to be perturbed about having to go and get working papers. Mitch had blown his top shouting that nobody would expect the Beatles to go and stand in line for anything. Finally the promoter, Mike Goldstein, said that he would take care of it, and that was that.

On February 25 the *New York Times* called Jimi "the black Elvis" in a laudatory review of his albums and shows.

On February 27 they appeared in Chicago. He was waylaid by the infamous "Plaster Casters," a couple of young groupies who made plaster casts of rock stars' genitals. In their diary of the event they use London hip parlance. "Plater" refers to the one who administered fellatio to Jimi's "rig," which means his penis.

CAROLE: Plater

DELORES: Mold and plaster caster

MARGE: Delores's assistant

We needed a ratio of 28:28 and found this barely sufficient. He has got just about the biggest rig I've ever seen! We needed to plunge him through the entire depth of the vase. In view of all these dodgy precedents, we got a BEAUTIFUL mold. He even kept his hard for the entire minute. He got stuck, however, for about fifteen minutes (his hair did) but he was an excellent sport—didn't panic . . . he actually enjoyed it and balled the impression after it had set. In fact, I believe the reason we couldn't get his rig out was that it wouldn't GET SOFT! We rubbed a little warm water around the top of his balls and eventually it slipped out. A beautiful (to say the least) mold with part of a ball and some random embedded hairs. Dig this—the plaster cast was a flop. Delores got uptight and didn't mix enough, and then after she'd gotten it set into the mold, she got anxious to get the finished product out before it was finished, and so it all crumbled. But it was kept intact in its crumbled heap for a couple of days and it subsequently dried together and was only broken in three divisions—head, rig, and ball. A little Elmer's Glue and we had our plaster cast—a little on the Venus De Milo side, but it's a real beauty.

On February 29 they played Hunter College in Manhattan. Counterfeit hand-lettered tickets were sold outside the sold-out auditorium.

On March 3, 1968, the JHE played to an SRO crowd at Veterans' Memorial Hall in Columbus, Ohio. In Cleveland, where the Experience was to appear three weeks later, the papers reported that thousands waited in line for tickets. By March 8 a second show was sold out. The *Cleveland Plain Dealer* held a contest "to give a definition of Jimi Hendrix in fifteen words or less" for free tickets to the show.

On March 9 lawyers for Jimi Hendrix enjoined Capital Records and PPX Productions (Ed Chalpin) in a temporary injunction to halt the distribution and sales of an album entitled *Get That Feeling*. They argued that the album cover was confusing to the public because it showed a large colored photo of Jimi Hendrix and featured his name, when in fact he had been only a side man on those sessions of Curtis Knight.

That night the JHE and the Soft Machine played the State University of New York at Stony Brook (which was often referred to as the Berkeley of the East). John Hammond, Jr., opened the show. His mike did not work and he broke a guitar strap as well. His set did not go well at all. The Soft Machine's set went on for forty minutes with a coordinated light show that burst bubbles of color that flowed as

Barely escaping fan at Cleveland Music Hall
March 28, 1968   RICHARD T. CONWAY

keys shifted and volumes changed. When it was the JHE's time to appear, the police and hired guards hassled the capacity crowd about smoking and standing in the aisles. They finally had to make an announcement that Jimi Hendrix would not go on unless the edicts were obeyed. The JHE blew their minds even though the equipment suffered breakdowns throughout the set.

On March 15 *Life* magazine hailed Jimi Hendrix as the "Most Spectacular Electric Guitarist in the World." That night Jimi threw a wild party at his suite in the Waldorf-Astoria. A caravan of cars swathed in psychedelic colors deposited an entire tribe of hippies at the Waldorf's entrance before a stunned doorman.

Jimi had thought he would just throw a little get-together, but *everybody* in New York showed up at his suite of rooms. A cross section of all kinds of people—a typical hip New York party and they were all talking about him and they were all celebrating him. It was really blowing his mind.

Tom Wilson, Bob Dylan's producer, was telling some people that Jimi was "the dominant force in pop-rock today. He combines the phantasmagoric splendor of a Hieronymus Bosch painting with the funky essence of rhythm and blues.''

Harvey Cooper was comparing Jimi to the English cats: "Beck is actually better than Clapton at playing four guitars over dubs and then fusing them together. Hendrix is better than them both; he does it all at once.''

Eric Burdon was in characteristic form: "Everyone likes Jimi because they think his cock is bigger than theirs.''

Jimi was talking about the wah-wah. "The wah-wah pedal is great because it doesn't have any notes. Nothing but hitting it straight up using the vibrato and then the drums come through and that there feels like that, not depression but that loneliness and that frustration and the yearning for something. Like something is reaching out.''

Mike Bloomfield was talking about some of the dates he played on the same bill with the Experience a couple of weeks ago on the West Coast. "We were playing a gig at the Shrine at Los Angeles—he and I were standing backstage fooling around with our guitars. And I was playing and playing. And I'm hearing these insane sounds. And Hendrix was just playing with his toggle switch. He was taking the toggle switch off the guitar, tapping the back of the neck and he's got his vibrato in his hand and he's moving the toggle switch and tapping the neck and using the vibrato and it sounded like sirocco winds coming up from the desert. And here I am playing, hunched over and playing all these notes and there's this guy just lightly tapping the back of his guitar and fooling with his toggle switch and these desert breezes and sounds are coming out.''

Truman Capote, slightly tipsy, looking like a matron in drag, talking in his high-pitched gossipy voice about Bianca, the South American heiress who was clearly the toast of the party: "She is a totally self-invented person. One night I went to a dinner party . . . given by an *extremely* superfashionable lady who was having a dinner party for about six, no, just about eight people, and Bianca came. And she *kept* getting up from the table and going and dialing this number on the telephone continuously. And she told this woman who was giving the party, she said, 'I have a friend who is coming by here to pick me up—you mind?' She said, 'Noooo, I don't mind at all.' And finally, about eleven o'clock at night, just as we were all leaving, arrives Jimi Hendrix. And I must say I didn't know who Jimi Hendrix was at the time—I don't think anybody else there did. . . . He came in and he was very—very, ah, not like anything that I would subsequently know anything about him, you know. He was a very polite subdued rather shy guy. He stayed for about a half an hour and we all left. And she was just absolutely *maaaaadddd* about him. . . . Later in the next week or so we got all about Jimi Hendrix in the whole country. They were around that winter for about three or four months—I guess it must've broken up. She's a real adventuress—but at least she knows what it's all about."

Eric Clapton was going on and on about Jimi's "strong fingers" to jazz guitarist Larry Coryell, who laughed and agreed: "He sure knows how to shake them strings." Although Coryell knew Jimi had had no classical training, to him Hendrix "had the talent of someone like a Stravinsky or Berg."

By the time the party was over Jimi had been notified that he was being kicked out of the hotel. The security force escorted the stragglers to the street.

Mike Bloomfield kept rapping to a journalist friend after the party ended. "The first time I saw Jimi play he was Jimmy James with the Blue Flames. I was performing with Paul Butterfield, and I was the hotshot guitarist on the block—I thought I was it. I'd never heard of Hendrix. Then someone said, 'You go to see the guitar player with John Hammond.' I was at the Cafe Au Go Go and he was at the Nite Owl or the Cafe Wha?—I went right across the street and saw him. Hendrix knew who I was, and that day, in front of my eyes, going off, flying missiles were flying—I can't tell you the sounds he was getting out of his instrument. He was getting every sound I was ever to hear him get right there in the room with a Stratocaster, a Fender Twin Reverb amp, a Maestro Fuzz Tone, and that was all. He was doing it mainly through extreme volume. How he did this, I wish I understood. He just got right up in my face with that ax, and I didn't even want to pick up a guitar for the next year.

"I was awed. I'd never heard anything like it. I didn't even know where he was coming from musically, because he wasn't playing any of his own tunes. He was doing things like 'Like a Rolling Stone,' but in the most unusual way. He wasn't a singer, he wasn't even particularly a player. That day Jimi Hendrix was laying things on me that were more sounds than they were licks. But I found, after hearing him two or three more times, that he was into pure melodic playing and lyricism as much as he was into sounds. In fact, he had melded them into a perfect blend.

"Jimi had been fooling with feedback, but when he heard the Yardbirds, he realized its huge potential. Hendrix would sustain a note and add vibrato so that it sounded just like a human voice.

"He uses an immense vocabulary of controlled sounds, not just hoping to get those sounds, but actually controlling them as soon as he produces them. I have never heard such controlled frenzy, especially in electric music. Jimi said that he went to England to wipe them out, and he did.

"I have never heard a sound on a Hendrix record that I have not seen him create in front of my eyes."

Bloomfield did not know how Jimi kept the guitar in tune. Usually if you jerked a whang bar your guitar went out of tune. "But his didn't apparently. He could bend it in tune.

"Somehow, by tapping the back of his guitar neck (which he constantly did), and by using the bar, Jimi could control feedback. You hear a rumbling start and then Jimi hits a note he knows will feed back. He knew which note would feed back and what harmonic he was shooting for, and then he controlled it. Somehow, when he has all the notes open, he raises the pitch level by using the bar and he gets a higher note to feed back, or he makes the bass note feed back harmonically. He was listening for such things, and I believe he heard them on the English records, particularly by the Yardbirds and Jeff Beck."

But Jimi, as he was very modest, never said that he took feedback farther than the Yardbirds. He said, "I fool with it, and what I'm doing now is the fruits of my fooling around."

"You can't tell what Hendrix is doing with his body. He moves with all those tricks that black guitarists have been using since T-bone Walker and Guitar Slim—playing behind his head and with his teeth. He takes exhibitionism to a new degree. He crashes his guitar against his hip. It is a bold gesture, and he would get a roaring, fuzzy, feedback sound. His body motion is so integrated with his playing that you can't tell where one starts and where the other leaves off.

"Many of his sounds are things that Jimi stumbled on and a lot he shopped for. They become part of his musical language. It's not something he can just tell you how to do. You have to understand the way he hears sound. The way he wants to feel sound and get it out to create music."

Mike Bloomfield noticed that Jimi used two basic scales: "The blues minor scale (E minor) and its relative major. If Jimi played A minor, he would go to C major and make it a major seventh scale.

" 'All Along the Watchtower' is a perfect vehicle for minor- or blues-scale improvisation, while 'Bold as Love,' 'Little Wing,' and 'The Wind Cries Mary' are perfect vehicles for major-key explorations."

Bloomfield heard Jimi defining electric music before his eyes. Jimi turned sound into music. Sound derived from devices and gadgets that he made come alive. "Jimi's playing went beyond music into realms of pure sound and music combined."

Bloomfield watched Hendrix perform many times but never could understand his hand positions or the chords he used. Jimi could play left- or right-hand, with equal facility. "Sometimes he didn't even restring his guitar—he just played it upside down."

Hendrix was, to Bloomfield, by far the greatest expert he had ever heard at playing rhythm and blues, the styles of playing developed by Bobby Womack, Curtis Mayfield, Eric Gale, and others. Bloomfield got the feeling there was no guitaring of any kind that Jimi had not heard or studied, including steel guitar, Hawaiian, and dobro.

"In his playing I can really hear Curtis Mayfield, Wes Montgomery, Albert King, B. B. King, and Muddy Waters. Jimi is the blackest guitarist I've ever heard. His music is deeply rooted in pre-blues, the oldest musical forms like field-hollers and gospel melodies. From what I can garner, there was no form of black music that he hadn't listened to or studied." But Jimi especially loved the real old black musical forms, and they pour out in his playing.

"Jimi's musical approach, as he explained it to me, is how to lay out the entire song and decide how it should be—horns, strings, the way it will wind up. He plays the drumbeat on a damp wah-wah pedal, the bass part on the bass strings of his guitar, and the pattern of the song with just the wah-wah pedal. Then he fleshes the pattern out by playing it with chords and syncopation.

"Jimi plays a bass pattern, and then fills it in with chords, and at the exact same time he plays lead by making a high note ring out while using very unorthodox chord positions. He has a massive thumb, which he uses like an additional finger, so his hand positions are very unconventional for every chord.

"... He told me once that his whang [tremolo] bar was customized on all of his guitars, so he could pull it back much farther than a whole step. He wanted to be able to lower it three steps."

Bloomfield was surprised to find that Jimi was extremely interested in form. In a few seconds of playing Jimi could give him an idea of the entire structure. "That's why he liked rhythm guitar playing so much—the rhythm guitar could lay out the structure for the whole song." Jimi would always say, "This is a world of lead guitar players, but the most essential thing to learn is the time, the rhythm."

Bloomfield laughed, "He once told me he wanted to burn Clapton to death because he didn't play rhythm."

Backstage at the Fillmore East. Sly Stone guffawing his hacksaw laugh. Wearing a glossy white Gabriel suit, with a brief, winglike cape across the shoulders. The brothers in the band wearing gorgeous Las Vegas showgirl wigs. Little Sister with a blond Brigitte Bardot model, Larry Graham with a Jane Russell model, and Cynthia, the big round saucy trumpet player, with her California Afro *au naturel*. Sly's natural rose a foot above his forehead in an elongated pompadour. They were ready to go. Sly was crazy.

Sly opened the show. He was out to kill from the git.

In a flash the Fillmore East is consumed with the baddest, asskickingest, hard-bopping soul music in America. Larry Graham's bass walking seven-league boots on everyone's head. Freddie, Sly's brother, next to Larry on rhythm electric guitar. Both of them gutbucking walking kicking boogeying proscenium steps. Cynthia, in the horn section, bending her sweet red lips to the soul trumpet, calling down Jericho. Calling down Sly Stone in his Gabriel whitecaped white-on-white satin suit. Sly getting down on his Beulah Baptist holiness organ, counterpointing the guitar between the peak licks of the punctuating horns.

Sly *physically* rocks the Fillmore. It is like a battleship in rocking and rolling waters. This Oakland mack man has all his pieces instrumented as rhythm. All sounds are in motion—mixed down to equal value under Sly's exhorting lyrics.

Sly didn't sing "Try a Little Tenderness" like Otis Redding, although it was Redding's arrangement. It was more like a musical shrine to Redding, like a jazz funeral, celebrating Redding's spirit in song. Redding had perished in a plane crash shortly after the Monterey Pop Festival. Sly didn't sing it exactly as *he* would have, either. He merged his voice with Redding's version, as if Otis Redding were onstage singing with him. He moved in between Redding and his own version, and remained true to the original. Toward the crucial climax of "Tenderness"—that beautiful building up Redding did that made you burst in anticipation of the clashing woodwinds and Otis's plea—a screaming *"got to got to try and please her"*—Sly suspends "Tenderness" in a heart-sinking abyss. Sly holds the *"got to got to,"* slowly repeating it, and then staggers the phrase. His brothers join; the pendulum swings wider and wider and pretty soon the three brothers are into a time-suspended chant: *"got to got to now now now/got to got to now now now/got to got to now now now."* The chant continues and pretty soon you have ceased to hear the original words. You hear something else, something closer to the utter archetypal root of the words in the melody. And then after what seems like an eternity, a trip at the speed of light over conti-

nents and centuries, they end "Tenderness" in the resounding glory
of Otis. The light-show screen's purple orbs merging and exploding
into an immense twilight blue. Then Sly breaks into a fire-and-
brimstone rhythm and then as quickly into the hambone (the
thump of hand and chest and the slap of the palm on the thigh, dual
rhythms in hump position). They do it to it. Then they jump into
traditional Apollo dance steps and the freight train is off once more.

Jimi loved to play against a group as heavy as Sly and his band.
Second on a two-bill show, Hendrix comes out and wastes no time.
A signal twinkles in the distance, coming faster and faster, rushing
atonal and crashing notes. Billows of molten metal wafting exhaust
into purple plumes of funk—"Foxy Lady." And Jimi is off burning
from the onset, Mitch and Noel forming a flying *V.*

Hendrix assaults the mind, sublimating horrible noises of the
city. Subways busting through violent tunnels, exploding Mack
trucks, jet exhaust fumes, buses; he turns the fascist sounds of energy exploitation into a beautiful music with a pyramid base of
urban blues guitar. B. B. King's looney obbligato screams, Blind
Lemon Jefferson's beautiful justice of country space, and Jimmy
Reed's diddy-bop beats; Jimi exalts them all into a personal mastery
of primordial sound itself, beyond ken and imagination. We hear
spaceships landing in the heavy atmospheric gases of fantastic
planets, we hear giant engines changing gears, we hear massive tur-
bines that run cities, Frankenstein life-giving electric-shock blasts,
jets taking off and exploding into melody. We hear the thunder of
Volton, Shango, and Shiva mixed with the ethereal melodies of our
cosmic sphere, evanescent and eternal.

Jimi began having trouble with his amps. They were great in the
upper registers and shit in the lower ranges. He was trying to make
like his constant going back and forth to the controls of the amps
was a part of his choreo-delivery by going into a split after each visit
to the amps. His exhortations to Gerry Stickells, who stood help-
lessly behind the amps, were to no avail. Every time he tried to get
into a fusion of metals, fuzz, and feedback the system would falter.
He threw his white Stratocaster over his shoulder and plugged it
through his legs, getting a roar from the crowd. But he could not play
what he wanted. He began to feel burned. He began to make a few
offhand comments to the crowd, presaging the moment when he
would have to tell them he could not go on due to equipment fail-
ure. Then he thought of a song he could play that would cool out
the final disappointment. "Gloria." It had little of his heavy metal
pyrotechnics. Instead he grooved in upper registers on the rhythm
within the ensemble.

Jimi, splendid in the lights, bumping and a-grinding to "G-L-O-R-I-A." Every move displaying total mastery over both the instrument and his body. The sound surging panning back and forth in huge continuous waves of vibration. Holding everything together and taking it into another realm blended into a heavy bliss within the awe. G-L-O-R-I-A . . .

Jimi plays three guitar parts simultaneously: long sustained chords, picking rhythm in electrostatic harmony, and doodling tips of fire between it all. The sound is unbelievable. You can't get enough. It's too much. You want more. You can't stand it. Sound overdriving the conscious mind and reaching right through to your subliminal centers. And then Jimi is down on his haunches weaving and bobbing like a limbo dancer to the beat and in double time. He holds the guitar up with one hand—it plays by itself.

Jimi set to work on his next album. He moved into a suite at the Drake Hotel, seventeen floors above its plush velvet lobby. He began to get into the New York City social scene by bringing himself up-to-date on the fly ladies.

Devon was on the scene. They both knew they would be getting together soon, although just when and where and how still had to be worked out. Linda Eastman showed up at the Record Plant, where he was laying some preliminary tracks for his new album. She took many photos and got them back very quickly for him to see. They were beautiful flicks. She has a relaxed, offhand manner, and with her charming blond good looks, she helped the flow of energy move naturally and got good pictures at the same time. And she was not hung up about ten or twenty dollars. She was very cool about bread. She came from a wealthy family.

Steve Paul's Scene Club was happening, so were the Hippopotamus and the Salvation discos, but while Jimi was hanging out, he had the album on his mind, too. Mike Jeffery and Chas Chandler were giving him static about costs. Studio time was more expensive in the States. They would have preferred shorter hours in the Record Plant, but Jimi was seriously thinking of booking it around the clock, twenty-four hours a day. He could feel that he and Chas were drifting apart. Chas was engaged to be married and wanted to complete their business and return home. But for Jimi, he *was* home. He could see that Mitch and Noel were impatient to return to England as well. They had not been scheduled to return until the fall of 1968 anyway, but the scene was still strange to them. They did not necessarily want to groove on the scene. Their attitude was largely one of workers out to do a job. Noel had taken an inexpensive three-room suite in the nondescript but clean Penn Hotel across the street from Madison Square Garden on West Thirty-fourth Street. He was determined to save his money. He wrote down everything he spent—down to the dime, the penny. He wrote in a diary religiously. Mitch was a bit looser. He was having a better time, but he too was lonely for England.

Gradually Jimi took more control of the sessions. Chas felt left out, especially since he figured Jimi was wasting a lot of valuable studio time on maddening details. Jimi took take after take of seemingly irrelevant phrases and passages—even on the basic tracks. He would sit down and piece together a raggedy wah-wah pedal for hours, even though studio time cost more than a hundred dollars an hour. Mitch and Noel took to napping while they waited for Jimi. They even took to laying up with their girlfriends while they waited. Jimi would scrap seemingly perfect tracks and takes right at the point when they seemed completed. They all began getting pissed with each other.

More and more hangers-on appeared at the sessions. They effectively buffered Jimi from Mitch, Noel, Chas, and even Mike Jeffery. Jimi seemed to give a lot of control of the scene to Devon. She became an unofficial watchdog of the sessions. She would order people out when Jimi wanted the scene cleared. She would say who could stay and who could not. Her attitude was perfectly suited to the task. She seemed to enjoy her powers over the scene-makers. Tall, sassy, and well put together, she also had the street shit together and was known to tote a razor—*and use it*. She was not afraid of incurring the wrath of *anyone*—even Jimi. Yet he felt that her presence and seeming omnipotence were necessary to his scene. It was obvious he needed help in the handling of many mundane tasks, and Devon was glad to do it. When he decided he wanted to get an apartment, she got right on it. It did not take much persuasion to have her put on the payroll as a kind of girl Friday to Jimi. She could check out pads and once they got one she could keep it together for Jimi while he took care of business.

Jimi let Devon handle more and more of his affairs. She became essential to the "office" as well. Relations began to break down between Jimi and his management. Chas Chandler was ready to split any day, and Jeffery was in a difficult position. Devon made no bones about serving as liaison between the two factions. Jimi did not want to hear it. All he wanted to do was make the most beautiful album imaginable.

Opposite: Devon   © BARON WOLMAN

In her platforms Devon was taller than Jimi. Beautiful, but sometimes ugly within the throes of junk, but always charming. With a type of cunning akin to Jimi's. Never at a loss. She had the most unique set of problems imaginable. Able to be just about any way she wanted to be, she could charm and recharm with equal ease. Not one to be put off, she could usually get at any time of the night what no one else could. Be it smack, coke, or a second girl for a sexual *trois*, she could deliver. Cunning like a streetwalker, pulling chicks like a pimp, she could satisfy the mama's boy and the sadomasochistic urge. Devon.

Devon, a street urchin who evolved from Milwaukee. Hick in the Big Town getting over by wits and charm—the artist. Devon's art was the con with a fifty-fifty chance of delivery. Yet to her, the superwoman of the groupies, Jimi was a part of her scheme. From Duane Allman to Mick Jagger to Miles Davis to Quincy Jones, she knew the heaviest people in music and could deal the heavy shit. Survival for a beautiful woman with no special talents did not come easy. Even rich men or men with money could assume that this elegant, luscious woman had no need of bread, and it was not her game to project those needs. Yet the utter necessities of life merged with the vicious drug habit she had—inseparable from her cool and her energy—made her subject at times to quite unwomanly conduct.

Quincy Jones met her in Vegas, years ago in the early sixties when he worked for Sinatra. A fifteen-year-old runaway who looked like twenty-five, full of street hip and hustle, Devon was nevertheless a poor, confused, homeless girl who had not had time to grow up. A fifteen-year-old girl may be able to hustle successfully in the streets, but she is not as hip as the older woman who *has* grown up. For Devon, tricking in the trick capital of the world often meant getting ripped off. Her lack of savvy meant that she could have a few thousand dollars in her hand one night and be without cash or a place to stay the next. Quincy took her under his wing, adopted her as his cousin, and took her on to Los Angeles, where at least she had a place and people she could relate to as a person without the exploitation of Las Vegas.

In the realm of the glamorous but hip beauties of the rock world, Devon became a counterpart of Hendrix.

As Jimi constantly practiced, whether simply jamming, writing, or sitting up in bed with the acoustic singing the old blues he loved, Devon practiced her craft as well, constantly maintaining her mastery of the groupie syndrome. This took a similar degree of energy and devotion, as did the constant competition of beauty and deliverance. Trickery became one of her catchwords. Even after a ripoff, or burn, she could, unlike most other beauties of the realm, reconcile even the hardest minds to her ways and make them like it—almost. She had a way that few could reject of copping out when caught red-handed at some shit. Haughty and proud even if one were to catch her, a smile, a shrug, a twinkle of the eye, and perhaps a quick jive story or a little loving were usually enough.

Jimi dug Monique as soon as he met her. Devon introduced them. Devon knew what Jimi liked and she also knew that pulling a woman like Monique for Jimi would cement their relationship even more. Monique was very much like Jimi, especially the side of him that was the fun-loving get high and ball and laugh and look at everything like a cosmic good time side. In so many of Monique's ways he saw himself.

Monique, long white-brown slender joyous total ease in smile, and very much like Jimi. Same five-eleven height, always thin, but the kind of thin that is lithe yet soft and cuddly. A sensuous space between her even white teeth that always range between a kittenish smile and a full-faced Cheshire cat grin. Of Moroccan-Jewish ancestry. Monique loved the good times. She loved Jimi, perhaps more than anyone else, in the romantic way.

Although she had been in the States for some time, her French accent was still very much there. It gave away her lack of many English words that dealt with complexities. But in the delights of the senses and the flesh she was expert.

A perfect person to have fun with. Laughter spilling from her lips as if she were a bubbling fountain of joy. She exuded a champagne high at all times. Before you knew her or even talked to her you would be impressed with her carriage; tall, graceful, and elegant, she moved in the unhurried pace of one who does not have a job to appear at. In fact, she gave the impression that she lived life totally on her own terms and did not *really* have to be anywhere at any time. Her smile was warm, at ease, and sensual. Not in the sexpot way, but just easy and warm, saying everything can happen in its own time. The affable tilt of head when talking, her musical voice, light and soprano, making you like her immediately, making you want to be pleasant around her, to bask in her smile.

Always there, Monique's smile is her trademark. And if perhaps she knows you better it might be a greeting or a kiss, a long luminous tongue in your mouth, directly between your lips parted in surprise. Followed perhaps by a one and one of coke, or whatever was being enjoyed—perhaps some excellent smoke.

A gourmet, she strikes one as always enjoying the best and seeing really no other reason for anything else. She eats like a bird and drinks lightly. She loves music, getting high, and making love the most.

Monique was a stranger to America. An outsider. She had to struggle to understand the ways. Hendrix, black, introverted, from Seattle, then the South, then Harlem, the Village, and then London, never really felt American in the strict sense. Dislocated and estranged, he found that Monique's view of the newness and wonder of this place was close to his outsider's awe. Although Jimi Hendrix was famous when he returned to America in the middle of 1968, he was also a stranger. He would live in the Village, close to the pulse of the Empire City. He would live in the heart of the city, and it was Monique more than Devon who made him feel at home.

Devon had just gotten Jimi his pad and was there to help him, but they were not yet as tight as they would be later. He stayed with Monique before Devon found his apartment. But Monique was married, and her husband, who was away, would return. Jimi had to find a place of his own. So he moved up the street a couple of blocks on Twelfth Street off University Place. Monique explained to Jimi that she was intent upon maintaining her relationship with her husband but that she could come there every day and be with him a great deal of the time. She knew marriage and a home with Jimi was out of the question, but she would be with him and help him as best she could under the circumstances.

But Hendrix did not want to leave her home. He wanted her with him. The compromise they reached was more a part of their love and mutual understanding. Neither Jimi nor Monique could make a concrete and long-standing commitment. Monique was fun-loving and gay, but she was also as shrewd and survival-oriented as her North African ancestors.

So Hendrix moved to Twelfth Street and Monique came every day and decorated his pad in Neo-Moroccan. They acted like newlyweds, shopping for decorations and furnishings, going over lists, and talking with salesmen.

Hendrix was greatly insecure upon arriving back in America. Monique's love and quiet ease and sense of peace gave him confidence. She was a woman who knew how to do for a man. Another man's wife—no matter—Hendrix needed her very much, and they both realized it and acted upon it. The other person who knew what he needed was Devon, and while she was not exactly *in* at that time, she would make the moves, the calls to Monique to get her to come over, as well as occasional calls to others; but for now it was

Monique. Jimi soon found Devon essential to his life, even if only to make sure that Monique could be with him without blowing her life with her husband.

She knew sensuality as he knew guitar. Her long brown sun-blonding hair swirled as languorous as her long limbs and arms. She could curl up or have him curl into her with ease, as if it were the most natural thing in the world. Her brown steady eyes staring directly into his, her faint freckles, the lilt of her playful voice, the way she had of ducking her head and listening intently to what he was trying to say. And with music, he could feel it through her, he could listen with her and be sure she was listening and responding as he was, not only because she was with him, but also because she loved music. She had her own. She was no groupie. She was in total control of her life, at ease with life; her easy elegance gave him confidence on the street or inside the house when they were alone.

She designed clothes for him with special colors and fabrics, lots of velours and crushed velvet, soft cloths in magentas, deep blues going into purple, turquoise, starked-out reds that related to him astrologically and musically.

Monique spent a lot of time in a dress shop on the Lower East Side that was owned by two friends of hers: Colette Mimram and Stella Douglas. Jimi would sit in the shop at 321 East Ninth Street with Monique, Colette, and Stella while they did their thing with clothes. Jimi would even play salesman, blowing a customer's mind by coming out from behind the curtain that separated the back from the front and telling them how good they looked in something. It was a joke, but it was good, too. People bought things and he was glad because he wanted the dress shop to succeed. Sometimes he bought an item for a customer as a spontaneous gift. He also bought a lot of things for himself. He loved Monique and her friends.

Monique, Colette, and Stella would turn him on to expensive restaurants, good things to eat, how to order, and how to pronounce the foreign words to the waiter.

Monique decorated his apartment like she decorated him, in bluesy space colors, canopies billowing out, exotic East African fabrics and spreads, pillows spread on the floors. You had to really get down and be comfortable because there was no perching on the edge of chairs. A get-down pad. You really had to get down to enjoy Jimi's home, because if you were uptight and upright you would have to leave; there would be no place for you.

Monique, Colette, and Stella turned him on to paintings—especially the paintings of Mati, whom Colette often posed for. Mati's spaced landscapes, often with intricate designs that turned out to be people making love in all kinds of erotic positions out of the *Kama Sutra*, if you looked closely. Monique encouraged Jimi to look closer at things and appreciate finer things with the same sensibility he had for music. And he wanted that and she gave it in the laid-back sensuous easy way she gave everything.

Jimi soon found the Scene Club irresistible. In London there were many hip clubs to hang out in, and they were always changing, but in New York City there was only one—the Scene Club. Fans did not hassle you there. It was dark and intimate, almost labyrinthine, yet you could go there and party, or play and just sit alone and drink, and no one restrained you either way. And most important of all was that he could *play* there. He could jam any time he wanted to. *He could woodshed right in the middle of New York City.*

The Scene Club was like a miniforum model for every arena he would ever play. The shouting stark frenzy of the close room is what he brought with him to every stage around the world. It was always the small intimate room he was really playing to. The thousand and one nights of playing long into the Scene Club's night. When the chairs would finally be upside down upon the tiny tables. When Steve Paul himself would finally have to pull the plug, while Jimi alone in his universe would be totally unaware of the hour or of the devotees and workers who patiently waited within the exhilaration of his sound.

At the Scene, Jimi would completely let himself go—playing all he knew and didn't know, going beyond sharing—playing all. Trying to get it *all* out.

Jimi slowly and surely got to be good friends with Willie Chambers and Ray Warner of the Chambers Brothers. Sometimes it was difficult to tell the five brothers and cousins apart. They were all tall and dark with brilliant eyes. They all wore black brims in the country way, with the crown head full and the brim riding low. Willie and Ray and then Joe and Julius and silent George all made Jimi an honorary Chambers Brother. They were from Mississippi and had a beautiful rural simplicity. They still talked in southern accents, although they worked hard to round out their *r*'s by speaking as crisply thin-lipped as possible. But when they got excited they dropped right back into their back-home raps. Their career in music began when they were teen-aged gospel singers, out of the black church in the early sixties. Later they found work in "folk" scenes, coffeehouses and at civil rights affairs. Folk singer Barbara Dane did an album with them. Then they abandoned both gospel and folk at the same time and went straight into hard blues/rock. The Chambers Brothers then went to L.A. and became regular musicians on the Shindig national TV music show. After that they signed with Columbia Records—John Hammond was their producer. Their "Time Has Come Today" was a hit single.

Jimi was closest to Ray Warner. They got to talking about the meaning of "the axis" and went on with it for hours, days, weeks. Ray Warner was well-read and planned to go back to college to complete the small amount of time he had left for his degree. A psychology major with broad intellectual interests, he found through talking with Jimi that the strange title of Jimi's second album, *Axis: Bold as Love*, had far greater significance than he had imagined. Jimi had said once:

I just thought about the title. There might be a meaning behind the whole thing: the axis of the Earth turns around and changes the face of the world and completely different civilizations come about or another age comes about. In other words, it changes the face of the Earth and it only takes about one-quarter of a day. Well, the same with love. If a cat falls in love or a girl falls in love, it might change his whole complete scene. *Axis: Bold as Love* . . . 1-2-3, rock around the clock.

Ray was curious as to what else was there. He was not satisfied that it was as offhand and simple as all that.

Yet when he and Jimi got down and rapped seriously about it he found that Jimi's whole conversation was full of things that sounded one way yet meant something else. It was a trip just to hear the normally shy and retiring Jimi open up and really rap about where he was at. He had other speech trips. He would talk backward, saying something was *bad* when he meant it was good, together. He would say something that sounded completely simple and normal, but by nodding his head, winking his eye, or slightly altering the sound of a word, give it a completely different meaning. What Ray finally deduced from talking with Jimi many times was that the man had a concept that boggled Ray's mind because it encompassed so much.

Jimi's concept of the axis was hooked up like a freeway from Earth to space to infinity. The axis was like a bridge or crossing over a threshold from one reality to a deeper reality, or from one dimension to another. He looked upon the Earth as a single creature. Jimi

wanted to help the whole world, the entire universe. The wars and
the bloodshed were terrible to behold—the wounds and the swords
and the poverty. But as the Earth turned on its axis, the people
turned on to the music; even the image of a record on a turntable
was a representation of the axis. It was like the axis itself was a
living form of energy music, a mass of love and creativity all rolled
up into one thing that came out positive. The axis was like a step-
ping-stone to a greater understanding.

He was trying to say that he could take you to a holy place without even moving your body—and he wanted to do that. It was not
about LSD or any hallucinogenic—he was the drug, he was the high.
He saw music in the sky. He saw his music as a living life form that
had the potential to give people a direct feeling, a direct understanding—that would open their eyes to cosmic powers by simply directly experiencing his music. He had a way to work that was going
to reach across the nation. And any extraterrestrial beings out there
would have to pick up on it. It was a heavy communication thing.
Jimi knew he could not tell a whole lot of people about where his
head was at and what he wanted to do, but he could give little hints
in interviews and some of it in the songs and all of it to a few. Ray
Warner began getting the distinct feeling that Jimi Hendrix was not
of this Earth.

Jimi got into a heavy hanging-out thing. He had been working
steadily for nearly two years straight. Recording in New York was
great. For one, recording freed him from touring. Although Chas was
still balking because he felt Jimi was taking too much time, Jimi
was enjoying the recording of an album for a change. Not like the
rush jobs on the first and second albums, but a relaxed yet intense
run of sessions, which also allowed him time to reflect on what was
happening in the music and to do something he had always wanted
to do: compose an extended piece. And while he was recording he
had the run of Manhattan as well. Indeed, it was like a vacation.

He had his buddies who all hung out at the Scene, or the Salvation
or the Hippopotamus, and he always had some fine ladies up front or
on the side. He had the best recording studio on the face of the Earth
in the Record Plant, and several pads besides his official residence
where he could disappear to. It was a perfect setup.

He got really tight with Hugh Masekela, who was still tripping
behind his hit "Grazing in the Grass." It was the kind of hit everyone hoped for. A monster that stayed up in the charts for months.
Hugh was enjoying it to the hilt. Flying back and forth between L.A.

and New York, Hugh was into a heavy party scene. Sometimes he would stop what he was doing for a moment and say, "You know, I haven't slept for months!"

One day some chick from *New York* magazine talked her way into his suite at the Drake Hotel and then rushed into his bedroom and began taking pictures of him as he awoke from the commotion. Jimi was happy to find that she was a good-looking chick. They had a nice time talking and laughing and getting high. Next, Eric Barrett, the new road manager, came in very upset. Bad news. The equipment truck had been stolen. He looked like he expected his head to be cut off. Jimi was more philosophical. New York City was at least notorious compared to London. Eric Barrett offered to go looking for it himself. He had already contacted the police, but their nonchalance gave him the impression that they had more important things to do. Eric rushed out frantic. Jimi thought for a while and then called Manny's on West Forty-eighth Street.

Jimi had dealt with Manny's Musical Instruments and Accessories store since he had come to New York City to live in 1964. The store was a family business. The elder Manny had given way to his son Henry after thirty years at the helm. Jimi had established an open account and would come in once a week to try out all the new instruments, distortion devices, and accessories. Usually he would take all of them home. Every other week Jimi would buy three or four guitars. He could count on Henry to deliver several guitars to him by car, or to ship the necessary stock ahead for a worldwide tour. Henry was fascinated by Jimi. Henry knew that any new little "toy" or sound effect he got ahold of would be bought by Jimi on the spot.

The Fender Stratocaster, like its predecessor, the Telecaster, was designed by Leo Fender to be easy to build, play, and service. Their fretboard was standardized for accuracy down to a thousandth of an inch, the very best the tool-and-die shops could do. The cutaway body made it easy to play all twenty-one frets; its solid body made the Fender electric guitar accessible to the most modern of technology. Up until the advent of the Fender Telecaster in 1948 electric guitars (which had been inspired by the popularity of Hawaiian steel guitar music of the thirties and then through country-and-western music and finally popular music) were acoustic hollow-bodied instruments with pickups for amplification. Leo Fender introduced the solid-body Telecaster in 1948. Its sounds were pure-toned and accurate and were loud enough to drown out an entire orchestra.

Jimi films Janis Joplin and the Fugs at Winterland, 1968
© 1981 JIM MARSHALL

The feedback that had plagued the hollow-bodied electric guitars was virtually eliminated by the Telecaster and subsequent Stratocaster. Leo Fender had started on his quest for the perfect electric guitar by concentrating on the pickup. The pickups deliver the sound of the guitar through the amplifiers and loudspeakers by electromagnetism. The pickups are actually magnets or several magnets wound with coils of superthin wire. The guitar strings are slightly magnetized and when they are plucked they vibrate through the magnetic field, making the current pulse through the coils and on through the amps and speakers as sound.

The designed serviceability of the Stratocaster made it easy for Jimi to modify the instrument for his own use. First he would bend the tremolo bar by hand for several hours to get it to go down three steps, instead of the customary one, and also to get it near enough to the body so he could tap individual strings and raise and lower their pitch without it being an obvious manipulation, the proximity making it able to be done quickly. Also, because of the tremolo bar proximity to the other tone controls, he could play with all of them at once while whanging the tremolo bar at the same time. Sometimes he removed the back panel so the strings would be accessible from the back. It would achieve another kind of sound. This also enabled Gerry Stickells, his roadie, to be able to change the strings onstage while he continued to play. Jimi made his own adjustments at the bridge and the pickups. The adjustable solo-lead pickup had a snap-on cover that housed three elevated screws that enabled Jimi to balance the tone; this was connected to the lever switch, which had three set positions. Similarly, the rhythm pickup was adjustable by removing the pick-guard panel and working the elevated screws. The micro-adjustable bridge was beneath the snap-on cover. Three longitudinal screws adjusted string length for proper toning and six elevated screws adjusted the height of each string, therefore enabling Jimi to get loose action on the bass strings for a deeper twang, and fast, close-to-the-neck action on the treble strings. Jimi varied the selection of his strings for his particular sound. He used very heavy strings on the bottom, medium gauges on his A and D, a Hawaiian G string, a light-gauge B string, and a superlight E string. The head of the Strat was styled with all the tuning pegs on one side of the neck, which made it very easy to tune the guitar even while actually playing. A neckplate was anchored by tempered steel. This extrasturdy construction made it possible for Jimi to bend the rosewood or maplewood neck of his Stratocasters without breaking them. That way he was able to get more unique sounds. Since Jimi made sure the tremolo bar was bent down as close as possible to the control knobs, he could also manipulate the tone-control knob—which functioned as a lead pickup modifier when the lever switch was in the lead position at the same time. The lever switch had two other positions: a middle position for straight rhythm work and a forward position for deep soft rhythm. The volume-control knob was between the two; Jimi kept it at full volume 10 at all times. Roger "The Valve" Mayer rewired all of Jimi's guitars and built him an individual and fantastic fuzz tone.

In modifying his guitars, Jimi concentrated on the pickups. He also re-coiled them to get a personal sound and range. They were the tiny poles of the "axis" that propelled his sound and made his control of feedback possible.

It seemed that Jimi was trying to set an endurance record for jamming. In June of 1968 he and Jeff Beck got in two good jam sessions at the Scene. The first was with Eric Clapton also—three incredible guitars. The patrons couldn't believe it. Soon after that

Jimi and the Jeff Beck group played a benefit at the Scene for Reality House, a drug rehabilitation center. Jimi came out and played "Foxy Lady" and then got behind Beck on bass and let him blow his brains out, while he covered the bottom territory with his lightning-fast fingers.

Jimi played with the McCoys, challenging young cocky guitarist Rick Derringer. Then Derringer got on bass while the Chambers Brothers sang and Buddy Miles played drums. Jimi played with Jim Morrison and Harvey Brooks and Willie Chambers at the Scene. Jim Morrison got so excited he got down and started kissing Harvey Brooks's feet. Then Mick Taylor of the Stones took over on drums, and Johnny Winters plugged in his guitar, and they played a strange version of "Red House" and an ultrafast version of "Sunshine of Your Love."

Jimi sat in with Muddy Waters at the Cafe Au Go Go and it was beautiful. Jimi sat in with Howling Wolf at the Scene but "The Wolf" put him down and really made him feel bad.

Jimi and Buddy Miles started going around jamming together at different places. They would scat Albert King solos.

Jimi and Johnny Winters got together on a Guitar Slim tune— "The Things We Used to Do"—Winters playing slide and Jimi playing lead and singing. They went right down to the Record Plant and taped it.

Finally, Jimi got a chance to play with the entire Chambers Brothers group at the Electric Circus. Of course, they did "Time," their big hit. Jimi was glad and eager for that because the song had incredible spaces for his lead, since Willie (their only regular guitar) played only rhythm all the way through.

Jimi dug hanging out with the Chambers Brothers. They were a big family and they accepted him as another one of their brothers. Willie Chambers *looked* like a guitar.

Once they were all at the Scene Club playing a benefit for the Biafra war victims. During a break, some of the people from the audience had gone out to get a breath of air and got busted in the parking lot. Jimi was the first guy to jump in his Stingray and go down to the police station to bail the brothers out.

Another time Jimi and Willie and Ron Hobbs, bass player for Johnny Winters, rode around New York City for hours to score some grass. They had about eight chicks back at the apartment. When they finally copped and returned to the apartment, Jimi sat up there and put on a show. He told jokes, did his Harlem queen bit—he was as loose as a goose. This was a side of him Willie had never seen before. Then Willie realized that although he had known Jimi for years they had always encountered each other before hundreds of people or backstage at a gig, but never anywhere approaching one to one. He had always thought Hendrix was shy. He was, with lots of people around. But with a few friends in the room he was truly one of the fellas.

People would always be trying to get Jimi stoned. They *assumed* he wanted to be loaded all the time. Willie and Jimi were in a bar once and someone came up and put something in Jimi's drink. Willie was astounded. They just assumed that Jimi would want to get high—and most likely he did not. A lot of people thought it was real funny to do that with acid. Willie would hear people saying that Jimi shot LSD into his temple, into the side of his head.

Jimi enjoyed recreational drugs, but not all the time. What he always wanted to do was play. He would come into the Scene at midnight or so, and at five o'clock in the morning they would try to drag him off the stage. Steve Paul would say, "Please quit, quit—I'm going to get a summons."

Sometimes Jimi and Joe Chambers would just sit at a table drinking without saying anything. Jimi had several places where he stayed. Sometimes it was not cool to go to one place, so he had others to go to. He had a place in the Village that Devon kept for him and a "business" suite at the Drake Hotel. Sometimes he kept a room in the Howard Johnson Motor Lodge on 53rd Street and Eighth Avenue near the Scene. He had a place in the Bronx, too. Plus a couple of others that nobody knew about. All of his pads had lovely young ladies taking care of them. They would mend his clothes and sew special things. Jimi was not at all possessive. The girls were free to see who they liked. Sometimes Willie Chambers or Hugh Masekela would be seeing the same lady at the same time. One of the ladies gave Willie a turquoise ring to wear that belonged to Jimi. When Willie became concerned that Jimi might object, she said that it was cool but if Jimi wanted it back she would just ask Willie for it.

Offstage, among his employees and ever-broadening entourage, Jimi was a strange, retiring, self-effacing fellow. Not about to let fame turn his head, it seemed as if he were trained and groomed for humility from birth. Able to see through situations involving undue adulation and parasitic dependency, he would still not say anything, not rock the boat. He would not let it bother him at the moment, but he seemed to store it up and then release it all onstage where Jimi was completely transformed. All the pent-up violence, frustrations, and personal harassments were sublimated into the music.

And the audience, his fans, the lovers of his music, would come to see him with pretty much the same feelings pent up inside of them. He would provide them with their release as well as his own.

But there were other ways in which he got release. He loved the pretty young ladies who followed him around. His pad, which had become a curse to his privacy, was at the same time a blessing for his great love appetite. He would come home to find a bevy of ladies lying all over the pad and in his bedroom a special one naked with her legs open upon the bed.

Hugh Masekela would often come by looking for Jimi and find instead a houseful of chicks. Many times Hugh just came looking for chicks knowing that Jimi's pad was a sure place to find them. One night he came by to find Jimi conducting his special orchestra, each chick in the place had some kind of instrument (mainly elementary percussion), and Jimi on guitar conducting them in a special concerto.

With all the people in his life, the only place Jimi could be alone and not hassled was on stage or in the recording studio. Many nights he roamed through Manhattan, eventually winding up at a studio. One night he recorded "Midnight," a tune that reflects his nocturnal quest. "Midnight," one of the rare instrumental recordings of Hendrix, has a staggered shuffle beat that remains the same throughout the entire piece. Mitch's box shuffle snare is in the time dimension of midnight. Jimi begins by playing the bass line, the only sound. Climbing three steps quickly and then falling deep into a slow-motion funk abyss, Jimi distorting fuzz, delays a rag in syncopated 4/4 time. The bass, matching every shuffle/skiffle of the drums, takes off behind Jimi. A stately city journey. In the city most are asleep when he is awake. His day begins in full force around midnight. Arising when the sun is down at twilight, freaky spirit thrills those who live on the other side of time. "Midnight," the beginning of the day. The midnight creatures glowing resplendent through the dark nights. The midnight cruise illuminated by treble beacons and electric fire fuzz, connecting souls through the quiet caverns of midnight. To the sound-cushioned rooms where music blasts to the midnight musicians playing thousands of gigs, recording thousands of tunes, all over Earth. Up in the sky at midnight, wild stars visible by thousands and the moon reflecting sounds. A soul satellite beaming magnetic messages to the heads in midnight nirvana. Searching crosstown, the rhythm changes at the bridge. Jimi walks his bass as he transfers lightning-fast squalls to treble tremolo gliding through the night. In love upon the midnight tides, the waters and the flow of moist mucous membranes, the flush flow of fluids undammed flowing into screams of joy. A choir of soprano orgasms and unconscious atonal winds breaking bonds. A chord breaking open into three shards of feedback streaking across the sky in a flying *V*. The overtone of the middle note departs upward from the rest, and then all three of the notes revolve into a pure synthesizer signal. Sliding along the back of the neck in a beautiful moaning glide into a yelp, the guitar says "OH WOW" just like a girl and then back to the life of the night as the theme returns. Jimi plays his sitarlike trademark of writhing vibrato sweeping into lissome grace figures that are then driven to the sky. And then suddenly the sound blossoms into broken feedback and a lonely aloft figure disappears beyond the sky.

"Midnight" was recorded during the period in which Hendrix was completing work on the *Electric Ladyland* album. But it was not included on the album. Hendrix was interviewed as he neared the completion of the album:

When I was upstairs while the grown-ups had parties listening to Muddy Waters, Elmore James, Howlin' Wolf, and Ray Charles, I'd sneak down after and eat potato chips and smoke butts. That sound was really—not evil—just a thick sound.

Guitar is the basic thing for me, voice is just another way of getting across what I'm doing musically. It's hard for me to think in terms of blues anymore—so many groups are riding the blues bandwagon, blues groups today that might be classic groups tomorrow. The blues are easy to play but not to feel. The background of our music is a spiritual-blues thing. Blues is a part of America.

We're making our music into electric church music—a new kind of Bible, not like in a hotel, but a Bible you carry in your hearts, one that will give you a physical feeling. We try to make our music so loose and hard-hitting so that it hits your soul hard enough to make it open. It's like shock therapy or a can opener. Rock is technically blues-based. Rock is like a young dragon until the establishment gets hold of it and turns it into a cabaret act with the big voice and the patent-leather shoes and the patent-leather hair.

Lots of young people now feel they're not getting a fair deal, so they revert to something loud or harsh, almost verging on violence; if they didn't go to a concert they might be going to a riot. They are young; the establishment hasn't put them in a cage yet. Their music hasn't been put in a cage yet. It's more than music. It's like church, like a foundation for the lost or potentially lost. That's why the kids don't mind when you take fifteen minutes setting up for a concert. It's like watching something being born. The guys come out and set up instruments; they turn their backs to the audience taking time to get ready. The kids like it. It's not the establishment. . . . They become like fathers to the music.

We're in our little cement beehives in this society. People let a lot of old-time laws rule them. The establishment has set up the Ten Commandments for us saying don't, don't, don't. Once you say "don't" you've made two points against yourself. Then all of a sudden kids come along with a different set of brain cells and the establishment doesn't know what to do. The walls are crumbling and the establishment doesn't want to let go. We're trying to save the kids, to create a buffer between young and old. Our music is shock therapy to help them realize a little more of what their goals should be.

Almost anyone who has the power to keep their minds open listens to our music. Black kids think the music is white now, which it isn't. The argument is not between black and white now. That's just another game the establishment set up to turn us against one another. But the black kids don't have a chance too much to listen—they're too busy trying to get their own selves together. We want them to realize that our music is just as spiritual as going to church.

The soul must rule, not money or drugs. If you can do your own thing, just do it properly. A guy can dig ditches and enjoy it. You should rule yourself and give God a chance. The drug scene came around and looked good for a while, but we found that was just another thing to get hung up on. . . . Definitely I'm trying to change the world. I'd love to! I'd like to have my own country—an oasis for the gypsy-minded people. My goal is to erase all boundaries from the world. You have to set some heavy goals to keep yourself going. As long as I know there are people out there who aren't fully together I can't withdraw to lesser goals.

If I quit making money I would still want to change the world. The money scene can turn you into a slave to the public, a zombie, a penguin. If I starve tomorrow it would just be another experience to me. I don't want to be so big that I'm a slave to the public. That's why people get so sad when someone dies. They haven't finished using him. They're selfish. . . .

I'm trying to keep my music from being prostituted. I just call it raw, spiritual music and it's up to the person himself to make what he wants of it. Singing is letting off a certain frustration that I'd have to get married and beat up my wife to do otherwise. . . . If our music were really an assault we wouldn't have an audience after the fourth or fifth gig.

The establishment is so uptight about sex that all it wants to do is make the groupies look bad. Any art has its group of female admirers (we call the groupies Band-Aids). They are just innocent little girls trying to do their thing. But the insecure man puts labels on them—suck your favorite star. They don't talk about the ones who bring flowers and then go home to their mothers . . . kids are wiser than grown-ups in some respects. If parents really want to love their kids they should be aware of their music. . . . Conflict comes when insecure older people overprotect their young.

The content of the old blues was singing about sex—problems with their old ladies—and booze. Now people are saying so much more with music; music is such an important thing now; people have to realize that.

A long black limo drives up the West Side Highway of Manhattan taking its time. The funk of the Hudson River breezes through the windows. A glistening ghostly white moon shimmers over the waters. The high cliffs of the Jersey Palisades take the land higher, dispersing the land into little homes, and tiny lighted streets that diminish into the spread of greater America.

Living and working in New York City like any other person. Fixing up your pad with a beautiful lady who you live with who loves you. Lying back in a long, soft, smooth ride with Devon watching the river. The sky and the moon go by. And she is tall like you and slender, not lanky. Her smooth black sheath curves across her long-limbed body. Long legs bumping against each other, so warm and so cozy.

Off the highway, through the streets, to the Scene. On the edge of Times Square. Out front, a big lighted entrance; inside are narrow rectangular panels leading up to a dim box office. You sweep past into a zigzag-shaped mazelike room with tiny tables and tiny-backed chairs. But up on the tiny stage, two feet off the floor, the music happens as it happens in all major cities in the Western world.

He wears a red velvet cape that swirls about him in the dim blue lights like a red molten forcefield charging the air: his aura.

And there is Fayne Pidgeon, sitting with the owner of the Record Plant, Gary Kellgran, and his sister Michelle. Jimi stumbles over chairs and tables. Devon flows regally behind. Fayne is laughing already. Her long smooth brown impeccably clear face with steady mysterious black eyes looks even more beautiful than Jimi remembered. Jimi sits in Fayne's lap. The perfect thing, as he well knows, to make her laugh uproariously as if he were tickling her. Gary and Michelle look on pleasantly as Devon moves into a check position.

Jimi fondles Fayne and does fast-talk ecstasies aimed at Gary and Michelle. Laughter rises all around the room; some because of him directly, some because of the delight everyone now feels for being here, for being alive, for being so fortunate to be with each other, to be there when Jimi comes in cutting up 'cause he's happy.

Fayne sparkles copper gems. She is loud-talking, high-laughing, happy street people. She looks total uptown, her up-sweeping pillared hair style with black locked curls illuminated against the dim air. Perfect sound system pumping rock. Devon is superelegant, her sleek black hair splaying out at the nape of her olive neck. She takes the scene in slowly, giving Gary a stroke, a slight dyke slur to Michelle, an appraisal of Fayne, who is starting to crack up all over again because Jimi is still in her lap. Then Devon checks out the adjacent tables. But she does not crane her neck; she will wait until she goes to the ladies' room to powder her nose and then she will really get a look at what's happening.

Jimi is back to Devon. He is explaining how he hasn't seen Fayne for over a year. Devon is vaguely interested. When she and Fayne have sufficient eye contact, Devon invites her to the ladies' room. This is a distinct invitation to some nice blow. Fayne is again delighted. Delights upon delights.

Devon leads the way. Weaving expertly through the narrow paths. Swooping down to say a few hellos, an occasional kiss. Fayne, much shorter even in heels, has to stop each time Devon stops, allowing enough room so she won't bump into her. Fayne is impressed. Devon moves with a measured ease and does not take too much time at any one table.

In the ladies' room Devon goes immediately for the coke. From a jeweled snuffbox case she solemnly and expertly offers Fayne a generous spoon, lifting it reverently to her nostril, as if Fayne's nose were the most beautiful part of her body. Another in the other nostril, then Devon gives herself a one and one. Devon takes her hits hastily, as if abhorring the delay, and then hands the entire case and spoon to Fayne for her to go for herself. A sign of healthy respect and comradeship. As the fine-ground powerful white powder connects with the mucous tissues of the sinuses they begin to talk. Devon says that Fayne looks like she knew Jimi well. Fayne laughs. "Yeah, I knew that nigger when he was uptown, just came from the South. I took him from some faggot in the Palm Café." Fayne laughs her constant chuckle, as if there were much more she could say. Then she goes on. "Did you see Gary's face when he sat in my lap? I nearly died, Jimi's always doing something like that. You never know what he is gonna do next."

"Yeah, we're fixing up our pad down on Twelfth Street in the Village," Devon said. "You got to come down and hang out, get loaded, and have dinner. We have a ball. You get enough? Here, for the road."

Devon led the way back, walking right into a befuddled Eric Clapton, who looked like he had been hanging outside waiting for Devon to emerge. Devon laughed and hugged him. He continued his befuddled puppy dog kind of spaciness, very English yet very much in a way like Jimi. Devon introduces him to Fayne. He acts silly and shy but sweet and serious, absurd in his slick American hippie clothes.

Devon sweeps him back to the table, allowing Fayne to go first. She brandishes him like a statue of war from a London minipark. Now she will have some fun tonight. Eric really goes for her. He acted as if he didn't understand his attraction, himself, as if he were drawn to her by a mysterious force. He and Jimi were so in awe of each other, so shy and respectful, so all-giving, that she would have free rein over the situation. She could fuck with Eric and fuck with Jimi and they would smile genially at each other and be ever so polite and reserved that she would want to scream and whoop with hilarious delight. Their only respite, their only refuge would be the stage where . . . well ain't that a bitch, where Jeff Beck stood ready to jam with the McCoys, who were set up and raring to go.

Fayne wound up coming home with Devon and Jimi and spending the night. The night's party lasted until the next day and then they crashed through the day. They awakened in twilight to eat, drink, and toot, and start the party again into the endless night. Put on your clothes and get into what happens, a fascination from moment to moment, for days. Fayne stayed for several weeks.

The Record Plant, situated very close to the Scene Club, was near enough to take a good night of jamming right to the recording studio with the energy and inspiration still high. It soon became necessary to rent the Record Plant around the clock. Regulars at the Scene became the audience for several jams that appear in their entirety on the *Electric Ladyland* album.

The entire vista of his sound accelerated at the Record Plant, as it had at first in the London studios. The Record Plant had the latest equipment, young engineers with good ears, and an older, more experienced engineer who knew what could be done and would work with Jimi on exploring new sounds. No more working night and day with two four-track machines just to layer the sound correctly. And it was great that Fayne was there; a solid crazy friend from the old days who was as excited as he amid all the debonair New Yorkers.

Long hours were spent in the studio working with the extensions of what could be done. Now there were eight tracks to work with, increasing the layers possible. And more sophisticated equalizers extended the tonality of the bass, especially on the low registers, without distorting, and allowing a rounded, deeper throb. Now he was able to use three or four mikes on the drums, thus getting more subtlety on the tom-toms, high hats, and cymbals, and getting a good kick from the foot-pedaled bass drum. And he still has several tracks for himself and the voices.

The night they recorded "Voodoo Chile" was a gas, with streams of people going back and forth between the Scene and the Record Plant. The recording simulated a live session, and the nearness of the Scene gave the set the freshness Jimi wanted.

"Voodoo Chile" captures the atmosphere of a funky nightclub within the music. The busy sounds of the crowd are mixed into the song as if public witness to a ceremony The ceremony, late-at-night partying, and secular blues are mixed down within a Voodoo creation tale—"Voodoo Chile!" There are shouts of pure joy, shouts of encouragement—"YEAH! *YEAH!*" Tinkles of glasses, small talk, and simply the alive hush of humans in a room as if their breath itself is being transferred to the grooves of the recording.

Jack Casady, the regular Jefferson Airplane bassist, starts the set off by signifying in terraplane bass growls. The mood is set. Jimi's beginning licks alternate between an octave high-unison formation with Casady and some tenor doodling, the whole effect setting up a tension of anticipation.

"I'm a Voodoo Chile, Lordy I'm a Voodoo Chile." The guitar dubbing in sharp soprano every word sung. Stevie Winwood hitting a single organ note, the thrilling tonal key to the melody.

Still suspended in mystery, Jimi begins with rhythm licks at the precise staggered tempo that will carry this "song of creation" throughout. Punctuating the licks by zooming his bass strings, he hits a figure opposite his rhythm licks—it seems to talk, saying, "OK, boys, let's go."

In a rambling, loping, yet stately stride, the rhythm section starts out. Winwood's organ blossoms into the modal underpinnings for Jimi's voice. Mitch hits like he has been waiting all his life for this moment, his double kit sounding like the clean strikes of an ax into fresh oak.

That was the sound. That was the sound he wanted. It came bopping out at him strong and round, bubbling like lava and wide and all-encompassing.

And against the ensemble sound you can feel the room. It is alive. Though all voices are hushed, you can hear the air respire. A resounding southern roadhouse effect. The long banking lines of Jimi's guitar are borne through the air over great distances, over land and sea to the summit where he begins this teaching tale, this personal catalytic of the mysteries.

The night I was born the moon turned a fire red
The night I was born, I swear, the moon turned a fire red
My poor mother cried out, well the gypsy was right
And I seen her fell down right dead

Mountain lions found me there and set me on an eagle's back
Well, mountain lions found me there and set me on an eagle's
*   wing (an eagle's wing baby)*
He took me past the outskirts of infinity
And when he brought me back, he gave me Venus witch's ring

The music begins to muster, building and charging into a crescendo. The guitar stalking up ahead like a purple-flamed dragon. The organ sweeping upward. Jimi's primordial tone flashing below the organ urging it on.

Hey, and he said fly on FLY ON
'Cause I'm a VOODOO CHILE, VOODOO CHILE,
*   VOODOO CHILE*

Well I'll make love to you
And Lord knows you felt no pain

Well I'll make love to you in your sleep
And God knows you'll feel no pain

'Cause I'm a million miles away
And at the same time I'm right here in your picture frame

'Cause I'm a Voodoo Chile
Lord knows I'm a Voodoo Chile

There is a happy energy, a buoyancy that comes through the live studio setting. Jimi has Stevie Winwood's organ pipes to play against. This gives a surprising depth-of-sound plane. The organ is a perfect opposite to Jimi's talking guitar. Mitch is kicking ass on drums—the stomp of his kick meeting the bass in its deepest tone, the shimmer of his cymbals contrasting the deep cavern echo. Winwood plays intelligent blues changes that build to Jimi's solo. Midway through, Winwood hits a series of brilliant runs and Jimi comes in at the peak to quickly drop an octave and push a liquid delay that moves beautiful deep tones into underwater depths. The shimmer of metal vibrating, atomic particles, and human tissue in the air. The song becomes a night-train spaceship zooming off in a shimmering whine of primordial energy.

> *My arrows are made of desire*
> *From far away as Jupiter's sulphur mines*
>
> *My arrows are made of desire*
> *From far away as Jupiter's sulphur mines*
> (Way down by the methane sea . . .)
>
> *I have a hummingbird and it hums so loud*
> *You'd think you were losing your mind*

The song almost stops, but picks back up again to the cheers of the studio audience. Jimi's guitar growls in appreciation.

> *Well I float in liquid garnets*
> *In Arizona new red sand*
>
> *I float in liquid gardens*
> *way down in Arizona red sands*
>
> *I place the honey from a flower named Blues* (way down
>   in California)—
> *And then New York drowns as we held hands*
>
> *I'm a Voodoo Chile*
> *Lord knows I'm a Voodoo Chile*
>   *Voodoo Chile*
>   *Voodoo Chile*
>   *Voodoo Chile*

They had just about walked out of the studio when a camera crew rushed in. They ask Jimi to give them something they could film. Jimi and company went back to their instruments and right into "Voodoo Chile (Slight Return)."

The rhythm is brighter and nearly a hambone. The intro figure from the guitar is stark old blues. It descends as if from on high into an atomic explosion, billowing out a bottom bass of gut-bucket clouds that range, staggering and talking, across a deep terrain. Jimi has his guitar making primordial monster growls and roars. Then he gets into serpent movements, darting lizard tongues, and to cap it all off he achieves the sound of a sacrificial lamb being slaughtered.

Well I stand up next to a mountain
Chop it down with the edge of my hand

Well I stand up next to a mountain
Chop it down with the edge of my hand

I pick up all the pieces and make an island
Might even raise a little sand

'Cause I'm a Voodoo Chile
Lord knows I'm a Voodoo Chile

I didn't mean to take up all of your sweet time
I'll give it right back to you one of these days

I didn't mean to take up all of your sweet time
I'll give it right back to you—one of these days

I won't see you no more in this world
I'll meet you in the next world—So don't be late

In the midst of work on his *Electric Ladyland* album, Jimi suddenly took off for the West Coast, much to the consternation of Chas Chandler, who was used to a closer working relationship with Hendrix. New York was hip, but L.A. was outasight. Bevies of the freakiest and loveliest ladies, resplendent in the tropical enclosures of Hollywood/Beverly Hills. Days and days on end of parties by poolside, or in someone's private jungle high above L.A. Hugh Masekela, Sly Stone, and of course Buddy Miles were on the set. The Whiskey A Go Go replaced the Scene as Jimi's chief jam stand.

Chas Chandler, in the traditional paternal/maternal manager's role, felt that Jimi was beginning to lose control. For Chas and Noel and Mitch, England was home, England was their scene. Crazy America was like an aberration to be tolerated at best. Chas felt that England was Jimi's power base, that he had an important duty to retain England as his official and real headquarters. But Jimi, after two backbreaking years of emergence, of becoming a star, wanted to have some fun.

Jimi and Buddy Miles quickly became legends that summer in L.A. Jimi stayed at Miles's home, which was just up the winding road past Schwab's Drugstore in the Hollywood Hills. Running with Buddy was a gas. There is nothing like two high-powered brothers on the loose who are down to party. Miles, from Minneapolis, and Jimi, from Seattle, often acted as if they had been sprung from their respective hometowns for the first time.

They hung out at a club called the Experience. It had a huge face of Hendrix painted upon the façade, with the entrance being the mouth of the likeness. Buddy was working on his first album. Hendrix was listed as producer but he mainly sat in the booth while tracks were being laid and while Buddy sang. He produced the album by just being there and being himself, Buddy would say. Jimi did not play but just indicated his taste for the music. Jimi worked the dials some but mainly let the sessions take their own course unfettered. Jimi wrote the liner notes for the album entitled: *Expressway to Your Skull* by the Buddy Miles Express.

> *The express had made the bend, he is coming on down the*
>   *tracks,*
> *shaking steady, shaking funk, shaking feeling, shaking life . . .*
>   *the conductor*
> *says as they climb aboard, . . . we are going to the electric*
>   *church, the express*
> *took them away and they lived and heard happily and funkily*
>   *ever after and—*
> *uh—excuse me but I think I hear my train coming. . . .*

The lines of young ladies waiting to see whether they would be chosen to enter Miles's handsome white Tudor house became a part of the Hollywood sightseer route. All into the night long white legs wound down the steps of the circular front entrance.

Jimi began to drink a lot, to throw some money around, and speed his silver-flecked Stingray, packed with foxes, through the winding hills of Hollywood night and day. He was having a good time. Letting it all hang out. He knew that Chas, Noel, and Mitch felt that he was being that legendary "nigger on Saturday night," but he didn't care. They treated the music as if it were a career, as if they were clerks in the British Post Office.

Jimi had a lot of fire to burn off. He had not been able to properly run the streets with a brother while he was in England. More importantly, he was in a highly productive and creative period. All the hijinks in a weird way balanced with his creativity. *Electric Lady-land* was a bitch!

He smashed up his Stingray. Yeah, he had been loaded and probably shouldn't have been driving, but those Hollywood Hills were the weirdest roads anyone would ever want to maneuver. Trying to get back to Buddy's pad, he had to make turns up a winding one-car-wide road that swung in ninety-degree angles. He missed a turn and put the car through the fence. Well, big deal. They towed the car off and he went out and bought another one. Everybody made a big thing about it. But he *had* the money, shit, he had the cash. Why wait when you need a ride? Miles dug the limo scene, which was cool for him, but whenever possible, Jimi liked to drive his own machine. Sometimes Miles's limo bills ran into the tens of thousands, but if Jimi put up ten for a new ride everyone made a big thing about it. But what bugged Jimi most about the incident was Noel's insistence that he needed glasses. That his eyesight was poor and that was why he had the accident. Noel just wanted everyone to wear glasses, live in England, and count every penny like he did.

The brick-throwing incident was something else. Jimi didn't know whether he had thrown this brick at some chick or not. He did know that he had been getting pretty consistently loaded. Not so much acid now as booze, the hard stuff. Sometimes he wouldn't remember what he had done. And then to watch the glee of those who told him of his antics. He did know that the novelty of the chicks hanging around day and night was wearing off. They began to get on his nerves. He had given a couple of chicks a whole pocketful of money, just to get rid of them, really. He was stoned and they were nice chicks. Later, word swept Sunset Strip that he was giving away thousands of dollars at a time. After that, traffic jams ensued outside Buddy's pad. There were hundreds of girls, and many not so nice.

But the best time he had was with the music. It was nice to do studio work in L.A. and then come out into a balmy night. It was a different perspective and he heard different things there than when he was back East or in London. The West was more expansive. Sometimes he could hear his guitar bouncing off of the canyons and mountain ranges and diving into the ocean.

Jimi would work late into the nights at the many amazingly modern studios in L.A. There he had the brand-new sixteen-track machines to choose from. He felt free to work on the expansiveness of "1983" in L.A., especially with the extra tracks. A multimovement sound painting, "1983" seemed to lend itself to the L.A. lifestyle. In many ways L.A. reminded him of the last stage before the deluge. L.A., earthquake-prone and absolute in its insanity, seemed to hold both great promise and imminent tragedy in a strange balance.

One night at TTG Studios on Hollywood Boulevard, Jimi completed one of the countless guitar overdubs on "1983." There were several brothers in the studios doing work, also, who were really gassed to see him there. Jimi voiced his concern over the lack of black support for his music. But the brothers told him differently. There were a lot of black people who dug his music and bought his records. They saw him perform when they could, but they were outnumbered by the simple fact of his overwhelming popularity. This was the first time Jimi had heard this point of view. It was heartening. He opened up to the brothers and told them stories about his most recent tour. He had gone through the South and found a very nice vibe there—it had surprised him. In a way it related to what the brothers were telling him about his black support. The newspapers said one thing, but once you checked it out for yourself, you discovered something closer to the truth.

Jimi had been working all day and now he wanted to play. He wanted to go to the Whiskey, but rather than call a limo or cab, or call Buddy's for someone to come and get him, he put his problem on the floor and immediately got an offer of a ride. It was a gas to ride in someone's ordinary car for a change through dark and warm Hollywood with his lovely lady companions by his side. He always sought to be as close to his people as possible, and he enjoyed this simple, innocent, brief ride a few miles down the road more than his benefactors imagined.

August 23, 1968. The Singer Bowl, Queens, New York, former site of the World's Fair. Jimi Hendrix and Janis Joplin face each other in the narrow dressing room. Between them is a fifth of Jack Daniels, which they share amid the hustle and bustle. They are having a little party with each other. So seldom can folks get together and relate. They cherish the moment through the twelve-year-old whiskey.

They had not planned anything. It had just happened. The Chambers Brothers had just gone on, and Jimi would follow Janis to the stage. Through the walls the crowd hummed and crackled, cheering as the lights came up on the first big chord from the Chambers Brothers.

At first Jimi just sat and listened to her talk. She had an extraordinary set of pipes. She could sound like a university-educated Texas schoolteacher one minute, and an insane, lascivious teen-ager the next. The more they drank, the more resonance began coming out of her voice. A subtone, like the strange intonations of a heavy drinker, yet at the same time timbres and pitches that came closer to what she sounded like when she sang. She had a squawk voice, and a husky voice that could almost sing bass. Her range increased the closer it came to the time she would go onstage. It was like her rap was a vocal exercise—the drinking, too—getting all those funky and freaky edges and vectors together.

They had started talking about the old blues. They both solemnly acknowledged how much the old music contributed to their inspiration. Then Jimi took out his stage prop for that night, a Confederate flag the size of a handkerchief, and blew his nose. That blew Janis's mind, she cracked up. She howled. Her high wheezy laugh, for a moment, reminded him of Brian Jones. She lost her breath, laughing, tears rolling down her face. That broke the ice. They talked enthusiastically about their favorite blues singers, singing little snatches from their songs. Janis's soul was into Bessie Smith, while Jimi's was somewhere among Elmore James, Robert Johnson, and Muddy Waters.

Jimi began to play some blues, like he always did before a concert. Janis fell right into the patches of melodies and runs, humming softly, repeating phrases, swaying her head to the implied beat. They were loaded. The fifth of Jack Daniels was dead.

Then a sudden flurry of activity in the dressing room had her onstage in a flash.

Her voice amazed him. He could sense the energy latent in the low tones. Her sound was Texas country crossed with Louisiana blues. The energy and the volume of her singing at full tilt in many ways matched the intensely high volume he played at. She had the voice of a wailer, a belter, who could switch to sultry blue tones with no effort. She gave all. It was not perfect and precise, but her feeling outshone everything.

She could reach up high and sing over her range, as a free jazz man would blow over his reed, producing scaling screeches. The power with which she sang produced overtones in both the upper and lower registers. Sometimes she hit three notes at once, producing weird chords of pure freak. But then she could come right down to

Earth and talk, singing with such naked sincerity that you *loved* her. In song she was a goddess, irresistible. Onstage now she jumps up hollering like a field hand, pushing breath through herself seemingly at the velocity force of hurricane winds. Janis also had a foreign-like quality in her middle range that made it feel sometimes like she was not singing in English, but in languageless tongues swirling eternal. Her croony moans trailed off in unique figures you could never predict. There was something spooky about her singing that was thrilling and scary at the same time.

The huge PA system of the medium-sized stadium bowl was a perfect vehicle for her sound. You heard every piece of her eerily beautiful cries, her guttural moans, and her freaky slides as they swayed in the winds. She intertwined them all and they gave up guessing where she was coming from and totally surrendered to her power. Somewhere inside, beyond herself, she wrought it out, spread it around, and shared the power.

She was power.

Janis Joplin was total inspiration. He really felt like playing after hearing her performance.

As the Experience set up, Jimi murmured something about "making it up in spades" for all the equipment problems he had had at Fillmore East when he played on the same bill with Sly earlier in the year. The crowd doesn't care what he is saying. They are going wild. The cops are scampering about. And wow—the stage is revolving like a lazy Susan.

Jimi goes through "Purple Haze" and "Foxy Lady." He could see how weird it must have been for Janis, facing thousands of screaming fans you can hardly see, turning all the time.

He sees Mike Jeffery and Gerry Stickells come to the edge of the stage. The house lights flash on, revealing two equipment men pulling a kid off the stage. He is resisting. They get him to the stairs and leave him there. The lights go back down. The Experience continues to play. Gerry Stickells is hassling the kid on the stairs because he is blocking the way. A cop comes up and yanks the kid off. A swarm of cops rain sticks down on the protesting kid. The crowd responds angrily. A few skirmishes start up near the stage and the momentum spreads back into the crowd. A man takes up a long two-by-ten from one of the police barricades. He is waving it at the cops. People begin to smell riot. The audience takes in a collective breath of air. Some move toward the revolving stage area, some recoil in fear. A gang of cops quickly hustles the kid out through the musicians' entrance, and as the music continues the crowd settles back into a jagged groove.

Jimi ends his set by charging the amps like a knight, with his guitar as the lance. He skims the fret board against the felt covers of the amps, achieving a frenzied bottleneck effect. Then he squats over his white Stratocaster and swirls it around and around under him while still playing.

Jimi was interviewed by *Circus* magazine, a New York-based publication, early in October of 1968. The possibility of Nixon winning the upcoming election was on a lot of minds.

Circus wanted to know what he was working on right now.

Jimi answered, "There's one song I'm writing that's dedicated to the Black Panthers, and that's the sort of thing we might go into. It doesn't just pertain to race but to symbolism and today's things and to what's happening today. By that time, the president will be elected."

Would that mean a big change for Jimi or no change at all?

"Well, we plan to make it a whole new thing *regardless* of who is elected."

The interview was full of references to "the masses," America, and the present political situation. Jimi suggested that if everyone spent three to five minutes a day to be by themselves they would find more peace of mind. Taking the popular slogan of the time, "Make love, not war," Jimi warned that there are "evil folks around and they want you to be passive and weak and peaceful," so that they can take you over. "You have to fight fire with fire. I mean, I'm getting myself personally together in the way of music and what I'm going to do."

Toward the end of the interview *Circus* wanted to know how much contact Hendrix had had with the Black Panthers.

"Not much. They come to the concerts, and I sort of feel them there—it's not a physical thing but a mental ray, you know. It's a spiritual thing."

At last the new album was finished. November 2, 1968. *Electric Ladyland* entered the charts and went immediately to Number 1.

The album opens with ". . . And the Gods Made Love," setting the tone for the sound paintings that would follow. Jimi would say the title with such serious reverence that people did not know whether to laugh or to listen more closely.

When Hendrix first played the melody "Electric Ladyland" in the Record Plant studios, it had only a spare solo guitar feel. It sounded

**Backstage at the Oakland Coliseum, Jimi
fixes Mitch's hair** © 1981 JIM MARSHALL

acoustical, crooning out a Manhattan rhapsody. The polished grace-
notes trilling and turning between the strangely winsome yearning
melody. Alternating chops between the bass line and the chord, and
descending steps downward to break out in garlands of incredible
gypsy-flavored trills. His playing indicating all four of the guitars
that would be on the recording.

In the final recording the solo intro (and also the initial mood) is
sacrificed for instant vocal choirlike overdubs and layered guitars
refraining with the voices. Getting to the heart of the melody at
once, Jimi, in these voices, harmonizes with himself in beautiful
falsetto overdubs.

> Have You Ever Been—Have You Ever Been
> To Electric Ladyland?
> The magic carpet waits—for you
> So don't you be late,
> I want to show you
> Different emotions
> I want to ride through

The sounds and motions.
Electric woman waits for you and me
So it's time to take a ride
You can cast all your hang-ups over the side
While we fly right over the love-filled sea
Look up ahead
I see the love land
Soon you will understand
Make love make love make love make love
I want to show you (Angels will spread their wings)
I want to show you
Good and evil lay side by side
While electric love penetrates the sky
I want to show you
I want to show you
I want to show you
I wanna show you

When they recorded the song in the studio, Jimi jumped out of the barricaded enclosure where he hid himself while he sang, and shouted, "I can sing, I can sing." He was literally jumping for joy, it sounded so pretty.

A faint whine of metal flying above the treetops fades the song out.

"House Burning Down" starts off as if it's in the middle of a splendid Hendrix solo with the drums rolling and the bass-rumbling finale. Then it quickly breaks down into a sprightly 4/4 funk march with Jimi shouting "HEY ... HEY ... HEY" over rooting treble guitar licks that harmonize with his shouts.

Look at the sky turn a hell-fire red
Somebody's house is burning
Down down
Down down

Then he falsettos *"Down, down, down"* into a break where Jimi briefly solos twin guitars:

Well, I asked my friend
"Where is that black smoke coming from?"
He just coughed and changed the subject
And said, "Uh, it might snow some,"

So I left him sipping his tea,
And I jumped in my chariot and rode off to see
Just why and who could it be this time.

Sisters and brothers, daddies, mothers
Standing around crying
When I reached the scene
The flames were making a ghostly whine
So I stood on my horse's back
And I screamed without a crack
I said, "Oh baby why did you
burn your brother's house down?"

Jimi goes back to the refrain and then out into a solo that reveals lightning-fast picking blended perfectly with just a touch of raunchy feedback. The solo streaks into a break where Jimi just plays rhythm, calling and refraining with the twin guitars.

Well someone stepped from the crowd
He was nineteen miles high
He shouts, "We're tired and disgusted
So we painted red through the sky."
I said, "The truth is straight ahead
so don't burn yourself instead.
Try learning instead of burning
Hear what I say."

So I finally rode away
But I'll never forget that day
'Cause when I reached the valley
I looked down across the way
A giant boat from space
Landed with eerie grace
And came and taken all the dead away.

Jimi takes the song out with three guitars all playing rhythm figures. One emerges across the top burning a treble pinnacle. Then Jimi growls a turn, jacking his tremolo bar to cause a slight rise in pitch that gives the effect of a great vehicle in a torturous turn.

"Crosstown Traffic," a bouncy back-beating boogie, reveals Jimi's ability to simply get down with amusing lyrics and basic rock 'n' roll.

Opposite: JIM CUMMINS

You jump in front of my car
When you know all the time
Ninety miles an hour, girl
is the speed I drive

You tell me it's all right
You don't mind a little pain
You say you just want me to take you for a ride
You're just like   Crosstown Traffic
So hard to get through to you   Crosstown Traffic
All you do is slow me down
          And I'm trying to get to the other
          side of town.

I'm not the only soul
Accused of hit and run
Tire tracks all across your back
I can see you had your fun!
But darling, can't you see
My signals turn from green to red
And with you I can see a traffic jam
Straight up ahead
          You're just like
                    Crosstown Traffic
                    Crosstown Traffic
                    Crosstown Traffic
                    Crosstown Traffic

Recorded in late 1967 in London, "All Along the Watchtower" by Bob Dylan bursts forth with an enchanting sound. Later, Jimi was able to remix it in New York on advanced equipment that enabled him to enhance the sound. Chanting guitars set up sharp harmonics of yearning. Settling against a flurry of back-beating drums and blossoming out with the bass, the twin rhythm guitars mew violin lines. Slightly delayed in the rotation of the beat, Jimi emphasizes breathtaking violinlike sustains and pure treble reach. His lines are so delicately drawn they seem classical in their phrasings. A high drone constantly peaks in the background. An incredibly wide expanse opens between the bass and guitar and drums. They ride upward to the tip of emotion, where Jimi shouts from the summit:

There must be some kind of way out of here
Said a joker to the thief

There's too much confusion
I can't get no relief

Businessmen they drink my wine
Plough men dig my earth

But let us not talk falsely now
The hour is getting late

"Watchtower" from Mount Olympus, majestic and grand the sound towers in the sky. Below, the ocean breaks against the rocks. Jimi takes off from the rhythmic theme and creates a solo that ranks with his very best. The ensemble sound is splendid.

Dew tinkling droplets, liquid electric lines, and a jazz saxophone blowing through the rhythms of the heavens begin "Rainy Day, Dream Away." The congas come out commanding a mixed-down chugging ensemble. A sleepy voice says, "Hey man, take a look out the window and see what's happening." A pause in space as the ensemble slowly establishes a dreamy interior. A sleepy muffled voice says, happily surprised, "Hey man! *It's raining.*" The saxophone riffing bluesy against the mellow mood. Jimi's guitar trades licks and duels with Freddie Smith's saxophone on a free terrain as the beat takes a jump in tempo and brightness. Jimi's voice comes in blending perfectly with the beat and the space between.

Rainy day, dream away
Let the sun take a holiday
Flowers bathe and see the children play
Lay back and groove
On a rainy day

Well, I can see a bunch of wet preachers
Look at 'em on the run!
Carnival traffic noise
It sinks to a splashy hum
Even the ducks can groove
Rain battering the parkside pool
And I'm leaning on my windowsill
Digging everything (and-uh you, too)

Rainy day, rain all day
Ain't no use in gettin' uptight
Just let it groove its own way
Let it drain your worries away

Lay back and groove on a rainy day
Lay back and groove on a rainy day

Neptunian bass throbs atmospheric fog in the cosmos, ranging along the planet of the key. Mike Finnigan's organ tightens the ensemble sound with its chords and Buddy Miles keeps the beat funky and well-defined on the raining earth, fading out.

"1983 (A Merman I Should Turn to Be)" starts delicately. Hammering up fret, Jimi produces a distant vibrating peal. It sounds like fingers gliding up fretless electric violins in weird harmonics. The hammering-on goes into sonic feedback. The squealing violin sound scaling the peak of itself, the feedback tight-roping distort and wobbling on the signal's edge.

A simple chord lick says, "We're about to start," within the midst and marks the beginning of the peaked feedback coming in on a pan, getting stronger and stronger, the chord sounding like the expellation of human breath—OM. Then a perfect bluefolk run (reminiscent of "House of the Rising Sun") as the feedback and the piercing metal sounds gliss-slide up and out. The repeat of the run meets the hollow ghostlike whooze of a high wind upon a summit.

The ghostly howl pans stronger, phasing into the taxiing sound of a long-range jetliner. Then the "deep six" submarine descending, buoy gongs-bells fade into the distance giving way to skittering plucks. The bluefolk run ends in the low registers leading to the bass line that will run for the entire piece. It dips deep in a yawning diving arc, like the culmination of a seagull's arc sweep to the waters and back to the sky.

The sound comes full up. Mitch Mitchell's chopping military snare rolls pan louder into the sound level. The bass guitar (played by Jimi) takes the bass line over from the Stratocaster and plunges the line an octave deep, creating the interior wall of an underwater mountain.

The sound comes up a bit too fast. Two wailing Cry-Babies dub a lament, both doing the same note yet one slightly sharp, adding an echo effect.

His guitar goes out of control momentarily on a feedback whistle. The bass, the drums, and a single guitar chord dubbed in, sustain a note constituting a break. The drum, picking up from its somber taps, establishes a stately polyrhythmic march that preludes Jimi's vocal.

The ghostly swoons continue as Chris Wood comes in on flute, picking up on the ghostly woooos. Playing against the effect, Wood plays single sotto lines with a variation on the key that sustains a minor mode against the finely tuned feedback effects stroked in pinks against the upper canvas. His flute is a mellow complement to what could have been a somber song. Yet the words, although painted against the bleakest landscape, are an uplift and a relief.

Jimi croons in his most appealing *pull* voice as the bass plunges to its deepest range.

> *Hooray I awake from yesterday*
> *Alive but the war is here to stay*
> *So my love, Catherina and me decide to take our last walk*
> *   through the noise to the sea*
> *Not to die but to be reborn*
> *Away from lands so battered and torn*
> *Forever*

A flying signal wavers over the scene, hovering a moment in the break. The voice sustaining in a shadowy echo reverb tagging and extending the word *torn* the same length as the signal.

> *Oh say can you see*
> *It's really such a mess*
> *Every inch of Earth is a fighting nest*
>
> *Giant pencil and lipstick tube-shaped things*
> *Continue to rain and cause screaming pain*
> *And the Arctic stains from silver blue to bloody red*
> *As our feet find the sands and the sea—it's straight ahead*
> *   (straight up ahead)*
>
> *Well it's too bad that our friends can't be with us today (it's*
> *   too bad)*
> *The machine that we built, it would never save us (that's*
> *   why they've not come with us today)*
> *They also said it's impossible for a man to live and breathe*
> *   underwater forever*
> *That was their main complaint*
> *And they also threw this in my face*
> *They said, "Anyway, you know good and well it would be*
> *   beyond the will of God (God, God)*
> *And the grace of the King" (grace of the King)*
>
> *So my darling and I make love in the sand*
> *To salute the last moment ever on dry land*

Our machine, it has done its work, played its part well
Without a scratch on our bodies and we bid it farewell
Starfish and giant foams greet us with a smile
Before our heads go under we take a last look at the killing
    noise
Of the out of style, of the out of style . . . out of style

Reverbing into chamberlike passage that sounds like a Bach pre-
lude. In three-part harmony, the bass and the guitars sound like an
organ switching at the peak of its passages to overtone harmonies.
Then abruptly back to the initial three-part harmony that breaks up
in a slow flurry of intervals. Jimi feints a classical guitar solo while
he plays over his own backward tape riffs of shimmering high frequency that spaces into a sustained drum solo, which presages the
next movement.

The kinds of sounds the seagulls make in their orbits, circling
above the waters. So similar to the sounds of metal bodies arching in
space at sonic speeds, approaching the soundlessness of space. As if
the depths of the waters were synonymous with outer space.

The rhythm continues as if the drum in its spare essence is the
continuance of life. More than just the beat in the pulse, but an
entity against which all objects of harmony must resolve.

"1983" segues right into "Moon, Turn the Tides . . . Gently,
Gently Away":

Down and down and down and down and down and do
    we go
Hurry my darling we mustn't be late for the show
Neptune champion games to an aqua world is so very dear
"Right this way" smiles a mermaid
I can hear Atlantis full of cheer

The end of "Moon, Turn the Tides . . . Gently, Gently Away" is
also the end of "1983." With the return of the "1983" theme, the
two guitars in harmony enliven their mournful tones. The top guitar
nearly peaks into feedback with its wail, while the lower guitar is
playing blue tremolo. With the thrilling qualities of a snake charm-
er's horn the emotion and the movement twine, wrapping themselves about you. A heightened ecstasy winding through the
third-eye charka. A cello sound joins in, perfect-toned and classical.
Jimi begins to wail it all out. Returning to the "sound painting"
terrain they jam some heavy blues striking toward freedom.

Jimi Hendrix's face flaming in red yellow specter fire glow is the cover of the *Electric Ladyland* album. Looking like fire elemental, the salamander that lives and glows in all that is fire—including the greatest fire of all—electricity.

The Great Britain edition of *Electric Ladyland* had another cover.

20 NUDES DISC IS BANNED

Two record dealers have banned a new pop disc—because they are shocked by the record sleeve.

The LP, *Electric Ladyland*, by the Jimi Hendrix Experience, has on its cover eight lounging nude girls.

The other side of the sleeve shows twelve more in similar pose.

The owner of one of the York shops which has banned the record, Mr. Hugh Robertson, declared yesterday: "This has gone too far. There is no need for covers like this."

ARTISTIC

A shop manager has also complained to the distributors and several shops are keeping the record cover hidden from view.

A spokesman for the company, which designed the sleeve, Track Records, of London, replied: "The cover should be looked at from an artistic point of view.

"In view of the title, we thought it appropriate to have nude women on the sleeve. I don't think it's pornographic."

Sunday Mirror
November 1, 1968

Weeks later the British edition of the *Electric Ladyland* album was still in the news.

DISC DEALERS HIT AT SEXY COVERS

Britain's disc dealers hit out last night at the trend towards "vulgarity" on pop record covers.

Mr. Christopher Foss, secretary of the Gramophone Retailers' Committee, said the trend could only lower the industry's image in the eyes of the public.

He claimed that twenty-one naked girls pictured on the cover of Jimi Hendrix's new LP, *Electric Ladyland*, were unnecessary. "This type of album sleeve is almost certain to reduce the sale of records," said Foss.

But a spokesman for the Jimi Hendrix Experience said last night that more than 35,000 copies were sold within four days of its release in Britain.

Sunday Mirror
November 21, 1968

Noel and Mitch left the band at the same time that *Electric Lady-land* was becoming Number 1 on the U.S. charts. The Experience had officially broken up. Chas, fed up with the hassles of dealing with Hendrix, sold his share of the JHE management to Mike Jeffery for three hundred thousand dollars cash and future considerations. Chas, Noel, and Mitch returned to England. Jimi remained in New York.

Jimi understood that Mitch and Noel wanted to be back home in London, especially with the Christmas holidays coming up. Jimi had to just let it hang for a while, rest for a minute. He did not have much to say to the press.

"Mitch and Noel want to get their own thing going—producing and managing other artists. In the New Year we'll be breaking the group apart from selected dates.

"Oh I'll be around, don't worry . . . doing this and that. But there are other scenes we want to get into."

SEVEN

... **I** can explain everything better through music. You hypnotize people to where they go right back to their natural state, which is pure positive—like childhood when you got natural highs. And when you get people at weakest point, you can preach into the subconscious what we want to say. That's why the name "electric church" flashes in and out.

There's no telling how many lives your spirit will go through—die and be reborn. Like my mind will be back in the days when I was a flying horse. Before I can remember anything, I can remember music and stars and planets. I could go to sleep and write fifteen symphonies. I had very strange feelings that I was here for something and I was going to get a chance to be heard. I got the guitar together 'cause that was all I had. I used to be really lonely.

A musician, if he's a messenger, is like a child who hasn't been handled too many times by man, hasn't had too many fingerprints across his brain. That's why music is so much heavier than anything you ever felt.

Life magazine, 1969

The Experience went back together after the beginning of the New Year, 1969. Noel Redding had rehearsed a band he was calling

233

Fat Mattress for three weeks over the holidays. It was a kind of boast, for when he split the Experience the month before, it was common knowledge that Redding had saved the most money out of everyone in the Jimi Hendrix organization. He achieved his mass of cash by severe penny-pinching, and he used it as part of his reason for leaving and as part of his bargaining position for returning. He knew Mike Jeffery would have him back under any terms. A tour through England, Europe, and America was already booked, from January 5 in London through June at the Newport Festival in Los Angeles.

The bargain was struck. Noel Redding's band, Fat Mattress, would be the official opening band of the tour, regardless of whether there was another band on the bill or not.

The big news of the New Year was that Cream had broken up (and remained so) over the holidays. Eric Clapton was adamant about leaving—and there could be no Cream without him.

The JHE appeared on Lulu's TV show, which was very popular in London. She was both a hit singer and a movie star. She had co-starred in "To Sir with Love" with Sidney Poitier and the movie had been a smash both in London and in the States. Lulu's show was live.

Jimi, Noel, and Mitch came on, and after a bit of variety-show patter they played "Voodoo Chile (Slight Return)" from *Electric Ladyland*. Then they swung into their first hit, "Hey Joe," but midway through, Jimi startled everyone by stopping the song, announcing a tribute to Cream, and going right into a jam of "The Sunshine of Your Love." The director, the producer, the star, and the technicians all began tearing at their hair and gesturing at their throats— Jimi was going way overtime. Lulu might not be able to say a proper good-bye. Jimi, Noel, and Mitch paid them no mind as they climbed, fell, and rode through Cream's greatest hit. Jimi was tearing into the lead guitar lines that Clapton had established as a near classic. Jimi bore into the solo space with searing lines that turned up into atonals or turned over into funk moans. That was the way "The Lulu Show" ended January 7, 1969.

HALLELUJAH!
IT'S HENDRIX IN HANDEL'S
OLD HOUSE

Another musician has moved into the London house where the great composer Handel lived and died more than two centuries ago.

Not that Jimi Hendrix pretends to know much about the old tenant.

"I didn't even know this was his pad, man, until after I got in," he said, "and to tell you the God's honest truth I haven't heard much of the fella's stuff. But I dig a bit of Bach now and again."

Luckily, Jimi's words didn't fall on the ears of some students who had come to gaze at the blue-coloured plaque in memory of the old master.

Hendrix, fuzzy-haired, wild man of pop, 1969, in scarlet trousers and yellow shirt, may not meet with the approval of classical students. But millions of pop fans across the world hail him as the world's No. 1 musician.

It is in this house in fashionable Brook Street that Handel is said to have composed "Messiah" and the "Water Music."

Hendrix promises not to let tradition down and says he, too, will compose here. Music he defines as "twenty-first century" and that "sort of scene."

Hendrix is 23, an electric man with a 240-volt electric guitar. When he plays it onstage, he may set it on fire, smash it or play it with his teeth, depending on his mood.

His music seems an uninhibited collection of jarring sounds without melody.

The grandson of a pure Cherokee Indian, he looks a rebel, and a man many could hate without meeting—someone you're sure smokes pot, has a lust for birds and likes his hooch.

VALUES

Hendrix pleads guilty on all counts—or the experience of those happenings.

He laughs: "That's how I got the name of my group, the Jimi Hendrix Experience."

That's what I like about Hendrix. Not his music, but the man. His honesty. His sense of values may be wrong, but he creates his own values which, he feels, reflect the way young people want to live without suppression today.

The attic of the house, which has become Hendrix's favourite room, contains an assortment of bric-a-brac and a bed with a Victorian shawl pinned to the ceiling as a canopy.

At two in the afternoon, Hendrix is making the bed neatly folding back the black sheets and straightening the colorful

Persian bedspread. Then he grins and calls Cathy to open a bottle of wine.

Cathy Etchingham is a 22-year-old redhead from the North who shares the flat. Jimi explains her presence: "My girlfriend, my past girlfriend and probably my next girlfriend. My mother and my sister and all that bit. My Yoko Ono from Chester.

"We won't marry. Marriage isn't my scene; we just live together. Those bits of paper you call marriage certificates are only for people who feel insecure."

There is no alarm in the face of Cathy, who was once a hairdresser and met Jimi by chance on his first day in England three years ago.

GROOVY

"There is no shame in living with sin," she says quietly and without defiance. "My mother knows and she thinks that Jimi is groovy."

"One day I wanna become a parent," Jimi announces. "Now that is what the world is all about. Having kids. Like planting flowers . . ."

We move on to Jimi's music. "I would describe my music as electric church music," he explains. "Church meaning religion and not meaning God, that is.

"I know," he adds with a long stare at me, "that many people are blocked out but I hope they will come to understand my music soon. In fact I'm gonna write a new album which will simplify it all and bridge the gap between teen-agers and parents."

NAKED

"I'm moving away from what I've done so far. I don't want to play the guitar with my teeth any more or clown around, but I did it because fans, having seen me do it once, expected me to do it always and I came to do it out of self-satisfaction."

Jimi, from the cluttered mantelpiece, took a copy of his new album, Electric Ladyland, *the sleeve of which shows twenty-one naked girls. Many record shops won't display it.*

"Man, I don't blame them," said Jimi. "I wouldn't have put this picture on the sleeve myself, but it wasn't my decision. They messed about with the picture and although the girls were pretty they came out disfigured."

Jimi grew up in Seattle and was expelled from school; more recently he was given the freedom of the city.

He admits he has been in jail: "Spent seven days in the cooler for taking a ride in a stolen car. But I never knew it was."

He admits, too, that he was fined £250 for smashing a hotel room in Gothenburg when he got drunk. And once an American moral society got him banned because his act was "too erotic."

But a wild man? "No, I'm just natural all the time. What others think or say doesn't worry me, man."

Jimi says: "People still mourn when people die. That's self-sympathy. The person who is dead isn't cryin'.

"When I die I want people to play my music, go wild and freak out an' do anything they wanna do. . . ."

Obviously, Jimi Hendrix won't need a plaque for any of us to remember him by.

Don Short
Daily Mirror
January 11, 1969

In the studio. Could be any studio in the world. The same sense of being closed in against the world. The soundproofed walls, the whir and click of advanced machinery, sensitive and delicate, smooth gloss and metallic. Soft interior lighting, not a glance of sunlight. It was like a spaceship. The smooth dials of the electronic magnetic reproducers, perfect red, green, white. The turned-down lights make it even more cozy, more tunnely, like in the center of the Earth, making the rooms indistinguishable in true size. Wafts of incense. Every sound capable of being captured, every vibe of the room submissive to the sound, everybody in the room supporting the sound. This was Jimi's workshop. The endless timeless space where he was most at home.

Take after take. Seemingly for days and weeks. Getting the right sound, the right pitch and intensity. Getting a swan-diving tremolo to glide right within the ensemble sound on time. It's what he's hearing. People look at him like he's crazy. Musicians and engineers exasperated, but it's his session. But that love, when it's happening, when it's right, makes everything worthwhile. The blown minds, the beaming faces, smiles silly to behold—beatific.

Most could not hear the sounds he was after, yet were greatly touched by the final product. Its close perfection, surrendering to the final moments when it came together. Especially the electronic gadgets. He would fiddle with one for days to get it to flow with the other parts and gadgets he had hooked up. From Mellotron, to Cry-Baby, to wah-wah, to Fuzz-Face, to Univibe, to Octavia, to Phase-Shifter, he had his own recipes, his own methods of combining what seemed like mumbo jumbo. Especially to the English engineers, neatly trimmed workers gazing idly through the control-room window at Jimi on his knees in a corner fiddling with a tiny box.

But when it was all working it was like a triumph of magic. Everything going at once and Jimi completely on top of it dancing between foot pedals orchestrating the frantic peaks of his sound at the speed of light.

February 24, 1969, Royal Albert Hall, London. The recording people and the film people had been setting up since sound check. Chas Chandler had been called in to help sort it out. It was a hectic scene to play against.

There was a new feeling about the Experience—their brief recent breakup had put some distance among them, especially Noel and Jimi. Noel was into asserting himself as an individual player and the essential link between guitar and bass did not have the unified fire of a healthy Experience. And the drums, so essentially keyed into polyrhythms around the time since Noel and Jimi both played rhythm, had to relinquish some of their freedom to keep time. Something the Experience was never known to do. Jimi took a lot more solo time than usual as they ranged through "Lover Man," "Stone Free," "Getting My Heart Back Together Again," "I Don't Live Today," a thirteen-minute "Red House," "Foxy Lady," and a long version of "The Sunshine of Your Love." The band was not really working as a unit, and Jimi's solos—as a result—are not as brilliant as when there is an ensemble sound with good ideas coming from all sides of the flying wedge.

Then Jimi did a new song, a blues: "Bleeding Heart" by Elmore James. The time was in twelve bars, very much like "Red House," but it was apparent that the song had variations that were not coming through.

Then they hit "Fire," "Little Wing," "Voodoo Chile (Slight Return)," and the finale, "Room Full of Mirrors," another new song Jimi had written over the holidays, with Dave Mason, Chris Wood, and "Rocki" joining them onstage.

I used to live in a Room Full of Mirrors
All I could see was me
Then I take my spirit and I smash my mirrors

And now the whole world is here for me to see
Now I'm searching for my love to be

A broken glass was solvin' my brain
Cut and screamin' crowdin' in my head
A broken glass was loud in my brain
It used to fall on my dreams and cut me in my bed
It used to fall on my dreams and cut me in my bed
I say making love was strange in my bed

Jimi ranges out in a solo against Dave Mason's scratch rhythms
and Rocki's klok-mokking congas. They reach a free terrain where
"Room Full of Mirrors" extends into a jam all the way out, conclud-
ing with a few bars of "The Star-Spangled Banner."

Amid the cheers and applause of the crowd emerge calls for various songs. They sound taunting, insolent, brash—as if they had
not just sat through an entire concert. Jimi mumbles that he is not a
jukebox as he slows the pace and waits out the shouted song titles,
which sound like catcalls. He reannounces Chris Wood on flute,
Dave Mason on guitar, and Rocki on congas. He calls for an *A* from
Dave Mason and goes into an extended tuning-up process. It is clear
that he is not happy with the crowd. Then Jimi feints two beats of
"Purple Haze" (those famous two beats) and then goes into an amp-
scorching feedback-rumbling free jazz distort over free percussion

accompaniment. "The Star-Spangled Banner" starks out in weird tonalities. It rages out in manic white and pink noises as full-range distortion. Audio destruct. Now he does not need to break up his guitar—he can create the effect with sound.

The concert is over.

Chas Chandler told him that the original Experience reunion had sounded as if three guys were soloing at the same time. He felt that their former unity was gone. Perhaps it would return, but they would need time and a conscious unity of purpose. Jimi had been glad to see Dave Mason, Chris Wood, and Rocki, the African conga player, join him on stage. If they were sounding like they were jamming with three pieces, well then, they jammed properly with six. But he had to admit, it did not really hang together. The crowd was a useless monitor of how they really played. They cheered anything he did.

He was glad of one thing about the concert. He had gotten a chance to see Rocki and some other African musicians on the London scene. They had gone to a studio before the Albert Hall concert and recorded some tunes with Jimmy Page, Denny Laine, and a lot of African percussionists, including Ginger Johnson on talking drum and Rocki on his handmade carved congas. Jimi liked experimenting with a lot of drumming sounds. It gave him different ideas from the usual power trio rock trip. He found it a pleasure to play rhythms against their polyrhythms. They would totally get outside, into another kind of space that he had seldom been in before.

He and Rocki rapped for a good while. What Rocki had to say about himself and the music fascinated him. Rocki had played with the Rolling Stones, Ginger Baker, Georgie Fame, Spooky Tooth, and with a whole lot of other people. He was considered *the* journeyman conga player of the London scene.

They went to the Speakeasy and hung out. Jimi and Rocki first played together at the Speakeasy while Jimi had been jamming with Amen Corner. He and Jimi took over the set and that was how they met and became friends.

Rocki's father was a voodoo priest and the chief drummer of a village in Ghana, West Africa. Rocki's real name was Kwasi Dzidzornu. One of the first things Rocki asked Jimi was where he got that voodoo rhythm from. When Jimi demurred, Rocki went on to explain in his halting English that many of the signature rhythms Jimi played on guitar were very often the same rhythms that his father played in voodoo ceremonies. The way Jimi danced to the rhythms of his playing reminded Rocki of the ceremonial dances to the rhythms his father played to Oxun, the god of thunder and lightning. The ceremony is called voodoshi. As a child in the village, Rocki would carve wooden representations of the gods. They also represented his ancestors. These were the gods they worshiped.

They would jam a lot in Jimi's house. One time they were jamming and Jimi stopped and asked Rocki point-blank, "You communicate with God, do you?" Rocki said, "Yes, I communicate with God."

The hip *International Times* dispatched its foxiest reporter to interview Jimi. Jane De Mendelssohn wanted to know about his American Indian heritage.

"Well, my grandmother's a full-blooded Indian, that's all. She used to make clothes for me. And everybody used to laugh at me when I went to school, you know—the regular sob story. She's full-blooded Cherokee (laughs). . . . [She lives] Up in Seattle, Vancouver, British Columbia now."

"Was she living on a reservation?" Jane wanted to know.

"No, she lives in a groovy apartment building. She has a television and a radio and stuff like that. She still has her long silver hair, though."

Jane wanted him to comment on the "whole Indian heritage scene. . . ."

"It's just another part of our family, that's all. . . ."

"Do they still take peyote?"

"Oh yes, it's all over the place. . . . But you know all Indians have different ways of stimulants, their own step toward God, spiritual forms, or whatever . . . which should be kept as nothing but a step, mind you. . . ."

She wanted to know how being such a "real pop giant," and "*Rolling Stone* performer of the year," was affecting him as a "human being."

Jimi gushed, "Oh don't tell me those things (laughs). . . . Well, I'm trying not to let it affect me at all. It's nothing but a brand . . . but I don't think that way. . . . I just happen to have a chance to be heard."

Jimi drifted into talking about his writing: "I just don't go around too much, except when I find a certain little scene going, and just go there if I want to go anywhere. But I stay in bed most of the time, or go to the park or somewhere. That's where I write some of my best songs, in bed, just laying there. I was laying there thinking of some when you came in. A really nice piece of music that I'm getting together for this late-summer LP that I'd like to do with this cat named Al Brown, in America. It's called 'The First Ray of the New

Rising Sun,' and it gives my own solution. You know, anybody can
protest, for instance, like in records or whatever you use your music
for, anybody can protest but hardly anybody tries to give a decent
type of solution, at least a meantime solution, you know.

"A lot of times I write a lot of words all over the place, anywhere,
on matchboxes, or on napkins, and then sometimes music comes
across to me just when I'm sitting around doing nothing. So I go
back to those few words if I can find them and you know, just get it
together. Sometimes it all happens at the same time. All depends on
what you might want to say. Different moods you might be in. . . ."

Jimi was glad his songs were not analyzed and intellectualized by
reviewers, as Jane put it. He said, ". . . our songs are like a personal
diary. . . ."

Jimi returned to the States at the beginning of April. On April 4,
he sat in the Village, in the Generation Club, with B. B. King and
Buddy Guy. Martin Luther King was dead. Shot down in Memphis
minutes ago. The faces of Buddy Guy and B. B. King are so much
alike. The little mustaches, the straightforwardness of their gaze
and talk. Southern fellows polite and direct. But now with Martin
Luther King dead, Jimi read in their faces the blood thing. And he
felt it. They shared the hurt that so many like them were feeling all
across the world. A pall hung heavy in the air, in the heart, a heavy
soddenness. Too easy to cry, but it was more than that. Not a
momentary pain, but a dead lasting reality. Death, the eternal
reminder, especially of treachery: an assassin in the free world. B. B.
King and Buddy Guy made him feel like a kid. In their grief-stricken
faces he sees their age. They are ageless. In the dark underground
room within the earth there is a stillness, silence. James Cleveland
is up at the Apollo. That would be the place to be if it were not for
the reports of violence. You knew Harlem would blow up. But down
in the Village, integrated like King and those before him had fought
so hard for, a moral force of right and good had been taken from
these people just like the people in Harlem. Yet in times like this
you want to be home where your people are. But then again, he *was*
home. Martin Luther King in so many ways made it possible for the
Village to be his home. But danger was all around and it got into the
music. There was nothing left to do but play. The music is high
gospel blues directed upward. The solos are in flight. No heavy earth
soddenness, although it's there. But just a taste of the danger, and
then the release, soaring out of view.

They had to play. They jammed the blues. Deep into the lower Manhattan night, three guitars pulled pure emotion from the mournful faces before them. They jammed the blues for Martin. Three guitars in tear-drenched tremolos, guitars singing a down-South jazz funeral.

When the club passed the hat for contributions to the Southern Christian Leadership Conference, Martin Luther King's organization, Jimi slipped in a check for five thousand dollars.

And then the three guitars of Buddy Guy, B. B. King, and Jimi Hendrix played on.

The JHE's "gig list" for April/May 1969 began on April 11 in Raleigh, North Carolina, at the Dalton Arena. They stayed at the Triangle Motel. The seating capacity of the Arena was 9,100. Fat Mattress was the supporting act. The JHE's potential gross: $45,000. Their motel was at the airport where they flew out in the middle of the morning for Philly where Jimi headlined the Spectrum. The potential gross was a high $105,000. The JHE and Fat Mattress returned to New York City, while the road crew and equipment drove down to Memphis for the gig of April 18 at the Mid-South Coliseum. The next day they were due in Houston for the Sam Houston Auditorium and the next day in Dallas at the Memorial Auditorium. The potential gross for each of the three dates was $60,000. They flew to L.A. on April 21 for dates at the Forum on April 25 and 26, for which they had p.g.'s of $105,000 each date. They flew to Oakland for a show on April 27 at the Coliseum Auditorium and back to L.A. that same night. They went to Detroit for two days, where they played Cobo Hall with Cat Mother. And then their largest potential gross, Maple Leaf Gardens, Toronto, Canada, for $110,000. They went back through the South. Hitting Tuscaloosa, Alabama, on May 7, Charlotte, North Carolina on May 8 and 9, Charleston, West Virginia, on May 10. Then to the Midwest for the Indianapolis State Fair on May 11. The JHE returned to New York on May 12. Their next date was in Baltimore on May 16.

Mike Jeffery suddenly came up with an easy addition: a return one-nighter in Toronto at the top-grossing Maple Leaf Gardens. Hendrix would be coming to New York for a five-day layover. A night of work for a possible $110,000 would still leave him four days in New York to rest.

Jimi had just leased a house in upstate New York; he would have time to cool out there before gigs in Baltimore and Providence and New York City. He had to fly back across the country for gigs on the Coast after May 22.

Toronto, Canada, May 12, 1968. Going through customs, as the Experience had done many many times without a hitch, was usually a relaxed laughing and smiling occasion, with many fans and reporters waiting for Jimi and company. But this time there was a weird delay. Jimi had not really checked out his luggage and was looking away when the customs official called his superior. They spoke together low-keyed and ominously, and then the officials asked Jimi if he had brought any illegal substances into Canada.

They produced a small bottle that contained several glassine packets of heroin and some hashish that they said had rested on top of the clothes in his luggage. Jimi had seen packets like that before. It was out of the question that he would ever carry around heroin, especially across a border. But then he knew that it was no use saying anything about his sense of propriety: He was being busted. Arrested on the spot.

His party was in an uproar. He was hustled away in such a hurry that it was unreal. One minute he was on top of the world, the next minute he was in the custody of Canadian police as a drug smuggler.

Although he was bailed out immediately, his arrest caused a sensation. He was able to make the gig at the Maple Leaf Gardens with no problem.

After the show was over and he was returning to the States, the impact of his arrest really hit him. Sure, he would have the best lawyers that money could buy. Sure, it was obvious that even if he used heroin he would not be stupid enough to leave it on the top of his luggage. But the obvious had nothing to do with it. The fact remained that he could be put away for quite a long time. It came to him in a flash how he would have to change his life around with a jail sentence hanging over his head. For one, he would have to make sure that he did not get into any other hassles with the law. That meant that the house he had leased in upstate New York had become, in the space of a few hours, the most important place for him to be. Away from the New York City scene he would be away from the influences that could possibly add to his problems with the authorities. He could keep a low profile upstate and really get into working on his music. In the event that he was put away, at least he would have some music together and in the can so he would not be forgotten.

He had the feeling that he had been set up. He searched back in his mind trying to recall the exact circumstances of his packing. Trying to recall who was nearby, close enough to slip something in his luggage. But it was no use. He had been so rushed and enveloped by people that it was all like a whirlwind. All he saw was the expression on the customs official's face. Jimi had known something was wrong in the way the man's manner suddenly changed toward him. He had felt an icy chill in his gut that spread all over his body. Before he knew it consciously, his body had already reacted.

He knew he would have to change his music now or never. Either he would be remembered as a freaky rock 'n' roll musician or as a serious creative musician. He might have to serve time in prison. The choice was his and he had to make it—fast. He wanted to get much closer to jazz. That meant that Noel would probably have to go. Noel had strong ideas about rock 'n' roll and would not change. There was a wider range of musicians Jimi wanted to work with. He wanted to relate to musicians who were into new sounds, who were not tied down to rock 'n' roll or rhythm and blues. Jazz was what he thought of. Not pure jazz, but new elements added to his sound that would extend it and make it possible to merge with other realms of music. The house upstate would be perfect. He could have who he wanted to have up there and be free from the restrictions the city placed on him. Before he had been toying with the idea of a new direction but now it was a serious quest. He would have to have some new music together that would appeal to more than just the fickle rock 'n' roll crowd. He did not want to be forgotten if he had to serve time in jail. The maximum sentence was seven years.

A couple of weeks later, in June, Jimi got permission from the authorities to split from the U.S.A. for a vacation in Morocco with Stella, Monique, Colette, and a woman named Luna. It was a time to reflect away from the turmoil.

It was a strange trip. They were followed by several strange men wherever they went.

They got to Morocco and headed out into the countryside. They met up with the Living Theater people along the way; Judith Malina, Julian Beck, Rufus, Jenny Hecht, and the rest of the troupe. Jimi and Colette dropped acid and tripped out in the magical countryside.

They wound up in Essaouira (Mogador), 100 miles west of Marrakech and 180 miles south of Casablanca. Timothy Leary was there with a whole bunch of followers. So was the Art Ensemble of Chicago, a black avant-garde experimental jazz unit. It was like a prearranged pilgrimage. They partied, took acid, and generally got to know each other. They traveled all over Morocco, received and feted by aristocracy and royalty. Jimi was often mistaken for John Claude Vigon, the popular Moroccan singer. That was a switch.

Leaving Morocco he was body-searched by their customs authorities.

Coming back to the States, Jimi and company found that they were still being followed.

The Experience was still able to tour while Jimi's drug case was pending in Toronto. It would be months before the case was settled.

June 20, 1969. Jimi appeared at Devonshire Downs, a racetrack in the San Fernando Valley, for the Newport Jazz Festival—L.A. He received the highest sum ever paid a rock act for one appearance: $125,000. Unsatisfied with the performance and police violence against the crowd, he returned the next day and jammed with Buddy Miles for forty-five minutes. It was the first time that Jimi and Buddy had played before a large audience together. Returning to the mobile home dressing room after the concert Noel Redding found Jimi talking to several Black Panthers. Redding made a fuss about their discussion disrupting his dressing room. He was more uptight than usual.

In L.A. Jimi finally got to meet Herbie Worthington. Buddy Miles always spoke highly of Herbie. They had been roommates once. Herbie was the kind of guy who helped you to get your thing together by his very presence on the scene. Herbie had helped Buddy Miles get his horn section together for his band. Jimi was interested in horns, too, but even more so in a good friend. They were hard to find. Since Jimi's bust, he had begun to notice strange machinations among those who were supposed to be his friends. Herbie had a reputation in music circles as a good solid person who could be counted on in tight spots, and who never tripped out on anything. Jimi dug Herbie right away. Herbie was not a musician. He took photos and studied books on a wide range of subjects.

Vishwa was on the scene also. He and Jimi and Herbie met at the hotel just as Jimi was getting ready to split for the June 29 "Denver Pop" concert. Vishwa, by then, was a regular member of Jimi's entourage. It was obvious that Herbie wanted to go to Denver with them as well. Jimi finally asked him to go at the last minute. Herbie said that he would like to go but that he did not have the bread. That was a laugh. Jimi probably had about ten thousand dollars on him at that moment. Herbie was so glad to be going that he picked Jimi up clear off the ground in a spontaneous gesture, cradling him like a baby. They all had a good laugh.

They flew in to Denver on June 29, 1969, and checked into the hotel. Herbie and Jimi dropped some fine acid just before the ride to the gig. Herbie confided to Jimi that his favorite song was "Bold as Love"—he dug the relationship of the colors to the emotions.

Mile-high Stadium was in an uproar. There were forty thousand screaming kids bursting forth from the stands and not enough security. The stage was located on the infield diamond and the fans were desperate to get down close to the music.

Jimi and Herbie felt the acid coming on as they clambered onto the stage. Sedulous, fluent, and delicious waves of energy pulsated from everything.

Jimi got right into "Bold as Love." "*Orange: so young and full of daring/But very uncertain on the first go-round.*" He could not resist a peek at Herbie, who stood in the wings. The acid exhilarated through the air and they had a moment of pure contact that made both of them crack up. Jimi stood on the stage laughing for a moment—then, keeping his face averted from Herbie's side of the stage, Jimi started the "Bold as Love" all over again, from the top.

As Jimi rode toward the end of the song the crowd started rushing toward the stage. The police hastily assembled on the turf. The police began firing tear-gas bombs into the boisterous, onrushing crowd. The wind shifted and the tear gas began blowing onto the stage. It was not long before the crowd had completely overrun the police and security guards, and charged the stage. Barrett and Stickells and the rest of the JHE road crew raced against time and the mob. They quickly backed up the equipment truck and jammed Jimi inside, followed by Herbie, Mitch, Noel, and the others. Barrett and Stickells locked the truck and then they proceeded to slowly wade the huge truck through forty thousand rampaging kids. Jimi and Herbie giggled in the black interior of the slowly moving rocking truck. It was wild! Some kids got up on the top of the truck and began stomping on it as if they wanted to bash it in. Others rocked the truck as if they wanted to topple it. Barrett and Stickells raced the motor so the kids would think they were going to speed off. Jimi suddenly remembered the girls he and Herbie had brought with them from the hotel. Jimi also panicked before Herbie laughed and told him that the girls were in the truck but were too scared to talk.

They went to a private party for Jimi at a club. All the best guitar pickers and the prettiest young ladies of Denver were there. Jimi jumped up on the tiny stage and played for two hours straight. Then they went to an outdoor wedding celebration and Jimi jammed until dark with the Rich Brothers and "Snip" Milton on drums. They jammed on an old Junior Walker tune: "Cornbread and Buttermilk."

Back at the hotel, Jimi, Herbie, and Vishwa shared five groupies among them.

Soon after the "Denver Pop" concert Jimi went into virtual seclusion.

On July 2 Noel Redding and Mitch Mitchell turned up in London announcing that they had left the Experience for good. Noel Redding told Stan Reed, of the *Evening Standard*, "I suddenly heard that Jimi was planning to expand the group, bring in other musicians, writers, and composers, and drop the name of the Experience and I hadn't been consulted." Mitch Mitchell concurred that the group had definitely split up completely. But Jimi was more involved with the sad news from London that Brian Jones had died.

Billy Cox, the bass player Jimi knew from the army, and Buddy Miles were waiting in the wings. Although they were still basically a jam-rhythm section for Jimi, he planned to make them the core of his new musical direction.

Soon after, Jimi appeared on the "Tonight" show, which was guest-hosted by Flip Wilson. Jimi, accompanied by Billy Cox on bass and the drummer from Doc Severinsen's band, dedicated a new song, "Lover Man," to Brian Jones. The television studio amplifiers blew up midway through the song, something Brian Jones would have probably found amusing.

The word was out that Hendrix was into something. Since the bust in Toronto he had maintained a very low profile. He was commuting between three locations, always moving fast in seemingly laid-back elegance. His Manhattan apartment was maintained by Devon, as an employee. The Record Plant had extensive studio time reserved for him. But it was his retreat in upstate New York where he was putting it all together.

Miles Davis was into something, too. He had been carefully moving his new band to a place where they could sail right into a new thing and hit it right. Miles Davis had stuck (since *ESP*, an album that signified a new "official" band of sorts) with Wayne Shorter on tenor sax, Herbie Hancock on piano, Ron Carter on bass, and Tony Williams on drums since 1965. George Benson's guitar was added to the same personnel on his *Miles in the Ski* album. *Filles De Kili-manjaro* was the summit for this band. It was also a perfect setup to follow with something totally new.

Impeccably orchestrated, *Filles* had a song dedicated to his new wife, Betty Davis, née Mambry: "Mademoiselle Mambry." Best of friends with Devon, Colette, and just getting to be friends with Jimi, Betty Davis had just written a Chambers Brothers hit, "Uptown to Harlem," a song that celebrated the jumping black fervor of "uptown" blackness. Miles Davis was suddenly catapulted into the midst of the hip young funky music crowd.

Betty Davis threw a dinner party at their townhouse on West Seventy-seventh Street and invited all the finest chicks she knew. Miles Davis did not like men visiting his home, but it was understood that Jimi would escort Devon. At the last minute Miles was unable to attend the party due to an engagement. That left Jimi as the only male in attendance among a roomful of lovely ladies. Miles had left a sheet of music that contained part of a score for Jimi to check out. When Betty gave it to Jimi he told her that he could not read music. Miles called later and asked Betty to put Jimi on the phone. They discussed music in general but were unable to talk about the written music Miles had left.

Alan Douglas, a friend of Miles and husband of Stella, Colette's best friend, business partner, and confidante, was dying to get Miles and Jimi together in studio sessions. Miles Davis was said to be the more reluctant of the two but they both had a reluctance to work together. Aside from their mutual respect was their knowledge that the hip musical ideas they had developed independently could as readily be absorbed and applied by either one. But Miles was willing to help Jimi put together his new band. Horns would be the biggest problem for Jimi—and who knew horns better than Miles? Figuring out how to add horns to Jimi's virtuoso one-man-band guitar that would heighten what was already there became a cross-conversation among Jimi, Miles, Al Brown, Quincy Jones, Gil Evans, and Alan Douglas.

Jimi neither wrote nor read music. Many of his bends, runs, harmonies, cross-rhythms, and chords were not score-possible. While Jimi desired very much to be able to notate, he also knew that he wrote most of his material as he went along, culminating largely in the studio or in jams. His compositions were not based on notes as much as *sound*. His compositions compressed incredible pieces of blues funk with jazz and black classical modes including heavy electronics. He had the ability to go down to the hardest rock 'n' roll or up to his personal improvisational signatures, where it was pure pleasure to hear his mind and imagination work out at such high speeds.

Miles Davis began to go public with his recognition of a wider spectrum of black music than just jazz. He publicly praised Jimi

Hendrix, Stevie Wonder, and Sly Stone. He declared that they were the music he was listening to. Critics like Ralph Gleason and Leonard Feather were astounded. Miles talking about Jimi's band said, "It took a black cat to make two white dudes play their ass off." Miles even gave offhand praise to Mitch and Noel in the process of his growing love for Jimi's music. Jimi was astounded: Miles was the living legend of jazz. He had played with "Bird": Charlie Parker. He had helped to launch bebop.

They got into long conversations on the phone. Miles felt that Jimi was doing good as he was. Miles was fascinated by Jimi's untrained ear—its incredible correctness in the most advanced spheres of music theory. Wilfred Mellers, the famous musicologist, often talked about how the Beatles had in their unschooled ears somehow a direct communication with ancient pagan, tribal, and magical essences of old English traditional music; some of their music he traced back to the Middle Ages. By the same token, Miles heard in Jimi solutions to the wedge that had grown over the years to separate jazz from popular music. It was difficult to explain, but then Jimi did it so well, so often, and so unconsciously that it would have done him little good to understand in words or even to try to score what he did naturally.

Miles knew it would be difficult to really help Jimi musically. Yet the problem was intriguing. You could talk about it for hours. At its center was the growth and direction of the most powerful region of black music. It was more than jazz and funk. It was the touches that Miles had already worked with while in another place. The cadences of *Sketches of Spain*, the random moods of *Filles* that often had it totally in sync with a flowing consciousness.

Jimi Hendrix's "sound paintings" from *Electric Ladyland* had been soundly knocked by the rock 'n' roll press (including *Rolling Stone*), yet those who followed him loved "1983," "Rainy Day, Dream Away," and "And the Gods Made Love." Jimi had been painted so one-dimensionally by the rock 'n' roll press that they failed to realize his art and his humor.

Jimi held back from doing more "sound paintings." His new works were more sculpted celestial "sky church" guitar balancing with "social realism."

But his "sound painting" concept grew stronger and stronger as *Electric Ladyland* became the type of album no one could sensibly be without.

Jimi was getting in a lot of jamming up in Boiseville, while in the studio he worked more with his sculpted pieces. Two prominent

musicians who spent significant time jamming with Jimi on his
new direction were Larry Young, the incredible keyboard jazz man,
and Harvey Brooks, Fender bass whiz. Both later played on the
album for Miles that was his breakthrough: *In a Silent Way.*

The land increased the farther from New York City they drove,
heading north where hills merged into mountains, where trees and
sky began to take over; the rough gray of Manhattan fading in the
distance, fading in the mind.

They stopped off for refreshments at the Red Apple, a highway
food and gas complex. Plain country folks. It seemed as if nothing
hip could exist so far away from everything. Miles of highway leading into nothingness. Was this the peace he wanted?

Entering Woodstock he could see the signs. Long hair, hip restaurants, funkily painted houses, and broadly smiling stoned people
taking it easy. Right then he could feel it. The earth commanded the
space of the mind.

After a couple of days of lying around, his daydreams came back.
His mind quickly adapted to the country space. His visions were
less frenetic and harried; long legato graceful dreams, lasting longer
with more texture and involvement.

As always, he counterpointed his dream meditation with acoustical blues playing. Out of a simple bass line that flowed along
endlessly, coming back to its beginning, dipping deeper, then coming back again like an eternal cycle. They were long and peaceful
days, the first in a long time, and the music began to jell.

Upon reflection it seemed that in his music he had advocated a
speeded-up "A" head type of version. He strongly wanted to contrast
that with another side of his existence.

It was amazing the way that simple bass line had inspired him.
The peaceful yet syncopated line spun off countless variations in his
mind. It was like it could go on forever. Moreover, the tune set his
mind at ease. What greater gift to get from yourself than something
that helps you? He decided to call the tune "Pali-gap." "Pali-gap"
was like an ode to the mind, the spaces of the mind when stilled,
where marvelous visions and sounds came through.

He began to call people on the phone. Musicians. He wanted to
play. He wanted sound around him, not only sound to support his
playing, but also musicians who were into something of their own.
Jimi had met Juma, a conga-playing brother, one day while shopping
in Woodstock. He had played with a lot of heavy jazz dudes like

Archie Shepp, Sonny Murray, and Larry Young. Jimi was very shy
about approaching jazz musicians. Very often they had negative feelings about the kind of music he played. But talking with Juma, Jimi
found his vibes were very different. Not only was Juma positive, he
also was enthusiastic.

Juma had been living up there for some time. He owned a forty-
acre farm. He knew all the other brothers living in the area. There
were a lot of bands up there like Paul Butterfield's Blues Band, The
Band, The Blues Project, and others. Juma volunteered to help round
up some cats to come and jam. In no time at all they had Ron Hicks,
the brother who played bass with Paul Butterfield, Phillip Wilson, a
drummer, also with the Butterfield band, Larry Young, keyboards,
Larry Lee, guitar, and Jerry Velez, congas. There were also some
hangers-on, like this spaced-out "A" head, Avocado, but everything
was cool. Everyone was really into playing.

Jimi had had a conga player, Larry Faucette, on one of his cuts on
the *Electric Ladyland* album, and Rocki, the African conga player,
had sat in with him during a live recording session at Albert Hall
earlier that year, but Jimi had never lived with one before, playing
continuously. It was a new and exciting feeling. The rhythmic com-
plexity that Mitch had hinted at in his busy playing was resolved in
the conga and bongo—African drums. Jimi could play softly and
have the proper subtle effects he wanted on the percussion. And
• when he wailed, the African drums added to the drive without being
too loud. Every trap drummer feels that he can cover all the percussive effects, and Mitch (who had returned to Jimi, leaving Noel in
London) was no exception, but it was time to change and grow, and
Mitch had to go along with it.

Mitch hung around, coming up regularly to "practice." It was
strange hearing his hobbitlike English accent. Jimi found himself
missing Noel and Chas, their accents and timbres. But he had been
dominated by those English voices. Now it was different. Mitch was
in the minority.

Jimi had not spent so much time with brothers for what seemed
like ages. He dug it. It was like coming home. In the singular world
of rock there were few blacks. Buddy Miles was one of the few. But
now with a whole bunch of cats around every day he began to
recapture some of the soul feelings he had been apart from.

Jimi was most impressed by Juma, college-educated, well versed
as a musician, and totally black, not in a militant, unyielding way,
but in an intelligent, dedicated way. Juma had been operating the
Society for Aboriginal Music, which was basically a promoter of

serious black and African music on a research and performance level. A merging of African and American music took place in the jam situation where the different elements of both had a chance to blend in an unrestricted atmosphere.

Juma organized a concert at Tinkerville Playhouse for the jammers back at the house. Way after midnight, the Band of Gypsys assembled.

Jimi really got into it with Larry Young, the jazz organist. Young was well-known on the European jazz circuit, which featured the works of the younger jazz instrumentalists and composers. He was into both avant-garde music and Herbie Hancock rhythms, electronic music and funk. He had that mystical, selfless surrender to the music they played, and his drive made it possible for him also to be himself.

The *sound* of the organ live in the wooden-walled space of the little old theater like an old frontier church was thrilling; merged with Jimi's Stratocaster, the combined sounds exhilarated chills in the nervous system. Tuning slightly down, using only two Marshall amps, Jimi would overdrive through the pre-amps to get the bell and gonglike effects. Then he would concentrate on the Leslie dubbing with the organ reaching the outer ranges of the scale. Sliding up in a bottleneck trill and zooming down the neck in an all-fret distortion dive, then switching to fuzz tone on the way to grind in the bottom ranges as the organ droned in the deeper ranges.

The congas popped and rumbled, shaking, vibrating the wood slats of the room. The sound making one very aware of the earth beneath. The bongos sounding sometimes like *tabla*, sometimes like hands slapping thighs, chasing Jimi up a run, a fraction of a beat behind him. Billy Cox on bass holding the bottom, with cautious and deep alternating phrases. At one point there were twenty-five musicians playing onstage.

Jimi exulted in the new dimensions his music was taking. He was discovering incredible new realms he could play in and invent out of. The new sounds meshed with the feelings he had been hoping for, the emotions he sought to express. He was listening to jazz a lot now, and enjoying it too. He was into John Coltrane, Rashied Ali, McCoy Tyner, Ornette Coleman, and of course Rahsaan Roland Kirk, who was like an idol to him.

The Boiseville house gave Jimi a lot of good times, especially after big Claire came up to cook. She was a friend of Juma Sutan, and could really burn. She cooked Jimi's favorite dishes. He loved to have a big pot of soup on the stove—ready to eat, with lots of goodies in it. He dug sweets too. His favorites were tollhouse cookies made with chocolate chips and nuts. They would pick blackberries and make fresh blackberry pie.

The place had huge grounds. You could go horseback riding for miles without ever leaving the estate. But the grounds were not guarded and all sorts of people took to camping about and hanging near the house hoping to get to Jimi. One chick showed up after having walked miles in the rain. She parked herself in the doorway. It took days to get her to leave. There was an underage chick from Texas staying there whose father would often call at odd hours. Jimi was extremely kindhearted. One cat, who had been posing as Jimi while running up an enormous hotel bill in Manhattan, wound up inside the house as a guest. Claire doubled as the one to keep people away from Jimi. Devon, who usually took care of such things, was strangely absent. There had been a big fight. No one would talk about it.

Jimi's bedroom, with beautiful Moroccan rugs and a precious French antique makeup table, looked out over a huge reservoir. It had a large sitting room off to the side with a wood-burning fireplace—as did all the bedrooms.

Very often at three in the morning they would go down to the Woodstock movie theater and jam. Santana came up and so did Janis Joplin. All kinds of beautiful musicians were coming up to jam.

The house was always full of chicks, besides other hangers-on. The musicians began staying there, too, due to the late hours the music began. Juma, who was staying there, began to help Claire with the house-cleaning duties. It was getting out of hand. It got so bad that Jimi would have to call before he came and tell Claire to clear the house. Always all of the seven or eight chicks around would claim emphatically that they were not the ones who were supposed to leave.

One day Jimi went to town and brought back a whole lot of magic markers, colored pencils, and crayons, and had everyone sitting around drawing and coloring. Then everyone got an instrument and played; even the groupies got little percussion things. Later he grabbed an engraved Spanish guitar that Devon had given him and said, "Now I'm really gonna play y'all some music." He played a full solo concert on acoustic guitar—all pure Jimi.

Billy Cox came along slowly but very surely. He had no problems about playing Jimi's dictated bass lines. After a while Billy began to really get what Jimi was after: not just playing the notes, but also playing the sound; the contrasting double bass lines and the drum bass drone of Earth and its bodies of water that enabled Jimi to take off and soar beyond planet reach.

There was the feeling especially among those in his management office that Jimi wanted Billy more as an old buddy, a crony, than as a bass player. While it was true that Jimi dearly needed a friend, an old friend he could trust, Jimi also felt that Billy had more potential as a bass player than Noel. Besides, Billy's progress with the music was coming along so wonderfully that it served to cement their long friendship. Unlike Noel, Billy trusted Jimi. Billy did not believe it a put-down to play dictated bass lines.

The bass lines were not difficult, but the feeling and philosophy behind them were. It was a subtle thing. String-bending nuances only brothers who had played in the South knew. More than the notes, it was the texture of the sound interwoven with the patterns the bass and guitar made in rhythm that made the sound happen.

Jimi knew that Billy Cox was a down-to-earth, Southern homeboy with simple tastes and few excesses. Since their days playing in the army and in Nashville as the Casuals and the Imperials they had known containment and poverty. Jimi hoped that Billy's mind would not be blown by the sudden wealth and weird scenes. Jimi hoped that he succeeded in communicating to Billy that he was not as much into the weird scenes as it seemed, or as many thought. And Jimi hoped above all that nothing would happen through his scenes that would really trip Billy out.

Being around brothers made Jimi appreciate his relationship with Billy Cox and Buddy Miles more. They always had fun on sessions. Buddy's style was pretty predictable, but also always predictably strong.

One night at the Record Plant they had some tape to use up to end the reel. Jimi played the intro to "Hootchie Cootchie Man" knowing that Buddy and Billy would pick right up on it. He had one of his jokes planned for them. He sang the first lines in an imitation of the mannish "country" Delta blues phrasings of Muddy Waters, making about ten *b*'s out of the line "Before I was born":

The gypsy woman told my mother
Before I was born . . .
I got a boychild coming

And then in his famous Harlem drag queen voice Jimi pipes in falsetto:

GONNA BE A SON OF A GUN!

Buddy and Billy burst out laughing (much against their will, as they all had a deep and abiding love for the older blues men; in fact, Buddy had just finished a session with Muddy Waters for the *Fathers and Sons* album). Jimi kept going, raunching the lines:

He gonna make pretty womens
Jump and shout
Then the world wanna know
What this all about

And then they all began to smoke. Jimi sliding into the first solo as he shouted the chorus:

'Cause you know I'm here
Everybody knows I'm here
Yeah, you know I'm a hootchie cootchie man
Everybody knows I'm here

Ed Chalpin's suit against Jimi Hendrix, Reprise Records, and Mike Jeffery for breach of contract had been going through motions, countermotions and delays for over a year. His evidence was a contract that consisted of merely one piece of paper.

PPX ENTERPRISES

Master Producers and Agents
1650 Broadway, New York, N.Y. 10019 Tel.: 247-6010
Cable: Chalprises, New York

Agreement made as of October 15, 1965 between PPX Enterprises, Inc. and Jimmy Hendrix, Hotel America, 145 W. 47th St., New York, N.Y.

In consideration of the sum of one (1.00) dollar and other good and valuable consideration it is agreed to as follows:

1. That Jimmy Hendrix will produce and play and/or sing exclusively for PPX Enterprises, Inc., for three (3) years from above date.

2. Jimmy Hendrix will make available his services at the request of PPX with a minimum of ten (10) days notice to pro-

duce no more than four (4) titles per session, a minimum of three (3) sessions per year.

3. That Jimmy Hendrix services will include singing and/or arrangements, which at the option of PPX shall be written out by other copyist or arranger.

4. That PPX shall pay all cost of studio, musicians, etc., and shall be reimbursed from first profits received.

5. Jimmy Hendrix shall receive one (1) per cent of retail selling price of all records sold for his production efforts, minimum scale for arrangements he produces.

6. That Jimmy Hendrix shall play instruments for PPX at no cost to PPX Enterprises, Inc.

7. That PPX shall have exclusive rights to assign for all masters produced in conjunction with Jimmy Hendrix.

Agreed To:

PPX Enterprises, Inc.

Agreed To:

By /s/ Jimmy Hendrix   By /s/ Ed Chalpin

     Jimmy Hendrix   Ed Chalpin

Chalpin had had the diminutive Curtis Knight as a witness. All of Jimi's royalties due from Warner-Reprise were ordered placed in escrow by the court pending a settlement.

Instead of woodshedding, instead of working on his musical growth, instead of a measured deep reflection and a consolidation of direction—he would have to work, work like a nigger. He would have to gig like mad to stay afloat. And there was still the Canadian bust hanging over his head.

The worry that had started the last part of 1968 would reach a height by the end of 1969. Litigation seemingly goes on forever, weeks and months and years. But yet as he ached to soar, the weekly scorecard of suits, courts and dates, motions and appeals began to absorb more and more of his consciousness.

Devon knew that the best way for Jimi to beat the shit against him was to move on ahead with his new musical ideas, build the studio he always talked about, and concentrate on gaining more control over his destiny. Racing against the clock. Racing before the final toll of judgments and evil human vibes.

Devon, on the other hand, treated the matter with the seasoned scorn of a junkie burn. They had made up and gotten even closer, and she still kept up his New York City apartment. A typical ripoff in a fucked-up world. What *concerned* her was the effect it was having on Jimi.

Her concern reached its height when Jimi's hair started coming out in clumps, in his hand, in the comb, on his sweated pillow. He began to sleep with his hat on. It was then that she gave him what she had. She gave him her most important possession: her circle of friends who kept *her* together. Included in that circle was Finney, the hairdresser.

Finney, Miles Davis's hairdresser, was a hair specialist who was known to be able to prevent men from growing bald (he had saved Miles's hair) and to enable women to have long, luxuriant locks. Miles Davis had gone through bouts of hair loss, due in large part to the conflict of trying to create amid tremendous legal and business pressures.

Jimi was in really bad shape at the prospect of losing his hair—the youthful allurement and staple part of his image. He wouldn't take his hat off, even wearing it to bed. Devon called Finney in desperation. Finney had his own shop at that time and invited Jimi to come over, but Jimi did not want to go anywhere in public where the state of his hair would be exposed. After a couple of weeks, Finney finally decided to go to Hendrix. They met at Jimi's suite at the Drake Hotel.

Hendrix beat around the bush for a long time. He took Finney through his closets, showing off his wild array of stage costumes, casual togs, and fancy threads. Then he ordered dinner. While they ate he told Finney about dreaming of his mother. Jimi said that he often saw his mother while he was wide awake. Finney, strangely, had had the same experience. Finally Finney took a look at Jimi's locks. Hendrix's hair was a common case. Often straightened, conked, and curled, his hair had been weakened by artificial straighteners and had begun to come out. The fact that Jimi had begun to worry a great deal also weakened his hair. It had to be cut, the split ends pared, and allowed to grow back out fully. This was truly traumatic for Jimi—cut his hair? But it had to be done. Finney began to cut, clipping quickly and expertly with long thin scissors. Jimi was scared to death watching much of his fabled long hair plop to the floor. He picked up a newspaper and read intensely. Once the cutting was over he sprang to the bathroom mirror. After staying a long while in the bathroom he came out smiling—it looked good.

Finney and Jimi became fast friends. Devon always said how

much they resembled each other. Now, Finney, small, compactly built but spare with a soft voice and laid-back, relaxed, totally self-controlled air, became a part of Hendrix's intimate circle.

Jim Robertson was one of Jimi's favorite engineers at the Record Plant. He put up with Jimi's eccentricities like the dobo barricade Jimi insisted on singing behind, or his penchant for recording some vocals in the bathroom. They got stoned together, and Jimi amazed Jim by snorting meth or coke through one nostril without the aid of a straw or rolled dollar bill. Jimi often dropped several tabs of acid daily. And the thing Jimi liked most about Jim Robertson was that he could engineer while seemingly stoned.

Jim Robertson had quickly distanced beyond Tom Wilson-protégé status and had become a damn good engineer in his own right, recording Jimi at the Record Plant. Mike Jeffery began noticing him. He liked Jim's vibe. Jeffery felt he could trust him. Jim Robertson had a young naïveté and a pleasant touch of perception. He worked hard without seeming to be working at all. He had a loyalty to music as well as to interpersonal relationships. The sessions at the Record Plant were arduous, yet Jeffery and Hendrix seemed to get on better around Robertson, who seemed to like them both equally.

Jim Robertson became very important to Jimi. He was one of the few engineers he could communicate with. Jimi and Ed Kramer had had a falling out. The pressures of building a new studio coupled with Jimi's seemingly eccentric recording habits had taken its toll on their intense relationship. Robertson was relatively new to the business and found no problems with Jimi's philosophy regarding recording. In fact, he seemed to enjoy the long stoned hours.

Jimi discussed his feelings about recording with Meatball Fulton, one of his favorite interviewers. Fulton was taken by Hendrix's frustrations regarding the recording process but could not quite understand it. He generalized about the differences between LPs and singles, between the U.S.A. and London, but Hendrix got very specific: ". . . the cutting of it . . . that's a whole scene, the cutting of it. You can mix and mix and mix and get such a beautiful sound, and when they cut it, they can just screw it up so bad."

Fulton did not understand.

Jimi explained: "I wouldn't understand that either 'cause we, you know . . . ooooh, it comes out so bad. 'Cause they go by levels and all that. Some people don't have any imagination. . . . See when you cut a record, right before it's being printed you know, when you cut the master, if you want a song where you have really deep sound, where you have depth and all this, you must . . . almost remix it again right there at the cutting place. And ninety-nine percent don't even do this. They just say, 'Oh turn it up' so their mixture doesn't go over or their mixture doesn't go under. And there it is you know. It's nothing but one-dimensional."

Hendrix went on. "I want to have stereo where it goes . . . up . . . and behind and underneath. . . . 'Cause all you can get now is just across and across. . . ."

Jimi went on to talk about some songs he had written that had never been recorded and probably would not ever be. Length was a problem. "Eyes and Imagination" was one. It was about fourteen minutes long and had four movements, and every verse told a completely different story.

". . . they're so many songs I wrote that we haven't even done yet and we'll probably never do. It's because . . . it's a really bad scene. . . . You know, we must be Elvis Presleys and rock 'n' rolls and Troggs. We must be that (laughs). And there'll be no smoking in the gas chamber."

He told how "Purple Haze" originally had many more verses about going through mythical lands. "They got the Greek gods and all that stuff, well you can have your own mythology, see?"

Jimi often thought up his own mythologies lying in bed, but sometimes other things happened. "Have you ever laid in bed and you was in this complete state where you couldn't move? And you feel like you're going deeper and deeper into that, and it's not sleep, but it's something else. And every time I go into that I say, 'Ah hell I'm scared as hell' and you get all scared and stuff and so you try to say, 'Help help.' You can't move and you can't speak but you say, 'Help help,' and you finally get out of it you know. You just can't move. It's a very funny feeling. But one time that feeling was coming through me and I say, 'Ah here we go. This time I'm just gonna let it happen and see where I go.' I just wanted to see what happens and it was really getting scary, man, it was going whooosshhhe, like that, you know. And I said, 'I'm not even asleep, this is really strange.' And then somebody knocked on the door. I said, 'Oh' . . . Because I wanted to find out."

Fulton asked, "Can you remember some things really far back? Like when you were a baby?"

Jimi's memories had merged into dreams. Like one he had when he was a "real little" boy: "Like my mother was being carried away on this camel. And there was a big caravan and she was saying, 'Well, I'm gonna see you,' and she was going under these trees, and you could see the shade . . . you know the leaf patterns . . . crossing her face. You know how the sun shines through a tree, and if you go under the shadow of the tree the shadows go across your face. Well these were in green and yellow. Shadows. And she was saying, 'Well, I won't be seeing you too much anymore you know.' And then about two years after that she died. And I said, 'Where you going?' I remember that, I always will remember that. . . .''

The new jamming with the Band of Gypsys Suns, Moons and Rainbows was also helping Jimi with his laborious studio work. It seemed to take seasons just to move from one point to the next—the final mix was always elusive. Continuously laying down new tracks, working on older tracks, mixing, adding touches, remixing. The thought that he had new music before him and a studio under construction made him more efficient with his open-schedule account at the Record Plant. He could not wait until Electric Lady Studios were completed.

His office (Mike Jeffery and crew) really froze on his upstate jams. They resented him taking on other directions when they were burdened from day to day with the details of building Electric Lady Studios. They had just found out that the site (formerly the Generation Club on West Eighth Street in the Village) was over a subway tunnel. Extra soundproofing would now be essential, at outrageous cost.

He felt that Mitch might be spying on him for the office. Mitch's loyalties were to the rock 'n' roll star sound, as were the loyalties of the office. Jimi *knew* that Devon was shaky sometimes. But you never know who can be bought. Even Juma, as much as Jimi respected him, could be a spy. Jimi even asked Juma. Juma laughed, ''Man, you're really paranoid.''

Jimi told Juma why he was paranoid. A very bizarre and frightening act of violence has happened to him recently. He has told no one about it except Big Claire. One early morning, alone in his apartment in the Village, he answers the doorbell. Strange men are at the door. He is taken forcibly from his apartment and stuffed in the back of a car by four dudes. They act tough yet they still handle him more gently than would be expected. He is blindfolded. One of the guys kneels on him, his knee in his back. He is shunted and reeled through black vectors to a dry brick-smelling bare cement floor. In very tough voices the guys tell him how they are going to hurt him. His mind has resigned itself to that. He waits. But they don't hurt him. He just sits and sits. Then after a while there is a commotion. Sounds of struggle. Shouts and curses. Doors slamming and feet running. He hears people running toward him. His blindfold is ripped off. It is Mike Jeffery and the guys from the office. His bonds are untied. He is relieved. He is grateful. They hustle him out of the building, talking some shit. He is dazed, wondering. . . . What kind of shit is this? How did they know where I was? What happened? They jabber a story at him, but he is too busy wondering in his mind. . . . Was it a setup or was it for real?

It was hard to tell. The atmosphere around the music was always too spacey and trippy. It was hard to tell what kind of influence the office had over the people close to him. Any type of official business that went down involving anybody put them in direct touch with the office. Jeffery would not even pay the weekly salaries that had been agreed upon for his jam band, nor even help them with transportation.

But he could not let that bother him. His obligation to the music was where he was at. But he could see his office's point about rock: They had made a lot of money with it and they wanted to continue.

He had met over the past year new people who were into his music and were very sure of his abilities: Tom Wilson, Jim Robertson, Al Brown, Quincy Jones, Miles Davis, Gil Evans, Alan Douglas, and on another level, Timothy Leary. Alan Douglas had produced Eric Dolphy and other jazz artists, usually in their formative stages. Douglas was the producer of the infamous "Last Poets," who had entered the national charts with poetic chants set to African drum accompaniment. *Performance*, the movie that starred Mick Jagger, used a cut from their album in the movie and in the sound-track album.

Douglas was also recording at the Record Plant at the same time as Jimi. They knew each other fairly well through Stella, Douglas's wife, who was partners with Jimi's private designer, Colette, in a dress shop on the Lower East Side. Alan Douglas had Timothy Leary in the studio doing a spoken-word album entitled *You Can Be Anyone This Time Around*. Jimi visited their sessions a few times and even contributed a few guitar licks and effects to a varied montage score that played behind the voice.

Jimi remembered some of the lines Leary spoke:

You can be any *one*, this time around. You can be anything, this time around. . . . You can do anything, this time around. . . . You're the first generation in human history to know how to control your own nervous system, change your own reality. Blow your own mind. Make up your own mind. . . .

Douglas took to acting as a go-between for Jimi in various transactions. Douglas knew many jazz musicians. He brought Tony Williams, the brilliant jazz drummer, by while Hendrix was doing some solo overdubbing. Hendrix and Williams jammed for a while, feeling each other out. Tony Williams was the young prodigy who had joined Miles Davis's band at seventeen years of age. That had been almost six years ago. Tony Williams was in the process of recording his own band. He had sent for John McLaughlin, the English electric guitarist, to record with him, but Miles had used him on the *In a Silent Way* sessions. Williams preferred McLaughlin's colorless high technique to Hendrix's free-flowing funk and blue noise. Williams and Hendrix did not click together. They stopped jamming after several minutes.

Even though they had not hit if off, Hendrix had been impressed that Douglas had come up with Tony Williams and brought them together. Douglas felt that Miles Davis would eventually come in the studio and record with Jimi. Although *In a Silent Way* had just gotten in the can, word was out that Miles had gone very strongly toward rock. This was earth-shaking news in the music world. Tony Williams rebelled against it. Herbie Hancock stood on the fence. But Miles was completely into *his* new sound. Hendrix was impressed with just the fact that Miles had moved musically in a way few jazz men had the guts to move: to challenge rock's dominance over popular music. In Jimi's mind, it endorsed what he was trying to do in moving closer to jazz and African percussive realms. At one point Douglas had Hendrix, Tony Williams, and Miles Davis ready to record together. The deal fell through after Miles demanded $50,000 for the sessions.

Back at the house in Boiseville, word had begun to come through the grapevine about a proposed rock festival to end all rock festivals. They were calling it "Woodstock" and it would be given somewhere in upstate New York. People were beginning to freak out over it already. Woodstock—Oh well, he had some new shit for them.

The cars began coming weeks before. Everybody in the thirty-mile radius had strange cars parked out in front of their houses, visitors from all over. Traffic in Woodstock got noticeably thicker day by day. The single-lane roads that branched off to other small towns nearby like Boiseville and Liberty began to look like Twelfth Street and University Place in Manhattan.

The week before Woodstock, cars began to show up parked and

Larry Lee, who played rhythm guitar at Woodstock, August 1969
JIM CUMMINS

Juma Sultan, percussionist with the Band of Gypsys, at Woodstock
JIM CUMMINS

locked on the side of the roads. Backpackers trudged through the fields. The Woodstock area was miles from Max Yasgur's farm, the actual site of the festival. Three days before Woodstock the roads were closed to automobiles. Cars were backed up for ten miles.

The day before Woodstock was insane. Everybody was in town. Stevie Stills came by plucking out a song on acoustic that Joni Mitchell had just written for the occasion. Stills was part of a new band, Crosby, Stills, and Nash; Woodstock would be their first appearance together. Jimi felt that Woodstock was also his first appearance with a new band as well. It seemed amazing that Woodstock was happening at this time, when so many new things were coming together in the music.

But then again, it was the last summer of the 1960s.

The day Woodstock opened was manic. The producers still had not finalized their agreement with Jimi's office. The phone rang all day. Cars were now lined up thirty miles in all directions. Folks were beginning to abandon them en masse. Friends were coming by and leaving so quickly their names began to melt into a faceless procession.

The deal was finalized that night: $18,000, promise of $42,000 more (which they would probably get burned for); a helicopter would have to bring the band. There was no other way. Jimi would play last, as usual. Ever since Monterey, and then Fillmore (when the Jefferson Airplane refused to follow him), no group would follow him on any stage in the world.

The vibes were high. The air was charged with mass magnetism. Instead of taking the helicopter, they wound up in a funky caravan. Big Claire's Dodge Dart and someone's Rambler station wagon, led by and followed through the countryscape by the looney-sirened cruisers' flashing lights and motorcycles of the state troopers.

The day Woodstock officially opened, Miles Davis assembled the most ambitious group of musicians in his musical history to record at Columbia Studios in New York City: August 19, 1969.

Missing from his basic unit of the past six years were Herbie Hancock and Tony Williams. Replacing Hancock on keyboards were Chick Corea, who had made the last session (In a Silent Way), Joe Zawinul, of the Cannonball Adderley band, and most notably Larry Young, straight from Boiseville jams with Jimi Hendrix. Miles employed several drummers of different textures to cover for Tony Williams (Jack DeJohnette, Lenny White, and Charles Alias); most notable was the addition of a percussion man, Jim Riley, who played everything from bells to bongos to congas to triangles.

Wayne Shorter on soprano sax instead of tenor and Dave Holland on bass were the only carry-overs. Bennie Maupin appeared on bass clarinet. John McLaughlin again on electric guitar. And the biggest surprise was Harvey Brooks, the journeyman rock bassist, on Fender.

The title of the sessions was Bitches Brew. It was to make musical history as the first serious synthesis of jazz and rock. It was to be Miles's biggest-selling album to date. And strangely enough, it was recorded under the full influence of the Woodstock vibes.

Jimi came out on the Woodstock stage following Sha-Na-Na, with Jerry Velez on bongos, Larry Lee on rhythm guitar, Juma Sultan on congas, Billy Cox on bass, and Mitch Mitchell on drums. Since they arrived, it had been a hard three days of getting the music together and partying. Jimi had not slept the whole time. Big Claire held his full purple cape in the wings, looking on very anxiously. Everyone was stoned but keyed entirely into the incredible vibes of history staring them four hundred thousand strong in their faces.

Jimi and company go into "Red House." Then an upbeat instrumental improvisation, with everyone getting in some good licks. They segue into a formal jam called "Villanova Junction Blues" and another jam by Mitch called "Jam Back at the House," which is governed by Mitch's rhythmic patterns rather than melody. They hit "Izabella," one of Jimi's new songs, as a bit of rock in the midst of their jam fever. And then they go back to the train station for "Getting My Heart Back Together." Jimi tearing out huge chunks of pure blues soloing off the two chord changes. With the bass string tuned down a fifth, Jimi really gets into his own bass accompaniment, bending the bass string to gut-trembling vibratos while he hits weird modal pitches in fast eighth-note runs, then quickly repeats them twice as fast in sixteenth notes and triplets as well. Like sixteenth notes to the second power, as if he is splitting the atom of the notes, which then come out in thirty-second-note cascading waterfalling runs. They slide into distort at the edge of overamplification where Jimi's speed-of-light attack overloads the amps. Jimi takes that distort, just at the peak of feedback, and glissandos back down into the modal space-station pitch and then back down to the two-chord blue earth.

They go into a jam pattern with Jimi's lead mixed far out in front on the monitors. They bomp into "Purple Haze" on a nice groove. There is a full battery of percussion and rhythmic sounds going behind Jimi. He is exulting in the heights of the sound. Jimi leads a segue into "The Star-Spangled Banner," the congas and bongos and the military-drum kit all rolling strong polyrhythmic statements, Billy Cox holding the bottom drone and Larry Lee hitting key notes of the changes as he and Jimi sustain long lines in the all-time greatest hit of the U.S.A. Jimi moves from a raging finale into a genuflectingly lyrical improvisation melody told in sparse Spanish-Moorish tones that is both sad and beautiful, almost mournful yet exquisitely sculptured. The melody, making the total more than any of its emotional parts. This is the last set of the festival, the last festival of the summer, of the year, of the sixties—and Hendrix's solo is a lament, through human cries of divine ecstasy.

The African holy drums confer a blessing upon all.

Woodstock is over.

Jimi walks offstage and collapses. Panic ensues. A doctor runs up and checks him out. Severe exhaustion. Jimi is helicoptered to a hotel suite in Woodstock with a lovely young lady named Lesley, who stays there with him. Jimi sleeps for three days.

The recordings of the Woodstock performance were disappointing. As usual, Jimi's guitar dominated the sound; Larry Lee's rhythm guitar, Billy Cox's bass, Juma's congas, and Jerry Velez's bongos were hardly heard above Mitch's drum kit. The sound the African drums made in the air was lost, an entire acoustical realm lost in the air.

He wished he had done more with Wally Heider and his crew in hipping them to the new kind of sound he wanted recorded. It had sounded fine onstage. But it was disappointing that it *all* did not get on tape.

The rock 'n' roll press was very cautious about his new band. He had not come out with a new album in 1969, although *Electric Ladyland* had spanned the bridge between 1968 and 1969. Rumors were beginning to crop up about this being the end of Jimi Hendrix. He knew better than that. He continued to work on the new album and push through on the completion of Electric Lady Studios. His office was nervous about his new band. They clearly wanted Noel and Mitch back with him, and there were few dates lined up for the fall of 1969. Jeffery felt that the fielding of an all-black band would ruin his image.

Jimi was interviewed by Ritchie Yorke, a sensitive English journalist, who had come over for Woodstock:

> I plan to use different people at my sessions from now on; their names aren't important. You wouldn't know them anyway. It really bugs me that there are so many people starving, musicians who are twice as good as the big names. I want to try and do something about that.
>
> I feel guilty when people say I'm the greatest guitarist on the scene. What's good or bad doesn't matter to me; what does matter is feeling and not feeling. If only people would take more of a true view and think in terms of feeling. Your name doesn't mean a damn, it's your talent and feeling that matters. You've got to know much more than just the technicalities of notes, you've got to know sounds and what goes between the notes.
>
> When you first make it, the demands on you are very great. For some people, they are just too heavy. You can just sit back, fat and satisfied, or you can run away from it, which is what I did. I don't try to live up to anything anymore.
>
> Really, I'm just an actor—the only difference between me

and those cats in Hollywood is that I write my own script. I consider myself first and foremost a musician. My initial success was a step in the right direction, but it was only a step, just a change. Now I plan to get into many other things.

What it all comes down to is that albums are nothing but personal diaries. When you hear somebody making music, they are baring a naked part of their soul to you. *Are You Experienced?* was one of the most direct albums we've done. What it was saying was, "Let us through the wall, man, we want you to dig it." But later, when we got into other things, people couldn't understand the changes. The trouble is, I'm a schizophrenic in at least twelve different ways, and people can't get used to it.

Sure albums come out different. You can't go on doing the same thing. Every day you find out this and that and it adds to the total you have. *Are You Experienced?* was where my head was at a couple of years ago. Now I'm into different things.

There's a great need for harmony between man and Earth. I think we're really screwing up that harmony by dumping garbage in the sea, air pollution, and all that stuff.

And the sun is very important; it's what keeps everything alive. My next album, coming out in late summer, will be called, *Shine on Earth, Shine on*, or *Gypsy Sun*.

There might also be a couple of other albums in between. A live album which we cut at the Royal Albert Hall in London, and a Greatest Hits thing. But I have no control over those. All I know is that I'm working on my next album for summer release.

We have about forty songs in the works, about half of them completed. A lot of it comprises jams—all spiritual stuff, all very earthy.

I couldn't possibly take a year off. Even though I am very tired. In reality, I might get a month off somewhere but there's no way for a year. I spend a lot of time trying to get away but I can't stop thinking about music. It's in my mind every second of the day. I can't fight it so I groove with it.

To each his own. In another life the people who were trying to do it may have been Beethoven or one of those cats. But this is a rock 'n' roll era, so the people get into rock. Every era has its own music.

What I don't like is this business of trying to classify people. Leave us alone. Critics really give me a pain in the neck. It's like shooting at a flying saucer as it tries to land without giving the occupants a chance to identify themselves. You don't need labels, man. Just dig what's happening.

A couple of years ago all I wanted was to be heard. "Let me in" was the thing. Now I'm trying to figure out the wisest way to be heard.

Ritchie Yorke
September 1969

Hendrix made his management cancel the big *big* outdoor concert planned for the Boston Common in September of 1969. They prepared a press release that said that he was suffering from nervous exhaustion and would have to have at least a month's convalescence. They even got two doctors' names on it.

Jimi was tired of being run all over the country without any concern for how he felt. That he had had to cancel a benefit for the Young Lords at Randalls Island to appear on "The Dick Cavett Show" really got Jimi's goat. His management was all in an uproar over his alleged "Black Power" turn of mind, as if it were unnatural for him to have concern about his people in a political way.

There were other things. All the money he was supposed to be making failed to jibe with his bank account. He never quite understood why all the publishing money had to go to the Bahamas. He had been pressured into signing a release that freed Jeffery from any liability in the settlement with Chalpin. The lawyers would go into their raps and he would feel like a kid. It seemed like what they were saying was that while he could make the money, it was beyond his ability to handle it. He knew he would have to get his own lawyers. Lawyers who worked for him, who could not be bought and who he could trust. He shared Henry Steingarten's law firm with Jeffery. This did not seem right from a commonsense viewpoint, although his present lawyers were indignant when he voiced even the slightest reservations about the setup.

While the word was going out about his "nervous exhaustion," he sat up with Jeanette Jacobs, an old friend from his Village days, laughing and watching television. Finally the boredom got to him and they went to The Scene. Eric Barrett was amazed to see him. Barrett thought Jimi was sick. Jimi laughed it off, saying that there was no particular time limit on getting well—was there?

But in the back of his mind he realized that he would have to make a complete stand against all the bullshit. He was getting hustled and bled dry. Jeffery complained about all the hangers-on and how they were hustling Jimi. But a couple of drinks, or dinner, or some exotic treats were chicken feed compared to the money that his trusted co-workers were losing, or seeming to lose.

Mike Jeffery took some friends along with him when he traveled to the house in Woodstock to talk with Jimi about the problems that had forced cancellation of the Boston Common concert. Juma and others who were part of the Gypsy Suns, Moons and Rainbows had been alerted that there might be trouble.

Jeffery drove up to the house with several tough-looking men. He and Jimi went upstairs to confer privately while the others in his party stayed in the yard. Jeffery had booked Jimi into the Salvation Club and was insisting that he make the gig. Many of the Gypsy Suns, Moons and Rainbows speculated that the Salvation was Mafia-controlled and balked at playing there. Jeffery knew that he had to have local support if Electric Lady Studios was to be a reality. The Salvation, on Sheridan Square, was less than two blocks away from the site of the studios.

As Jimi and Jeffery conferred, a member of Jeffery's party began to take some target practice. He emptied his Beretta into the side of a tree in the yard. He reloaded and did it again. Meanwhile, the Gypsys assumed battle stations throughout the compound. One of them, hatchet in hand, stole around the house in case Jimi needed help.

Jeffery and Jimi finally came downstairs appearing well disposed toward each other. Jimi would make the gig.

Jimi got to play in Harlem in September of 1969 at an outdoor street fair hosted by Eddie O'Jay, the popular DJ of WWRL, the black R&B station that reached all over New York City. The musicians from back at the house up in Boiseville were on hand.

Jimi found the intimacy of this unheralded street affair fascinating. Thousands of faces, it was almost another "Woodstock Festival," only the faces were all black and instead of being in a meadow, they were in the street.

Jimi waited to go on behind a police barricade. Some little black kids beckoned him over; he went to the end of the barricade and talked with several ten-year-olds. They were vibrant and fresh. They were awed by him but did not stand off. They touched his clothes, his pink pants and yellow blouse, his Moroccan vest, and stared at his Indian moccasins. They touched his hair and his wide-brimmed black hat and stared wide-eyed and innocent into his face. Jimi felt strangely serious. Although he could have just as easily laughed and jived, he felt a strange obligation to impart something meaningful. They had never heard of him before.

As Eddie O'Jay introduced Jimi, O'Jay seemed to be, amid his upbeat DJ patter of praise for Jimi's music, apologizing for the fact that he did not play Jimi Hendrix's records on his popular daily show.

In many ways Jimi Hendrix's appearance in Harlem brought up the true paradox of his fame. Jimi was known the world wide, but not in Harlem, his symbolic hometown. Both he and Eddie O'Jay knew that this reality was the result of corporate conferences. Eddie O'Jay nearly had to admit to the crowd that he did not control his own playlist (a horrible admission for any DJ). In fact, his playlist was controlled by the Sonderling Corporation of Dallas, Texas—a white corporation that owned a string of the biggest black radio stations in America and ran the stations as a component of specialized radio for black markets. Their seven-day, twenty-four-hour air time was the heaviest advertisement-saturated format in radio. Their interests in the cultural development of their listeners did not rise above black R&B Top Ten and the most legally allowable ad density.

Jimi followed Big Maybelle, a perennial Harlem favorite, to the portable stage. With Larry Lee laying down a nice rhythm guitar texture, and Juma's congas bouncing off the tenement walls, Jimi roared out of his Marshall amps, playing his ass off. He did his complete showtime routine while all the while wrenching the echo of human sounds from atonals, distortions, and feedback. He could imagine being able to play loud enough so that all of Harlem could hear. They played "Fire," "Foxy Lady," "The Star-Spangled Banner," "Purple Haze," "Red House," and then the finale (which he announced as "the Harlem national anthem"), "Voodoo Chile."

As he was walking back to the equipment truck after the set, a black nationalist type came up to Jimi and said, "Hey, brother, you better come home." Jimi quickly replied, "You gotta do what you gotta do and I gotta do what I got to do *now*."

Poet Jim Brodey interviewed Jimi for the *Los Angeles Free Press*. The first thing he wanted to know about was the bust in Toronto.

"I can't tell you too much about that because my lawyer told me not to. Anyway, I'm innocent, completely innocent."

"Do you think it was a frame?" Brodey asked.

"It must have been or either it was just a very bad scene, because it ain't anything it was. . . ."

Brodey mentioned the rumor that Jimi would go into a self-imposed "retirement" for a year. Jimi denied that, but when pressed for his "objectives," he mentioned a move "toward a spiritual level through music. . . ."

Part of his spiritual awareness had to do with a perception of advanced life in outer space:

"There really are other people in the solar system, you know, and they have the same feelings too, not necessarily bad feelings, but see, it upsets their way of living for instance, and they are a whole lot heavier than we are. And it's no war game because they all keep the same place. But like the solar system is going through a change soon and it's going to affect the Earth in about thirty years, you know."

Jimi went into his role in this change: "There's no whole lot of religions. Just one link because there's only a few chosen people that supposedly are to get this across; these chosen people, in the process, are now being distracted and they are drowning themselves. . . . In order to properly save them, they've got to take a break from people."

Although this was an interview situation, Hendrix seemed to be talking independent of the questions, as if he had some statements he wanted to make. "Like someone is going to have to go back to his childhood and think about what they really felt, really wanted before the fingerprints of their fathers and mothers got ahold of them or before the smudges of school or progress. . . . Most of them are sheep. Which isn't a bad idea. This is the truth, isn't it? That's why we have the form of Black Panthers and some sheep under the Ku Klux Klan. They are all sheep and in the beginning they were all following a certain path."

Brodey then asked, "But you feel the Black Panthers are necessary, though?"

"Yeah, only to the word necessary. You know, in the back of their minds they should be working toward their own thing. They should be a symbol only to the establishment's eyes. It should only be a legendary thing. . . ."

Al Brown, a highly educated and experienced composer, arranger, violist, and violinist, was a stable influence, a mentor to the young crowd that formed loosely around Devon. Al Brown, a roundish chocolate-brown man, had a wonderful beaming smile. Older—speckled-gray short black hair, the beginnings of a gray beard when he didn't shave—he is animated and joyous, very much the father figure. Upon greeting always a warm hug to heart and chest. Being a one-to-one person, Al Brown was closest to Devon. She brought him together with Jimi and he extended his personal one-to-one warmth to Jimi, including the run of his rambling apartment at Fifty-seventh Street and Tenth Avenue, which became Jimi's home away from home.

Jimi, subject to the vicious food of the road and many missed meals, glossed over with amphetamines, cocaine, cigarettes, and whiskey, had developed ulcers. Al Brown cooked well, especially West Indian dishes from his native Nevis Island. A particular dish made with beef, chicken, dumplings, and carrots was Jimi's favorite. Al Brown would have that dish every time Jimi showed up. Jimi would invariably meander into the kitchen and peek into the big kettle. "Is it OK if I have a little?" he would always ask, to the exasperation of Al Brown, who had to continuously repeat to Jimi that he was to treat the place as his own home. Al insisted they were sharing the place rather than being guest and host, but Jimi always acted as if he had come for the first time. Apologetic and sorry for every minuscule transgression even after he had many of his possessions there—jackets, notes, a red-velvet caftan with a hood, a guitar—enough stuff to actually be able to claim residence, he still continued his self-effacing, apologetic attitude.

One day when Jimi was leaving after an extended stay he said "Thank you" to Al at the door. Al chose that moment to lecture him. "Jimi," he said, "this is your home. We share this home. Ever since you first came I have always told you to treat this place as if it were your own. You are always free to come whenever you want to and stay as long as you like. You don't have to give me any thank yous; it is understood that this is your house as well as mine—we share it. No more thank yous, Jimi, this is your home." Chagrined, all Jimi could say was, *"I'm sorry."* They had a good laugh.

Jimi's running buddies began to note a drastic change in him. There was something deep going on around his career that made him more and more depressed as 1969 went on. There was some finagling going on with his head. He began to come into the Scene or Unganos, a new club on West Seventy-first Street, and be so deep in thought that it looked like he was going to freak out. Jimi would be sitting and drinking and then all of a sudden split out the door and get in his car and take off. At times it seemed like he could not handle a public place where there were other people. It would get so heavy that Jimi would jump up in a second and run out the door, leaving his chick and everything.

His friends saw the apparent torment and began to wonder what was really bothering him. It was more than an occasional depression, more than just being under the weather. It became obvious that it was something very, very deep. To his friends, his career was apparently going well, he was playing as excellently as ever, he had the love of many wonderful people—yet something deep down inside was eating away at his mind and his thoughts. And anyone who saw him could not fail to register Jimi's deep unhappiness. But his friends respected him so much that they never brought it up—and Jimi never volunteered. Very often they wanted to ask what was bothering him—but they did not dare.

Devon knew what was happening. For all the hassles Jimi and Devon had, she was still his confidante. She kept many of his most valued possessions and his New York apartment as well. She knew a lot about his business and what was bothering him, but she did not talk about it either.

One night at the Unganos Club, Jimi sat with Devon digging on Buddy Guy. Hendrix was supposed to sit in with the renowned Chicago blues guitarist. But when Guy introduced Jimi, he had already left. Buddy Guy was very hurt. He had been put on the spot in front of the crowd. Buddy Guy was near tears as he began his next tune.

There were many things that burdened Jimi during this period and probably intensified his erratic behavior. Jimi was worried about the impending court case in Canada, which might send him to jail for seven years (he was recording at a breakneck pace, so at least he would be heard on LPs if he were jailed), the lawsuit Chalpin had against him, a great deal of money that he had earned was not accounted for by his management, he was not gigging, his record royalties were in escrow, the studio he was building was months behind schedule and running way over projected costs, and Devon was fucking with smack again.

The out-of-court settlement with Chalpin would cost him a complete album to be delivered to Capitol Records for distribution for PPX. Chalpin received a cash settlement and a percentage of all future royalties earned by Hendrix. Warner Brothers had softened the blow by assuming payment of Chalpin's percentage of future royalties. They also bought out Jeffery's interest in Hendrix's royalties so that Jimi was actually better off from that point of view. Instead of having to give Jeffery the bulk of his royalties, Hendrix now would receive almost 10 percent for himself, instead of the 3 percent he previously shared with Mitch and Noel. But it was Warner Brothers and his management and legal advisers who had urged the settlement upon him. They did not want to fight it out in court. Jimi was still convinced that the contract was not legal and that he could have won the case, but he had no one on his side. The problem with Jimi was not the money, but control over his music.

Many people thought he was on top of the world, but his problems were monumental. For the first time in years he dreaded his upcoming birthday.

On November 27, 1969, Devon threw a birthday party for Jimi in producer Monte Kay's duplex on the Upper East Side of Manhattan. Devon invited all the guests, including the Rolling Stones, who, it just so happened, opened at Madison Square Garden that night. She and Mick Jagger had been linked romantically before. This was a subject not often brought up to Jimi, but whenever he was down on Devon he would always bring it up, not angrily, but with a grunting acknowledgment—calling her Dolly Dagger, punning on Jagger.

The hassles over whether Devon was his woman, his employee, his roommate, his running buddy—or just what—often came up. She played each role with great verve, as she went from one to the other according to Jimi's disposition toward her. Like Fayne, Devon was first associated with Jimi on a simple level, which then became complex. Like Fayne, Devon was an independent woman who could run dudes like Hendrix ran chicks.

Mick Jagger swaggered in dressed up like a gangster in a black-and-white checkered zoot suit and a Mafia-sized ruby ring on his pinky. Although it was Jimi's birthday, Devon paid uncommon attention to Jagger. The professional competition between Jagger and Hendrix had always been high, and so was their lover-man competition. Hendrix had tried to *pull* Marianne Faithfull from Jagger a few years ago in London. That Marianne dug Jimi was apparent from the public support she had given him. But Jagger had pulled Devon in the public eye. According to the gossip, Jagger had an uncanny possession of Devon. She was unable to go to anyone but him whenever he was on the scene.

Except for Devon's attention to Jagger, the party was rather uneventful.

Finney and Al Brown were there. Devon had scored some soma and everyone seemed spaced. Someone kept repeating a quote of Madame Blavatsky, "And those who are aware of the nature of the soma know the properties of other plants as well. . . ." Someone else was explaining that Marianne Faithfull had recently run off with an Italian count.

They just sat around listening to sides, getting stoned watching Devon go through her thing with Jagger. Flip Wilson, who lived upstairs, was telling jokes. Hendrix disappeared downstairs early in the evening. Finney, after waiting around for a while, exchanging small talk with the various Stones, especially Jagger, who he sat next to on the couch, excused himself to Jagger and picked up Sally, his date. He wanted to go somewhere else before the night was over where he could possibly have a better time.

They went downstairs to look for Jimi. The room was dark and his eyes had to get adjusted. He spied Hendrix and was surprised that he sat alone in the middle of the room. Sensing a delicate situation, Finney and Sally asked Jimi what was wrong. He said he was depressed, that's all. Finney and Sally quickly said good-bye.

They went back upstairs and through the party on the way out. It was clear to them that Devon and Jagger were leaving together. Not wishing to be around for the results, they hustled out.

Walking down the streets, rather early in the night, they discussed the scene at the party. They both were grieved that Jimi obviously did not have a good time, and would be left alone on his birthday for the remainder of the night. Before they had gotten too far away, Sally decided to go back.

She returned to the party to find it just about over and Hendrix still downstairs alone. He didn't have much to say, but he was glad that she had returned. She left with him and they went to his pad. There he told her of how so many chicks come on to him just wanting to do a physical thing. They laughed. Sometimes, he said, he just wanted to talk. They talked for a while, he venting his hurt. Sally told him she was from Antigua. She gave him a bottle with her picture on it as an impromptu birthday present. Then he said, you know what? You know what I'd really like now more than anything? Some ice cream and cake.

They ate birthday cake and ice cream together with great relish. Then they spent the night together.

Jimi arrived in Toronto on December 12 for, perhaps, the last trial of his career. With him was Sharon Lawrence, who testified on his behalf, and his old friend Jeanette Jacobs. Jimi, with his hair cut short and in a sports jacket and slacks, looked like a lamb. He and Jeanette looked like newlyweds on honeymoon in Canada. After eight and a half hours of deliberation, the jury returned a verdict of not guilty. Jimi was more then relieved—it was like he had been born again, brought back from death to life.

Because of the possibility of his internment in Canadian prison, he had not really known whether he would be able to play at the

Philharmonic on Christmas Eve. Now it was certain. Flying back to the States, he began to compose in his mind some funky renditions of "Silent Night," "The Little Drummer Boy," and "Auld Lang Syne." He certainly had the Christmas spirit this year.

Later that night Jimi entertained the crew at Al Brown's with his impressions of the various bands he had played with before he made it. He did an incredible impersonation of Little Richard and an equally incredible one of the notorious Harlem queens.

Jimi and Al Brown would talk long hours about plans for the guitar concerto they were writing together. This subject, as a plan for part of Jimi's musical future, made him glad, and he talked eagerly about the direction he wanted to go in. He loved the idea of his guitar backed by an entire orchestra, and especially the violins, violas, and cellos that Al had mastery over. Horns and voices, a higher plateau of sound. Right away several of the tunes he was working on took on the measured and thought-out pace of the concerto. Just thinking about it inspired him in his writing.

He had affirmed his African-American mystical/magical heritage in "Voodoo Chile" and was readying "Machine Gun," a protest against police establishment oppression, with Buddy Miles. His space thought had attracted many American mystics, spiritualists, and groups. Foremost among them was the Sufi Group from Tucson and its Hollywood counterpart led by Chuck Wein, who were getting together *Rainbow Bridge*, a movie intended to offer America a spiritual alternative through yoga, vegetarianism, psychicism, consciousness-expanding drugs, and an affirmation of intelligent and advanced life in outer space.

But for Jimi his magic was in the music, and the collaboration with Al Brown promised to move Jimi's music to a higher spiritual plane, which would at the same time take the growing stigma of being a rock 'n' roll star off Jimi's back.

Hendrix and Buddy Miles are in the studio with Alan Douglas listening to Alafia of "The Last Poets" run down this poem that was orally composed by black inmates. *Doriella du Fontaine* is a story about a chick, the choicest of the pimp's chicks, who sets out to make her man, her pimp, the baddest pimp of them all, the man of men. Like *Shine* or *Stagolee*, the poem is an epic from "the people," a true folk expression, dealing metaphorically with the black man's relationship with his women, as expressed through the pimp and the

Jimi celebrating with friends December 10, 1969, after being acquitted of two charges of drug possession UPI

whore. Two lovers living under oppression, underground, illegally—the ill-fated romance.

It was so ironic that this tale, this saga with its force and power, would remind Hendrix of Devon. She probably really loved him, and like a prostitute to her pimp, their understanding was inclusive of the myriad chicks he had. For a pimp the chicks are strictly monetary, but for Hendrix the chicks were release, part of his creative fashion, a way for him to maintain his drive and keep his energy peaked. That Hendrix's sexual appetite was enormous made him more the pimp in Devon's eyes, the superpimp, the master game pimp, which is the pinnacle of pimpdom: the pimp who has mastered the game, the pimp who has become so proficient in his tasks that he now has the choice to go legit, and once legit the pimp who masters that game is the master, the sage, the professor of pimpdom.

Doriella du Fontaine thus became a kind of parallel to Hendrix's life with Devon. Devon, who tricked at fifteen in Vegas, the big time for prostitutes, was fully aware of that role. She would trick and procure for Hendrix and then in the next minute do some shit to enrage him. But that was part of it: The prostitute demands the hard-edged discipline of the pimp, and the gentle Hendrix was sometimes prompted into "heavy" acts by the devilish, mischievous Devon.

Their mutual attraction seemed to have occurred in spite of themselves. Neither particularly wanted a romantic attachment. Devon, as efficient as she was devious, commanded enough presence to keep the creeps away, get him to the show on time, score some blow with minimal effort at any time, keep track of his shit, and maintain some line of intelligible contact and communication between Hendrix and his estranged management. Perhaps she would not have done that except for love, but she was paid to do that and paid well from the start. Perhaps her pulling him and getting his nose open was to her a part of her job security also. But she had her own shit going, too. Bisexual, it was said that she only loved women until Hendrix came along and straightened her out—or else she straightened out for him. At one point she even tried to have a baby by him. But she did not give up her female lovers for Hendrix; in fact, she often served both Hendrix and another woman in their famous threesomes. Her initial meeting with Hendrix had involved a train, with her and Angie calling up Quincy Jones in the process to announce the train they were running on Jimi. They also said that Hendrix's joint "was damn near big as his guitar."

Devon also had a vicious heroin habit, a habit that cost plenty and cost every day as well. Maintaining it with rare cool, she did get uptight on occasions and put people through some very weird changes. In addition to keeping up the glamorous image of the supergroupie, she also had to score and stock big. She required more bread than the occasional cab fare. She required bread that paralleled the turning of tricks, and she got it. Whether her love for Hendrix was part of the intrigue or not, it did cause them some very bad moments. But her tremendous appeal, mixed with her boldness and charm, always got her over.

Jimi had hoped that Fayne would be able to help Devon get her shit together and drop heroin, but Fayne came back with some weird stories. It was hopeless. Fayne talked about Devon needing a fix, going out in the street; fly, tall, and lean, getting some trick to go for a ten-minute blow job in an alley. To Devon it was a joke, yet a fact of life not too distant from where she was at the moment. Junk tends to erase memory, but in the throes of needing a fix, it all comes back. She had the bravado of a streetwalker. No happening could be *that* far out as to blow her mind. Her head erect like the Sphinx, regal and tall, her chin slightly jutted in arrogance, her black hair swept back severely behind her serene eyes. She was the Cleopatra of the groupies.

Jimi talked about Cleopatra as the absolute temptress. Cleo had been a fantasy. A fantasy that the myriad of women who surrounded

him all sought to emulate. But most imaginations were lacking.
Devon was *a* Cleo incarnate. But not the fanciful fantasy that
seemed to come out of Jimi's dreams. But a weird temptress demon
of the times whose being had edges he could only vaguely compre-
hend. A super *femme fatale.* He could understand the occasional
perfidies, and even understand the frequent bouts of lovemaking,
but the middle and outer grounds, the gray areas, often seemed to
suffuse the entire polarity. At times it seemed that her lies were a
simple mistake, while at other times they seemed like vast conspir-
acies. Her lovemaking often would make her seem as true as the
sloppiest love story, but then she would turn another side and become the biggest dyke, the biggest sadomasochist, the biggest
whore, the most relentless nymphomaniac, and the heaviest
doper—all rolled into one.

What began to scare Jimi most about Devon was the smack.

He had no trouble staying away from heroin. First he found out
that Devon snorted a little bit now and then. Well fine, lots of
people do. Then he gradually found out she was doing a little chip-
ping, using the needle, "a little bit." But his time was always so
fucked up he could not really check on her properly. After a while it
became obvious that she was heavy into smack. Usually he kept
enough space between himself and the ladies to be clear of whatever
trip they were into. But Devon was close, very close. She had gotten
next to him. Many times he remembered himself unconsciously
accepting the smack's presence. This he realized was dangerous.

Devon wanted the public thing to confirm their relationship. After spending several days with Mick Jagger she returned to the apartment she and Jimi shared and told a writer from *Rags* magazine, "So
what can I do for an encore? I don't know, probably marry Jimi. . . .
Will you publish my wedding pictures?" As much as Jimi loved her,
he knew she could destroy him.

Jimi walks across the floor of his room in Al Brown's large apartment. The many books lining the shelves give a time-lasting feeling,
a permanence, a feeling as old as the wisdom in many of the books.
Books written before his lifetime, some centuries ago. Books silent
and solid muffling the noise of the street, insulating the inhabitants
even more against the distant vibes.

Tonight is the concert at Philharmonic Hall in Lincoln Center.
Last year, promoter Ron Delsner had put up a big fight to have them
there. "The first rock concert at the Philharmonic," like it was some
big deal. The Philharmonic Hall officials had told them that the

event "must emphasize symphonic or an otherwise classical approach to music" and clamped down a tight framework for the performance before Hendrix could appear. Delsner lined up baroque harpsichordist Fernando Valenti and the New York Brass Quintet. Hendrix was supposed to accompany them but when the event took place Jimi flatly refused to do so. When the curtain went up, there was Mitch Mitchell in white tails sitting at his drum kit.

Al Brown bounced around his apartment, always busy, but happy in it. The phone always ringing didn't bother him, he had gotten used to it. That was the way Jimi wanted to get older: peaceful and confident, always composing and studying, having time for many new and old friends. Al Brown's people all cared about each other. They all looked after one another, making sure that everyone was all right.

Devon is involved in preparing for the concert; her casual fly look (basic black) with a slightly stoned interior as usual, but ready to run all the interference necessary. She operates just as well stoned. She swoops out of the bathroom, billows of perfume following her. She's busy now, it's countdown time. Jimi is laid back resting in his shy solemnity. Devon dials, talks, hangs up, dials again, talks, and hangs up to dial again. Get it together, girl! Al Brown is just happy, he likes Jimi and Devon as if they were his kids and it is like that, too. Devon has contacted Colette, who has his special costume on the way uptown in the limo. Al's apartment is less than ten blocks from the hall.

It is Christmas Eve, 1969.

Bill Graham, grand impresario of rock, had booked Hendrix in the Fillmore of San Francisco right after his historic performance at Monterey in 1967. He had steadily booked him every time he appeared in the States, but always inconveniently by long distance. When Hendrix moved to Manhattan he lived very conveniently less than ten blocks from the Fillmore East.

With New Year's approaching, Graham planned a big one for the beginning of the seventies—the end of the decade of the sixties, where rock and soul really took their rightful berths in worldwide music. Who better than Jimi Hendrix, Buddy Miles, and Billy Cox: the Band of Gypsys?

But Graham was nervous about it. Hendrix was always very standoffish, keeping to himself with his own personal friends; and now with the estrangement of his management at an all-time high, it would be necessary to approach Hendrix directly with an offer of such an important date. Graham had to be sure. The only way would be directly to Hendrix and then back through the management.

The good fortune of Hendrix staying right there in the Village paid off. A couple of days later Graham went over to the west side of the Village to a rented garage where Jimi, Buddy Miles, and Billy Cox rehearsed and jammed. They made a deal—Fillmore East New Year's Eve and Day—two shows each. And then, for the first time, they actually broke open a bottle, sat down, lay back, and rapped for a while. In the dark of a practice studio garage, they laughed and talked for the first time without being in a gig situation.

The night of the first concert, New Year's Eve, Hendrix and Miles and Cox rocked the Fillmore. The audience was jubilant, cheering Hendrix's every move. And Jimi put on a classic two-hour soul show—a minihistory of showtimes all over the U.S.A. in black towns, villages, and ghettos. The crowd was screaming after Hendrix came in after the third encore. Graham stood solemnly in the wings. Exuberant, Hendrix, passing through the wings, asked boss-like Graham, "How was it?" Graham, dark, swarthy, and terse, said, "All right, Jimi, all right." Taken aback a bit by the formal, almost prosaic rebuttal to his enthusiasm, Jimi took a strange look at Graham as he kept on to his dressing room. After drying off, changing, Hendrix sought Graham out in his office. Again he asked Graham, "How was it?" Graham again gave a noncommittal, "It was all right, Jimi, fine." Jimi couldn't believe his ears. He had had three encores, the crowd had screamed, they were still whooping in the streets of Sixth Street and Second Avenue below. He wanted to know why Graham was so contradictorily reserved.

Graham, on record as preferring Latin and soul music to rock, was outspoken: no bullshit. A shrewd New York streetwise businessman of Jewish origins, he was aware (as he was aware of every phase of the multimillion-dollar history of rock) that this historic occasion would go down in eternity through the live recording being done by Wally Heider's remote crew outside.

"You really want it," Graham said. Hendrix quickly agreed. The staff, sensing another typical Graham–artist confrontation and wanting none of it, left just as quickly.

It seemed to Graham that just as they had gotten a bit close as people, in a wink they were on the verge of a confrontation that could ruin their business relationship. But he also wanted a good performance for the recording and he felt Hendrix's wild showtime movements often slowed and stumbled the music. The crowd did not mind, they were enthralled by the spectacle and seemed to forget about the music completely as Hendrix moved so incredibly across the proscenium, under the great washes of rose and white violet lights, the huge tentlike screen exploding billows of subscan molecules, atoms, DNA RNA LSD pyrotechnics. Graham behind the stage only hearing the concert wanted more. He told Hendrix that the crowd would have loved him no matter what he did, and that his wild cavorts, swoops, and sex play only allowed him to play, in actuality, much below par.

Again, Hendrix couldn't believe his ears. And Graham elaborated on the theme. If he got cheers for only his antics, then the thing to do at the end of the show was to ask the crowd if they liked it. And when they cheer and scream to slowly intone in the mike, "Oh yeah? Well, you are full of shit!" Hendrix tried to interrupt, but Graham, on his horse, said, "You asked me, right? So let me talk." Graham intoned on about the responsibility of the great and truly gifted to avoid the trap of mass adulation, which is surface and illusory, to withstand that deception and *play* their very best at all times.

Jimi Hendrix had always loved his movements onstage—since he was a kid. He loved to go out like that before a crowd. But everyone had hated it, except the fans. His fellow musicians in the service and even in high school would complain that he was making a fool out of himself and all of them as well. In England and the U.S.A. it had helped establish his uniqueness as a performer—the press always scandalized, the promoters always bugged. Graham had questioned and challenged his integrity as a performer and also as a star who had earned the right to choose what he presents.

The next set Hendrix played stock-still, hardly moving at all. The crowd was breathless all the way through. Bill Graham danced in the wings. Sweeping back to the wings, after the tremendous ovation that seemed to pervade the walls, every nook and cranny of the great theater, Hendrix walks over to Graham and says, "All right, motherfucker?" Then he walks out and plays a fifteen-minute encore doing nothing but bumps and grinds and humps and tongue-ings.

That classic second set that Hendrix played standing stock-still formed the basis for the album *Band of Gypsys.*

"Who Knows?" and "Machine Gun" from the second set became the first side of the *Band of Gypsys* album. The other side was drawn from material recorded during the three other sets of the two-night performances. "Who Knows?" a new song, begins the set as Bill Graham's dramatic introduction nears the end. It is a bouncy, bopping tune with a lilting flow that is aided by a close call-and-response lyric sung by Jimi and Buddy. After an incredible ovation Jimi intones, "This next song is dedicated to all the troops fighting in Harlem, Chicago, and, oh yes, Vietnam. A little thing called 'Machine Gun.' "

Never before had Jimi sounded more funky. But it was also a scary funk. Syncopating the heartbeat in the hypnotic drone of an eternal caravan, the Band of Gypsys hit an awe-inspiring power. No psychedelic soars, no bump-and-grind humor. Jimi's tonalities grow from bending E-minor modes into the Eastern drone-sounding tonic and leap octaves into screams and howls. Slurring from deep within his range, Jimi uses his body between the amps and his Stratocaster to undulate a slowly building feedback howl. His sound over the drone shifts from a woman's scream to a siren to a fighter plane diving, all amid Buddy Miles's Gatling-gun snare shots building in intensity by Buddy's sheer power. His broad-girthed arms slowly rising on each beat to smash the dual cymbals which dangle in position above his head. His arms fall slowly, like a conductor's, to his snares beating out percussive licks that sound like marching music amid the report of a point-blank gun. Jimi sings, his voice almost breaking with sadness.

> machine   *GUN*   *tearin' my body*
> *OH*   *machine gun*   *tearin' my buddies all apart*
> *Evil Man make me kill ya*
> *Evil Man make you kill me*
> *Evil Man make me kill you*
>   *even though we're only families apart*
> *Well I pick up my axe and fight like a farmer*
> *And your bullets become like rain*
> *Well I pick up my axe and blast like a farmer*
> *But you still shoot me down*
> *Same way you shoot me down, baby*
> *You'll be going just the same with three times the pain*
> *Same way you shoot me down, baby*
> *You'll be going just the same with three times the pain*
> *And yourself to blame*

Jimi's voice veering at tenor peak to the pentatonic intonations of a Vietnamese or Bangkok nightclub singer.

Buddy Miles pauses, eyes closed, like a Buddha within a silver metal bubba flowing outward, his snare shots wide and strong. He beats into the depths of a groove, the snare shots *ratatatting*

Jimi with Johnny Winter © 1970 FRED W. MCDARRAH

stronger and stronger. Miles captures and entrances you with his repetition. The intensity of his shots ring out on par with Jimi's guitar.

At the bridge the pace of the song turns upside down into the juicy middle, where it gets more buoyant and funky. Jimi momentarily stops playing to go over and turn both Marshall stacks to their utter limits, and then in total feedback the maestro takes over. As Buddy Miles screams in the background a Delta moan, Hendrix lightly fingers the amp-busting guitar, his very touch emitting the cries of a woman beyond pleasure to the threshold of pain, the screams of electric fire, the looney cacophony of siren scream alarm pain planes in space bombing people screaming.

Jimi's Stratocaster emits very light high harmonic pings. And then the guitar gets to haranguing and shit. Double picking. Going back and forth between runs, cross-running them faster and faster. Filling with a rhythm lick turn, Jimi evokes a speed rush a coke rush a grass rush a DMT rush. It's total recall, total awareness, total light streaming, and you understand it all in the feeling.

They had a beautiful time. Jimi, Buddy, and Billy got off and made a political statement as well. It was a classic concert; they *rocked* the joint and said something, too. Bill Graham, a great showman, had urged them to make a historical musical statement as well, playing their best straight to the music. The end-of-the-sixties concert, Jimi, their prince, and Graham, their field marshal, taking them into the seventies.

But something was haunting Jimi that night. He was hurt and angry, and the vibes had made him take it out in the music. A big hurt hung over the 1970s for Jimi.

The recording of the performance was "owed" to Ed Chalpin of PPX Productions as part of the out-of-court settlement. An album *(Band of Gypsys)* would be released on Capitol Records. A large cash settlement and a percentage of all past and future record royalties was also part of the agreement with Chalpin.

Even Hendrix's original management contract with Chas Chandler and Michael Jeffery had been exploitative. They—Chandler and Jeffery—had received 30 percent of all of Hendrix's earnings. In addition, they had received 7 percent of his record royalties. Hendrix controlled 3 percent, he kept 1 percent and split the remaining 2 percent between Mitch Mitchell and Noel Redding. Hendrix's management had received 30 percent of his 1 percent record royalty earnings as well.

For live concerts, after management had deducted their 30 percent off the top, Hendrix had received 50 percent of the remainder and Mitch Mitchell and Noel Redding each received 20 percent. All expenses were, of course, deducted from earnings. Now with the Band of Gypsys, Billy Cox was on salary. So was Buddy Miles, who had officially joined Jimi in October of 1969. Buddy received a large salary plus other benefits.

The influence that the constant jamming and rehearsing with Billy Cox and Buddy Miles had on Jimi's writing is born out in "Message to Love," "Power of Soul," "Who Knows?" and the incredible "Machine Gun."

"Machine Gun" was a big departure from Jimi's usual celestial and/or love themes. The Vietnam war; the national repression of the Black Panthers, who for many were a symbol of the black struggle for self-determination within the United States; and Jimi's exploitation contributed to his somber, highly political mood. The FBI, aided by other intelligence agencies and local police forces, was waging war on the Panthers in an attempt to separate them from the youth culture and the peace movement. J. Edgar Hoover was determined to stop their momentum, which was garnering more and more public support every day.

Many influential and popular entertainers were becoming more and more outspoken in their support of the Panthers and the peace movement. Many of Hollywood's top entertainers supported both movements. Rock musicians and groups from the San Francisco Bay area had been the first to openly avow some sort of revolutionary stance. Folksingers like Joan Baez, Bob Dylan, Pete Seeger, and Peter, Paul and Mary had supported the civil rights movement in the early sixties. By the time Dylan went electric in 1965, San Francisco musicians were discovering acid and protest as one and the same. The coinciding of the Monterey Pop Festival of 1967 with the great Human Be-ins in New York and San Francisco had made rebels almost overnight of the majority of the youthful attendees.

By 1969 the sides were clearly drawn. Many within the establishment vowed that the 1970s would be a different story. And with Richard Nixon in power, the secret and uniformed police began a program of harsh repression. By the end of 1969 almost every Hollywood star of any consequence to the youth culture was attending peace rallies and Panther fund-raisers, and donating significant sums of money to both movements as well.

This was the popular mood of the time, and Jimi Hendrix as the *top* musical performer was called upon in various ways to contribute. To put his body on the line.

From all the evil and disturbing things that were happening to him as 1969 closed, Jimi began to feel the emotion of the struggle the Black Panthers were going through. He began to really feel what the brothers up at the house in Woodstock said about repression and racism.

Jimi felt he was being robbed by people close to him, people whom he trusted; and he could not be sure who was doing it, how it was being done, or why. It was hard for Jimi to relate to basic criminal greed. Everyone around him mouthed the same feelings about love and peace and getting high and hating the police—yet some of those very same people were robbing him blind. And some of those very same people who said that they were his friends—who swore by it—were full of shit. Jimi really began to feel the presence of evil close by.

He had been set up for a bust at an international crossing. He would never be so stupid as to take heroin *anywhere*—much less across a border. Heroin was an evil drug that he avoided; he even found it hard to be with people who used it. That was one of the

factors that made him so ambivalent about Devon. He had been
sued by someone who had said he was his friend, whose chief witness was another person who said he was his friend (a fellow musician, yet). The settlement of the lawsuit had taken more money
from him than he had thought he would ever make in a lifetime. But
the biggest drag was that he had to give an entire album over to
them—that hurt. That meant that he had to give of himself something he dearly loved—his music. That contract on one piece of
paper had given him all of one dollar for his signature. It was between friends.

It was ironic, to say the least, that the debut of the Band of Gypsys, doing his new "Protest" and teaching songs of social concern,
would be recorded for release in order to pay off this settlement. It
seemed that everyone was against him in the judgment: not only the
party that sued, but also the record company and even his own
lawyers. How could such a settlement come down? He truly felt evil
around him like he had never felt evil before. *Evil man make you
kill me/Evil man make me kill you . . .*

It was January 1, 1970.

EIGHT

Overleaf: *WARNER REPRISE RECORDS*

Although Jimi had mixed feelings about the New Year's Eve concert, favorable comments swept the grapevine. Never before had Jimi been so funky and so political as well. "Machine Gun" was the talk of the town. The song fused the international horror of the Vietnam war with the local horrors perpetrated against the Black Panthers.

The Panther 21 had been in jail in New York City since April 2, 1969, when they were charged with conspiracy to bomb various sites in New York and the tristate area. While the New York dailies sensationalized the upcoming trial, others close to the Panther Party were beginning to wonder if the Panther 21 and others were not the victims of infiltrators, provocateurs, and organized police and intelligence-agency repression.

Jimi was acquainted with Black Panthers on both the East and West coasts. Several high-ranking Panther Party members had had discussions with Jimi about a benefit performance. The bail of the New York Panther 21 had been set at $100,000 each, far too much money for the party to raise in the usual ways. The trial began in February of 1970. Hendrix, engrossed in building Electric Lady Studios and having legal battles of his own, was still willing to do a benefit, but Mike Jeffery was dead set against it. He was having enough trouble without Hendrix becoming more identified with the Black Panthers.

Others close to Hendrix were worried that he might be attracting the very same infiltrators and provocateurs who were operating within the black liberation movement. Those who knew about such things knew that if any one of the intelligence agencies decided to go after Jimi they would do so with only the most subtly crafted plan. Not only would it be difficult to detect such an operation, but also such an operation would wreak havoc with Jimi's creative life— after all, he was a creative artist. The kind of pressure well-seasoned political activists were used to could destroy Jimi. With Jimi's estrangement with his office at an all-time high it would be incredibly easy to manufacture incidents. And with Jimi's easygoing- unable-to-say-"no" personality, he could well be duped by almost any person who got within his good graces. All it took was persistence. The streetwise wit of Devon became very important. She more than anyone else would hopefully be able to deal with such an emergency if it ever came to that.

Jimi had been approached to play a benefit by people connected with the Vietnam Moratorium Committee. They were supporting negotiations between the warring factions in Vietnam. Negotiations would have more of a chance of success if there were a moratorium in the fighting. Jimi was all for it. It was not the violent faction of the antiwar community that was sponsoring the event, but a group that lobbied for negotiations. They would have the benefit called "Winter Carnival for Peace" to kick off a nationwide campaign.

On January 28, 1970, Jimi headlined in Madison Square Garden in a benefit for the Vietnam Moratorium Committee. Vibes were very high. It was his first concert of the New Year after the debut of the Band of Gypsys at the Fillmore East. Many personalities on the New York scene were backstage. It was not the usual professionally organized concert. Bill Graham would have never allowed so many unaccounted-for people backstage with the performers, but the amateur producers for this show had allowed many politicos and marginal persons to mingle backstage.

Jimi stood with his entourage and looked as if he were dead. He had been given some powerful and horrible acid by someone he did not know. In the hectic rush of backstage just before showtime, Jimi's head hung down.

Bad acid is the worst of all possible things to take anytime, and much more so before an important concert. It would have been better if he had been stone drunk.

While the opening speeches were going on, Jimi sat on his dressing-room couch with his head in his hands. It was unusually bad acid. Not only did it make him physically sick, but also the trip itself was a vicious psychic downer.

But Jimi struggled with it. It was important for him to be there, it was an important statement for him to make. He had not been able to do any major benefits to aid the progressive forces that were fighting for reform. Although he felt like shit, he went on anyway, with Billy Cox on bass and Buddy Miles on drums.

Jimi tried to play, but his body and his mind were in agony. After a few minutes he had to say to the twenty thousand in the audience, "I'm sorry, we just can't get it together. . . ." Jimi walked off, followed by Buddy and Billy. The entire place was in an uproar. They did not know what had happened.

The next day in the press Hendrix made a statement to the effect that he was not happy with the Band of Gypsys. He singled out Buddy Miles as having too much "earth" for his taste. Still recovering from the effects of the amazingly bad acid, Jimi, in one comment, totally alienated Buddy Miles, who was also a close friend. And to the delight of Mike Jeffery, Jimi seemed receptive to rejoining Mitch and Noel for the spring tour. Jeffery immediately arranged for *Rolling Stone* to interview Jimi.

Buddy Miles was dismissed as a member of the Jimi Hendrix organization by Mike Jeffery, who seemed to enjoy the heavy role. "This trip is over," he told the large and muscular drummer.

For Buddy, the biggest disappointment was that Jimi had not come to him and told him himself.

Jann Wenner, young editor of *Rolling Stone,* dispatched crack reporter John Burks to interview Hendrix and company at Mike Jeffery's apartment on February 4, 1970.

Hendrix had been quoted late in 1969 by a *Rolling Stone* correspondent, Sheila Weller, as being sympathetic to the Black Panthers' plight. Mike Jeffery had been after Hendrix to clarify his position regarding the Black Panthers in the press. The almost protestlike songs of his Fillmore East concerts and his involvement in the benefit for the Vietnam Moratorium Committee had, in Jeffery's view, given Hendrix the image of a radical rock singer. And, in fact, Hendrix had just been acquitted of a serious drug charge in Toronto. In Jeffery's mind, Hendrix had changed his music so radically since moving back to America that he was in danger of losing the audience that had propelled him to fame. Not only did Jeffery feel that the original Experience sound was the right sound for Jimi, but he also felt that Noel and Mitch were the perfect completion of the image. Even before Woodstock in August of 1969, Jeffery had been

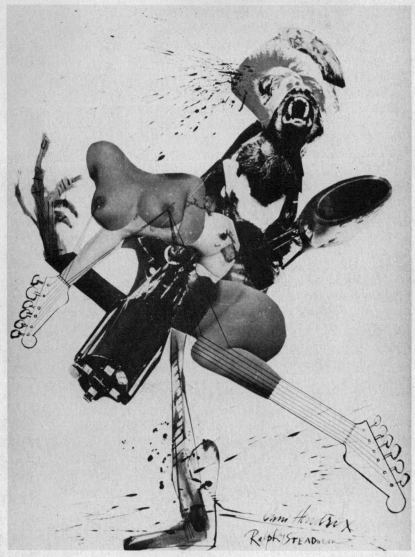

dead set against Hendrix appearing with black sidemen, especially when all of them were black. He had made sure they were far to the back of the stage at Woodstock. He did not like the wild-haired African-named Juma, nor the addition of his congas to Hendrix's sound. Jeffery marshaled a powerful argument against Hendrix going any farther in the direction he had been going in: Jimi had the lawsuit settlement to pay off and he had the Electric Lady Studios to pay for. They had little money coming in. Jimi could not take the chance of alienating people; and in Jeffery's mind, Jimi had already alienated his fans quite a bit in the past year.

Less than seven days after he had walked off the stage with Billy and Buddy, Jimi was being interviewed with the original Experience. Jimi, Noel, and Mitch were sprawled on the floor before a gas-burner fake fireplace. Burks felt it was a setup, like those done for fan-magazine reporters to give an image of solidarity and fellowship. Yet less than a week ago, Jimi had gone onstage at Madison Square Garden with the Band of Gypsys as his permanent band. The Band of Gypsys' marathon jamming sessions had been the talk of the town. Their performance at Fillmore East had been highly praised throughout the grapevine and everyone was looking forward to a return performance. So it was kind of embarrassing for all involved to greet each other and sit down as if it was not unusual for Jimi, Noel, and Mitch to be sitting around a fireplace together. They were close enough to hold hands. The power trio.

Jimi wore a dark green satin V-neck shirt, with a finely jeweled pendant balanced within the deep-cut V. Violet pinstripe bell-bottoms and pink loafers with high insteps that made them look like elf boots.

The presence of their press agent made it very clear that the Hendrix organization felt a dire need for some favorable publicity. The haste with which the interview had been arranged also pointed to that. And when a smiling Mike Jeffery entered with a tray of choice wine and wondrous cognac to counteract the bitter cold outside, Burks got the message. But Burks knew that it would be impossible for them to totally manipulate *Rolling Stone* for their own purposes. They knew it too. So there was a curious edge to the balance of desires in the room. Jimi seemed embarrassed while Mitch and Noel plunged right into Burks's questions.

Jimi seemed content just to listen. Then it was Burks's turn to be embarrassed a bit; although it was significant that Mitch and Noel were there, Burks's questions actually were only for Hendrix:

"Well, this is the band that you're going to record with? And not Billy Cox or Buddy Miles? Or will they [Noel and Mitch] be recording too?"

"Yeah, we have some tracks that we did, some jams that we did with them. That's another thing, though. It's a three-piece, it's a four-piece kind of thing. You know, you overdub the piano."

"I guess you'd call this the Experience and you'd call that the Band of Gypsys?" Burks pinned.

Jimi laughed.

John Burks addressed the room: "What I'd like to do is just launch into a whole thing here if you. . . . How much time we got?"

"As long as you want," Mike Jeffery replied.

Burks noted that there'd been lots of talk that "Jimi may be forming closer ties with black militant groups, possibly the Panthers, and all that."

Mike Jeffery led Mitch and Noel in laughter. The press agent stuttered incoherently.

Jimi murmured, "Start with a shovel, wind up with a spoon," then said to Burks, "I heard that too—tell me all about it?" He laughed.

"I don't know. I didn't write that," Burks said quickly.

Mitch piped, "We got the White Tigers."

Everyone laughed except Jimi, who cooed, "White-on-white."

Burks persisted. "But that's not—that's not so?"

"No man, listen. Everyone has wars within themselves. So like, you know, we form different things and it comes out to be war against other people and so forth and so on."

There was laughter and joking. Burks wanted to know, "Well, what do you do, man?"

Jimi, still laughing: "I can't solve that. I don't know. Anything: the Fat Gypsys and all those other cats."

Everyone laughed and talked.

Burks wanted to know about the jammers back at the house in Woodstock where Jimi had had "a bunch" of blues guitarists and avant-garde jazz players.

Jimi said, "Well, it was like a jam. They had different types of music coming in and out, mixing it with different types of sounds. . . ."

When pressed about public performances of that jam group, recordings, or simply what they sounded like, Jimi replied, "I'd like to say it's not effeminate. . . ."

After a while Burks got back to the Panthers; did Jimi feel they were into a good thing, or did he not relate to them at all? Did he feel a part of what they were doing?

"Yeah, I naturally feel a part of what they're doing, in certain respects. But everybody has their own way of doing things. I just don't know. They get justified as they justify others in their attempts to get personal freedom. That's all it is."

"And to the extent they do that—you're with them?"

"Yeah, but not for aggression or violence . . . I'm not for guerrilla warfare."

Burks mentioned the Toronto Peace Festival and wondered if Jimi would have any hang-up about returning to Toronto.

"Of course not. My *hang-up* is getting hung up with things that happened in the past."

"You told the court in Toronto that you'd, in your own term, outgrown dope."

Jimi laughed softly, "At least stop it from growing."

Laughter all around, comments traded, and then silence.

"It's true?" Burks asked.

"What is that?"

"About outgrowing dope."

"I don't know. I'm too . . . *wrecked* right now."

Laughter all around. "I'll have to check into it."

Jimi got serious. "Oh yes, it's true, it's true. I don't take as much. That's what I was trying to tell them."

The interview began to mellow out as Jimi talked about his music. He was writing. "Mostly just cartoon material. Make up this one cat who's funny, who goes through all these strange scenes. I can't talk about it now. You could put it to music, I guess. Just like you can put blues into music."

Then he talked about composing. The music in his mind: "The music I might hear I can't get on the guitar. It's a thing of just laying around daydreaming or something. You're hearing all this music, and you just can't get it on the guitar. As a matter of fact, if you pick

SAM SILVER

up your guitar and just try to play, it spoils the whole thing. I can't play the guitar that well to get all this music together, so I just lay around. I wish I could have learned how to write for instruments. I'm going to get into that next, I guess."

Jimi loosened up and got into the walkout of the Madison Square Garden concert for the Vietnam Moratorium. "It's like it's the end of a beginning. I figure that Madison Square Garden was like the end of a big long fairy tale, which is great. It's the best thing I could possibly have come up with. The band was out of sight as far as I'm concerned."

"But what happened to you?" Burks asked.

"It was just something where the head changes, just going through changes. I really couldn't tell, to tell you the truth. I was very tired. You know, sometimes there's a lot of things that add up in your head about this and that. And they hit you at a very peculiar time, which happened to be at that peace rally, and here I am fighting the biggest war I've ever fought in my life—inside, you know? And like that wasn't the place to do it, so I just unmasked appearances."

The interview closed on a musical note. Burks commented that Hendrix's tastes seemed "broader than the typical rock 'n' roll fan or listener."

To that, Jimi responded, "This is all I can play when I'm playing. I'd like to get something together, like with Handel and Bach, and Muddy Waters, flamenco type of thing (laughs). If I can get that *sound*. If I could get *that* sound, I'd be happy."

On February 21 the Hendrix office's press agent called John Burks back to see if it was too late to change his story. According to the press agent, Noel Redding had decided to tour with Jeff Beck, and Billy Cox would be the bass player on the spring tour. The press agent said that Redding would probably return to the group, so nothing really had changed.

It would be called Electric Lady Studios. It brought to mind the beautiful period during the recording of the *Electric Ladyland* album at the Record Plant and the grand experimentation that went on from the environmental setting for "Voodoo Chile" to the sound-painting composition, "1983—A Merman I Shall Be," the sounds of the depths of the ocean, sonar, buoys, gull cries, and submarine hydraulus, and included some monstrous engineering feats that both Hendrix and Ed Kramer, individually and together, fought for including the burning-guitar sound of "House Burning Down," and the sound of space in ". . . and the Gods Made Love."

He wanted Electric Lady Studios to be physically as beautiful as the sounds of music to be made within it. The outside would have a distinct shape—like a giant guitar wedged into the row of four-story brownstones that lined West Eighth Street. The studios would be below in the cavernous basement. They would be designed along circular cyclical lines that curved onward and out of sight in the dim light. Only the most modern of equipment would be in the engineering booths and beyond on the studio floor. The three stories above would house the offices of his organization as well as the offices for the running of the studio, which would book groups for sessions just like the Record Plant. John Stryk designed the physical layout for the studio in collaboration with Jimi.

Had Jimi known how much of a hassle building a studio would turn out to be, he might have changed his mind, or at least given it more thought. Although the site had housed the Generation (the same club where Jimi and B. B. King and Buddy Guy had played their blue guitar laments the night Martin Luther King was killed), all the walls of the basement had to be ripped out. The contractors took delight in charging superextra fees for circular walls that were ultra-soundproof as well. Even before they began to build, incredibly extensive alterations had to be made on the building at 55 West Eighth Street, both inside and outside. Permits to build a uniquely designed exterior were an incredible hassle to get. Jimi insisted on special colors for the walls downstairs in the studio section, whose building he was personally supervising. The walls had to be white carpet so they could reflect varicolored lights totally, green, red, purple, pink. A Hawaiian artist painted the mural of a space voyage on the hallway walls. Jimi ordered the best of everything for recording purposes, including the largest Moog on the East Coast and thirty-six Dolbys. There were two studios, A and B. All the mirrors on the walls faced each other, reflecting infinity. And then they discovered that the studio was over a subway tunnel. It would be even more expensive to soundproof.

There was another problem with the studios: the neighbors. Not the bookstore next door or the Nedicks on the corner, but the Mafia. It was rumored that they controlled the businesses along the commercial strip of West Eighth Street. There are subtle ways neighbors can make trouble. Jimi was glad that he had friends in the area, even glad the brother who sold the Panther newspaper was there.

It was said that the Mafia did not want Electric Lady Studios on

West Eighth Street. Jimi's management was only able to obtain a five-year lease on the space, and they could not buy it. Although Jimi had no real contact with his management, who were actually controlling the day-to-day operations concerning the building of the studio, he was held personally responsible by the Mafia. The Mafia did not want too much police concentration on the street. They knew that there was a drug scene connected with musicians and rock music. The Mafia also knew that the FBI had been sniffing around the studios already. They felt that Jimi would make it too hot for them to run business as usual. It was kind of unusual for the FBI to be involved in drugs; that was usually the domain of the local police. The Mafia sensed that something heavier was happening than just smoking pot or snorting coke. The Mafia had unusual trouble finding out the real reasons for the FBI's snoopings around.

All was not lost. Jimi had a go-between, Tom Nitelife, a small-time pimp and dealer, who talked to the Mafia regularly. Nitelife often assisted in the purchase of prime grass and coke and was a personal taster for Jimi. Not only did he help get it but he also guaranteed it through his internal system. He was a mainstay in Washington Square Park and was known as a person who could "fix things." The presence of the FBI on the scene put the Mafia in a double bind. Although they had control over most of the strip between Fifth and Sixth avenues, they had no control over Electric Lady, and if they tried to use some muscle they would have to outsleuth the FBI. Jimi's studio existed in limbo between two very powerful adversaries.

One night Jimi showed up at a gig some friends were playing at an out-of-the-way club in downtown Manhattan. They were surprised to see him just come in, out of the blue. He did not have his ax or his two TEAC recorders, so they knew he did not come to sit in.

As soon as they left the bandstand he popped a question to them: "Do you know of a hit man I can contact?" They hushed him up right away and whisked him out of there to a nearby place where they could talk privately. They knew that if word got out that Jimi was looking for a hit man then *his* life would be in danger—whether he meant it or not. Also, they did not want to know about the situation and they did not ask. If they gave him the name of someone and something had gone down, then they would have not only been involved but also be guilty of whatever outcome occurred.

They sat down and talked about it. The friends said, "Hey, there are hit men all over the place, but we're not going to turn you on to one because you'll get yourself in trouble." Then they talked over the situation in general. The main concern from their point of view was Jimi's depression. The way he would just up and leave places where his friends were. The way he seemed to be so overcome with unhappiness. They felt that a hit man was not the answer. That Jimi's state of mind would not be assuaged by hiring a killer. It would not end there.

Finally Jimi said, "Fuck it." It was kind of incredible to them that someone was messing with his head so bad that he wanted to have him done away with. He decided to put it in a song, in his music instead. Like sublimation, he would work it out where he was powerful and confident—in the music. Not in the underworld.

He wrote a song about it and went and recorded it right away. It had an old rural blues feel with subtle slide effects and almost no other accompaniment. It was called "Belly-button Window."

> *Well I'm up here in this womb*
> *I'm lookin' all around*
> *Well I'm lookin' out my Belly-button Window*
> *And I see a whole lot of frowns*
> *And I'm wondering if they don't want me around*
>
> *What seems to be the fuss out there?*
> *Just what seems to be the hang?*
> *'Cause you know if they just don't want me this time around*
> *Yeah, I'll be glad to go back to Spirit Land*
>
> *And even take along the rest*
> *Before I'm coming down the chute again*
> *Man, I sure remember the last time, baby*
> *They were still hawkin' about me then*
> *So if you don't want me now*
> *Make up your mind, where or when*
> *If you don't want me now*
> *Give or take, you only got two hundred days*
> *'Cause I ain't coming down this way too much more again*
>
> *You know they got pills for ills, and thrills and even spills*
> *But I think you're just a little too late*
>
> *So I'm coming down to this world, Daddy*
> *Regardless of love and hate*
> *I'm gonna sit up in your bed, Mama*
> *And just a-grin right in your face*
> *And then I'm gonna eat up all your chocolates*
> *And say I hope I'm not too late*
>
> *So if there's any questions*
> *Make up your mind*

'Cause you would give or take
Questions in your mind
Give or take
You only got two hundred days

Well I'm up here in this womb
I'm lookin' all around
Well I'm lookin' out my Belly-button Window
And I see a whole lot of frowns
And I'm wonderin' if they want me around

With Ed Kramer engineering, Jimi recorded "Belly-button Window" alone in the partially completed Electric Lady Studios, overdubbing solo electric wah-wah effects as touches over a straight blues accompaniment that had the feel of an acoustic guitar.

April 25, 1970, the Forum, Los Angeles. Jimi and company begin a selective tour that would last until August 1. Then the completion, hopefully, of the album *First Rays of the New Rising Sun* for worldwide release sometime that fall.

All the wild party times in L.A. now ceased without Buddy Miles around. It was kind of lonely secluded in the penthouse above Beverly Hills, facing out over Los Angeles, the amorphous smog making an infinite gray haze right in front of your face.

This is the first big gig with Mitch Mitchell back on his oversized double-kit drum. Jimi hopes Mitch's chops are up. They have not been on a stage together since the Denver Pop Festival nearly a year ago.

The crowd is enthusiastic at the sold-out Forum. It almost seems strange to Jimi. His thoughts about his music are far from where the audience is at. The last album release, *Electric Ladyland*, clashes with Jimi's new material that will be on the new albums, *Band of Gypsys* and *First Rays of the New Rising Sun*. The material for *First Rays* is considerable, enough for a double album, actually. He will include some new numbers in this concert and see.

Jimi starts out with "Spanish Castle Magic." There are cheers of recognition as he drones the intro. The staggered beat of the first few lines fades into the long boogie lines of the chorus. The crowd is happy at once. He could play this tune for the entire show and no one would complain.

The boogie is continued with "Foxy Lady." Mitch is not drumming with the confidence he had had in the past. Billy Cox on bass is consistent and steady as a rock, without the adventurism of a Noel Redding. Billy continues to improve the more he plays. As an extension of Jimi's guitar in the lower registers he can be counted on to always be there for Jimi's frequent unison and harmony lines.

Jimi announces a song that he has been calling lately "Getting Your Brothers' Shoes Together." Actually it is "Lover Man." The significance of this title selection is in regard to the increasing struggle he is having in bringing the music to the public. Segueing into "Getting My Heart Back Together Again," which is better known as "Hear My Train A-coming," Jimi has outlined his metaphysical dilemma: Love is the emotion that commands his devotion to the struggle to take the music around. Like in the blues, shoes, a difficult acquisition for the rural black, signified the ability to move and to do. Like Hermes, the early Greek messenger of the gods who flew with wings attached to his feet to render absolute love in his deliverance of the sacred words, which like sacraments nourished the multitudes.

In "Getting My Heart Back Together Again," Jimi is even more direct. Death is his adviser. Death, like the mythological train, chugs in the piston beats of boogie, measured and deliberate. Death is a celebration in that it propels him toward his destiny.

"Room Full of Mirrors," Jimi's theme song of sorts for the new year, is a twenty-two-minute-long set that includes, in medley, "Hey Baby (Land of the New Rising Sun)," a jam that ends in a drum solo, and then "Freedom." The wide range of the medley removes the sharp-edged drive from each tune, but overall it is a *tour de force*.

"Voodoo Chile (A Slight Return)" includes a section of a new song, "Midnight Lightning." The two songs flow into each other effortlessly, creating an added message to his natal song of creation.

"Machine Gun" is played like a hypnotic stately caravan with meditative delays in the beat. Military taps, the drape, the rolls of state funeral. Fading down, the beat lowers like a flag in the wind, as Jimi's solo comes up like human cries, screams, and emotional feelings of tragedy that are beyond human capability to produce in sound, but yet can be produced by Jimi's Stratocaster. Then he goes into the intro to "The Star-Spangled Banner," spinning off into the blues with a satirical Yankee twang to it.

It becomes clear that the cumulative message of the new Jimi Hendrix is much heavier than ever before. No longer straight-up boogie myths and rock 'n' roll blues, but now the political and occult overtones engender more meditative ponderance and less release and abandon. The cheers of the audience, though not the howls of Monterey, are nevertheless totally supportive. But it is difficult to assess from onstage the penetration that has been made into the ongoing consciousness of the crowd.

Jimi went into virtual seclusion after the first L.A. Forum concert. The feedback from the concert was muted but favorable. But of more concern to Jimi was a quiet contemplation in the penthouse above Beverly Hills. His mood was expressed in the sheaves of hotel stationery he filled with his thoughts:

> Forget of my name . . . Remember it only as a handshake . . . introduction to my Belief which is God . . . Ride instead the waves of my Interpreture . . . Music, Sound, Hypnotic if you choose . . . But truth and life regardless of your questionable timid compromises . . . which I intend to erase . . . which I will erase without hint of reward as I am only a messenger And you a sheep in process of evolution . . . almost at death with yourself and on the staircase of birth. Soon you may almost forget the smell of your family.

Meryl, a lovely Eurasian doe, shared his quiet suite with him in hushed reverence. Her Zen attitude was reflective of his mood. Vishwa was around, too. Sincere and intuitive, he sought to bring to Jimi what would help him to be happier.

Vishwa ran into Taj Mahal in Hollywood at the old Ashgrove where for years Taj had been a fixture in a range of tasks from doorman to performer. Taj sensed an urgency when Vishwa asked him to come to see Jimi. Taj went right away, driving up with Vishwa through the cityscape foothills into the semirural, suburblike expanse of Beverly Hills. He sensed a heavy mood before he got there.

On several occasions before, Taj had expressed, in his understated way, his concern for Jimi and his disdain for the scene Jimi was surrounded by. The hangers-on were legion, and in a way, were understood to be part of his rock-star imagery. But Taj also saw a carelessness behind it that bothered him. He loved Jimi brother to brother, and as a brother also saw that "Jimi's back was not covered." This left Jimi open to a number of dangers that could eventually culminate in his being snuffed—and only because of carelessness. Being surrounded by people who were into very unnatural ways, Jimi was walking a tightrope that was painful for Taj to see.

Devon was considered, by Taj, to be walking in a similar way. Her confusion, masked by bravado, concealed an intelligent and sensitive soul. That she was beautiful as well made her all the more poignant. She and Colette would come by whenever they were in the same town. They always brought a little present. Some wine and cheese, some good smoke, and in a way Devon brought herself—as if she were available for whatever might help him along. Taj, unused to being and unwilling to be approached in that way, would always rebel. He wanted her to show *herself* some respect. So *he* could in turn respect her. Otherwise, it was impossible for them to get together on any meaningful level. Her heroin, her sex thing ("with all her body hanging out of her clothes"), her strange desperation made him unwillingly ambivalent. He respected Jimi for taking a lot of time with Devon, but feared that Jimi would be sucked into a deathful void.

As they neared the hotel, Taj recalled the last time he and Jimi had been together: the previous year at Devonshire Downs, in the San Fernando Valley, for the Newport Jazz Festival. They were on the same bill with the Chambers Brothers and had ridden to the site together in two limos. As they rolled up to the gate the Los Angeles Police Department was seriously busting heads with specially prepared truncheons. As they coasted by in their limos their windows became life-size TV screens through which they saw the upfront violence of heads being directly smashed, blood splattering on the windshield, young people recoiling in panic, bodies falling, screams, and agonized groans. This is what they were entering. This is what the music was making happen. They all had been sick. Jimi had not really been able to play. He had had to come back the next day to make up for his truncated performance. Taj's revulsion had been more steeled. He had no illusions about the violence, but he felt that Jimi's whole spiritual stance had not prepared him for the true human nature that was apparent in what surrounded the music. George Wein wanted the crowd and the money. The surplus crowd got the shit kicked out of them. Jimi was still not prepared for these facts. And the time was late. He was too open. Too trusting. Too naïve. Taj hoped he would simply be able to survive.

Taj was surprised by the austerity of the penthouse suite at the Beverly Rodeo Hotel. Jimi's mood was as austere as the standard plush hotel furnishings. Taj had brought his Dobro acoustic, and Jimi was glad he had. Subdued by a light nervousness but still self-effacingly polite, Jimi got out his acoustic and turned on his reel-to-reel TEAC recorder. Taj put on his cassette recording of crickets singing in Topanga Canyon as background. Taj set the pace with a ruminating standard country blues. Taj liked to lie back and savor the meaning of the blues with an economy of notes that would feel in the air. To him this was the strength and reason within the acoustic guitar. To feel the vibrations in the air, and within. But Jimi soon took over the pace. He could not seem to relax within the dictates of the blues of the old masters they both loved so much. Jimi took to playing fast runs and atonalities against the measure. Taj still stayed in his economy, not letting Jimi take him over. Seeming to give Jimi the lead, but this was not the case. Taj was sticking to his guns, and Jimi was moving all over the place—each to his own head. Objectively, it was probably an interesting contrast, but subjectively Taj was further troubled by Jimi and where his head was at. The rural blues was like a test to a musician. Like Muddy Waters would say: The twelve-bar form is very simple, it looks and sounds easy, but it's not. It has a lot to do with how you feel. Sometimes the bars come out to eight or thirteen, but that has to do with a feeling for what was going down. You had to feel: That was the test of the blues. Taj dedicated himself to the axioms of the blues masters. And that was why his concern for Jimi went sky high. Jimi's *feel* was off. Whether because of depression, troubles, or worries—whatever—his feelings were off. Jimi's few other guests were being unnaturally thoughtful. Then, as if to punctuate and nail down his apprehensions, several Mafia-looking dudes swept into the room without knocking and proceeded to spread out on the coffee table a smorgasbord of killer dope. Taj was taken aback by the insult to the sanctity of the music and the space. Jimi was, as usual, apologetic and polite to all.

The next day Vishwa came by the penthouse with Ananda Shankar, the nephew of Ravi Shankar (who had dropped them off there). Ananda was very pleased to meet Jimi, and the feeling was mutual. Ananda had brought his sitar, of which he was a master, just as his uncle was. Ananda sat on the floor of the sumptuous room and tuned the sitar. He began to play, sitting Indian fashion, commanding the meditation it takes to play the difficult timings of the age-old ragas. Jimi soon plugged in his Princeton practice amp and began to play along. He played over, under, and around Ananda's timing. This truly astounded Ananda. It usually took years to master the timing of the raga. At the end of their session Ananda expressed his amazed pleasure at playing with someone as versatile as Jimi. They parted with a great musical respect for each other.

That night, after the last Forum concert of the tour, Jimi was in a strange mood when he returned to the penthouse. Vishwa was inclined to leave him be, he had noticed that Jimi's nerves were raw these days, but when Vishwa heard screams coming from the bedroom he ran in. Jimi had the beautiful Eurasian girl, Meryl, down on the floor and was beating her head against it. Vishwa tackled Jimi and held him as Meryl ran naked out the door. Jimi turned on Vishwa and began beating him. Although Vishwa was larger than Jimi and could have probably made a fight out of it, he elected to take Jimi's blows, defending himself as best he could without fighting back. Soon Jimi's rage was over.

The next day Jimi was all apologetic. Vishwa understood. He had a large sympathy for Jimi and the frustrations he faced as an artist. He also understood the great restraint that Jimi had to have in public and how the opposite would sometimes come out when Jimi was with his friends. It was not everyone to whom Jimi could vent his feelings of frustration. Vishwa forgave Jimi and forgot the incident. But he had seen the violent side of Jimi before and was more worried about his state of mind than about a few blows.

That night Herbie Worthington came by and gave Jimi a lovely ring that he had made out of petrified moss.

"What are you giving me this for?" Jimi asked.

"For your birthday," Herbie replied.

"It's not my birthday today."

"Well, keep it until your birthday."

Jimi was so touched that he looked like he wanted to cry. He tried the ring on. It was too big.

"That's all right," he said. "I'll eat more so my fingers will get fatter."

He rides with Devon and Colette in the deep black limo, Vishwa on the jumpseat, the bright sun of Berkeley, California, washing their dark clothes in white light. They are dressed for night. Devon's black lace blouse is open down the front, Saks Fifth Avenue supershades, hair back but loose. Jimi's glossy black shirt merges into his hair, which covers his ears in a medium-long stylishly cut Afro. Clean-shaven, his high cheekbones are stark against his lean face. Indian countenance. The trace of a goatee gives his pale, dark-sand-colored face even more angularity. Devon could be his sister, they look so much alike. She wears crazy chic jeans with embroidered erratic patches in blues and greens. Jimi walks through the Berkeley Community Theater stage door in low moccasins that look cartoonish, turquoise beads across the top like rows of corn kernels.

DAVID REDFERN/*RETNA*

The sound check is also a rehearsal. He goes over the bass lines with Billy Cox, playing higher octaves on his guitar as he gives eye and head signals. The same signals he occasionally uses onstage. They play the intro phrases to "Dolly Dagger," the bridge to "Freedom," a snatch from "The Star-Spangled Banner." Billy and Mitch run them over while Jimi checks the amps and the bottoms. He always depends on Eric Barrett to instantly fix problems with the sound system. Ten electricians and engineers scramble behind stage and scamper on knees across the facing bank of the giant stacks of Marshall cabinets. The dual stadium PA system's mammoth speakers are directed straight out across three thousand empty seats. They hit a song, the intro goes to a peak, where it stops. Jimi shouts, "Eric, the amps, man."

Berkeley was close to martial law. May 30, 1970. The "People's Park" protest coupled with the Cambodian invasion had led to rioting and trashing. There was an obvious beef-up of police everywhere.

Bill Graham sensed an even stranger mood among the crowd as he entered the Berkeley Community Theater later that afternoon.

Gate crashings common to many eastern arenas did not usually occur in northern California. The restraint of the Bay area's rock music lovers was one of the major reasons why Graham had stayed on the West Coast and terminated the fabled Fillmore East. By 1970 Bill Graham was phasing out the operation of his own halls, opting for the larger and easier to operate Winterland in San Francisco, the Berkeley Community Theater, the huge Cow Palace just outside San Francisco, and the modern Oakland Arena and Coliseum.

Graham's staff had noticed an unusual and continued demand for tickets. That night several thousand fans surrounded the Berkeley Community Theater.

It was an agitated, unruly, bellicose crowd, which began breaking windows, leaping walls, and charging the front doors when the announcement came that the two concerts were sold out.

Graham was shocked. They were the same mellow people who always came to his concerts. This was not like them. The crowd breathed an urgency that turned into manic disappointment that verged on mass hysteria. Many felt that it would be the last time they would be able to see Jimi play.

When the doors opened, Graham's security force was confronted with the most serious crowd-control problem they had ever encountered. The crowd was not only trying to rush the doors, breaking glass in the process and making it difficult for ticket holders to gain entry, but they were also on the roof of the theater. Some had scaled the thirty-foot windows and broke them trying to get in. Chaos reigned for the entire double concert, further compounded by Wally Heider's remote recording crew outside, and a film company shooting what was to be the film *Jimi Plays Berkeley*.

The first song they played that night was "The Star-Spangled Banner." It was greeted with a great ovation. It so befitted the mood of the entire city, the entire nation—at war. Using the guitar as a synthesizer. Hendrix gliss-slides rapidly up and down the neck of the guitar while he whangs the tremolo bar and shakes the instrument rudely, sometimes banging it against his hip. He does not *play* in the classic sense, but goes straight to the basic synthesizer sounds produced by the interplay between the guitar and amps. He begins with a crackling feedback effect, manipulating the position of his body in relation to the mike and amplifiers so that he gets a sound that is the sum total of all the systems in an overload situation. The sound is rerouted through the mike monitors, setting up an independent sound that Hendrix plays against. The cry of the system is heard from the onset, going out of concert key on ". . . *dawn's early light.*" Slightly bending the neck, Jimi brings it back into control, but it is clear that he intends to play against the distort of the system. Even though the words are not sung, everyone follows in their minds the lyrics so ingrained in their consciousness since childhood. Jimi wheezes his guitar on ". . . *proudly* . . ." staggering the sound into baroque figures. The feedback single tone is an atonal in strange harmony with the melody. Beginning with ". . . *hailed* . . ." the single feedback tone establishes itself in solitary station above Jimi's sound, to merge with it at certain peaks. At ". . . *the twilight's last gleaming? . . ."* the feedback tone entirely takes over the sound for two beats. At ". . . *whose broad stripes and bright stars,"* he sustains "stars" as if it is a shooting star attempting to maintain its height, but plummeting and wavering in flight. Then at *"And the rocket's red glare . . ."* he lets the system implode: The sound screams like a fighter plane strafing, coming out of a deep dive, the impact of bombs striking the earth, the cries of the Cambodian peasants merging with the impact of the bombs, metal striking metal, the high whine of machine guns chattering, the bombers fighting out of their dives to be able to strike again. At ". . . *The bombs bursting in air,"* Jimi plays *bonking* monotonous sounds of civilization back home going on as usual, traffic and machines, crowds going home after work, all safe and complacent amid the master machines. On *"Gave proof through the night,"* Jimi strings through in straight melody with no feedback tone at all. At ". . . *that our flag"* he sustains the note *"still there"* and then slowly ascends ever so subtly into a piercing peal where Jimi says ever so casually, into a perfect break, "Big Deal!" The crowd cracks up at his humor. *"Oh say does that star-spangled banner yet wave,"* he produces a sirocco wind coming up from the desert by flicking the toggle switch. *"O'er the land of the free"* breaks into a lovely figure produced by both the feedback of the system and his single-note sustain; *"and the home of the brave?"* Jimi grinds his Stratocaster's strings against the mike stand in rude bottleneck.

As the crowd begins to applaud, Jimi jumps right into "Purple Haze." The crowd roars, their voices forming a single sound of pure delight.

Jimi hits the intro run to "Johnny B. Goode" and the crowd roars with approval. And at that moment Berkeley becomes the rock 'n' roll capital of the world. Upbeat on the tempo, Jimi faces his Stratocaster to the crowd, picking incredibly fast and hitting chords that require superhuman stretches of his large hands up the frets. He moves between picking and rhythm chordings that run the entire fret board. Between the rapid-fire lyrics the chorus *"GO JOHNNY GO!"* becomes a chant, like an ancient high school cheer. Yet it is so keyed to the warfare outside the theater, in the world, on the campus, in the streets. This archetypal scene of rock 'n' roll history, thousands of young heads in high school auditoriums moving to the beat that changed the world. *"Go Johnny Go!"* The war will end: The spirit of the people is too high. *"Go Johnny Go!"* The song could have also been Jimi's life story.

> *Deep down in Louisiana close to New Orleans*
> *Way· back up in the woods among the Evergreens*
> *There stood an old cabin made of earth and wood*
> *Where lived a country boy named Johnny B. Goode*
> *Who'd never learned to read or write so well*
> *But he could play a guitar just like ringing a bell*
> *Go! Go! Go! Johnny Go! Go!*
> *Go! Johnny Go! Go! Go! Johnny Go!*
> *Go! Go! Johnny Go! Go!*
> *Johnny B. Goode!*
>
> *He used to carry his guitar in a gunny sack*
> *Go sit beneath the tree by the railroad track*
> *Ol' engineer in the train sittin' in the shade*
> *Strummin' with the rhythm that the driver made*
> *The people passin' by, they would stop and say,*
> *"Oh my, but that little country boy could play."*
>
> *Go! Go! Johnny GO GO*
> *GO Johnny GO GO GO Johnny GO*
> *Go! Go! Johnny Go! Go!*
> *Johnny B. Goode!*
>
> *His mother told him, "Someday you will be a man*
> *And you will be the leader of a big old band;*
> *Many people comin' from miles around,*
> *To hear you play your music till the sun goes down*
> *Maybe someday your name'll be in lights*
> *A-sayin', 'Johnny B. Goode Tonight' "*
> *GO GO GO JOHNNY GO GO*
> *GO JOHNNY GO GO GO JOHNNY GO*
> *GO GO JOHNNY GO GO*
> *Johnny B. Goode*

The album entitled *Band of Gypsys*, recorded live at Fillmore East, was released in June 1970. Jimi was not entirely satisfied with it. He had no control over the mixing and mastering, and no control over the album cover or the liner notes. Capitol Records could do virtually whatever they wanted. The ugly album cover made it look as if he were bowing in supplication.

Jimi's record royalties were still in escrow until the cash settlement owed Ed Chalpin had been entirely paid. Yet Jimi desperately needed cash to pay for the studio's completion. That meant that he would have to gig like mad wherever the bread was right. His management wanted the album out because they feared he would not draw as well without a new album, since the last album, *Electric Ladyland*, had been released well over a year ago. Jimi did not want *Band of Gypsys* to be thrown out like that, yet there was nothing he could do. A feeling of powerlessness welled up in him. And he had no way of expressing it.

The first total session at Electric Lady Studios took place on July 1, 1970. Everything was not finished yet. There was still a lot to do with the three floors of office space above. But behind the guitar-shaped front brickwork that rolled out at you like the hips of a vivacious lady, and down the long flight of stairs seemingly into the earth, the main studio was ready to go. The rest would have to be completed as they went along. Everyone agreed that the first step would be to have a functioning studio where Jimi could work in earnest.

Big Claire commemorated the event with a big feed, just like in the brief good old days up at Woodstock—days not really that long ago.

Jimi recorded important songs that he had nurtured through the long winter up in Woodstock. "Pali-gap" was a stone meditative piece flowing in rural magic. "Hey Baby" was the song that signified his new musical head direction. Subtitled somewhere between "First Rays of the New Rising Sun" and "Land of the New Rising Sun," "Hey Baby" was conceived as a piece that would form the basis of a concerto.

"Dolly Dagger" was a slick-flowing, capricious funk achieved through incredibly tight ensemble playing that got a unified and clear sound without the heavy metal bridges. It was about Devon, to Devon (in a way), and kind of cleared his head about her.

A lively diddy-bop bass line dubbing with lead guitar tools out the three-tiered theme. The fuzz-toned talking bass starts out in harmony with the bass drum's kicks.

Jimi shouts-sings "Here comes," then flows out legato "Dolly Dagger"

. . . her love's so heavy
Gonna make you stagger
Dolly—Dagger
She drinks her blood from a jagged edge

Juma's congas fill the interludes with Jimi's rap on top. The bass takes over and fuzzes down to the utter bottom as Jimi says, *"Drink up, baby."*

Been riding broomsticks since she was fifteen
Blowin' out all the other witches on the scene
She got a bullwhip just as long as your life
Her tongue can even scratch the soul out of the devil's wife
Well, I seen her in action at the player's choice
Turning all the love men into doughnut boys
Hey, red-hot Mama, you better step aside
This chick's gonna turn you to a block of ice—Look out!

Jimi pulls out into a solo that is light and whimsical, with a touch of sinister on the bends.

Devon would pull shit. She would cop sympathy and love and hate. All the while knowing very well her wit and courage would get her over. Loving her, not wanting to hurt her, her friends and detractors called her Queen of the Groupies. Her lovers called her the teacher of sex.

Jimi eventually went out on her and beat her ass, but even that extreme behavior could not tip the scales irrevocably against Devon in his mind. The song he wrote for her was bittersweet, but he knew she'd like it. She would be scandalized in ecstasy.

"She drinks her blood from a jagged edge. . . ." Dolly Dagger, Mick Jagger's black wife. But all in all, the song showed a real love for her life, her verve, her motion, her funk, but in bitter sarcasm. Jimi hated the choices she made, for they revealed her values.

Here comes
Dolly—Dagger
Her love's so strong,
Gonna make you stagger
Dolly—Dagger
She drinks her blood from a jagged edge
   Drink up, baby

Look at ole burned-out superman tryin' to shoot his dust on
    the sun
Captain Comet is dead on the run
The words of love, do they ever touch Dolly Brown?
Better get some highway and clear out of town

Here comes
Dolly—Dagger
Her love's so heavy
Gonna make you stagger
Dolly—Dagger
She ain't satisfied
Till she gets what she's after
You better watch out, baby—here comes your master
    Drink up, drink right on up, baby

(Watch out Devon, and give me a little bit of that heaven)

Dolly, everybody
Get it on, get it on, get it on

Dolly everyone
Get it on, get it on, get it on

Dolly, everybody
Get it on, get it on, get it on

Dolly, everyone
Get it on, get it on, get it on

get it on
get it on
get it on
get it on
get it on
get it on
get it on
get it on
get it on

Billy Cox on bass, Mitch Mitchell on drums, and Juma on percussion, with the Ghetto Fighters doing vocal harmonic effects on "Dolly Dagger." The sound of the congas fit the sound of the brand-new studio perfectly. Juma said it was because they were underground, with the earth's spirit.

July 1970. Maui, Hawaii. This was the last leg of the brief tour that had seemed to take an eternity. The tour had exhausted him. And suddenly you are in a plane, staring at an incorporeal self in the conical window, the landscape of sky merging with your reflection. Going yet another place, no matter where your head was at. Another terminal. Another set of changes. Another row of limos waiting, motors running.

Chuck Wein was not exactly the mogul type. He was round and soft, though not fat, slightly tipsy, yet gaily in control. "Jimi," he gasped, as if he were in the presence of a Greek god.

The island was physically impressive. Maui. He recalled reading and talking about the lost civilizations: Lemuria, Atlantis. He would have dearly loved to hang out, but he was working. Whatever sentiments to the contrary, he was indeed working—every minute.

One of the ceremonies upon Jimi Hendrix's arrival was to have his fortune told by the resident soothsayer. Clara Schuff, a German émigré octogenarian, intuits through the midsection navel area. She draws an etheric representation of Jimi, his past and present and future lives, on an ordinary piece of paper. She draws in red- and blue-colored pencils as she talks. Circles, bodies and heads, all circular and cyclical. Down through the ages, heads of Jimi's past lives, or those who have deeply affected his earthly sojourns.

She tells him to be careful of women. They mean him no good. She repeats this several times. She tells him also that he is descendant from Egyptian and Tibetan royalty, and that his next life will be most concerned with the magical systems of Tibet. She repeats the warning about women. For a moment "Bold as Love" comes into his mind. He had written of the queen behind him in jealousy and envy. It sounds so simple. No big mystical thing. What Clara Schuff told him was what he had once told himself.

He had the feeling that she was in touch with something deep. Not by her appearance, which was grandmotherly and old Germanic, but by her utter simplicity. She obviously enjoyed the fuss being made about her by all the young hippies. Yet what they talked about sounded much more complex and much more unreal. She was down-to-earth, uncomplicated, and very real.

But the place was a mess. Mostly everyone was stoned, even the camera crew shooting the film. He did not know what the sound would be like. Warner Brothers was paying for part of the flick and the recording, through some weird machination of Mike Jeffery to get him film exposure. Something did not seem right. There seemed to be no thought-out thing about what was to be done or who was in charge. Oh no!

Chuck Wein had introduced Touraine to Jimi a month before the concert. She was physically beautiful and heavy of mind as well. She had a three-hundred-page book that contained Jimi's music decoded into color vibrations that corresponded to internal bodily functions, neurological and philosophical elements, and radiant-energy levels. She was into color-sound healing and found that Jimi's music fit perfectly with her activities in that field. She and Jimi got into an instant and extended spellbinding rap. They talked about magic and the occult. They fantasized about being able to beam sounds of music over five thousand square miles. Touraine believed that the work she had done on color and sound healing would have a profound effect on all of the people who were within the sound of Jimi's music. Jimi told her that he was from another planet, an asteroid belt off of Mars, and that he had come here to show people some new energy. They talked about the axis a lot. They finally decided to buy an Arabian horse (Touraine was also an Arabian horse costume designer), name it "Axis: Bold as Love," give it a purple haze as a third eye, and never have it ridden. She would train the horse according to her sound and color charts to respond to those vibrations rather than the usual horse-trainer ones.

"The Rainbow Bridge Vibratory Color-Sound Experiment" was largely the inspiration of Touraine. The assembled sat in circles grouped into their astrological signs so Jimi could feel their celestial vibes. They were right on the side of the Olowalu Volcano, the Crater of the Sun. Jimi wore a special Hopi Indian medicine-man shirt, which was turquoise and black, that Touraine had gotten for him. Chuck Wein made the introductory remarks.

"Welcome, cosmic brothers and sisters of Maui, to the Rainbow Bridge Vibratory Color-Sound Experiment. We're here for a very very particular purpose. I think it applies to all our brothers and sisters all across the planet. The Rainbow Bridge is not just a bridge. Just as there are cells that make up our body, we are cells in the body of the planetary beings. And the purpose of the humanity for being on this planet is to build that bridge between the heart and the higher mental and spiritual centers of the planetary being. And every higher thought and higher action that each of us participates in builds that bridge. And the reason that we've all kind of dropped out to here; it's the first time that anybody has dropped out in any large numbers since the Christians dropped out of Rome, then we want to convey that vow to everyone else. So instead of just being like a reflective groovy audience that we have at every love-in and concert forever and ever up to now, if we just turn on harmony so Jimi can stick it to that and lead us across that bridge and everybody all over the world is going to pick up on that. So we're all counting on you and here's your chance and Jimi should be here in a few minutes. Thank you."

After Chuck Wein's intro everyone does "OM" until Jimi comes on the portable stage. The volcano looms in the background. Everyone, including the film and sound crew, is pretty well wrecked on LSD, hash, and booze, but most manage to function. The audience is rather stoned and laid back. They hardly remember to applaud.

"We have Billy Cox on bass. Billy Cox. Mitch Mitchell on drums and me, Jimi, on public saxophone." He mumbles something about playing an instrumental because the words are not quite together.

Jimi starts out with a majestic-sounding theme that does not seem possible to be coming from an electric guitar. More like cellos, several cellos and violas churning. The orchestra sound swells, rises, and falls seemingly with no connection to any song or melody. Then seemingly out of nowhere, Billy kicks down on the bass in a slow, moderate, yet funky rocking bottom that refers back to the theme in the last figures of the run as Jimi plays fills and augments the sound on top of a melody that sounds simple compared to the intro. Jimi steps to the mike and raps/sings, slurring words over the appropriate beats:

> "Hey gypsy baby,
>   Where are you coming from?"
>   She looked at me and smiled
>   And staring out into space said,
> "I'm coming from
>   The land of the new rising sun"
>
>   And I said, "Hey baby,
>   Where are you trying to get to?"
>   She said, "I'm gonna spread a lot of love
>   Around to everybody
>   A whole lot of peace of mind to you and you"
> "Can we come along with ya, baby?"
> "Yes, you can come along"
> "May I come along with you, baby? yeah"
> "Come along, aw, come along"

Jimi hits "In from the Storm" with great zest; it rides up and crests beautifully, just like the fury and emotion of a storm, with Jimi getting off on top waves. He is in fantastic form.

"Foxy Lady" is dedicated "to that lady over there, Pat Hartley." Although it is the same song, Jimi plays it completely differently. He has a new treble sound that wings high-scaling freaky peaks.

Jimi, totally stoned, raps an intro to "Getting My Heart Back Together":

> . . . he's gotta leave town because his old lady don't want
> him around. Because, you know, nobody wants him in
> town. The cat's all low and everything but then he's gonna
> get it together. Because he's going down to the train station
> with his little baby and his little pack on his back. Come
> back and buy this town and maybe—if the girl does it to
> him one more time—might even marry her and give a piece
> to her. Called "Get My Heart Back Together"—I don't
> know what it's about myself.

Jimi is bending strings over a wide tonal range. Not in the blues sense but in elongated notes that stretch beyond the B. B. King clichés and explore the meaning of the tonal range in between. Then he turns the exploration into cascading, waterfalling runs that are blocked against chords that move easily into pure electronic sounds. They all move so quickly against each other, producing a three-dimensional sound. The densities produced are a result of the linear clustering of notes that have a vertical effect because of Jimi's amazing technique. The lines move into pure sound distortion that obliterates all the notes into one sound.

Then through that distortion Jimi segues into "Voodoo Chile (Slight Return)," with Billy Cox hitting the change right on the head. Then they segue into "Purple Haze," with Billy Cox right on top of the action. And behind that they go into "The Star-Spangled Banner" to clear the smoke. And then they return to "Getting My

"I'm gonna sacrifice somethin' I really love"

Heart Back Together," where Jimi sings the line: *"Even tried my hand at being a voodoo chile, baby."*

"Red House" becomes more than just a twelve-bar blues. Jimi extends the blues vibrato, playing the most complex of the blues guitar clichés, molding them into multinote runs and then blasting them away with feedback distort.

Jimi played three forty-five-minute sets. After each set he retired to a special sacred Hopi Indian tent.

Later, witnesses on Maui testified that they heard musical tones emanating from rocks and stones. UFOs were also sighted over the volcano by people who called in to a local radio show. A cameraman on the set said that he fell from his perch after seeing a UFO through his lens.

Chuck Wein was a film director of the Andy Warhol school. Not much script, hand-held cameras, and a lot of improvisation. The film was to be called *Rainbow Bridge.* Jimi shot his only scene, outside of his performances, the same day. It turned out to be a rap involving himself, Pat Hartley, and Chuck Wein. The rap was going nowhere when Jimi decided to improvise:

CHUCK: Did you ever have a feeling of being totally out of your body? Actually going somewhere but not taking your body with you? Outer space? Tibet?

JIMI: Yes. Have you?

CHUCK: Where do you go, when you go?

JIMI: I don't know man it seems like there's this little center in space that's just rotating you know constantly rotating, and there's these souls on it, and you're sitting there like cattle at a waterhole and there's no rap actually going on there's no emotions that are strung out, so you're just sitting there and all of a sudden the next thing you know you'll be drawn to a certain thing and the light gets bright and you see stuff, a page being turned, and you see yourself next to a Viet Cong you know a soldier being shot down,

© *FROM THE FILM "MONTEREY POP" BY D.A. PENNEBAKER*

and all of a sudden you feel like helping that soldier up, but you're feeling yourself held in another vibe another sense of that soldier. It seems like the soul of him you know and then you whisk back to the water hole or the oasis and you're sitting there and you're rapping again or something eating a banana cream pie and sitting on the gray hardwood benches and so forth and all of a sudden somebody calls out again, but this is without words that whole scene, and all of a sudden the next thing you know you see yourself looking down at the left paw of the Sphinx and the tomb of King Blourr and his friendly falcons and these all-night social workers with mattresses tied around their backs screaming "Curb Service! Curb Service! Curb Service!" You know with a third eye in the middle of the Pyramid. Ah, then we find ourselves drifting across the desert sands dry as a bone but still going toward home and then finally things look up as Cleopatra is here giving you demands, and at the same time begging for fetishes. Invent something or else I'll kick your ass. Those kind of scenes, a girl who claims to be Pio Cleopatra, Pio What? And all of a sudden the Hawaiian mountains open up and rise another thirteen thousand feet, and we go higher and higher, and Cleopatra has this beautiful raven hair and what are you supposed to do man except lay there and play the part? And so I'm laying there playing the part and a grape chokes me almost but I can't let the choke come out, because, you know, I have to be together. Right? So I say, "PTTT, groovy grape wine you have there Cleo. Ah hell, I mean let's get it on. Forget about all that stuff back there and forget about you and your scene. Let's just go up in the hills and relax and live. No I have the conscience I must do this. I must do that, I must . . . Oh forget about it Cleo, man you're a woman, I'm a man, come on let's get it on. Let's go out and get ourselves a grapevine out in the valley somewhere on the side of Mount Vesuvius or something. I don't know, hell. No, no, no. My parents, my traditions, my snake. Ooh you bit me in the ass again you naughty asp." Then we found ourselves wrapped up in carpets, which was fine. And here I am.

Back in New York, Jimi sits alone in the partially completed studio of Electric Lady. In the dim muted lights, the white Stratocaster crosses his slender body pointing upward. Ed Kramer sits behind the plate glass that separates the control room from the studio. Jimi sits. His muted face happy. Only the two of them. Underground in New York laying new tracks within the subterranean womb of Electric Ladyland.

"Somewhere over the Rainbow Blues"

Well I see fingers
and hands and shades of faces
reaching up but not quite
touching the promised land
I hear pleas and prayers
and desperate whispers saying
"Whoa! Lord please give us a helping hand"

Way down in the background I can see
frustrated souls of cities burning
And on across the water, baby
I see weapons barking out the sting of death
And up in the clouds I can imagine UFOs
Chuckling to themselves rapping they saying
Those people so uptight they sure know how to make a mess

HEY, yeah yeah . . .

Back at the saloon my tears mix with mildew in my drink
Can't really tell my feet from the sawdust on the floor
As far as I know they may even
Try to wrap me in cellophane and sell me
Try to sell me and don't worry about looking at the store
yeah yeah yeah

Jimi had his management cancel his trip to London set for August 13, saying that he had sustained injuries in a surfing accident while filming in Hawaii. Those in London had no way of knowing that he had been on the set of *Rainbow Bridge* for only one day. They were very pissed about it. They felt that Jimi would not be able to get the proper exposure and the promotion for the upcoming European tour. He had not been to London for almost a year and a half. The expenses of the studio in the final stages of completion were enormous; Jimi would need this tour and even more work to cover the bills.

But Jimi wanted to be sure the studio was finished. He was there night and day. He even did a little painting himself. People thought he was really freaking out over the studio. It was said that he went about at night and talked to the machines and petted them and whispered to them. Stephen Christopher said that he was able to make the oscilloscope's signal configure the words "Fuck this shit." Jimi had been able to record there since the spring, and he used the full facilities July 1. He was there all the time. Recording and remixing for hours on end. When the recording stopped, he would spend hours upon hours mixing and remixing. The engineers knew he was crazy. Only Ed Kramer was accustomed to his fastidiousness, and it was Kramer whom Hendrix preferred to be with in the studio. But Edwin H. Kramer had a life of his own to lead and Jimi was known to work around the clock until he collapsed.

Jimi called Les Paul, the electric-guitar virtuoso and electronic whiz. Les Paul had done things with the electric guitar and studio electronics in the 1950s that people were still trying to catch up with in 1970. Jimi wanted to know some things about the recording board that only a guitarist who also knew electronic engineering would know. He wanted to know how Les Paul went into the board himself. And in general, any tips Les Paul might have about building a studio. Jimi found Les Paul to be very, very friendly, almost familiar. Paul's approach to electronics was as personal as Jimi's so it was difficult to explain in one conversation how he went about doing things. But Les Paul wanted to let Jimi know that he had heard him play in Lodi, New Jersey, way back in 1964. Even then Les Paul thought that Jimi was one of the most radical guitar players he had ever heard. He had dug the way Jimi was bending strings and getting a powerful funk sound out of his Fender. Paul had had to deliver some tapes to Columbia Records in New York, but he rushed back to the club only to find that Jimi had only been auditioning and that the club had not hired him because they said he played too crazy and too loud and too wild. That's what had really impressed Les Paul about him. So Paul started a search of his own, going all over New Jersey and Manhattan, even going up to Harlem asking around for him. Paul was interested in helping Jimi get recorded. Les Paul and his sons looked everywhere for Jimi. Finally they gave up. Jimi laughed out loud. "You mean I was that close and didn't know it?" he said.

Jimi had an idea he wanted to try out on Paul to see how it sounded to him: Would it be possible to mike a guitar amp from far away, like across a room, while having the guitar connected to the board at the same time? Les Paul knew what he meant in terms of sound. He wanted to get the same signal directly from the amp and directly into the board at the same time. There might be some delay in it akin to a kind of phase, the same signal at different mike sources giving like an echo of two different qualities of sound. Of course, the only way to find out about it was to do it, but it was interesting to talk about. After all, they both were after unique sounds. Les Paul told him how important the mastering of a record was, and how he used to sit in the parking lot while they mastered his recordings, listening to it through his car radio. While most studios had the equivalent of a car-radio speaker inside the studio, it was usually only used to listen back to the mixes. But Les Paul knew how much of the sound could be lost during the mastering stage. He told Jimi to be at the mastering of his albums and to try to have them remaster it two or three times so that the depth of sound and the heights of sound are true. And you will be able to hear them on a regular five-inch car-radio speaker and that is how you will know that it is being mastered properly.

Hendrix had changed a lot in the nearly two years he had been back in the U.S.A. More and more assertive, he was openly challenging his management, which had made just about every decision for him before.

Not only was he booking his own concerts, beginning in Pago Pago in late September, but also it was common knowledge that his management contract, up for renewal in October 1970, would be terminated. He also had a reputable lawyer checking his royalties and other financial statements. Now with the studio complete he could really do his Gypsy Suns and Rainbows, Electric Church Caravan thing.

The best bands, musicians, and singers in the world would be attracted to Electric Lady, paying top dollar for the facilities and the vibes. Juma knew nearly all the young jazz musicians. He could offer Electric Lady to people who could use a top-flight studio but, like many jazz musicians, could not afford the top prices. Now the tables could be turned on all those people who had made millions because of him. People he didn't even know. People he didn't want to know. People who cared very little about the music or the progress of his music, people who only cared about the cash money at the record shop or ticket-taker's booth. He did not need all the bullshit connected with his concerts anymore. His "caravan" idea was that all he had to do was show up and already they had an ample audience to fill any arena. All those middlemen made money just on the fact that he would be there. Now he could distribute the money more equitably, to the people who really needed it, and record and tour and have it all in front of his eyes instead of cut up and mystified in somebody's office through lawyer talk.

The official opening of Electric Lady Studios was celebrated with a hastily put-together bash. Jimi went all out to complete all the arrangements before he went on his tour of England and Europe. Electric Lady was one of his greatest achievements—a modern yet laid-back studio with the latest equipment. It spelled the Record Plant as the hippest place to record in New York. In the short month they had to record there, Jimi had burst out with a great wealth of material, as if he had been holding back for that moment. The tracks done at Electric Lady were the best work he had done to date.

The work on Electric Lady had gone on under great pressure: personnel changes back within the group, lawsuits, and lack of communication between Hendrix and his management, still headed by Michael Jeffery. But it was a great victory, they were able to complete the studio in spite of all the hassles. To celebrate would be a morale-booster as well.

Jimi personally called up certain people for the party. He especially wanted the lovely ladies he was very close to, especially Monique, Colette, Betty Davis, and even Devon. After all, the studio was called Electric Lady. He wanted to make sure everybody he loved came to his studio: a massive guitar growing out of the earth.

The carpeted stairway led to an underground reception area that was shaped like a flying saucer. A low, round cubicled mini-office was encircled by a soft, low couch. Passageways led to the first studio and, curving around a bend, to the second. Curving passageways disappear in muted lights, spacey spectrum colors gave the effect of endlessness. A sound-buffered, upholstered, cozy underground lab.

Jimi, Juma, Billy, Arthur and Albert Allen (the Twins) sit in Studio A listening to the tapes of the music that will be on the next album while the opening bash for Electric Lady Studios bashes on. Tom Nitelife is not with them as he usually is. He has turned up dead. A mysterious O.D. They refuse to let that dampen their spirits, but the strange death hangs in the air anyway.

As the tapes play, Juma comments on the conga sound he plays that is integrated within the sound, the Twins go through some of their background harmonies laughing at the prettiness, and Billy bomps his head along with the bass lines. Jimi is silent, totally into the sound, listening as if he were alone. When the tapes stop, another is put on, Jimi speaks in his fluttering rush about how it will be necessary to remaster the album and maybe master it again to get

In Electric Lady Studio with engineer Ed Kramer (left) and business manager Jim Marron © 1970 FRED W. MCDARRAH

the desired depth-of-sound terrain that balances the high sounds with greater contrast. *First Rays of the New Rising Sun* would be completely what he wanted it to be. No one would do work on it other than Jimi, with Ed Kramer at his side.

First Rays of the New Rising Sun was to be an official end to the rock 'n' roll image Jimi had cultivated and the beginning of a new direction. Jimi had been working on the tracks for well over a year. The songs were more sculpted than free-flowing; there were a couple of pure instrumentals that had classical flamenco and concerto-type movement, as in "Pali-gap" and "Hey, Baby (Land of the New Rising Sun)." He also had a funky instrumental called "Midnight," which had been in the can for a while, as had been "Tax Free." "Belly-button Window," "Somewhere over the Rainbow Blues," and the old session of "My Friend" were almost straight poetic lyric with only touches of accompaniment, almost as if he were playing solo acoustic guitar. "Hey Baby (Land of the New Rising Sun)" contrasted with "Dolly Dagger." One was about the ideal woman and the other about the demon woman. "Freedom," "Ezy Ryder," and "Stepping Stone" are rocking message songs, while "Drifting," "Nightbird," and "Angel" (with '50s R&B changes) are straightforward love songs. "Earth Blues" and "Room Full of Mirrors" had been recorded seemingly ages ago, although they had been done at the Record Plant only that last winter. They had a different sound, very busy, lush, and very freaky. Jimi had a wide range of material, more than enough for one album, enough for a double album at least, although his management was against it, but he would see how they flowed together when he returned from England. And since his management contract would be over by then, he would legally be the one to make the decisions totally.

The party was like a christening, not only of the studios, but of the music he had forged into a new personal statement. He listened to his new music, fixing it in his mind so as to hold him through the duration of the tour. That mad road. Warrior within, he listened.

Juma Sultan's tabla-sounding congas blending with the strong rhythms of Buddy Miles's drum kit begin "Ezy Ryder," recorded a year earlier at the Record Plant. Buddy is respectful of the African drums and uses more cymbal than snare bash to complement the added percussion. They establish a hand-jive rhythm as Jimi comes in sustaining a wailing blue-note howl. Jimi on another guitar track plays through two fuzz tones patched together, producing a mellow fuzz that jacks the rhythm at the same time as Billy Cox comes in playing double time against the bass drum in a way only he can. Jimi is still sustaining the blue howl against his own staggered rhythm jags. Buddy begins to kick as the rhythm guitars announce the turn into the song proper. The hand-jive rhythms really become dominant as Jimi plays the lead lines in his new violinlike treble sound. The sustain ends as Jimi begins the lyrics but comes back to punctuate the end of his phrases in abrupt metal howls.

Steve Winwood on organ and Chris Wood fill out the sound of what could have been the Band of Gypsys.

> *Here comes Ezy, Ezy Ryder*
> *Riding down the highway of desire*
> *He says the free wind takes him higher*
> *Trying to search for his heaven above*
> *—But he's dying to be loved*
> > *dying to be loved*

> *He's gonna be living so madly*
> *Today is forever so he claims*
> *He's talking about dying—it's so tragic, baby*
> *But don't worry about today*

We got freedom coming our way
    Freedom comin' our way

How long do you think he's gonna last
Can I forecast?
See all the lovers say, "Do what you please!"
Gotta get the brothers together—and the right to be free
In a cloud of angel dust I think I see me a freak
Hey look, motorcycle Mama—you gonna marry me?
    (Gonna be stoned crazy
    Love come in kinda easy
    Stoned crazy, baby)

There goes Ezy, Ezy Ryder
Riding down the highway of desire
He says the free wind takes him higher
Searching for his heaven above
But he's dyin' to be loved   *—LOVE*
Dyin' to be loved   *—LOVE*

    Here comes Ezy
        Ezy Ryder   *Ryder*
  LOVE
        Ezy Ryder   *Riding*
  LOVE
        Ezy Ryder   *Dyin'*
  LOVE
        Ezy Ryder   *Tryin'*
LOVE
        Ezy Ryder
LOVE
        Ezy Ryder
LOVE   *Love*   *Love*

The instrumental "Pali-gap" is three guitars blending beautifully, delicately, yet with a funky bottom. The lead guitar touches off a fuzzy feedback that is tastefully developed at the tips of phrases. A background guitar with a wonderful rhythm and strange yet appealing echo and yet another guitar track adds straight-chord touches at random yet consistently delayed intervals. The yearning of the lead lines develops the emotion, building and shaping.

There are Moorish flamenco flavors in the irregular repetitions of the two major phrases alternating against the meshings of Billy's kick-down bass lines and Mitch's shuffling, stately drums. The

Andalusian gypsy rhythm is tipped by a dervish fervor at points in Jimi's playing where he breaks with the beautiful harmonies of his guitars and peaks away in rapid triple meter. Jimi double-picks through a Leslie organ speaker getting sounds of water flowing. In the last passages Jimi completely changes the lead tonality. He goes into horn lines, then into ragtime, then a blues flurry, and then into celestial chordings that take off from Wes Montgomery, tagging out with a melody that could go on forever.

When Jimi had first written "Hey Baby . . ." he was calling it "Gypsy Boy," and it sounded real pretty on the refrains, *"Can I come along?"* going into lazy evanescent boy sopranos mixed back and flowing against the beat.

But it was pretty, too pretty, too laid back, winsome, and evanescent. Better to take it out and leave the weight with the song and the singer up front talking about it, like a testimonial rather than pretty slow-drag R&B.

A two-vamp song, the African change in melody is indicated by the blue-note stride slurring into nomadic pan-Sahara vibratos. It gives the English words and instrumentation an African feeling with the rhythmic and tonal meanings implicit in the flamenco style.

Fine harmonies of high-nut treble bending strings against a separate arcing feedback ring. Then the haunting Moorish sound that is basic to flamenco, hesitating in its deliverance, a saga of a search spread across Sahara sands and winds. Ecclesiastical tones of High Church emotions. Jimi's virtuoso picking cascades runs into microtonal notes. Then back to the swaying, sauntering rhythm, and then as if from out of nowhere, in surprise:

> *"Hey . . . baby, where you coming from?"*
> *She looked at me and smiled*
> *And staring out into space said*
> *"I'm coming from*
> *The Land of the New Rising Sun"*

Not limiting himself to major or minor scales, Jimi changes keys at will, sometimes on each note in weird modes. Since the fuzz tone changes the harmonics, and there are more harmonics in distortion, Jimi gets Eastern scales and pure freak sounds out of nowhere.

In "Earth Blues" the Ronettes are a joy of pure harmony and combined with the maleness of the Ghetto Fighters (the Twins) they get into a really nice sound. The engineer has the licks panning from

Opposite: © 1980 NONA HATAY

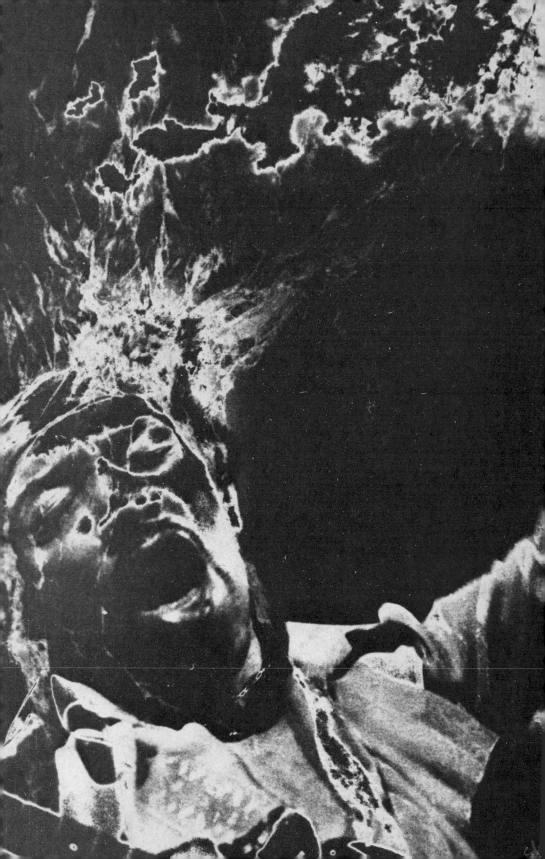

one speaker to the other. Billy Cox's bass lines have the feel of
Charlie Mingus playing bottom runs in his "Fables of Faubus."

Billy Cox has really arrived within Jimi's music. No more the
treble frenzy of Noel Redding as a frustrated guitarist. Billy Cox is
terse and tough. He covers the bottom without any yearnings for the
top. He has an understated funk groove that is so subtle that even
when he gets into off-tonalities it all flows in a fluid groove. He can
rev and snarl, strut and talk, and never blow the groove. His steady
jazzlike presence fuses the wide range of tonals on the bottom shelf
together. And that was just what Jimi wanted so he could have
complete freedom on top: a steady and consistent, yet creative, bottom presence.

> *Well I see hands and distant faces*
> *Reachin' upward not quite touching the Promised Land*
> *Well I tasted a whole lot of precious years wasted*
> *Saying "Please, Lord, give us a helping hand"*
>
> *ya ya ya   there's got to be some changes*
> *ya ya ya   a whole lot of rearranges*
> *ya ya ya   you better hope love is the answer*
> *ya ya ya   you better hope it comes before the summer*
>
> *Well everybody can hear the sound of freedom speeding*
>   *high*
> *Sirens flashing with earth and rockets stoning*
> *You better love me like this gonna be the last time*
> *And tell the child to bury Daddy's old clothes*
>
> *ya ya ya   yeah they talking about getting together yeah*
> *ya ya ya   together for love or blood*
> *ya ya ya   you better hope love is the answer*
> *ya ya ya   you better hope it comes before the summer*
>
> > *everybody   everybody!*
> > *everybody   every sister*
> > *everybody   every mother*
> > *everybody   got to feel the light*
> > *everybody   it's shining bright*
> > *everybody   Everybody's—gotta live together*
> > *Right on, baby . . .*
> > *Feel those surf blues coming at you, baby*
>
> *Don't let your imagination take you by surprise*
> *A queen I'll be I'll one day visualize*

My head in the clouds, my feet in the pavement
Don't get too stoned, please remember you're a man

ya ya ya   there's got to be some changes
ya ya ya   a whole lot of rearranges
ya ya ya   you better hope love is the answer
ya ya ya   you better hope it comes before the summer

  everybody everybody
  everybody gotta feel the light
  everybody gotta feel the light, baby
  everybody everybody
  everybody gotta get it together
  everybody keep it together
  everybody right on together
  everybody whooooo
   Now all sing for the Earth Blues jumpin' at
    you, baby

la la la
la la la
la la la . . .

"Drifting" is a slow ballad with beautiful layered violin-sounding guitar tracks. Jimi's lush-life vocal is one of his best.

Drifting—
On a sea of forgotten teardrops
On a lifeboat
Sailing for
Your love

        Sailing
         home

Drifting
On a sea of old heartbreaks
On a lifeboat
Sailing for
Your love

      Sailing home

Jimi loved the studio, his electric lady. He used to sleep with his guitar; now he could sleep *in* his studio. Amid the subdued fires of electricity, magnetism, and radiance.

They talked in the streets of dawn. On MacDougal and Eighth, the morning after the party, Jimi, Juma, Billy, and the Twins.

Juma and the Twins would not be making the tour. Jimi sat in the passenger seat of his Stingray, his feet dangling out on the curb where the others sat. The silence of New York City at blue dawn. A quiet time when words and thoughts come together. The party had been a success, one of the *events* of the season, like the newspapers say. They were not tired but they had no energy. They knew they would be tired sometime in the future, but in the euphoria of the christening of Electric Lady they huddled, drawing strength from each other like little boys in the street. They had just gotten through recording a few things over. In a way it was sad that Jimi was leaving so soon after triumph. Bread was needed. The bread for their concerts in Pago Pago was Jimi's responsibility, and he was going out to get it. They talked of Pago Pago, the American Samoans. They wore that Hawaiian-type hula stuff. Headdresses and thin soft material wrapped around themselves when they really got into celebrating their ancestral thing. But many related as Afro-American brothers. Some of them had Afros that were out of sight. They grew to tremendous sizes, especially the men and the women too. A three-hundred-pound Samoan was no big thing. Giving a concert in Pago Pago was an unusual move, but that's what the Caravan was about. The trial run would begin in the South Pacific. When they got it together they would be able to take the top names in jazz, rock, and blues anywhere and knock them out on short notice. Gypsy Suns and Rainbows, Electric Church Caravan.

Digging each other, reluctant to let go of that moment, they finally had to say good-bye. Jimi had become, strangely enough, a true leader, a leader of men. Their last words to each other were: "See you in Pago Pago."

NINE

Three or four different worlds went by within the wink of an eye. Things were happening. There was this cat came around called Black Gold. And there was this other cat came around called Captain Coconut. Other people came around. I was all these people. And finally when I went back home, all of a sudden I found myself bein' a little West Coast Seattle boy— for a second. Then all of a sudden when you're back on the road again, there he goes, he starts goin' back. That's my life until somethin' else comes about.

There are a lot of things you have to sacrifice. It all depends on how deep you want to get into whatever your gig is. Whatever you're there for. So like the deeper you get into it the more sacrifices you have to do, maybe even on your personality or your outward this and that. I just dedicate my whole life to this whole art. You have to forget about what other people say. If it's art or anything else, whatever you really, really dig doing, you have to forget about what people say about you sometimes. Forget about this or forget about that. When you're supposed to die or when you're supposed to be living. You have to forget about all these things. You have to go on and be crazy. That's what they call craziness. Craziness is like heaven. Once you reach that point of where you don't give a damn about what everybody else is sayin', you're goin' toward heaven. The more you get into it, they're goin' to say, "Damn, that cat's really flipped out. Oh he's gone now." But if you producin' and creatin', you know, you're gettin' closer to your own heaven. That's what man's trying to get to, anyway.

What's happening is, you, we, we have all these different senses. We've got eyes, nose, you know, hearing, taste and feeling and so forth. Well, there's a sixth sense that's comin' in. Everybody has their own name for it, but I call it Free Soul. And that's more into that mental kind of thing. That's why everything is beyond the eyes now. The eyes only carry you so far out. You have to know how to develop other things that will carry you further and more clear. That's why the fastest speed . . . what's the fastest speed you can think of? They say the speed of light is the fastest thing—that's the eyes—but then there's the speed of thought, which is beyond that. You can get on the other side of this theme in a matter of thinkin' about it, for instance.

Sometimes you might be by yourself writing something. And you come across some words and you just lay back and dig the words and see how that makes you feel. And you might take it at practice or rehearsal or something like that, and get together with it there, in music—see how the music feels. Or either sometimes you might be jammin'—when I mean you, I mean the group—the group is jammin' or something, and then you might run across somethin' really nice. And then you keep runnin' across that, then you start shoutin' out anything that comes to your mind, you know, whatever the music turns you on to. If it's heavy music, you start singin' things.

Once you have the bottom there you can go anywhere. That's the way I believe. Once you have some type of rhythm, like it can get hypnotic if you keep repeating it over and over again. Most of the people will fall off by about a minute of repeating. You do that say for three or four or even five minutes if you can stand it, and then it releases a certain thing inside of a person's head. It releases a certain thing in there so you can put anything you want right inside that, you know. So you do that for a minute and all of a sudden you can bring the rhythm down a little bit and then you say what you want to say right into that little gap. It's somethin' to ride with, you know. You have to ride with somethin'. I always like to take people on trips.

That's why music is magic. Already this idea of living today is magic. There's a lot of sacrifices to make. I'm workin' on music to be completely, utterly a magic science, where it's all pure positive. It can't work if it's not positive. The more doubts and negatives you knock out of anything, the heavier it gets and the clearer it gets. And the deeper it gets into whoever's round it. It gets contagious.

Bach and all those cats, they went back in there, and they had caught a whole lot of hell. All they could do was get twenty-seven kids and then dust away. Because the way the society was they didn't respect this. They didn't know how to say, "Well, yeah, he's heavy. We'll go to his concerts. We'll dig him on the personal thing." But like, see, you're not supposed to judge a musician or composer or singer on his personal life. Forget about that. I like Handel and Bach. Handel and Bach is like a homework type of thing. You can't hear it with friends all the time. You have to hear some things by yourself. You can listen to anything that turns you on, that takes you for a ride. People want to be taken somewhere.

I wish they'd had electric guitars in cotton fields back in the good old days. A whole lot of things would have been straightened out. Not just only for the black and white, but I mean for the *cause!*

They keep sayin' things are changin'. Ain't nothin' changed. Things are going through changes, that's what it is. It's not changes, it's going through changes.

That's the way evolution happens. You have little bumps here. That's why you have the number seven after six. You have six smooth and all of a sudden a little bump. There's gonna be sacrifices. You get a lot of Black Panthers in jail, a lot of—what do you call that war thing?—the moratorium. A lot of those people who are goin' to get screwed up, for instance, here and there. But the whole idea, the whole movement is for everybody to appreciate. It's not only for young people to get it together by the time they're thirty. It's for anybody who's livin' to really appreciate.

It's just like a spaceship. If a spaceship came down if you know nothin' about it, the first thing you're goin' to think about is shootin' it. In other words, you get negative in the first place already, which is not really the natural way of thinking. But there's so many tight-lipped ideas and laws around, and people put themselves in uniform so tightly, that it's almost impossible to break out of that.

Subconsciously what all these people are doin', they're

killin' off all these little flashes they have. Like if I told you about a certain dream that was all freaked out, and you'll say, "Oh wow, you know, where is this at?" That's because you're cuttin' off the idea of wantin' to understand what's in there. You don't have the patience to do this. They don't have the patience to really check out what's happenin' through music and what's happenin' through the theater and science.

It's time for a new national anthem. America is divided into two definite divisions. And this is good for one reason because like somethin' has to happen or else you can just keep on bein' dragged along with the program, which is based upon the past and is always dusty. And the grooviest part about it is not all this old-time thing that you can cop out with. The easy thing to cop out with is sayin' black and white. That's the easiest thing. You can see a black person. But now to get down to the nitty-gritty, it's gettin' to be old and young—not the age, but the way of thinkin'. Old and new, actually. Not old and young. Old and new because there's so many even older people that took half their lives to reach a certain point that little kids understand now. They don't really get a chance to express themselves. So therefore they grab onto what is happening. That's why you had a lot of people at Woodstock. You can say all the bad things, but why keep elaboratin'? You have to go to the whole balls of it. That's all you can hold onto, in the arts, which is the actual earth, the actual soul of earth. Like writin' and sayin' what you think. Gettin' into your own little thing. Doin' this and doin' that. As long as you're off your ass and on your feet some kind of way. Out of the bed and into the street, you know, blah-blah, woof-woof-crackle-crackle—we can tap dance to that, can't we? That's old hat.

We was in America. We was in America. The stuff was over and startin' again. You know, like after death is the end and the beginnin'. And it's time for another anthem and that's what I'm writin' on now.

> Jimi Hendrix
> from *Superstars*

Flying above the Atlantic he felt as he had felt when he had been a paratrooper. The same anticipation of descent, the same tingling in his belly. And he knew that this was the most important jump of his life. Yet it was not like a physical risking of his life, it was more that his heart, his spirit, his soul were being put up to risk for his music, his song. All he wanted to do was play. He would do anything as long as he could play. He thought of the plane crashing. Then from his window he saw the clouds break, they were low across the ocean as the plane pointed toward a land mass amid the waters.

Jimi checked into the Cumberland Hotel in adjoining suites 507 and 508. Because he had delayed his arrival in London to virtually the last minute before the Isle of Wight festival was to occur, Jimi felt especially obligated to spend as much time as possible with the press, the promoters of his tour, and various people on the London music scene. He went three days straight without sleeping, seeing folks, partying, and giving interviews to the papers and magazines in London and to reporters who reported to other points on the tour, which included London, Sweden, Denmark, Germany, and France.

Vishwa waited for Jimi as the helicopter landed at the Isle of Wight. He had not seen Jimi since the spring, when they were filming *Jimi Plays Berkeley*. Vishwa was an old hand at traveling with Hendrix. Since Jimi first came to Los Angeles after Monterey as a star, Vishwa often accompanied Jimi and company as a part of the entourage and helped out where he could. He had helped put together the deal for the film *Jimi Plays Berkeley* and had introduced Jimi and Jeffery to the special-effects man for the Kubrick film *2001*.

Jimi spied him as soon as he disembarked and waved Vishwa into his dressing room. The dressing room was a portable type that had a long history. Opulent and spacious, it folded out from its railroad-car size like an accordion. During World War II it had been used to smuggle arms.

Vishwa noticed Jimi's weariness right away. But it seemed like more than weariness. Jimi seemed resigned, down, almost fated. His vibe was the lowest Vishwa had ever seen, and as a highly trained TM master, Vishwa would not let something like that pass. At first Jimi and Vishwa talked excitely about what they had been doing and seeing since they had last been together. Then Jimi changed. Suddenly he seemed to go back into himself.

Vishwa helped some friends get through the security force into the dressing room. Jim Morrison was one. Jimi was happy to see them but there was something on his mind.

Besieged as usual by the press, Jimi continued to answer questions.

He told the *Times* reporter: "If I'm free, it's because I'm always running. I tend to feel like a victim from public opinion. They want to know about these girls, kicking people in the ass, doing the 'Power to the People' sign. I cut my hair—They say, 'Why'd you cut your hair, Jimi?' It was breaking up. 'Where'd you get those socks?'

'What made you wear blue socks today?' Then I started to ask myself questions. Did I take too much solo? Should I have said thank
you to that girl? I'm tired. Not physically. Mentally. I'm going to
grow my hair back, it's something to hide behind. No, not to hide. I
think maybe I grow it long because my daddy used to cut it like a
skinned chicken.

"When they (the audiences) feel, and smile with that sleepy, exhausted look, it's like being carried on a wave. We mostly build on
bar patterns and emotion. Not melody. We can play violent music,
and in a way, it's like watching wrestling or football for them—it
releases their violence. It's not like beating it out of each other, but
like violent sick. I mean, sadness can be violent."

He told free-lance writer Stephen Clarkson: "I am all alone and I
say, 'What are you doing here dressed up in satin shirts and pants?'
I've got this feeling to have a proper home. I like the idea of getting
married. Just someone who I could love."

It was evident Jimi was very tired, near exhaustion.

Soon the reporters left and Jimi prepared for the show. It was dead
in the middle of night, seemingly nowhere in time and place, only
the darkness of the expansive field, the roar of the crowd, and the
surges of the giant sound system. Richie Havens was on. He
sounded good. He always sounded good, his unique baritone swell-
ing out over the assembled.

Jimi did not have much to say to Vishwa, which was strange.
They were as tight as a star performer and a non-show-business
friend could be.

The Isle of Wight crowd was huge and loud. By the time Jimi was
to go on many that had been unable to get in had succeeded in
breaking in through barricades after a grenade had blown a hole in
the fence. The large security force with its trained dogs were unable
to prevent the widespread gate-crashings.

Just before going on Jimi said, to no one in particular, that he
would play until someone in the audience booed. It was a strange
statement for him to make since he was obviously exhausted. The
statement both indicated a weary bravado and his insecurities at
facing a large British audience after a nineteen-month absence.

Jimi comes onstage with flushed and youthful cheerfulness, his
voice wafting high greetings. Methedrine rushing through exhausted limbs.

Isle of Wight. Lying below the British Isles, longitude 50° 30'N by
latitude 001° 16'W. One degree from the end of time—Greenwich,
England.

Late night, early morning. Staring into depths of darkness, black shrouded crowd, lit only by the tortured surge of night fires, a few bodies visible in the haze. Blackness. The presence of thousands as far back as the eye can see merging with the horizon facing east toward the zero point of time.

Weird not seeing anyone—only voices from a black void. No faces staring back in the dead of night. "Yes," Jimi says. "It has been a long time, hasn't it?

"Stand up for your country and the police. Maybe you should sing along. Well if you don't want to stand then fuck you. . . ."

Crowd laughs. Voices up front speaking for the muted roar from the back, sounding like approval yet not really sounding like anything.

"God Save the Queen" comes on in a crash of volume, then drones downward. Almost like "The Star-Spangled Banner," but not as freaky. The same melody he used to sing as a schoolchild, "My country 'tis of thee/Sweet land of liberty/ . . . Let freedom ring." Only this is the original "God Save the Queen." The melody is so much like Handel, the anthem of long tradition and world domination.

Mitch beats out a brief drum solo as they segue into "Sergeant Pepper," the true national anthem of contemporary England. The jaunty fanfare of the song is replaced by Jimi's weird vibrato treble peaks that trail off close to feedback rather than bend roundly. He's rushing, but he can't stop. He is fighting the exhaustion, his body tone bone-weary. Harmonics began to pop up. Playing against the amps, his weariness seems to be reflected in the strangest electric tones he ever played. Sharp to piercing, the sound seems to want to take off from harmonics straight up into feedback, like a knife's edge sharpened to razor intensity.

Harmonizing with himself, fretting rhythm on the bottom strings and wild-trilled atonal licks on top—the sound was freaky, amphetamine-intense. Yet it swung, swung almost insanely. Teetering on the edge of manic annihilation.

He goes into "Machine Gun" and gets his mind blown. Cutting right through the introductory guitar phrases a clear middle-class Englishman's voice intoning, "Security force, security force . . . come in. . . ." He was floored. He almost stopped playing. He kept the show going, nodding at Billy and Mitch to keep on going. Sergeant Pepper had invaded his amps. Somehow the frequencies of the PA systems and the security-police band were feeding into each other. That was why he was having so much trouble controlling the sound. He was actually in circuit with the operating frequencies of the security police. Too much. At another time he might have laughed it off, but right then it was all he could do to remain standing. Every time his eyes would blink he was afraid he would fall. Head bobbing, directing Mitch and Billy, he was also directing himself, keeping himself going.

Mitch begins missing on drums. The steady drone of "Machine Gun" seemed to be eluding him. There are very weird vibes in the air. Jimi nods anxiously at him to pick up. But before he does he misses two entire beats. Mitch had stopped for two whole beats! Jimi could not believe it. Gritting his teeth, he turns to the crowd and grimaces in pyrotechnic agony and dances, taking his, the band's, and the audience's minds away from the pause. He moves into "Midnight Lightning."

I get stoned and I can't go home
but I'm callin' long distance on a public saxophone
my head is dizzy and shaken
Feel like I got run over by public opinion and the past. . . .

we gotta keep on walkin'
don't know where

we gotta keep movin'
we gotta keep on groovin'
gotta stay on both sides of the sky
we gotta keep on lovin'
good sweet lovin'
make love on my dyin' bed . . .

Suspended between Sunday and Monday, Greenwich Mean Time. Receding in time as if the sound that sprang from the giant amps and speakers rushed over the curve of the Earth into a vortex that separated other worlds.

"There must be some kind of way out of here. . . ." "Watchtower" stole up on him. Before he knew it, he was singing it. He had completely forgotten about the band, although he nodded unconsciously at them. The words of "Watchtower" seemed to come straight from his unconscious. In the past he had forgotten those words several times onstage. But this time they sailed out into the darkness of the Isle of Wight. Their meaning becoming clear as if he were hearing them for the first time. His voice almost breaking: *"But you and I we've been through that and this is not our fate/So let us not speak falsely now/the hour's getting late. . . ."* His guitar screams out in solo, rushing ahead of Mitch and Billy.

His heart thumped against his chest. The rhythm driving manic.

When he heard himself he sounded as if he were crying. As if something within had ripped from its moorings. He sang against the strange deep sleep that seemed to tempt him to collapse. He sang his ass off. Lest he cease to exist.

"Watchtower" in the cold distance . . .

Jimi's freaky vibratos spiraling out seaward toward the sonic sonority so close to the feedback range that they began to clash in peak vibratos that straighten out every so often into flat peals of pure signal. An earnestness clenched tight in fatigue. Nearly unconsciously he plays, pulling out his reserves to deliver what his top fee demanded. The bottom range of fatigue, one step from falling out, yet pushing forward in the black, bleak night, keeling seaward, signal distorting into fog.

Jimi played another version of "Hey, Baby (Land of the New Rising Sun)," an instrumental exploration of every conceivable note and sound possibility. Jimi ad-libbed new lyrics:

Coming back to England
Thank you, baby, for making it so easy
Going through changes in New York, Chicago
Thank you, baby, for staying with me . . .

They cheer. They always cheer. The blank faces he hates to face. No one to point at in the absolute blackness. No little girl to cun his tongue at. Only banks of nearly blinding super stage lights. Only screams of the same fatigue he feels in his bones coming back. One moment he feels he is playing lousily, the next moment it sounds OK. But he is dissociated from time, unaware of the lapses, wondering if he forgot a verse or movement. Trying to stay totally on top, lest his system stop and recede into nothingness.

He tries to listen to his voice. Then he stops trying to listen. It sounds strained, forced, a little higher than usual, emotions creeping in that he can't control. Songs sounding differently. All sounding new, yet far away, as if it might not be him onstage at all. Tears of frustration and rage are close to his surface, as close as the waters of the Atlantic. Tears of exhaustion and a burgeoning fear for what lies ahead.

"Red House," a blues, establishes a calm within the eye of the storm. Wishing, conjuring, feeling it, he tries to gather himself back together.

Jimi begins the lyrics of "Hey Joe," his first hit in England. Even though weary, he injects some musical humor into his solo when he starts off with a few riffs from the guitar intro to "I Feel Fine" by the

early Beatles and then goes into the tune of an old English dance
song called "Country Manor." And then on the tag-out ending, instead of singing, *I'm going way down South,*" he shouts, "Good-
bye, baby, good-bye."

"In from the Storm." The last number and he was so glad. He felt
like a boxer in the last round pushing through, wondering what the
outcome would be. Shrouds of depression sweeping across his consciousness like the predawn fog that moved through the arena, cast-
ing the lights garish.

He found himself singing in the same modality as "Watchtower."
He could not help the emotion in his tone. Overtones close to tears.
The song struck something within. It was true. It was what he
wanted to say. It was the way he felt right there at that moment. He
wished Emmeretta Marks were there to sing it with him. He felt so
lonely, so isolated—and it was only the beginning of the tour. Yet,
strangely, he did not want to leave the stage.

In the dressing room, exhausted, Jimi stands in the onslaught. The
security guards are admitting anyone into the tiny room. Jimi,
trying to catch his breath, smiles mechanically at the well-wishers.
He can hardly see. He feels he has played poorly, but then he does
not really know. He wishes there were someone there like Chas to
tell him, to talk it over. But now he is in the crush of the temporal
world. A star whom they touch and stand in the face of.

A helicopter awaits.

There is no rest. Monday, August 31, they would be at Gröna
Lunds Tivoli, Stockholm, Sweden. Tuesday, September 1, Liseberg,
Gothenburg, Sweden. Wednesday, September 2, Vijle Ruskow Hall,
Arhus, Denmark. Thursday, September 3, K. B. Hallen, Copen-
hagen, Denmark. Friday, September 4, Deutschland Halle, West Ber-
lin, West Germany. Sunday, September 6, Isle of Fehmarn Festival,
West Germany . . .

Jimi and company begin to move toward the helicopter, through
the throngs of well-wishers. Vishwa looks expectantly at Jimi as
they wade through. The dawn is breaking. Vishwa usually has never
had to ask to accompany Jimi anywhere, but this time he senses a
reservation in Jimi's demeanor. He searches Jimi's face for a nod of
the head, a twink of the eye, a smile, some kind of resumption of
their usual camaraderie—but it is not there. Vishwa has his traveling bag on his shoulder. Either he goes with Jimi or else he heads to
France to join the crew that will shoot *Le Mans,* a racing-car film.
But Vishwa would really like to groove along with Jimi through
Europe on tour. Finally they are standing at the door of the helicopter. Jimi turns and faces Vishwa. Expectancy plays on Vishwa's face

as they study each other. Finally Jimi says, "What are you—my old lady?" and disappears into the chopper.

Standing there as the helicopter creates its infernal racket in the takeoff, Vishwa thought through all the times Jimi and he had spent together, through good times and bad. They had shared women and had fought physically. Jimi had hit him in a frustrated night of rage once, but Vishwa felt the blow of Jimi's final words more than anything.

Wednesday, September 2, Vijle Ruskow Hall, Arhus, Denmark. They start the set with "Freedom." Moving into "Message of Love," something is obviously very wrong. Jimi stops playing. Mitch and Billy wonder at him. Holding himself together Jimi says to the audience: "I've been dead a long time" and walks off.

Never before had he come so close to falling out onstage. He felt that it was more than fatigue. There was a vicious vibe affecting him. Billy Cox was beginning to pick up on it. Jimi had been physically followed by strange people before, but this time, although he detected no one out of the ordinary, he felt marked.

The next day was all right. They sweated through a date at K. B. Hallen in Copenhagen and even did an encore.

The next day they were in West Berlin, at Deutschland Halle. Jimi was besieged by U.S. Armed Forces Radio personnel. Military brass was all over the place. The U.S. troops who occupied the U.S. section of West Berlin were, as usual, starved for any contact with the homeland.

Jimi, exhaustion telling in his voice, stumbled through an interview with Chris Romberg, a very nice cat from Armed Forces Radio whom he had known before.

They filmed an interview in Jimi's dressing room. The interviewers, assorted personnel from Armed Forces Radio, and a few other journalists were all nervous. The room was crowded and overlit. Jimi was bone-tired. His replies were in weary drawls between long, weary pauses.

Someone asked him about the Isle of Wight Festival.

"The people are really groovy. But I really hate to play at night. . . ."

"You couldn't see the audience?"

"Not too good. I couldn't see anybody, and that's what I play off of. . . ."

"We're not seeing you for very long—what have you been doing?"

"I've been doing like Yogi Bear. I been hibernating. . . . Because we received a lot of static in New York. A lot of aggravation in New York."

"Has your music of today changed?"

"We play a whole vacuum. A whole wall of sound. A wall of feeling. That's what we're trying to get across. Whew! I haven't slept in two days."

The interview meandered on with Jimi's replies getting more and more incoherent. When asked how Billy Cox came to him, he perked up for a moment: ". . . we used to play together before. We're doing a lot of bass unison, bass and guitar unison things . . . a lot of rhythms, we call it. It's like patterns, you know. . . . Noel is more of a melodic player . . . Billy plays more of a solid bass."

The interview ended with the question, how did he feel at the moment.

"Right now, you mean? I'm just worried a bit now. I sound . . . like a frog. Because last night we were playing so loud. I was just shouting on my tiptoes. I felt like my kneecaps were up in my chest (laughs). And just right now I feel a little nervous—but I think it will be all right. 'Cause now we're gonna go on and do our little gig. Like Mitch'll be playing drums and Billy will be playing bass and I will be playing guitar (laughter) . . . and I'll still be up there screaming. . . ."

The Isle of Fehmarn Festival, located on a dark and misty island, had succumbed to mob rule by the time Hendrix and company got there. Mad German bikers were shooting up the place, including the medical tent and even the stage itself, where the emcee had fled just prior to Hendrix's scheduled appearance. The bikers had robbed the box-office receipts and were charging exorbitant parking fees. They had taken over Isle of Fehmarn.

Late and tired and unwilling to go on in the madness, Hendrix, Mitchell, and Cox stayed in their camper while violence flared all around them. Rescheduled for the next morning at ten, Hendrix again failed to appear. Again the crowd was set to riot until Alexis Korner got up on stage and began to talk. By that time Korner was the sole emcee. He had been sharing the duties with another fellow, but when the shooting started, he had disappeared. Korner, who speaks fluent German, told the crowd that Hendrix was not there and that they'd have to listen to him play acoustic guitar or nothing. By noon the crowd was quieted down enough and Hendrix, Cox, and Mitchell came on.

"No more nights," he had been saying, but now coming on in the daylight of the Straits of Fehmarn, and wishing for darkness to shield the ugliness of the scene. Many of the crowd stayed only because Jimi Hendrix was scheduled to play.

People who had been beaten, people who had been robbed, staring, waiting for Hendrix to appear onstage. Along with the people who had done the robbing, the beating, the pillaging. No sympathy. Not even outrage or horror, just a weird acceptance on everyone's part, it seemed.

Alexis makes the intro. He tries to fanfare the occasion. But it is obvious that the crowd is in such agitation that only the music itself has a chance of getting through the grim mists. Jimi comes on out as usual: an octave higher voice vocally waving to the crowd, "Peace, peace, anyway." The crowd is divided between polite, cheerful applause and lusty boos. Jimi boos back. The booers in the crowd switch to that favorite Yankee-inspired phrase: "GO HOME . . . GO HOME." Jimi continues, "We were to come on last night but . . . it was just too unbearable. We couldn't make it together." As those who came to listen wait for the music, the booers take advantage of the lull in applause to fill the hush with raucous "GO HOME GO HOME GO HOME." Almost funny, almost ready to laugh—that's just where he would like to be, home. Hurriedly he whips through the platitudes: "Mitch Mitchell on drums, Billy Cox on bass, and Jimi on public saxophone. Like to play some music for you." As the boos and "GO HOME"s continue, he announces in German the title of the first tune: "The Killing Floor," and then in English, "I Should Have Quit You Long Ago," and here he appends a personal message to the booers, "You mothers. . . ." Jimi sets the tempo, as usual playing both lead and rhythm, and takes an upward climb progressing to the crest where the song proper begins. The tune is light-sounding but the message is quite clear.

I should have quit you a long time ago
I should have quit you a long time ago
Now you got me crying crying on the killing floor

Lord knows I should have gone
I just got here today y'all
And now you got me crying on the killing floor

The applause outsounds the boos. Again the music is in power, but those who love the music and have stayed here in violence's midst will have to find their way out at the end.

Jimi ends the quick snappy set with "Voodoo Chile (Slight Return)." No encores, no delay. They run for the camper, they speed to the helicopter that will take them across the Straits of Fehmarn to Rotterdam.

The bikers continued to loot the money, shake down the audience, and generally shoot up the place.

In Holland, Billy Cox was given, unknown to him, some acid mixed in some punch. He flipped out on the spot. Going totally manic, Cox had visions of people coming to kill them, to kill Jimi. Since he had never before had acid, there was no way to reorient Cox, so he had to be taken to a hospital where the customary Thorazine was administered. From the shock of acid-rush revelation to the sudden all-the-way-down of Thorazine—the drug given the violently insane—Cox became a vegetable. Several concerts, including the one at De Doelen of September 13, 1970, were canceled, and Hendrix took Cox to London to rest and work out the vicious combination of drugs that had made Cox a walking zombie.

Although it would have been better for Jimi and Billy to return to the United States, Jimi knew that Billy could not make the trip in the state that he was in. Fearing that Billy might freak out in public where he would run the risk of being institutionalized, Jimi hid Billy out in London in a borrowed apartment. Jimi was the only person there Billy knew well and trusted. Jimi still kept his Cumberland Hotel suite as a decoy official residence. He felt responsible for Billy's condition and was determined to make sure that Billy got back home safely. He would wait until Billy came back to himself. Until he was fit to travel. No matter how long that took.

Jimi was caught in a bind. It was a very bad time for him to stay in London. Ed Chalpin of PPX Productions, the same people who had been awarded the settlement, had pressed their fight to London, where Hendrix still had not been taken to court. Dodging messengers, process servers, and subpoenas, Hendrix was forced to live an underground existence while tending to the needs of Billy Cox.

Waiting for Billy to come around was rough on the nerves. He had much more time on his hands than he had had during his first days in London back in 1966. He checked out several friends on a regular basis. He spent a good deal of his time with Monika Danneman and Alvenia Bridges.

Alvenia had been staying at Pat Hartley's mansion up on Elvinstone Terrace since the spring. When Jimi first got to London, before the Isle of Wight, he called Pat Hartley's and got Alvenia instead (Pat was still in Hawaii). He was glad to hear Alvenia's voice. They had not seen each other in two years, since Alvenia had split New York for Switzerland. They had a lot to catch up on. They met at the Speakeasy and ate and talked, bringing each other up to date. Alvenia, who had gone to Switzerland with such love and hope, now nursed a broken heart, but she was happy to be back on the scene with her old running buddies. Jimi was tired but all right. He was having problems with his management doing the right things for him, but Electric Lady Studios was a reality.

Alvenia took to hanging out at the Speakeasy. It was an exciting atmosphere. Most of the people there were into music and into the Isle of Wight, which was being touted as England's Woodstock. It was like hanging out at the Scene Club. In fact, Alvenia met the girl who used to take the tickets at the Scene. She had married one of the members of Chicago.

One afternoon Alvenia called Jimi and said that there was this German chick named Monika Danneman sitting at her table at the Speakeasy who said she was a good friend of his. Jimi laughed and made arrangements to meet them.

Alvenia had been having lunch when Monika Danneman came over. They had known each other a couple of years ago when they both had spent time at a posh Italian resort. Monika had had to make Alvenia remember her. Somehow Danneman knew Alvenia knew Jimi. Danneman said that she had known Jimi very well. They had been lovers. He had been the first man ever to make love to her; she had been a virgin when they met. She began to cry. If Alvenia saw Jimi would she tell him that Monika was trying desperately to get in touch with him? At that point Alvenia left the table and called Jimi although she did not let Monika know what she was going to do.

They all got together. Monika and Jimi seemed to get along very well. Often the three of them would have dinner together somewhere, then they would drop Alvenia off wherever she wanted to go in Monika's blue sportscar.

Eric Burdon, another old London friend, was due in from L.A. to appear with a new band called War. The band consisted of brothers from L.A. and they were known to cook. Jimi was looking forward to meeting up with some stateside brothers who could blow. He dearly missed being able to play and record regularly.

Stella and Alan Douglas, Colette, Luna, and Devon were due in town any day now. Jeanette Jacobs, who was so kind in helping out with Billy, was cool. Kathy Etchingham was as vibrant as ever but he did not want to be close to that now. It would be good seeing Alan and Stella and Colette and even Devon; they could have some normal good times. And he and Alan could get together and talk about future plans.

Monika was sweet. He enjoyed being with her. And since she had her own pad and car and money she was very helpful to Jimi. She was of one of the richest families in Dusseldorf. She was attentive and warm and could share a joke like a trouper, but she was always worried about her father, her family interfering in her life. Her father disliked her being with that black rock 'n' roll singer. She was constantly worried about the family name being linked to drugs or some other youth-culture type of scandal.

Jimi was interviewed by *Melody Maker* in their offices. Billy Cox's condition had not changed. Fortunately it had not gotten into the press. Jimi continued to act as if everything was cool. As if he was just cooling his heels in London for a while. But he was harried, tired, and worried. It was beginning to show.

I've turned full circle, I'm right back where I started. I've given this era of music everything, but I still sound the same. My music's the same, and I can't think of anything new to add to it in its present state.

When the last American tour finished, I just wanted to go away and forget everything. I just wanted to record and see if I could write something. Then I started thinking. Thinking about the future. Thinking that this era of music, sparked off by the Beatles, had come to an end. Something new has to come and Jimi Hendrix will be there.

I want a big band. I don't mean three harps and fourteen violins. I mean a big band full of competent musicians that I can conduct and write for. And with the music we will paint pictures of Earth and space, so that the listener can be taken somewhere.

While I was doing my vanishing act in the States I got this feeling that I was completely blown out of England. I thought they had forgotten me over here. I'd given them everything I'd got. I thought maybe they didn't want me anymore, because they had a nice set of bands. Maybe they were saying, "Oh we've had Hendrix, yeah he was O.K." I really thought I was completely through here.

The main thing that used to bug me was that people wanted too many visual things from me. I never wanted it to be so much of a visual thing. When I didn't do it, people thought I was being moody, but I can only freak when I really feel like doing so.

I wanted the music to get across, so that people could just sit back and close their eyes, and know exactly what was going on, without caring a damn what we were doing while we were onstage.

I think I'm a better guitarist than I was. I've learned a lot. But I've got to learn more about music because there's a lot in this hair of mine that's got to get out. With the bigger band I don't want to be playing as much guitar. I want other musicians to play my stuff. I want to be a good writer. I still can't figure out what direction my writing is going at the moment, but it'll find a way. I won't be doing many live gigs because I'm going to develop the sound and then put a film out with it. It's so exciting, it's going to be an audiovisual thing that you sit down and plug into and really take in through your ears and eyes. I'm so happy, it's gonna be good.

By this time, Finney arrived back in London to do Hendrix's hair. Finney was now Miles Davis' *official* hairdresser but often doubled on Hendrix's head when the two did not conflict. He had gotten Miles's permission to stay on in Europe after the great jazz man's tour, which had included the Isle of Wight also, and do Jimi's hair for a while, before joining Miles again in time for his West Coast tour in the States. Finney found that Hendrix's tour had been canceled and that Hendrix was hiding out with Billy Cox, who was virtually a vegetable.

Billy Cox had not spoken a word since being out of the hospital for more than a week.

Hendrix and Cox stayed in a flat that had been abandoned by its owner for their convenience. They needed the privacy and also needed to avoid the press. Finney prepared Hendrix's hair daily and generally helped out. There was little else to do.

Keith Altham, probably the most sympathetic London reporter who regularly reported on Jimi, invited Jimi to a party given by Mike Nesmith at the Inn on the Park. Altham, who had been so influential in Jimi's rise to fame in London, noticed that Jimi was feeling pretty down. It is a big blow for one leading a band to lose a player, especially one who was so groomed and nurtured as Billy had been. Jimi could not help but feel that the intensity of the scene surrounding him was responsible for Billy's collapse. Jimi asked Altham what he thought he should do about a new band. Keith Altham replied that McCartney's advice to "get back to where you once belonged" was never a bad idea for a revival. Jimi laughed and said that that was what he was going to do. Both knew that Noel Redding was ready and willing to rejoin the band. But for Jimi, the new sound that he worked on for so long with Billy Cox was most important—and he knew that he would have to sacrifice it for the sound of the early Experience if Noel were to come back.

Ed Chalpin flew into London Tuesday, September 15, expecting to meet with Jimi.

Jimi was supposed to have appeared at a meeting between Ed Chalpin and representatives of Polydor and Track records. Chalpin's chief witness against Jimi, Curtis Knight, was Chalpin's hole card— always lurking somewhere in the background.

One of the big points of contention from Chalpin's point of view was that Jimi had still acted as if he were under contract to him by recording with Curtis Knight when he was in America right after Monterey but, as Jimi had asserted, he thought that they were only in the studio to jam and fool around, and to correct some stuff that Jimi had recorded earlier when he played as a sideman to Knight. And everyone who ever recorded with Jimi knew they could always call upon him to redo or correct what he had recorded. He was a perfectionist.

Hendrix wanted to make sure that he would not be anywhere where he might be found by anybody from Chalpin's legal team, the record-company people, or his own management. He was supposed to meet with them but that was very much out of the question. In the state of mind he was in, a meeting was impossible.

He dropped by Lorraine James's house, where she lived in a communelike situation with several other people. He had a lot of grass with him. Grass was rare in London, where the more easily obtainable hashish was the dominantly smoked high. Lorraine was astounded by the amount he had with him because she had hardly seen any grass in her life. To Lorraine, who had only seen Jimi before in the most romantic and sanguine of situations, he was a nervous wreck. One minute he would be grooving with her and two girls who were visiting from the States and the next minute he would go downstairs to the public telephone where he would spend hours talking and trying to reach people. One moment he was on top of the world and the next minute he was moaning about how fucked up his managers were and how he was facing imminent financial ruin. Jimi stayed at the flat all day and well into the night and early morning. He had taken a liking to the two American girls, and to Lorraine's chagrin had made love to them in her bed until 5:00 A.M. Then, instead of sleeping, he took them with him as he toured various flats in West London and Notting Hill.

In one of the flats they visited a man they had been talking to and getting high with all of a sudden leaped up and pitched himself over a banister, plunging to the floor below. He broke both his legs. An ambulance had to be summoned. Jimi and company left immediately.

Jimi felt as if he were going mad. He could not believe what was happening. Did he cause that man to jump? Did his presence so agitate the cat that he had to do that? Was he that high that he was not judging where people were at? He was just trying to stay out of sight so nobody would know where he was, moving from place to place at random. It seemed simple to do but it was not going smoothly at all.

Jimi returned to the secret flat where Billy Cox was kept. He was saddened to see that Billy had not improved for the better, although he had kept constantly abreast of his condition by telephone. Billy had still not uttered a word.

That morning Finney came by to do Jimi's hair. Billy and Jimi sat in the kitchen while Finney set up shop. Jimi had some hashish, which he was reluctant to offer to Finney because he did not want to smoke around Billy. Finney began to curl Jimi's hair, which he would eventually comb out into flowing waves. Although Jimi had been pretty much into the Afro he seemed to favor the older style in London. Jimi, the perfect polite host, finally offered Finney some hashish. He was relieved when Finney refused it. Finney had dug Jimi's hesitation and understood the circumstances. It all went by Billy, who watched Finney press curl after curl with almost moronic intensity. After one particularly pretty curl Finney and Jimi were startled to hear Billy Cox say, "That was a good one." Jimi could not believe his ears. Finney was blown away. It was a great moment. Billy had finally broken through his dreadful silence. That meant they all could return to the States. Jimi and Finney were overjoyed. They tried to act as if it was no big thing but a big load had been taken off their minds.

Jimi and Finney made plans to meet that night at Ronnie Scott's to celebrate. Finney went back to his hotel room to prepare for his return to the States. He had a tour to do and he wanted to get some rest in his New York apartment. Jimi went over to see Stella, Alan, and Devon, who were staying at Danny Secunda's apartment. They had been in London since Monday and he was long overdue for a visit with his running buddies. He felt liberated now that Billy was all right. He wanted to talk over some business with Alan. He wanted to be clear of a lot of the bullshit when he returned to the States, and Alan, as a friend and adviser, would help.

Devon was pissed off at Jimi. She had been looking for him for two days. Stella was her usual calm and intelligent self. It was like being home. They had been concerned for him and now they were all together, happy and at ease. Devon, who always had an attitude, cooled down and began to take Jimi through some familiar changes. She teased him about the blonde he was with. It seemed to her that he had to have a blonde a week or he was not satisfied. Jimi asked her about Mick Jagger. Devon said that he was in Dusseldorf, Germany, Monika Danneman's hometown. They traded Mae West impersonations and suddenly everything was all right between them again. Jimi got a limo and took the girls shopping.

That night they all met at Ronnie Scott's to check out Eric Burdon and War. Alvenia, Finney, Devon, Stella, Alan, and Angie Burdon were all sitting together. Finney had not known Devon was in town and expected Jimi to be furious when he found out. Jimi walked in with Monika Danneman, came by the table, and said hello, bussing Finney's hair and grasping Devon's neck in a mock stranglehold. He took a nearby table for two and then went backstage. He was very anxious to play. He had sat in with Burdon and War on a couple of previous occasions but had not played well. A couple of the brothers in War had thought that he had been slightly smacked out. His concern for Billy Cox had affected his entire existence.

During the last set, with Eric Burdon sitting in the audience, Jimi and War played an extended version of the Memphis Slim song "Mother Earth." It's a straight-up blues, and they played it with no affectations, shouting the chorus in unison.

> You may run at me all the time
> You may never go my way
> Mother Earth is laying for you
> 'Cause of that you got to pay
>
> Don't care how great you are
> Don't care what you worth
> When it all ends up
> You got to go back to Mother Earth
>
> You may own half a city
> Even diamonds and pearls
> You may buy an airplane, baby
> And fly all over this world
>
> Don't care how great you are
> Don't care how much you're worth
> When it all ends up
> You got to go back to Mother Earth
>
> You may play the racehorses

You may own a racetrack
You may have enough money, baby
To buy anything you like

Don't care how great you are
Don't care how much you're worth
When it all ends up
You got to go back to Mother Earth

Howard Scott and Jimi traded guitar leads and rhythm. Jimi got off a decent solo and enhanced the changes with skillful manipulations of the melody. Lee Oskar's harmonica and Charles Miller's saxophone blended remarkably well, with both taking excursions out over the melody. Miller tagged the tune out with a mellow solo and that was it.

Jimi returned to Monika and found that she and Devon had had a tiff. Monika had shown off a snake ring Jimi had given her recently and indicated that she and Jimi were planning to get married. Devon called her on that. Monika glossed over the threat but those who knew Devon made sure the ladies said no more to each other.

Jimi left with Monika and Alvenia. Alvenia seemed to be more upset than anybody about the argument. She wished she had known that Devon and Jimi had had a thing going in the States ever since she had been gone; she most certainly would not have helped Monika and Jimi get together.

Later that night/morning Jimi made it back to where Alan, Stella, and Devon were staying. He and Alan stayed up talking while Stella and Devon crashed.

Alan Douglas had performed various favors for Jimi. Their informal arrangement involved Douglas as a semiproducer and a semimanager. There was no doubt that Douglas wanted a more formal relationship from a business point of view. After all, he was no novice in the music world. He had pulled off some very interesting feats. Jimi was wondering whether they could operate on a more formal level in spite of Jeffery. Jimi talked about what he wanted to do when he returned to America and Douglas sought to see where he could fit in. It seemed that all plans stopped at Jeffery. He had such control over Jimi to the extent that it had been impossible for Jimi to even see the legal papers spelling it out. Every time Jimi had requested to see the legal documents that governed his and Jeffery's relationship as client and manager he was put off one way or the other. Jimi and Alan had bumped heads with Jeffery more than once. The last time was that spring when they had a big showdown meet-

ing with Mo Austin, president of Warner Brothers music division.
The meeting had resolved with Jimi staying with Jeffery. It had been
embarrassing, as if the meeting had been called to just let Jimi let off
some steam. Whenever Jimi and Alan discussed his management
they got bogged down, but when they talked about future projects
ideas flew. There was a question of whether the Caravan thing could
happen now that Billy had had a bad experience, but he would find a
suitable bass player sooner or later. But instead of having Jimi do a
heavy touring thing they talked of doing a tour for every season, fall,
winter, spring, and summer. They would film everything and then
send the films of the concerts around in between the seasonal tours.
Jeffery still remained the big hang-up. Finally they had a solution:
agree to pay Jeffery his management percentage for the remainder of
the contract. It was a great idea, they felt. If it was only money
preventing them from doing what they wanted then they would pay
Jeffery his money so they could do what they want. They got real
excited. Douglas would fly back to the United States the next day
and meet with Steingarten and Mo Austin. Steingarten would, as
Jeffery's lawyer, be informed as to what they intended to do. Mo
Austin would be informed that Jimi wanted to release a double
album that winter, not the single LP Warners expected. Jimi had
trouble communicating that to Warner Brothers through his present
management, so Douglas would do it.

The sleeping arrangements were limited at Danny Secunda's so
Devon and Stella had taken the bed and Alan was to sleep on the
couch and Jimi on the floor. In the morning they awoke to find Jimi
in the bed, Devon in the middle and Stella on the other side. While
the girls were still getting themselves together Jimi and Alan split
early for the airport in a cab. They conferred on the way and then
Jimi rode back into London.

Jimi felt elated and a bit afraid. He had made several decisions that
would affect his future. Alan Douglas would communicate some of
them and some of them he would do himself. He would definitely
avoid the court hearing Friday. By the time he arrived back in New
York the wheels would be turning.

That afternoon of September 17 he and Monika sat close together
in the garden of the Samarkand Hotel. He seemed rushed, yet very
much into communicating several things to her at once. On Monika's drawing pad he drew nine nine times, each nine inside the
other, flowing out like a nova. Looked a little bit like an Egyptian
eye, or a medieval sun. He talked of nine consciousness as being the

highest form of the intelligences. He then placed the drawings of the nine concentric nines against a reproduction of the solar system and talked about the radiation of the nine consciousness throughout the Milky Way. The two luminaries and the seven planets collectively were "nine-consciousness." Within the secrets of numbers were insights into "the grand design."

Monika found it difficult to grasp the meaning of the figures and symbols, but Jimi pressed on, urging her to remember it all, to remember all he said, even if she did not understand at the moment.

He knew she was very visual, a trained painter, she would be able to reproduce what he said on canvas. With that in mind he began to dictate some paintings.

A cross superimposed upon the Earth with faces of the four races. One evil, one enlightened from each race was the first of a series of paintings (he called them "cross paintings") that were to be done.

"You must remember this," he said. "You must remember all I'm telling you. . . ."

Jimi and Monika decided to go for a drive. He had been going at her with his talk for a couple of hours. It was time to take a break. They drove by the Kensington Market and decided to go in and browse.

Finney was in the gift shop of the Kensington Market doing some last-minute shopping when he bumped into Devon and Angie. He had just purchased an antique guitar pin for Jimi. They told him that they had just seen Jimi and Monika in another part of the market. Finney would have liked to give Jimi the gift himself but he realized that he only had enough time to catch a cab to the hotel, where his bags waited in the lobby, and continue on to the airport. He asked Devon if she would give the gift to Jimi and when she agreed he inscribed a note on the tiny card. It said, "I wish I were a guitar." He gave the package to Devon and split for the States.

Devon and Angie found Jimi and gave him the package. He had not seen them before and was surprised they were there. He excused himself from Monika and went with them to find Stella. They all greeted each other and went outside to chat. One of the older but hip wealthy Londoners they knew was giving a dinner party that evening; the girls wondered if Jimi would like to go. Sure he did. He knew people who would be there. They decided to meet and go together. While they talked Stella was struck by Jimi's eyes. They were fantastic, deep and wise. Stella, who knew Jimi well, had not seen his eyes like that often. He seldom looked in anyone's eyes, but today he seemed to be staring into Stella's soul. Devon picked up on it too. They saw something very special happening inside of him.

Stella was surprised when Jimi just tripped on with them back to their flat while she and Devon changed clothes. They went on to the dinner party in good spirits. Stella said they were having catered Polynesian food from a very special restaurant.

There were several groups of people in various rooms of the large floor-through when they got there. Stella, Devon, and Jimi found friends in the bedroom: Bert Kleiner, the financier; David Saloman, heir to the Wimpy fast-food chain; and Pete Cameron, music publisher, who was an old friend of Alan and Stella's. Jimi and Bert got into a long rap, both supine on the bed. There was nothing to get high with there, only liquor and conversation. Stella and Devon knew that Jimi, like them, wanted to get high. Devon came up with two blackbombers. She took one and Jimi took one. Later someone else came up with some pure Owsley powdered sunshine LSD in a small gold box. There was not much but the benefactor warned that it was very powerful. Jimi, Stella, and Devon took some hits of it through the nostrils. It got them all high. Stella stared at the crystals of her necklace for a long time, Devon seemed to almost pass out and Jimi continued to rap.

The food came and Stella took charge. She pulled the food out of the bags and containers and served up several bowls, but no one seemed to be interested in food. Stella called Jimi to the phone; she thought it might be Monika calling. After the call Jimi appeared to be leaving soon. Stella saw him trying to get Devon to come with him, but Devon was dozing off from the effects of two powerful chemicals. Stella heard a horn honk outside and going to the window she saw long blond hair in a blue car. She went and told Jimi that she thought someone was there to pick him up. Stella tried to let Devon know that Jimi was leaving and Jimi was telling her to come along with him but Devon did not break out of her lethargy. Jimi went back into the kitchen with Stella and talked and joked with her for a good while. Finally he walked out the door after sampling from the bowl of food Stella held in her hands. Stella went to Devon and asked her if she wanted to follow him and catch up. Devon said no. Stella said, "You know, you're terrible." Devon replied, "It's OK, it's all right—I'll find him later," and went back to sleep.

Monika was very puzzled by Jimi's behavior. First all the talk that afternoon and now he had her waiting in the streets for him. They drove to Elvinstone Terrace, picked up Alvenia, and went and had a drink in Soho. Later they dropped Alvenia off at Ronnie Scott's. She wanted to see Eric Burdon and also spend some time with some of the guys in War who were having trouble relating to London.

Monika and Jimi drove around some more. When they finally got to Monika's place she was in a quandary. Jimi was acting really mysteriously.

She was concerned about him. He had been telling her strange things all day. The nine nines, the cross paintings, and then going off to strange places and having her wait outside because they were not supposed to be good people. She could not understand why he would go to see them at all. There were parts of what he was saying and doing that did not make sense at all. Huge parts. He even had told her he did not want people to be sad if he died.

He was supposed to be in court tomorrow. He did not know what to do. He wanted to go back to the States. He had even called Electric Lady Studios and reserved some time early in the next week. He seemed to be unsure whether he was expected to be in court or not. If he went back to New York it might seem that he was contemptuous of the English courts. If he went into court feeling and looking the way he did he might blow it anyway. It was impossible for him to explain the circumstances of that contract. It was difficult to admit that he had been so stupid. There were strange vibes all around him. He did not want to stay at his hotel suite because it was a decoy suite, yet he did not know where it was cool to stay. Monika seemed to offer the only solution. Finney had split. Jeanette Jacobs had split, when Devon told her about Monika and the ring. Everyone else was staying with other people. And he knew it was not safe for him to stay somewhere alone.

Twenty-two Lansdowne Crescent. The dim trees of the gray day. The birds of dawn rest on the block of the consulates. In the Scandinavian hotel no politics, only ancient Buddha on the door zazen. As the dawn comes creeping up with birdsong and pastel blues he tells Monika that he wants to sleep for several days, at least a day and a half. He has not been able to sleep. Everything was acting up. His ulcer, his liver, and especially his nerves. He took a few of Monika's sleeping pills that she offered him and lay back. Yet when he tried to sleep he felt as if he were sleepwalking like he was awake and asleep at the same time. Some people used sleeping pills to trip off of, but he truly wanted to sleep. Maybe a few more sleeping pills would do. The pills were said to be twice as strong as stateside sleeping pills but everybody in England was used to them. Totally knock him out so he could sleep beyond Friday and September 18, the day of the trial, and slip out of London on Saturday or Monday. He might not be seen leaving at all. He wished he could have some advice, but he was not sure whom he could trust. He had tried to reach Chas but the only number he had was the Robert Stigwood

Organization office. He thought perhaps someone would be there but he only got a message machine. It is so difficult to get ahold of the big names in music, even if they are your friends. He left an urgent message for Chas. He wanted to make sure that Chas got back to him as soon as possible. "I need your help bad, man," he said over the phone. That was early in the morning.

Then, as Jimi often did when distressed, when he had a few free moments, or when he could not sleep, he wrote. It was a poem, conceived as a possible future song lyric:

(Slow)

The story of Jesus
so easy to explain,
after they crucified him,
a woman, she claimed his name

The story of Jesus
the whole Bible knows ·
went all across the Desert
and in the middle, he found a rose

There should be no questions
there should be no lies
He was married ever
happily after
for all the Tears we cry

No use in arguing all
the use to the man that moans
when each man falls in Battle, His
soul it has to roam

angels of heaven
flying Saucers to some,
made Easter Sunday
the name of the Rising
Sun

The story is written
by so many people who dared,
to lay down the truth
to so very many who cared
to carry the cross
of Jesus and beyond

We will guild the light
this time with a woman in
our arms

We as men
can't explain the reason why
the woman's always mentioned
at the moment. That we die.

All we know
is God is by our side

and he says the word
So easy yet so hard
I wish not to be alone
So I must respect my other
heart

Oh the story
of Jesus is the story
of you and me
No use in feeling lonely
I am you searching to be free

the story
of life is quicker
than the wink of an eye

the story of love
is hello and good-bye
until we meet again

Waking. Or a dream interval. Whatever—it's like tripping and sleeping at the same time. Dusky limbs in blue room. Monika, birdlike and truly innocent, her dancer legs spread, like her hair all yellows coming up, underneath cherry blossom pink puffed delirious. Her smile. Her semibroken English laughing golden white blond platinum. She championed the cause of the black man, the expression of alienation and rebellion in the music, that she likened to her situation and the restraints on her life.

Chinese junk. Like kitty litter. Crush it and it spreads out a lot. Snort. Sweet serene dreams. The top and the bottom drops out and all slows down to an effortless pace. Easy living. Love for the faces that show in your light. Rush of sudden concern for those surrounding. The din of the world outside is lost, forgotten, in the swell of well-being.

He thought of Chrissie for some reason. He saw her and felt her very close to him. She seemed to be in some sort of difficulty, but she was so glad to see him she was ignoring her problem. The moment seemed like hours. He urged her to go back, to go back and deal with it. He felt strange. Truly spacey, as if he were in a place he had never been in before.

Billy Cox was finally getting that really good tone in live performances that Jimi wanted. Billy was resolving his playing in relation to the ongoing happening-now music. Getting that good tone consistently. Bulbous blue funk in a bottom abyss. Mitch's drumming notwithstanding, Jimi and Cox had gotten into some nice things at the Isle of Wight, but the "Ezy Ryder" they had done at Copenhagen had really gotten off. They were riding very high on that teetering tip that Jimi was used to but that Billy was not.

Standing on an elevation looking out. Thousands of heartbeats through thousands of amps. Pure sound oscillating. Oscillating slow for bass, fast for guitar. Electric throb through him spiraling outward.

Peering into the darkness. Standing up there screaming, screaming like a madman. Screaming like a toad, kneecaps all up in the chest, to the emptiness to the darkness. Flying into the darkness beyond the continental shelf.

> *I just got back today*
> *I just got back*
>   *from the storm*
> *I was so tired and lonely*
> *Looking for your love*
> *Looking for your love*
>
>   *To keep me warm*

Jimi's tired face shows the bone of his high cheek in stark relief. Hair bouffant in soft curls slightly combed out. Eyes slightly closed, he directs Billy and Mitch: eye contact bone-weary. Each blink of the eye could bring sleep. Head keeping time nodding to the beat. Keep the beat for Billy and Mitch, widen the eyes for the change, sway abruptly for the solo entrance.

He sees his father crying. He sees himself setting his hair on fire. He sees himself cutting his wrist. He sees himself taking several sleeping pills. He sees himself lying in bed deep down in London. He sees the Isle of Wight he sees the Isle of Fehmarn.

Jimi turns in bed and tries to get up. He feels sick to his stomach. He does not want to disturb Monika. She has had as much trouble sleeping as he. He feels bile coming into his mouth. It takes a super-human effort for him to sway his body toward the edge of the bed. It is impossible for him to rise. He barely makes it to the edge of the bed. A stream of bile comes through his mouth. His cheek rests against the sheet. The sheet absorbs the bile. His retching ceases. Suddenly he does not care anymore. He falls quickly back into semi-unconsciousness.

Jimi feels the presence of Monika. He has awakened her, what a drag. Still he cannot move. Still he feels himself suspended between waking and sleep, a realm that is much stranger than he had imagined. It seemed he remembered being in this state only when he was actually in it. At other times it was absent from his memory like a bad dream. He feels Monika rise from the bed. The release of her weight gives him even more the sensation of floating. He wants to call her to wait, to come and help him wake up. But he cannot move. He cannot speak. He becomes aware of the stench of vomit close to him. He desperately wants to move away, but to no avail. He hears the door slam and he panics. Was it someone coming to get him? To do him in? Or was it Monika leaving? He did not want her to leave but there was nothing he could do to prevent her. Fear wells up inside him.

Lansdowne Crescent has come alive. Porters sweep the outsides of their buildings, the black cabs grind up Notting Hill Gate, pedestrians on their way to work pop from every doorway, and the birds have muted their songs as the humans take over the day. Monika drives toward Talbot Road to get cigarettes. She wonders if Jimi's vomiting is serious. Should she have wakened him?

When Monika returns she feels a strangeness in the room. She rushes over to Jimi and tries to wake him again. The vomit she had seen before she went to the store had dried, but now there is more. She panics. The effects of the sleeping pills she had taken earlier quickly wear off as she realizes Jimi is in trouble.

Alvenia awoke to the phone ringing. Eric Burdon picked it up. She had wound up spending the night in his hotel suite. It was Monika Danneman on the phone. She was saying that Jimi would not wake up. Eric shouted into the telephone, "CALL THE FUCKING AMBU-LANCE." Alvenia grabbed the phone. Monika was frantic, she did not know if she should, she was worried that Jimi might get mad. Alvenia spoke to her very nicely, "Call the ambulance, call the ambulance right now." Monika said she couldn't wake Jimi, he seemed to be sick in his sleep. Alvenia said, "I'll be right over. Hang up and call the ambulance." Alvenia hung up and began dressing hurriedly. Clothes on, she dialed Monika back. Monika was hyster-

After Jimi's death, his girlfriend Monika Danneman is helped to a waiting car by road manager Eric Barrett . *LONDON DAILY EXPRESS*

ical. "What hospital are you going to?" Alvenia asked. Monika had not called the ambulance yet. Alvenia was astounded. "CALL THE AMBULANCE."

Eric grabbed the phone and screamed, "CALL THE FUCKING AMBULANCE." Monika did not know if she should, Jimi might be mad about the scandal. Alvenia got hysterical too and said, her voice on an emotional par with Monika's, *"There's no time to lose. You have to call an ambulance."*

Then he sees his own body on the bed. The door is wide open and Monika tearfully admits several men in white coats. They roll him onto a stretcher.

He feels himself being carried through the door into the outside air. Its briskness shocks him. They carry him up the winding stairs with great difficulty. As they reach the top of the stairs he begins to feel sick to his stomach again. They carry him into the ambulance. Instead of laying him down, they sit him in a chair and strap him upright. He tries to bend over so he can vomit but one of the attendants quickly pushes his head back and straps him even tighter. Jimi's head lolls back as the ambulance takes off, the knell-like wail of its siren clearing the busy streets. The speeding ambulance presses his body back in the chair and makes it even more difficult for him to get his head down. He feels bile and vomit near his Adam's apple. He tries frantically to get his head forward, but one of the attendants is making sure it does not tip forward. Jimi is unable to speak. Even if he could, the ball of vomit in his throat would prevent him. More vomit wells up from his stomach. He cannot breathe. The vomit is strangling him He tries to open his eyes. He tries to scream. He tries to move his body over sideways, but he is strapped in tight. The vomit masses in his vocal cords. Jimi's lungs become congested. His heart begins to pump harder and harder, the right ventricle dilates. Fluid begins to seep into his lungs. He is rushed from the ambulance into St. Mary's Abbot Hospital. The doctors work on him for over an hour. The fluid in his lungs and his overworked heart are difficult to overcome.

Alvenia tried to call Jimi's road manager, Eric Barrett, then she tried to reach Noel or Mitch. She could not seem to get the numbers right. She reached Steve Gold, Eric Burdon, and War's manager. He gave her a car to use and she drove to the hospital. Monika was crying hysterically in the parking lot. A nurse came up and said that Jimi's heart had stopped and his lung had collapsed but that there was a good chance the doctors could revive him. Alvenia rushed off to call Eric and Gerry Stickells. When she returned from the phone Monika was crying, "No, no," and being physically restrained by a nurse. The nurse looked in Alvenia's eyes and said, "Jimi Hendrix is dead." Monika cried, "You're lying, you're lying." Alvenia pulled her well-put-together body up and with all the sister in her grabbed the nurse and said, "I don't believe you. You have to *show* me."

They finally agreed to let them see him. Alvenia and Monika went into a very clean and quiet white room, which was dimly lit and strangely peaceful. They saw Jimi lying there.

He looked so beautiful.

CODA

More than five years of research and writing went into this biography. I traveled to London, Amsterdam, Seattle, Vancouver, New York, and Los Angeles and conducted over one hundred interviews. Reams of press material were collected, studied, and charted, as well as related articles, tape recordings, and books. The music of Jimi Hendrix was my active inspiration and abides as such.

In most cases I have fused the information derived from all sources into a narrative. I also used Hendrix's own words in informing the narrative at crucial junctures. I have refrained from editorializing both the subtle and the obvious in my desire to be objective. I have used some quotations of what others have said about Hendrix in the construction of several scenes that serve to coalesce bodies of fact. There are also some scenes that are biographically interpretive, yet they too are informed by facts and sources that give themselves to such construction. In the few instances when I have been asked not to reveal the sources of information, names have been left out or changed. Where I have found source information to conflict I have included both versions, or several versions.

Jimi Hendrix was a classic black ghetto "smoothie" whose mania and genius was electric guitar. He achieved an unmatched virtuoso

369

style and became a musician's musician, a player's player, and a priest of the new age in Afro-American ceremonial music.

His music and words, studio or live, written or sung, are the best way of figuring him out—if that is the goal desired. Witnessing Jimi Hendrix playing live was a joy for many.

The particulars of his secular existence parallel everyman's. He ate, he slept, he made love, he worked (often harder than most men work), he made his mistakes and had his triumphs. The key to his life was creation. The most important thing in life for Jimi Hendrix was to create. And with pen and guitar, voice and ensemble, he kept his beliefs' bargain with his soul and left a wonderful legacy to us all.

In an intimate social setting, Jimi Hendrix was slender, elfin, and appeared even smaller with his traditional guitar-player slouch than his five-foot-ten-inch, broad-shouldered frame. He appeared "girl-ish" and even "jivey" to some, yet once Hendrix got onstage and played he underwent a complete transformation. His body seemed to grow into the gargantuan sound the powerhouse amplifiers gave his guitar. Ablaze in the brilliant stage lights, his long arms and large hands were intensified. His Indian-boned jaw, high cheek-bones, Tlaloc-like nose and mouth (that often chewed on a piece of gum), his slanted Afro-Asian eyes (and bouffant Afro, curls or conk) gave him an incredible presence. Long-legged and tautly muscled in the trunk, he had a dancer's body that choreoed effortlessly with his music.

In these pages I quote liberally from his songs and interviews, public and intimate. The reason is clear: Hendrix documented his life through his verse and through his oral improvisation on the interview.

Perhaps it was the contemplation of his mother's death and her love of music when she had been alive that inspired Hendrix to fall so deeply in love with music—to the extent that he often lost himself completely within its magic. Both he and his mother died at age twenty-seven.

Hendrix demonstrated a high order of voodoo. Not the pulp maga-zine tales of horror or the elementary sympathetic formulas—Hen-drix showed the voodoo that related to the stars and to magical transformations. Milo Rigaud, an authority on Haitian voodoo, has written of the crossovers between voodoo and Freemasonry and other high orders of Western mystical systems. *Voudou* is an ancient African religion of tremendous power that unites the land by the codification of every tribe's drum battery rhythm to the solar offices: to the solar chromosphere, photosphere, and nucleus.

Voodoo, as a religion, has been forced to dwell underground in America, as have other cultural and artistic manifestations of black people.

The song "Voodoo Chile" is a tale of creation that unites the religion with its transition to the West and its relationship to the solar systems. It speaks of legacy and transformation upon a "place of power" (a mountain summit), and then upon the wings of an eagle we are transported to the near planets. There we partake of the funk of life (methane seas) and the talismanic gems of love and power. At the beginning of the song Hendrix's mother's death is related in symbolic terms. At the end of the song supernatural powers are celebrated.

Jimi Hendrix often used death as his adviser. From "Hear My Train A-comin' " to "Voodoo Chile (Slight Return)," where Hendrix sets up a meeting in the next world if it cannot be accomplished in this one, the message is clear, as he intones, *If I don't meet you in this world, I'll meet you in the next world, so don't be late.*"

As a warrior, his sword and his salvation were his guitar. Throughout his life Hendrix produced an amazing amount of songs, chronicling them with a running philosophical commentary that ranged from the joys of sex to the mysteries of the universe. His musical compositions and performances coalesced all his words and beliefs into pure energy at a stellar level of creativity. His is a wonderful example of a gifted and productive artist.

Jimi Hendrix was one of the few top rock stars to come out against the war in Vietnam and in support of the black liberation movement in the United States. His "Machine Gun," recorded live at the Fillmore East during the height of the Vietnam war, was a devastating antiwar statement. Jimi made his declarations as an individual artist, he had no group to support his public stance.

He told Buddy Miles and Sue Cassidy Clark:

In American riots you see these masochist kids. Some of 'em will say, "Well, we don't have nothin' else to live for anyway. This is our scene now." They go in there with no shelter, no anything. They get beat. I mean you can see, you see how desperate the whole case must be if a kid's goin' to go out there and get his head busted open. Without no protection. Just gettin' things together. But then you look over in Japan. Now these students got it together and you must put this in the book, 'cause I'm tired of seein' Americans get their heads split open for no reason at all. The kids in Japan, they buy helmets, they got their little squadrons. The pink helmets for the left side, and they go in wedges like this. They got all their stuff together. They've got their shields. They're wearin' steel supports—protection. You have to have all these things if you're goin' to go up there; you might as well make it together. Just go on and do it together. I'd like to see these American kids with helmets on and big Roman shields and then do their thing! Really together. America. That music is goin' to tell 'em anything they want to know, really.

He did not seclude himself from the populace like most other superstars. He was not into Dylanesque reclusions, Rolling Stones traveling fortresses, or English countryside retirements like the Beatles. In Greenwich Village, Jimi was out there among the people who loved the music as much as he loved performing his own. At the Salvation disco on Sheridan Square, on Eighth Street where he was building his dream studio, or at Unganos or the Scene, both in midtown, Jimi walked among the people. And although he was extremely shy he was always ready to talk to those who came up to him in the street or in a club. Most of the time he was virtually alone in public with a couple of girlfriends and a male friend or two. But he had no full-time bodyguards or entourage to protect him. He did not design his public movements to shield him from the people. He had no fear of rapping with a stranger. He took every chance imaginable, from his music to his love life to the safety of his person.

At 11:25 A.M., September 18, 1970, Jimi Hendrix was pronounced dead at St. Mary's Abbot Hospital in the Kensington/Chelsea section of London. Immediately the London offices of the major wire services reported worldwide that Hendrix died of a drug overdose. Later, the inquest returned an "open verdict," which, according to the *New York Times*, "meant that the court was unable to decide the exact reason for Mr. Hendrix's death. . . ." *Jimi Hendrix did not die of a drug overdose.*

The death certificate listed as "cause of death":

Inhalation of vomit
Barbiturate intoxication (quinalbarbitone)
Insufficient evidence of circumstances
   open verdict

While Gavin L. B. Thurston, coroner for Inner West London, is listed as informant, he did not sign the death certificate.

Above: Friends carry him from the church after funeral services
WIDE WORLD PHOTOS
Below: Al Hendrix mourns the death of his son　*WIDE WORLD PHOTOS*

Monika Danneman was the only person who spoke to reporters and close friends about Hendrix's whereabouts and states of mind that Thursday night and Friday morning. She made several statements during the days that ensued. To Eric Burdon, whom she had called that Friday morning to ask for advice while Hendrix lay dying, she revealed a poem he had written earlier that morning. They agreed to keep the poem from public knowledge. They felt that it might indicate a suicidal state. To her brother, whom she called in Germany, she indicated that Hendrix had been exhausted and wanted to sleep for several days; and that was why, apparently, he took so many sleeping pills.

At the inquest she gave the following statement:

I am an artist and I live at the Garden Flat, 22 Lansdowne Crescent, London, W.11.

I have known Jimi Hendrix for about two years; we met in Germany. I had been in touch with him by telephone and letter while he was in the States. I met him when he came to this country in August. I have not known him to consult a doctor while in this country. I would say that all the time I knew him he was exhausted. As far as I know he always fulfilled his engagements. He took sleeping tablets from his doctor because he was nervous, but they were not that strong. I have not known him to take hard drugs, he tried them once, just for experience. I do not know whether he took amphetamines. I have not known him to have a vomiting attack.

He had been staying with me since Tuesday, 15th September. Nobody else was staying at the flat. He slept well on the Tuesday and Wednesday night. I do not know about Thursday night. We did not spend a tiring day on Thursday and arrived home about 8:30 P.M. I cooked a meal and had a bottle of white wine about 11:00 P.M. He drank more of the bottle than I did. He had nothing to drink other than the wine. He had a bath and washed his hair and then we talked. At this time there was no argument or stress, it was a happy atmosphere.

When we came back we were talking. I took a sleeping tablet at about 7:00 A.M. I made him two fish sandwiches. We were in bed talking. I woke about 10:20 A.M. He was sleeping normally. I went round the corner to get cigarettes, when I came back he had been sick, he was breathing and his pulse was normal but I could not wake him. I saw that he had taken sleeping tablets, there were nine of mine missing. I phoned for an ambulance and he was taken to hospital, where he lived for a short while. I would take one or two Vesparax. There were nine missing. I think he knew exactly what he could take in the way of sleeping tablets. When I last saw him before he went to sleep he was very happy. The tablets were in a cupboard, he would have to get out of bed to get the tablets.

As far as I know he had not taken pep tablets. He said he had had cannabis at the flat. There was no question of exhaustion on this particular evening. He was not a man to have moods. He was not tensed up or agitated. I have never heard him say he wished he were dead or that life was not worth living. He had business stresses but this did not worry him.

Later, to the press and to friends Danneman was to reveal more about the evening. The poem was allowed to surface after the inquest and the "open verdict." Danneman's accounts of the last hours of Hendrix's life revealed several hours when she was not in direct contact with him. The last half hour when she went out to buy cigarettes while he lay in his own vomit was the most crucial.

Other versions of Hendrix's death were to surface. One had to do with the "Cointelpro" program of the Federal Bureau of Investigation, which sought to neutralize an array of black leaders who were considered to be potential messiahs. (There are documents of FBI activity around Hendrix.) Another account had him overdosing on heroin at a friend's house on the outskirts of London and taken from there to Monika Danneman's place. Yet another account had him flown to Hollywood, where he was murdered and then flown back to London in a private jet. Other accounts have him dying at a well-known rock star's apartment with Devon by his side.

At no other time in Hendrix's life as a star had he faced so many problems in his professional and private life. Ed Chalpin's lawsuit and the entreaties of his management and record company lawyers posed more threats to his creative freedom. The loss of Billy Cox left him high and dry and vulnerable in highly visible London. He could not elude the bad vibrations by the sheer mobility of touring, as he usually did. And worst of all, he could not play, he could not record. Adrift in random London scenes and virtually homeless, weariness set in. His resistance lowered dangerously by his mental oppression, abundant London hashish and some tastes of the abundant pharmaceutical heroin snorted through the nose on occasion took him to a torpid yet anxious level. But the wheels kept on turning and he remained spaced-out in London, with the court date coming up and the new contracts for a continuation of the tour with the original Experience arriving any day, any hour. He wanted to be back into

Electric Lady, back in Manhattan where he could complete the album, where he could rest.

Keeping his whereabouts secret, Hendrix pondered and agonized over whether to appear in court, sign up for another Experience tour, or simply split back to the States. According to Monika Danneman he had decided to sleep through Friday and Saturday. Monday he could have been back at Electric Lady working on the album. Danneman said she saw him take only one sleeping pill, but one sleeping pill for a rock star accustomed to them is not enough.

Further analysis of the pathologist's report indicated that Hendrix had a very high level of alcohol in his blood. Much more than the bottle of wine he and Monika drank with their meal. It would seem, according to Danneman's testimony, that he had nothing to drink after their meal and after the dinner party, yet the alcohol blood level remained unusually high. There are hours that Danneman does not account for during that evening, and her information gets extremely fuzzy after midnight.

Apparently Monika Danneman felt it was all right to go to the store for cigarettes when she awoke at 10:00 A.M. In other accounts, she said she noticed vomit coming from Hendrix's mouth and could not rouse him. Hendrix managed to hold on to life until he got to the hospital. But there his heart swelled up and the meninges in his spinal column congested. His heart was too slowed by the barbiturates and alcohol in his blood to meet the emergency in his system. Unable to simply cough out the vomit, Hendrix's system failed and he died.

Jimi Hendrix left no will. His father was the sole heir of his estate. Al Hendrix named Henry W. Steingarten as administrator of Jimi Hendrix's estate at a court hearing in New York City. It was soon reported that the estate was worth some $400,000. This figure shocked many close to Hendrix, who knew that he had amassed much more than that in royalties alone. The $400,000 seemed to be only the monies Hendrix had earned on the last tour of England and Europe.

Al Hendrix was straightforward in declaring his lack of ability to handle the various legal and economic decisions required of him. He quickly fell victim to a couple of charity scams, and the estate, as headed by Henry Steingarten, was unable to add substantially to the $400,000 figure originally left. Al Hendrix began to ponder other courses of action.

Leo Branton took over the Hendrix estate after Herbert Price, Jimi's former valet, urged Al Hendrix to retain him. Immediately

Branton took action. Henry Steingarten cooperated by stepping aside as administrator of the estate after Branton threatened to take him before the bar because of the obvious conflict of interest implicit in the fact that his partner, Steve Weiss, was the lawyer for Michael Jeffery, Hendrix's personal manager. Ed Chalpin's suit against Hendrix in the English courts had been hanging the estate up, but Branton broke the contract by pointing out the obvious exploitation of the $1.00 contract.

Leo Branton felt that if Steingarten and Warner Brothers had fought the litigation of Chalpin in America they would have won easily. That would have saved Jimi a lot of heartache.

Electric Lady Studios were sold to the Michael Jeffery estate. The Jimi Hendrix estate began receiving updated royalties from Warner Brothers. A Bahamian tax shelter scheme that Jeffery and Steingarten had advised Hendrix to join had taken in considerable revenue from Hendrix's music publishing companies. The money had disappeared. Noel Redding and Mitch Mitchell received $100,000 and $300,000, respectively, as settlements for alleged oral agreements between them and Hendrix regarding record royalties. A paternity suit in Sweden was adjudicated in favor of Eva Sundquist and son. It had no bearing on heirs to Hendrix's estate since paternity suits in Sweden are traditionally settled on the sole testimony of the mother.

The posthumous manipulation of Jimi Hendrix's music is somewhat depressing to his true fans and followers. One of his biggest battles in life was the production, merchandising, and packaging of his music. It is a shame that *Electric Ladyland* is his only LP totally controlled and produced by himself. Of the albums after that, only *Band of Gypsys* was not issued after his death. The *Cry of Love* and the *Rainbow Bridge* albums were more or less the tracks that would have been on the double album *First Rays of the New Rising Sun* had Hendrix remained alive. Two of the studio-recorded songs on *Rainbow Bridge* ("Pali-gap" and "Hey Baby . . .") form the nucleus of the live concert performed in Maui that was supposed to have been the live soundtrack album for the motion picture *Rainbow Bridge*. But Chuck Wein, director and producer of the movie, lost the soundtrack to thieves after Hendrix died. *Loose Ends* was the last album put together by Ed Kramer, Mitch Mitchell, and others who were on top of his music at the time of his death. *Hendrix in the West*, *War Heroes*, and *Loose Ends* give pure Hendrix tracks. Although not up to the level Hendrix would have preferred, they offer some splendid surprises like "Midnight," an instrumental,

"Hootchie Cootchie Man," "Bleeding Heart," "Drifters Escape," a Dylan song, "Look Over Yonder," and "Room Full of Mirrors," among others.

First Rays of the New Rising Sun would have been a fabulous album rivaling *Electric Ladyland* in popularity. The tracks (which were split up into *Rainbow Bridge* and *Cry of Love*) reveal a lovely range and a new direction for Hendrix. Yet without his final mixes, follow-through mastering techniques, and other touches there are subtle and obvious lapses and flaws that Hendrix would not have permitted.

Jimi and Devon Wilson were a love story unto themselves. Their love, hate, and ambivalence created a parallel legend. Many related to Jimi through Devon, more than they related to him through his music. Jimi vacillated about his deep feelings for Devon as he did in many other essential areas of his life. But it was clear that he had a concern for her he could not shake. Devon impressed the women on the rock superstar scene almost as much as Jimi. Betty Davis, a close friend of Devon's who was married to Miles Davis during a good deal of their friendship, remembered Devon through a song: "I. Miller Shoes."

> *She could have been anything she wanted*
> *Truly fine from her head down to her toes*
> *Instead she chose to be nothing*
> *So nothing flew from the East to the West Coast*
>
> *Became a thief*
> *She was a dancer*
> *Became a harlot*
> *She was a black diamond queen*
> *Music men wrote songs about her*
> *Some said her sweet*
> *And some said her very mean*
> *Rock music played loud and clear for her*
> *Rock music took her youth and left her very dry*
> *She was abused and used by many men*
> *Ask the guitar grinder*
> *He'll tell you why*
>
> *She could have done anything that she wanted*
> *She had bells from her head down to her toes*
> *But instead she chose to do nothing*
> *So nothing flew from the West back to the East Coast*

She rendered her services easily
'cause her services were all she had to give
But after the passing of her savior
She did and tried everything she could to stay here

Dark glasses used to hide her mourning face
Dark marks found a place upon her arm
And when they told me that she had died
They didn't have to tell me why or how she'd gone
She came to the jungle from Milwaukee
Stepping high in her I. Miller Shoes
She came to the jungle from Milwaukee
And she stepped out in her I. Miller Shoes

Copyright © 1971 by Betty Mabry

Following Hendrix's death it seemed as if every guitarist in the public eye was making a personal testament to the beauty of the man's style. Many of his licks became immediate additions to every electric guitarist's vocabulary. All of what was possible was absorbed.

Robin Trower, former lead guitarist of Procul Harum, became a devotee of Hendrix's. While staying clear of Hendrix's compositions he often captured similar moods and effects. Frank Marino, lead guitarist of the Canadian group Mahogany Rush, plays several of Hendrix's compositions almost verbatim. Marino claims to have been visited by the spirit of Jimi Hendrix soon after his death. Ronnie Isley, of the Isley Brothers, acknowledges his debt to Hendrix in many of their early 1970s releases.

This task seemed impossible when I first started. Jimi Hendrix's inner circle of friends was even tighter than I had realized. Many had been put off by the poor and notorious accounts of his life that were published soon after his death. Hendrix kept no diaries. His notebooks, letters, collections of poems, and the myriad scraps of paper and matchbooks he wrote lines for lyrics on were all missing. His apartment had been raided and all of his personal effects distributed without any supervision or thought toward keeping his stuff together for posterity. Much of his wardrobe was traced to various itinerant clothes freaks. His priceless private tape-recorded collection of jams in clubs, in concerts, and solo (alone in his room at home or on the road) was gone. The two persons closest to him on a personal and a business level, Devon Wilson and Michael Jeffery, both died strange and violent deaths soon after he left this world,

Devon in an ambiguous plunge from the upper stories of the Chelsea Hotel in New York City and Jeffery in an exploding commercial airliner. Other close associates died, got strung out, or went mad soon after his death.

He was as much into himself offstage as he was flamboyant on-stage. He knew many people and many people knew him, yet many of his closest friends had been his friends long before his fame. Buddy Miles, Billy Cox, Fayne Pidgeon, The Twins, Jennie Dean, Jeanette Jacobs, Bobby Taylor, Tommie Chong, Linda Keith, Devon, and others all were his oldest friends and knew him well before he made it big. With the exception of Chas Chandler, his relationship with his English management and band that formed the Experience was as close to a purely business arrangement as could be in the small world of high international rock. His relationship with his American recording company was distant. One of his European labels, Track, distributed by Polydor, never paid him a royalty at all, according to Leo Branton. But it came to pass that close friends, record companies, and personal management all played a crucial role in his death.

Most of the people who were closest to Jimi Hendrix denied a close knowledge of him. Very often those who were somewhat re-moved from his ongoing intimacy felt they knew him better than their information indicated. One person who was interviewed early in the research said that those who knew Jimi Hendrix the best were those who loved his music. It took years, literally, to win the trust and confidence of many of those who formed Hendrix's inner circle of friends.

At first I was incensed by his death (like many who dearly loved his life, his music, and his style) to the point that I clearly bore a visible anger. It took me two full years and a trip to England to get over that hard-boiled, almost private-eye-like intensity. Once it en-tered my mind that the most important thing about the man was his life, I was home free. I must have encountered every causeway and roadblock imaginable. But I found it was more trial than error be-cause every effort toward uncovering his essence was almost magi-cally rewarded. Many beautiful people came forth to help me out, especially Herbie Worthington of Los Angeles, and Caesar Glebbeek and Don Foster of the Jimi Hendrix Information Centre in Holland. Because of their help and the help of many others, instead of hating his death, I too began enjoying Jimi Hendrix's life.

A SELECTED DISCOGRAPHY OF THE RECORDINGS OF JIMI HENDRIX

Jimi Hendrix released only five albums during his lifetime; these were issued by Warner Brothers/Reprise, his official label in the United States, and by Polydor and Track, his official labels in Europe and the United Kingdom. They are: *Are You Experienced?* (Reprise RS6261) September 1967, *Axis: Bold As Love* (RS 6281) January 1968, *Electric Ladyland* (Double 2RS 6307) September 1968, *Smash Hits* (MSK 2276) June 1969, and *Otis Redding/ Jimi Hendrix Experience at Monterey* (MS2029) July 1970. *Band of Gypsys* was released by Capitol (STAO 472) after the tapes from the historic Fillmore East New Year's Eve concert of 1969 were used to settle a lawsuit.

After his death, several albums appeared under varying circumstances, all lessened to some extent by lack of Hendrix's participation in the postproduction process, which he often considered the most crucial phase in the making of an album. These albums are also available through his official companies: *The Cry of Love* (MS 2034) January 1971, *Rainbow Bridge* (MS 2040), *Hendrix in the West* (MS 2049), *War Heroes* (MS 2103), *Sound Track Recording From the Film Jimi Hendrix* (2RS 6481) June 1973, and *Loose Ends*, which is only available in England (Polydor Super 2310 301) and Europe.

Loose Ends was not released in America because his official company felt that the tracks given them by the Jimi Hendrix estate were of inferior quality. This led the Hendrix Estate to contract independent producer Alan Douglas to spin off some albums from a mass of some 600 hours of raw, unedited tapes that Hendrix had left in his Electric

Lady Studios and elsewhere. *Crash Landing* (MS 2204) and *Midnight Lightning* (MS 2209) were released as a result of the agreement in February and November of 1975. Both albums sparked controversy because of Douglas's decision to erase tracks featuring original sidemen (Buddy Miles, Noel Redding, Juma Sultan, Larry Lee, and others) in favor of Los Angeles studio musicians and background singers. Many who were close to the tracks recorded by Hendrix that appear on the latest LPs state that the originals were far superior to their subsequent "versions." Douglas cited problems in the tracks themselves, which often changed key or tempo suddenly.

The Essential Jimi Hendrix Vol. I (2RS 2245) July 1978, and Vol. II (HS 2293)—including the seven-inch EP "Gloria" (EP 2293)—July 1979, are anthology compilations of songs and compositions released in prior official albums. *Nine to the Universe* (HS 2299), produced by Douglas, was released in 1980. It is a splendid album featuring largely instrumental tracks. Jazz keyboard man Larry Young is featured along with guitarists Jim McCartey and Larry Lee and bass player Roland Robinson. It was recorded at the Record Plant in late 1969. The triple LP *Woodstock* (Cotillion SD 3-500) has only a brief selection of Hendrix and the fabled Band of Gypsys, Suns, Moons and Rainbows performance. But the difficult-to-obtain *Woodstock Two* (Cotillion SD 3-500 Double) contains an entire side of their work. The *Isle of Wight* performance of Hendrix is available only in the United Kingdom (Polydor Super 2302 016) and in Europe. It was the first gig of his last tour. In Germany Polydor has released a twelve-volume set of all official European albums, including a "maxi" single of "Gloria": *Jimi Hendrix* (2625038).

Early in his career Hendrix participated in recording sessions with Arthur Lee (of the 1960s group Love), Little Richard, Curtis Knight, the Isley Brothers, and Lonnie Youngblood. "My Diary," 45rpm Revis (1013 mono), as sung by Rosa Lee Brooks and produced by Arthur Lee, was recorded in 1962–1963 in Los Angeles and is the earliest known recording of Jimi Hendrix. The LP with Lonnie Youngblood (with Herman Hitson and Lee Moses) has been entitled *Roots of Hendrix* (TLP 9501) and *Rare Hendrix* (TLP 9500), both from Trip Records, as well as other titles in the United States, Italy, France, Germany, and England. The sessions were recorded in the United States in 1964–1965. *In the Beginning, Shout* (SLP 502) features Hendrix apparently leading his own sessions (circa 1963). His instrumental version of "House of the Rising Sun" by Leadbelly is a refreshing and quite modern interpretation of the blues classic.

The following selection of tapes exist in private collections and archives:

With Noel Redding, bass, and Mitch Mitchell, drums.

January 19, 1967, London, England. "Top of the Pop's Show:" "Hey Joe," with the Breakaways, background vocals.

February 5, 1967, London, England. The Flamingo Club. Entire concert. JHE plays R&B standard, "Have Mercy."

March 2, 1967, London, England. Marquee Club. "Hey Joe," "Purple Haze."

June 18, 1967, Monterey, California. Monterey International Pop Festival. "Killing Floor," song left off of official release.

September 5, 1967, Stockholm, Sweden. Radiohus Studio. Entire concert.

October 6, 1967, London, England. "Top Gear Show." "Radio One Theme (BBC)" and a jam with Stevie Wonder on drums, "Midnight Hour/I Was Born to Love Her."

October 9, 1967, Paris, France. L'Olympia. "Hey Joe," "Wind Cries Mary," "Purple Haze."

October 17, 1967, London, England. "Rhythm and Blues Show." "Please Crawl Out Your Window," "Hootchie Cootchie Man," "Drivin' South."

December 15, 1967, London, England. "Top Gear Show." "Spanish Castle Magic," "Daytripper."

February 25, 1968, Chicago, Illinois. Civic Opera House. 30 minutes.

August 23, 1968, Queens, New York, Singer Bowl. Entire Concert.

November 28, 1968, New York City. Philharmonic Hall, "An Electric Thanksgiving." Entire concert.

January 17, 1969, Frankfurt, West Germany. Jahrhunderthalle. Entire concert.

May 25, 1969, Santa Clara, California. San Jose Pop Festival. Entire concert.

June 20, 1969, Northridge, California. Newport Pop Festival/Devonshire Downs. 30 minutes.

July 10, 1969, New York City. "Tonight Show," hosted by Flip Wilson. Billy Cox, bass, and unidentified studio drummer. "Lover Man," dedicated to Brian Jones.

Band of Gypsys: Billy Cox, bass, and Buddy Miles, drums.

December 1969, New York City. Record Plant. "Auld Lang Syne," "Silent Night/Little Drummer Boy."

December 31, 1969, Fillmore East. First show. Entire concert.

With Mitch Mitchell, drums, and Billy Cox, bass.

April 25, 1970, Los Angeles, California. Forum. Entire concert.

May 30, 1970, Berkeley, California. Berkeley Community Theater. Second show. Entire concert.

July 4, 1970, Atlanta, Georgia, Atlanta Pop Festival. Entire concert.

July 30, Maui, Hawaii, Rainbow Bridge concert. 45 minutes.

August 30, 1970, Isle of Wight, England. Isle of Wight Festival. Entire concert.

September 1, 1970, Gothenburg, Sweden. Lisebergs Tivoli. Entire concert.

September 2, 1970, Arhus, Denmark. Vijle Ruskow Hall. 25 minutes.

September 3, 1970, Copenhagen, Denmark. K. B. Hall. Entire concert.

September 6, 1970, Isle of Fehmarn, West Germany. Love and Peace Festival. Entire concert.

Miscellaneous

October 1969, Woodstock, New York. Various house jams with Juma Sultan, percussion, and Michael Ephron, electric piano.

March 1968, New York City. Scene Club. Live jam with Harvey Brooks, bass, Buddy Miles, drums, an unidentified guitarist, and Jim Morrison, vocals.

April 1970, Los Angeles, California. Beverly Hilton Hotel. Taj Mahal and Hendrix accompanied by a tape of Topanga Canyon crickets.

1969–1970, New York City. Apartment house jams. Solo acoustic blues, electric guitar duos with unidentified guitarist, and songs such as "Neptune Rising," "Astro Man," "Room Full of Mirrors," and an acoustic version of "Manic Depression."

1969–1970, New York City. Record Plant. Jam with John McLaughlin, guitar, Dave Holland, bass, and Buddy Miles, drums.

1972, New York City. Electric Lady Studios. Ed Kramer, engineer, breaks down the tracks of "Dolly Dagger" and explains the mix and the various effects.

1974, London, England. "Crawdaddy Radio Review." Johnny Winters accompanies Hendrix on "Things I used to Do." Also some jams with Larry Young.

1979 and 1980, Berkeley, California. The Third World Department of KPFA-FM Radio produced a 12-hour documentary, "Jimi Hendrix: A Slight Return."

ABOUT THE AUTHOR

DAVID HENDERSON was born in Harlem, later moving to Lower Manhattan, where he lived for seven years and where he helped found the *East Village Other*, one of the earliest and best journals of the alternate press in the sixties. He was active in the civil rights movement and in several anti-war groups, including Poets for Peace, Angry Arts Against the War, and Resist. An award-winning poet who has published three volumes of poetry and recorded for the permanent poetry archives at the Library of Congress, he has been Poet–in–Residence at the City College of New York, and a teacher of English and Ethnic Studies at the University of California at Berkeley. He has performed and recorded with jazz musicians Ornette Coleman, Sun-Ra, David Murray and "Butch" Morris, and wrote the book, music, and lyrics for the funk opera GHETTO FOLLIES, which premiered in San Francisco in 1978. He is the author of FELIX OF THE SILENT FOREST, DE MAYOR OF HARLEM and THE LOW EAST, and his work has been widely published in anthologies and in magazines which include: *The Paris Review, Essence, Saturday Review, Black Scholar* and *The London Poetry Review*.

That has to be A classic line.

You know, I'd do anything to get out of
feeling loneliness; Do you really believe that. I know
you would, wouldn't I, and with this choice I have
chosen as you would, I hope you never know, I know
I wouldn't. If you did I hope you would
understand as I can See it, apart of
the whole.